A Survey of Buddhist Thought

Alfred Scheepers

A Survey of Buddhist Thought

Olive Press

ISBN 9789077787403, *Buddhist Philosophy*
Published by Olive Press,
Leeuwerikstraat 4-B, 1021 GL, Amsterdam, The Netherlands
www.olive-press.eu / info@olive-press.eu

Transliteration of the Sanskrit Alphabhet

as in	as in
a – c*u*t	ā – f*a*ther
u – p*u*t	ū – p*u*t
i – tr*ea*t	ī – b*ee*r
e – l*a*te	o – f*oa*m
ṛ – th*ir*st	
kh – *c*ow	g – *g*et
gh – *gh*ost	ṅ – thi*ng*
c – *ch*apter	ch – *ch*oke (aspiration)
j – *J*ohn	jh – *j*oke (aspiration)
ñ – a*ñ*gel	dh – *d*owry (aspiration)
ś – *sh*anty	ṣ – *ch*auffeur
y – *y*es	v – *W*asser (German)

The following sounds are retroflex: ṭ, ḍ, ṇ. They correspond with the normal English dentals. The same consonants, but without diacritical marks, are pronounced like their continental counterparts, e.g. as in Italian. ṁ is used as an abbreviation of n, ṅ, ñ, ṇ, or m, or it represent a sound similar to 'm' in French 'faim'. ḥ sounds as a soft aspiration.

Chinese is translated according to the Hanyu Pinyin system. For melodic pronunciation one should consult a dictionary or grammar.

Buddha, dhyāna mūdra

Contents

Preface 15
Introduction 19
Destiny 22
From origin to destiny 24

I Buddhism in India 27

Chapter 1, The Buddha and his Teaching 29
The scriptures in three baskets 29
The basket of sermons 30
The life of the Buddha 31
The Path to Freedom 33
Ethical rules 34
Meditation 34
Liberating insight 35
Thoughts behind the Method 36
The four noble truths 36
The influence of ignorance 39
Dependent origination 40
Explanation of the chain of dependent origination 42
Elucidation of the separate elements of the chain 43
Ignorance and thirst 45
The circle of life 48
The five groups of grasping 48
Feelings, positive, negative, and neutral 49

Hope and fear are without any base. 49
Ultimate reality. 50
The subject. 51
The absolute. 55
Ethical causation.. 56
History. 57
Retribution. 57
Retribution as a psychological law. 59
Realms of rebirth.. 60
The middle way. 61

Chapter 2, Early History 65
The five heretical theses. 66
De sects 68
Sthaviras.. 71
Mahāsaṁghikas.. 72
Vātsiputrīyas and Dharmaguptakas. 72

Chapter 3, Abhidharma 75
Theras and Sarvāstivādins. 77
Nature of the Abhidharma. 79
The Thera Abhidhamma 81
Freedom and bondage.. 82
Mind and 'saṅkhāra.' 82
Consciousness and rebirth. 86
The process of conscious apperception.. 87
Psychical factors. 89
Wholesome and unwholesome mental factors. 94
States of mind.. 96
Matter. 98
Time. 99
General characteristics and interpretation. 100
The Sarvāstivāda Abhidharma. 102
Retribution. 104
Visible deed and invisible result 104
Whose is the deed 105
1) Volition and fruition 106

2) Five substrates 106
3) Will and space 107
Death and after. 108
Knowledge and volition 108
Mental faculties. 110
Wholesome and unwholesome mental faculties 114
Matter. 116
Perception. 118
Time. 119
The concept of Nirvāṇa 120

Chapter4, Sautrāntikas 123
The stream of mind. 123
Action and fruit. 124
Forms, volitions, mind. 125
Subtle consciousness. 126
Knowledge.. 126
Time versus space. 128
Development in time. 128
Nirvāṇa. 125

Chapter 5, Mahāyāna 133
Mahayana as philosophy.. 136
The dharmas are without self 137
The truth and the illusive power 138
Scriptures 139
Origin 142
History 143
Kāṇvas and Śuṅgas. 143
Scyths 144
Kuṣāṇas. 144
Cedi and Sātavāhanas 145
The Guptas 146
Puṣpabhūtis and other houses 147
Cashmere and Gndhāra 1 4 8
Decline of Buddhism inm India. 149
Magadha as the melting pot of ideas 150

The Path of the Bodhisattva 151
The ten stages 152
The Bodies of the Buddha. 157
The apparitional body 159
The body of enjoyment 160
The body of Dharma 161
Truth. 163
Suchness 163
The veils of affliction and of thought 165
Conventional and highest truth 166
The Unity of Saṁsāra and Nirvāṇa *167*

Chapter 6, Madhyamaka 169
Criticism. 170
Life of Nāgārjuna. 171
Works ascribed to Nāgārjuna. 171
Short history of the Madhyamaka 173
Dialectic 175
The tetralemma. 176
Relativity. 178
The goal of dialectic 179
Substance or Fleeting Events 180
The Highest Wisdom. 183
Nature of wisdom. 184
Wisdom is freedom. 185
Absolute and Phenomena 186
Ignorance. 191
Two truths. 192
Freedom 192
Freedom is spiritual. 193

Chapter 7, Idealism. 197
History 199
Dignāga 204
The reality of the external world. 204
Theory of knowledge. 206
Sensation. 207

Inference. 208
Dharmakīrti. . . . 210
Two levels of truth. . . . 211
Ontology. . . . 212
Momentariness. 212
Causality. 213
Mind. 214
The means of knowledge. . . . 215
Perception. 216
Inference. 217
Buddha. 218
Goal and practice.. . . . 218
Understanding. . . . 220
Apoha 220
Logical implication. . . . 221
Representations 222
Meaning and judgement 223
Word and sentence 224
The idealist solution of the problem of knowledge. . . . 225
Three aspects of consciousness 226
The pure light of true knowledge 228
The problem of intersubjectivity. . . . 228

Part II, Buddhism in China 233

Chpater 1, The Assimilation of Taoism 235
The Six Houses. . . . 235
Sēngzhàu. . . . 238
Movement. . . . 238
Existence. . . . 239
Wisdom.. . . . 240
Dàoshēng. . . . 242
Retribution. . . . 242
Instantaneous enlightenment 244
The Immortality of the Mind. . . . 246
World-denial and the state 250

Chapter 9, Later Buddhist Developments 251
Jízàng 251
Xuánzàng 253
All is relative to the mind. 254
Four levels of consciousness. 255
Store-consciousness. 256
The seven active forms of consciousness. 258
All consists of the mind's immanent differentiation. 260
The three natures of reality and their true essence. 281
The road to wisdom.. 263

Chapter 10, Three Schools 267
The Făzāng and the Huà-yán School 267
1. Origination through causation.. 268
2. The emptiness of 'matter.' 268
3. The three natures. 269
4. Revelation of what is without quality. 270
5. Non-generation. 270
6. The five teachings. 271
7 The mastering of the ten mysteries. 272
8. Embracing the six qualities. 274
9. The achievement of bodhi 275
10. Entry into nirvāṇa.. 275
Epilogue.. 276
The Fàhuà, or Lotus School of The Tiāntài Mountains 276
Absolute mind. 277
Three natures. 278
The universal and the individual mind. 280
The integration of all things.. 280
Cessation and conumplation. 281
Pure and impure natures. 283
Ignorance and enlightenment. 283
The intellectual position of the Tiāntài school 284
The Chán School 285
Wisdom 286
1. The highest truth is inexpressible. 288
2. Wisdom cannot be cultivated. 288

3. In the last resort nothing is gained. 290
4. There is nothing much in the Buddhist teaching. 291
5. In carrying water and chopping wood lies the wonderful Dào. 292

Part III, Buddhism in Japan 297

Chapter 11, The Character of Japanese Buddhism 299
Chapter 12, Buddhist Sects 303
Chapter 13, Zen Buddhism. 313
Tbe universal and individual aspects of consciousness. 315
Two Schools.. 317
Dōgen 319
Against syncretism. 321
Enlightenment. 322
Time and Being. 325
Causality.. 326
Zazen. 327
Hakuin 328
The realm of the absolute. 331
Karma and liberation. 333
The analogy of man and society.. 333

Bibliography. 337
Index and Glossary 353

Preface

This book is not a detailed history of Buddhist thought, nor is it a history of Buddhism in general. A like work should yet be written. I focused on the philosophical aspects of Buddhism, omitting others. But even Buddhist philosophy covers so wide a field, that I only was able to select some highlights. In spite of these limitations, I believe, many readers may find in this book brought together things, that until now had to be gathered from a multitude of sources. I treated some subjects – such as Abhidharmic philosophy, or the epistemology of Dharmakīrti – carefully avoided by other general works, either because most authors don't know anything about it, or, because they think it to be too difficult for the general public. Moreover, I wrote this book from a philosophical understanding. Most authors specialized in Buddhism lack a thorough education in philosophy. That's why they render Buddhist concepts by fanciful terms that have no known connotation in the West, unaware of the fact that many terms may be rendered by means of standard European equivalents. For instance, the logical concept of *vyāpti* is often rendered through 'invariable concomitance,' but, in fact, in many Buddhist works it is just the term for what in the West is called 'logical implication' (If A is, then also B is, but the givenness of B does not necessarily imply A; A does not occur without B, but B may occur without A). Another example: a key-concept in Buddhist thought, *vijñāna*, is most often rendered through 'cognition,' while another key-concept, *saṁjnā*, is rendered through 'perception.' But internal evidence of Buddhist material shows, that it is *vijñāna*, that means 'perception,' since the concept is used in composita combined with the names of the five senses, indicating visual, olfactory perception etc. *Saṁjñā*, on the contrary, literally translated means 'cognition,' which translation, moreover, is etymologically cognate. Up to now no translator has chosen this, maybe all too obvious, solution. I myself have chosen to render the concept also through 'apperception,' or 'apprehension'. To avoid further confusion. 'Understanding' also would not be far off the mark. With so much unclarity, even in the translation of key-concepts, how could it hitherto have been possible to understand Buddhist thought?

The reader of this book will find, that much of the old Buddhist philosophy has a modern ring. We are reminded of positivism and of phenomenology, but these thoughts have appeared in Buddhism already two thousand years ago. Yet we hear people like the German expert Lydia Brüll say in her book *Die Japanische Philosophie* that in the West philosophy is the object of a full grown scientific discipline, and that this is not the case in India, China, or Japan. Apart from the question whether it is fair to compare contemporaneous developments in Western philosophy with ancient Eastern thought, one may wonder what philosophy she is talking about: Plato, Aquinas, Descartes, Kant, Nietzsche, Wittgenstein, Heidegger, or, God forbid, Derrida? Either all these thinkers were (or are) not philosophers, or the term 'scientific' is a meaningless concept, that may be applied to anything; but then, why not to Buddhistic philosophy?

As I believe it to be, the history of philosophy, in the East as well as in the West, is just the history of human ideas about reality and existence. There are flashes of insight, thought-structures, some persuasive, others less, but there never has been a system of philosophy that could claim absolute validity. If any philosopher ever claimed such a thing, he was already criticized for it by his immediate successors. But we need our illusions, don't we? Besides, if the concern for the validity of knowledge be a mark of science, then it must be pointed out that the Buddhist logicians had something to say about the subject.

This book is divided into three parts, one dealing with Buddhist thought in India, one dealing with its sojourn in China, and one coping with its reception in Japan. I omitted Tibet, and South-East Asia, for which omission only my own incompetence is the reason. The method I used in treating the subjects varies in those respective parts.

The basics of Buddhistic thought originated in India. Therefore, in the part dealing with India I treated these basics thoroughly, using my own philosophical understanding to penetrate the matter. While coming to China, I found good work was already done by Fung Yu-lan in his *History of Chinese Philosophy*. I closely followed his treatment of Buddhist thought in part two of that work. For Japanese Buddhist thought such structured prior study was not available. But philosophically Japanese thought takes over the ideas and concepts of the Indians and Chinese. For the sake of not falling into endless repetitions, it therefore seemed only necessary to state the typically Japanese character of Buddhism. I took some representative examples of japanese Buddhism, concentrating on Zen, only saying something about the thoughts of Dōgen (12th century) and Hakuin (17th century). The book is left with an open end. This indicates the fact that Buddhism in Japan is still in full development, and cannot be considered as a closed chapter, as it can be, to a certain extent, in India and China. I am not able to give a full exposition of it, also covering the present time. Therefore the reader must be content with my few sketchy remarks.

Introduction

What impels a man to undertake the study of history, and in particular, that of the history of ideas?

When I was beginning as a student in philosophy, there were two questions I thought that ought to be answered, one concerning the principle which forms the foundation of our life and the world or universe that it inhabits, the other concerning its destiny. Our established religions have had something to say, especially about the latter. But even if it be true what one or other religion preaches, the fact remains that as long as we merely believe in some religious doctrine, we can by that very fact never know whether it is true. And it is just that what we want. Thus religion, instead of providing us with answers to our fundamental questions, rather stimulates us to search for them. Otherwise we would never get to know what we really believe, since all religion cannot escape being interpreted within the context of a world-view that lacks the knowledge that may appease our restlessness. So we are caught in a vicious circle. Modern man has thought that science should fill the gap left open by religion. Objective knowledge might provide for the sound interpretation of our religious believes. But, alas, there has been no scientific knowledge in the past that is not modified by our present insights, and we may hardly expect that our present insights will not be changed by future investigation. Moreover, science is not a unity, the humanities and the physical sciences do not seem to stand on a common ground, and their respective viewpoints of freedom and determinism appear to be diametrically opposed. If such is the case we might almost give up hope to find in scientific development, as it is, the ultimate answer to our questions. Even the methods of both groups of scientific culture have little in common; the one wants to understand, the other to explain.

As life is one, and cannot at one and the same time partake of two conflicting universes, it became my conviction that a third way of interpreting existence should be possible. Instead of the prevailing scientific model, shaped by geometry and not being able to include the facts of human life, I thought, there should be searched for a model based on a principle that can account for both, mental and physical phenomena. I have not been the first in search for this principle. The gigantic work of Russell and Whitehead, undertaken in their *Principia Mathematica,* to reduce mathematics to logical principles, was prompted by the same need. After partial failure of the endeavour, Russell relapsed into physicalism, but Whitehead continued in another way. He tried to find a common denominator of all phenomena, physical, biological and human. To that end he postulated feeling as the inner essence of whatever can be presented by outward appearance. In doing so, physical phenomena became principally at least – accessible to the hermeneutics of understanding. History showed that Whitehead's leap into metaphysics, and Russell's relapse into the mechanistic worldview, came out of unjustified discouragement. Although the development of quantum-physics issued in ideas which do not suggest Whitehead to be a complete fool, this branch of science did not force the desired breakthrough. It led to the discovery of many new facts, but at the same time it revealed fundamental contradictions within physical science itself, especially regarding the basic characteristics of its object. Here no unified interpretation of existence could be established.

In recent times, although scientists are frantically trying to make us believe the contrary, physical science has come to an impasse. Not being able to decide questions as to the fundamental characteristics of matter and the origin of the universe, leading physicists start re-stating the old philosophical problems, e.g. the question of time, hardly aware of the fact that they have left the domain of empirical research and have entered the field of the *a priori.*

The truly dynamic development was to emerge in the field of logic, resulting in cybernetics or computer science. Finally here was given a model that could simulate the workings of intelligence without deviating from the laws of physics. Slowly more and more people get convinced that, maybe, after all, the impossible – for being a contradiction in terms, viz. an intelligent machine – is possible. Now then, let intelligence and mechanics, understanding and explanation, coincide, what may then be the underlying principle of this unity? This principle was formulated already centuries ago by a man who kept fascinating me with his thought since I heard of him. He was the one who paved the way for modern symbolic logic, and for the computing machine, even for Whitehead's conception of being as essentially perceptive. His name was Leibniz, and he coined the idea behind it all; the *principle of sufficient reason*.

Whence did this principle come? Genius? The hint to search for it in Buddhism I got from Whitehead. It took a long time of severe mental trouble before circumstances made me take up that advice. But finally in Buddhism I rediscovered Leibniz's principle of *sufficient reason,* now called the 'principle of dependent origination' *(pratītya-samutpāda).* I am still not sure whether the appearance of this principle in such different cultures and times is a coincidence. After all, Leibniz lived after the Portuguese and Dutch seafarers had found their way to the East. The painter Rembrandt had already copied Indian miniatures, and Leibniz knew enough of China to admire its culture and thought. I am in the dark as to the exact nature and extent of his knowledge, but it does not seem impossible that somehow he picked up from it the principle of sufficient reason. In short, the statement of the principle by Leibniz may itself be conditioned by it.

In recent years I have been studying the history of Buddhist thought. And I discovered how much my approach differs from that of the philologists who dominate this field of study for obvious linguistical reasons. While they are content establishing the meaning of words and to base on it an account of the ideas held in those days, this cannot offer me any satisfaction. The philologist often takes for granted the patent progress of science and technology that characterizes the Western world, and his interest in the other culture has something of romance, even of escapism. It also has something of the collector's mentality; one wants to collect the oddities of the human mind to put them into the museum of the modern age. In this endeavour philological correctness is the highest virtue. If our translations do not make sense, so much the better. As long as they are based on established usage of the meaning of words, this only proves the advance of our logical thought in comparison to that of other cultures. And that confirmation of our own ego pleases us to the highest degree. How can you expect logical consistency in the realm of ignorance? Personally I find little satisfaction in this approach, bothered as I am by the inconsistencies of the intellectual frame of our own time and culture and desperately searching a medicine for the collective schizofrenia that upsets our whole intellectual life. I stick to the principle that things would not have been said if the people who said them, would not have had the feeling of expressing a consistency of meaning. It seems more probable that philosophers deviate from the daily usage of words in expressing the intricacies of the mind, than that they are talking nonsense. We should before all pose the question: 'What reality did they want to elucidate?' Here we find more profit in Wittgenstein's idea, that the meaning of words is derived from their usage, than in the postulate that words are used in accordance with an established meaning.

For al this, in interpreting the history of Buddhism, I do not content myself with just rendering so-called objective descriptions, no matter how awkward, but I try to find a standpoint from which the data seem to fit together into a coherent whole, even to the point of stretching the 'established' meaning of terms. But then, the history of Buddhism becomes more lucid than ever. We see that there never have been major differences of opinion, and that the basic ideas of early Buddhism have developed throughout history until the present time without ever having been abandoned. They have been elaborated, refined, slightly modified, and, above all, clothed in ever different terminology. But they always retained the same inner logic, that of the principle of sufficient reason, a principle that is now causing a major scientific revolution.

Destiny.

As regards the second question, that concerning the destiny of life, one can only approach it personally. I was young in the seventies of the 20th century. Whoever experienced these years in the sensitive age knows there was something in the air. Young people attacked the prevailing, established, and often hypocritical morals and rejected a life of 'progress,' industrialization, and accumulation of wealth. They – for a part at least – returned to the simple values of love and peace, a life close to nature, and they searched in non-Western cultures for ideas and techniques that might realize this ideal. But on the whole there was a strong accent on experience at the expense of knowledge. Abandoning tradition and possession one tried to regain oneself after having been banished by one's parents to an alien world which seemed to offer nothing human.

The new movement was mainly expressed in a music characterized by a fresh, sometimes naive non-conformism. Listening to it, remote and slumbering recesses of the soul were brought to life and opened up a world, free, new, colourful, nourishing, never heard of before, but yet more intimate than anything until then familiar. One could – even without irony – believe in happy and 'beautiful people,' as Melanie (Safka) sang.

After those years I never have been able to see anything worthwhile in gaining a position in the world, procuring a good income, buying a house, or planning a family. My parents had a caravan on an island bordering the North Sea. I often stayed there from early spring and walked through the unpolluted stillness of the dunes. As summer approached, I saw the cars of the tourists occupying the hitherto deserted roads, damaging the whole scene with their noisy ugliness. Then it became clear to me that what we call progress is really destruction. Since then I go along searching to re-locate early spring, or the untrodden morning dew, or the beach from which the traces of human carelessness have been recently washed away by the flood or by heavy rains.

Back to the beginning before al complexity! What do I search for in the ungrazed meadow, or in the forgotten roadside studded with flowers in the moment in which it seems forgotten by everyone, forgotten to be spoiled? It is perhaps what I have come to call the moment of absolute birth, the birth that is not a development of something else, but that lies at the root of all growth, the mystery that lies between the mute silence of eternity and the peace of life's elixer, not yet fermented, but in which the yeast is on the verge of becoming active. Here we have the inconceivable, yet it is unavoidably there. In it we find the calm preceding every free and creative act that is able to change our life from the root. Only standing in this calm we can decipher the meaning of life, which is always our life.

I think, that to stand in this calm, never more deviating from it, has been the sole aim of the Buddhist path, nothing more and nothing less. From this calm one acts without any coercion, one understands without any distortion, one feels without any depression. One is clearly conscious of the beauty around, as things are when one is not shaped or conditioned, when one is not part of, and not incorporated in anything. We should not call it 'autonomy.' For in that there is still a will commanding and coercing a human frame. In that there is not the unharmed freedom of this spontaneity. If we are not like this, if we do not stand in that calm, and act in the love that wells from it, cognize in the wisdom surrounding it, feel the joy of conciliation, atonement, of home-coming, that accompanies it, then we are maimed in our humanness, the son of man – with empty hands, without pretention, without claims, with nothing to call his own, because he does not have, but lives, is all this – is not yet there. For the more one has, the more one maintains, the more one is imprisoned, the more constricted, the less one *is* – that is, *is free*.

Thus destiny is a beginning, but a beginning starting from an ever different whole, from a perpetually changing context.

From origin to destiny.

If you have lost your way in the forest and cannot find your way home, you may start crying until somebody finds you. If you're lucky some helpful guide takes care of you, if you're not, you keep on crying, or some robber comes to take your money and maybe also your life. If you want to depend on yourself there are some rules to cope with the situation. Descartes advised to advance always straight ahead, then sooner or later you emerge out of the wood. From there it is easy to proceed further safely. But there are other methods: one can climb a hill or a tree for orientation, or look upon the sky, the sun, moon, and stars, to choose a safe direction; the type of vegetation may reveal your position, or, if the soil is soft, you may return on your own footprints. In any way, don't panic, and don't start running hither and thither or in circles: you will exhaust yourself and diminish your chance of rescue.

The rules for coming where you want if you don't know the way have been called laws. The most important of them can be used in any situation. For the lost soul there have been made some rules of conduct, also called morals, which in all main religions of the world have been formulated more or less the same: do not kill, do not lie, do not steal, and, mind your appetites! For those who do not want to leave anything to chance, different religions have prescribed more refined rules, which, if practised conscientiously, bring you straight away home. In Judaism and Christianity such a rule is e.g. to have unremitting faith in the Lord, in Buddhism the proper practice of meditation is prescribed.

Rules are to be followed if you don't know the way, but not necessarily if you know what you do and why so. This explains the paradox that the same God of the Jews who forbids the killing of men, is enraged against the one who left someone alive. For they who are not lost travellers on the road, but are fulfilling a divine plan, do not live under the guiding rules but under direct command. Similarly, the *Yogācāras* of Buddhism thought it was permissible to kill one man-slaughtering tyrant to save many lives. As already Machiavelli remarked: being too absolute in goodness may cause more damage than the amount of wickedness required in curbing evil. But caution! This insight has too often been used as an easy excuse for violence. Generally speaking, the one who lives out of spontaneity, love, and wisdom, does not need fixed guiding rules, but this does not mean that he usually transgresses them. He only does so in extremities, if in any other way he would betray himself, if by not transgressing he would lose his freedom and his stand in the primordial calm.

Thus we have enumerated the few principles of Buddhism: nature of reality, destiny, and the right path. We shall now see how the Buddhist mind coped with these throughout its history.

Part 1
Buddhism in India

Buddhism does not want to catch the world in a system; it makes no effort to explain the origin and constitution of the world as a whole. It rather addresses itself to the human condition, and concludes that life is suffering. As suffering is highly undesirable, man should be freed from it. Buddhism has contrived methods to achieve this aim; all its ideas, thoughts, and analyses are ultimately subservient to this goal. Buddhism, accordingly, is a way of salvation, it has a soteriological character. All attention is directed at man's bondage in the circle of rebirth, and at how this bondage can be overcome. That is why Buddhism did not start as a philosophy. We might better describe it as a psychotherapy. The method used is derived from medicine: first one makes a diagnosis, then one searches for the cause of the disease, and finally its cure is prescribed. The early Buddhists saw their teaching as a method of spiritual healing in analogy to the bodily healing practised by the physician. Their intention was not the finding of theoretical truth, but the healing of the suffering of mankind. They even taught, that an overdose of scientific inquisitiveness might obstruct the healing process they had in mind. That we consider the thinking of the Buddha here in the context of a history of philosophy, is, because of his thinking having – in the course of its development through the ages – many philosophical repercussions. On the one hand it developed into an institutional religion, on the other hand it gave rise to sophisticated philosophic systems in the fields of the theory of knowledge (epistemology), and that of metaphysics. But these never were considered worthy to be striven after for their own sake.

Chapter 1
The Buddha and his Teaching

In the following we will try to give a survey of the life, method, and thoughts of the historical Buddha. Much of it is tentative, since we must base ourselves on scriptures recorded not before 200 years after his death. The scriptures that we actually possess are based on versions that are dated even between 200 and 400 years later. We cannot know for sure what of it presents the genuine word of the teacher, and what is later addition, or a restatement of earlier, even perhaps pre-Buddhistic thought.

T*HE SCRIPTURES IN THREE BASKETS.* Traditionally the canonical scriptures of Buddhism are divided into three 'baskets' *(piṭakas)*. That's why the collection of it is called *tripiṭaka*. These are: the basket of *sūtras*, consisting mainly of sermons believed to be spoken by the Buddha in person, the basket of order rules, and the 'metaphysical' basket or Abhidharma. Of these three baskets the last one is of considerably later origin. Its content is coloured by the convictions of different schools, and it does not give reliable information about the historical thought of the Buddha. Therefore we let the discussion of it rest a moment, and confine ourselves to the first two baskets.

The basket of order rules gives much information about the way of life in the early Buddhist community. The rules themselves were considered a matter of convention, time-bound and not of absolute truth. Such absolute truth was to be found in the sermons of the Buddha, which were written down in scriptures called *sūtras*. In these the Doctrine or Law was expounded, which forms the heart of all Buddhistic teaching. For an understanding of the Buddha's thought, it is therefore necessary to scrutinize this basket of *sūtras*. This basket – as the other baskets – is in whole or in part preserved in many recensions, of which the Pali-recension used in Sri Lanka, Thailand, and Burma is the most complete and best known.

The baskets of rules and of sermons may well date back in their origin to the earliest Buddhist community, and may give a fair account of what the Buddha preached. They probably were originally written in Ardhamagadhi, the lingua franca of the Maurya-empire (3d century BCe). Afterwards they were translated in many local and foreign languages. Of these the Sanskrit and Pāli are the most important, since these are the languages in which most is preserved. For Buddhism the Pāli-language is of special importance, since in this language of the sacred scriptures of Sri Lanka, the old canon is, as far as we know, preserved completely. There is much debate about the origin of this language. It is certainly not an archaic form of Singhalese (the language of a large part of the population of Sri Lanka), and it is also not a language of the Magadha-region where the Buddha himself preached. It is an archaic language, akin to the Vedic, but it is characterized by a strong agglutination of consonants. Most scholars search the cradle of this language in Central India. The estimations range from Kaliṅga in the east (Orissa) to Avanti (near Ujjain) in the west. The regions of Sarnāth and Kauśāmbi also are mentioned.[1] If these scholars are right, the Sri Lanka scriptures may not be so ancient as to guarantee complete authenticity. They seem to have been written down in the first century BCE. On the other hand, most of the Pāli scriptures are confirmed by canons in other languages, such as Sanskrit or Chinese. This pleads for their trustworthiness, and their being rooted in more ancient tradition.

The basket of sermons.

The basket of sermons or *sūtras* is, in Pāli as well as in Sanskrit, divided over five collections, called *āgamas* in Sanskrit and *nikāyas* in

1 Avanti is mentioned by Étienne Lamotte in his *L'Histoire du Bouddhisme Indien*, p. 626, Kauśāmbi and Sāñci by Erich Frauwallner in his *Geschichte der indische Philosophie,* 1st volume, p. 150.

Pāli: that of the long sermons, that of the middle ones, the mixed, the ascending, and small ones. The first two groups of sermons (and other anecdotes) are classified according to their length, the 'ascending' collection gives an enumeration of truths in order of importance, and the small collection is a compilation of heterogeneous material. The heart of it is constituted by verse *(stanzas)*, which may partly even be older than the Buddha himself. He heard it singing and approved of it. This collection also contains the stories of former births of the Buddha, the so-called *Jātakas.* In the table on the next page we give an enumeration of the contents of the baskets of sermons and of order rules, to which is added the Pāli content of the 'small' collection.

T*HE LIFE OF THE BUDDHA*. A commonly accepted date concerning the life of the Buddha is the year 486 BCE for his death. In some traditions there is also accepted a date some hundred years later. Depending on these different dates, different chronologies are used, the so-called long and short ones. Most Western scholars have adopted the long one, but recent evidence seems to indicate that, after all, the short chronology, accepting the later date, is the correct one.[2]

It is believed that the Buddha was born around the year 560 (or 442) BCE in a town named Kapilavastu at the feet of the Himalayas in present day Nepal. This region seems at the time to have had a busy city life with much trade, a developed bourgeoisie and a vivid intellectual life. The Buddha was a member of the nobility and belonged to the clan of the Śākyas. That's why he was later called Śākyamuni (sage of the Śākyas). His proper name was Siddhārtha, and his father was a king or better, clan head. As a youth he lived the life befitting his status. He married a girl named Yaśodhara. With her he had a son named Rahula. Siddhārtha was destined to follow a similar career as his father. But something came in between.

In the flowering of his youth he decided to abandon the world and

2 Hajime Nakamura mentions Hakuju Ui as the first modern scholar accepting the short chronology. According to him the Buddha lived from 466-386 BCE (*Indo tetsugaku Kenkyū*, vol 2, pp. 1-112, Tokyo Kōnisha 1926). Nakamura follows him, putting both dates, of birth and death three years later (*Indian Buddhism*, p.14. In Europe H. Bechert has recently come to similar conclusions in *Die Lebenszeit des Buddha*, Göttingen 1986.

Scriptures

Vinaya

Bhikṣu-pratimokṣa & Vibhaṅga – *Rules for monks and commentary*
Bhikṣuni-pratomokṣa & Vibhaṅga – *Rules for nuns and commentary*
Skandhaka – *Rules on regulation of certain details*
Mahāvagga & Cullavagga – *Large and small collections*
Parivārapāṭha – *Summary in Pāli*

Sūtras – Sermons

Dīrghāgama (Skr.), Dīgha-nikāya (Pāli) – *Long sermons*
Madhyāmāgama (Skr) Majjhima-nikāya – *Middle length sermons*
Saṁyuktāgama (Skr), Saṁyutta-nikāya (Pāli) – *Mixed sermons*
Ekottarāgama (Skr), Aṅguttara-nikāya (Pāli) – *Ascending Enumeration*
Kṣudrāgama (Skr), Khuddaka-nikāya)Pāli) – *Small writings*

Khuddaka-nikāya, Small writings

Khuddaka-pāṭha – *The small rehearsal*
Dhammapāda – *Verse on the Dharma*
Udāna – *Elated utterances*
Itivuttaka – *Things thus said*
Suttanipāta – *The emergence of the sūtras*
Vimānavatthu – *Story about heavenly mansions*
Pethavatthu – *Ghost stories*
Theragātha – *Stanzas of the monks*
Therigātha – *Stanzas of the nuns*
Jātaka – *Birth stories*
Niddesa – *Index*
Paṭisambhidāmagga – *The path of discrimination*
Apadāna – *Legends*
Buddhavaṁsa – *The Buddha familiy*
Cariyapiṭaka – *The basket on conduct*

become an ascetic. Seeing the reality of old age, sickness and death he became despondent, and forsook all the material advantages he enjoyed. He started now as a homeless wanderer to study Yoga under two teachers, Arāḍa Kalāma and Udraka Rāmaputra. They wanted to bring their pupils by way of meditation to higher levels of consciousness, the first to the level of nothingness and the second to that beyond consciousness and unconsciousness. The gifted pupil Siddhārtha quickly achieved these states, but without being freed from his unrest. He decided to find by himself the way to liberation, and he started to practice asceticism *(tapas)* to the extreme, but without result. So he rejected it. Not long after, one night, at the foot of a tree in the land of Magadha, he found for himself the liberating knowledge. He was then thirty six years of age. He doubted whether he should make this liberating knowledge known to the world, but finally he went to Benares to preach in the park of the gazelles, to his old companions in asceticism, what he had found. Then followed the life of a preacher. His preaching was not class-oriented; he preached to kings, artisans, Brahmins, merchants and prostitutes. He called himself (or was called) the Buddha, the enlightened one, or the one who has come to awakening, and also was he called the *tathāgata*, the one who has thus become or the perfected one. He died at the age of about eighty years in the town of Kuśinagari. During his life an order of monks and nuns had come into existence.

T*HE PATH TO FREEDOM* It seems that the Buddha had already since his youth an aversion of speculation. He felt a closer affinity with the practical approach to the problem of life as found in Yoga and asceticism. His attitude towards speculation is even clearer revealed by his negative characterization of liberation; it is the escape from the circle of rebirth *(saṁsāra)*. There is no speculation on the nature of some ultimate entity, but simply the promise of the end of suffering. The only positive thing that can be said about it, is that it is constituted by some kind of liberating knowledge.

Ethical rules.

Two tenets lay at the base of the Buddha's insights: one that man is trapped in the rebirth circle, the other that he can be freed from this trap. But this can only be achieved by those who can fully devote themselves to the liberation job, the monks and nuns who live in celibacy. Those living in this world as a householder can prepare for future liberation in a next life by supporting the community of monks and observing the lay rules: it is forbidden to destroy life, to steal, to commit illicit sexual behaviour, to lie, and to drink intoxicating liquor. For the community of monks and nuns *(saṁgha)* count the same rules, only here sexual behaviour is forbidden at all, and some rules on verbal behaviour are added. Monks should refrain from slander, brute language, and talking nonsense.

Meditation.

The monk carries all he has on his body and keeps his senses under control. Being thus without distraction he must practice wakefulness and attentiveness. Such behaviour is a prerequisite for a liberating meditation. Further preparations are the disposing of the hindrances. These are: avarice, angriness, anger, inflexibility, weakness, excitement, remorse, doubt, and unclarity concerning what is wholesome. One should practice these preparations in a remote and quiet spot, e.g. under a tree, in a cave, or on a graveyard. The best time is during the night. It cleans the mind, which is brought to a clear awareness. This abandoning of all unwholesome phenomena is the beginning of the sinking in a first of four stages of meditation. Guided by reflection and deliberation one reaches the contentment and pleasure that are the characteristics of this first meditation-state. This meditation is accompanied by breathing exercises.

When reflection or thinking and deliberation come to rest, the second stage of meditation is obtained. It consists in the finding of an inner tranquillity and concentration. The novice stays in it; and again from it emerge contentment and pleasure. In the third stage there is a turning away from this contentment in an equanimous perseverance, and again there returns a physical experience of pleasure. Finally, in the fourth stage, the aspirant does away with both pleasure and pain or suffering, and he finds pure equanimity and wakefulness. He is now ready to accept the liberating knowledge. This knowledge is introduced by paranormal phenomena, such as the appearances of gods and many other miraculous things, amongst which the coming free of a mental body from the material body. The aspirant starts to see clearly his former births and lives, periods of world-creation and world-destruction. Then he contemplates the birth and decay of the creatures on a more general level, and he sees how they return to a new life in accordance with their works *(karma)* in previous lives; those having accomplished good works going to heaven, and those having committed bad deeds going to hell.

Liberating insight.

Then the monk directs his attention to the causes of his bondage in the world, and he understands, that these are both subjective and objective. The subjective causes are suffering and its origin: desire. For without suffering there can be no (experience of) bondage. The objective causes are the defiling 'influences' *(āsravas)*, viz. those of attraction *(kāma)*, making you desirous to have and to enjoy, of becoming *(bhava)* [personality formation], making you desirous to be someone important, and of ignorance *(avidyā)*. When the monk becomes clearly aware of them, by contemplating them with a detached mind, and without personal interest, he becomes free from these influences and from the suffering they cause, and there arises the following insight:

> 'This is suffering, he acknowledges according to truth. This is the origin of suffering; this the abandoning of suffering, and this the road that leads to the termination of suffering. These are the defiling influences, he acknowledges, this their origin, this their abandonment, and this the road leading to their termination.'

When he has acquired such insight, he is freed from the influence of attraction, from the influence of becoming, and from the influence of ignorance. The knowledge of liberation breaks through: 'Destroyed is rebirth, accomplished the noble path, fulfilled the duty. There is no more return into this world.[3] The aspirant is now an arhat, a holy one, and when he dies he enters into *nirvāṇa*, the final extinction of all activity and craving.[4] In all this, the liberation method of the Buddha has much in common with that of Yoga, save that nothing positive about the content of the liberating knowledge is stated.

T*HOUGHTS BEHIND THE METHOD*. The way of liberation as described above is an instruction of the mature Buddha to an already developed community of monks. Three important thoughts lay behind it. The first is that of the *four noble truths*. This thought was conceived by the Buddha as a direct result of his experience of enlightenment. It was expressed in his first sermon, addressed to his former companions in asceticism in the Park of the gazelles near Benares. The second thought was that of the influence of ignorance, which is the condition for the forming of a mundane personality (with its status and worldly importance), which alone can be the subject of suffering. This idea may have arisen in the Buddha's mind as a result of discussions with other schools of thought. The third thought is that of dependent origination. This thought represents the final synthesis of the previous thoughts.

The four noble truths

First we discuss the thought of the four noble truths. This thought is a development of the medical method: making a diagnosis of the hu-

3 E. Frauwallner, *Indische Philosophie*, vol. 1, pp. 161-170, based on *Dīgha-nikāya* 2.3 etc. and *Majjhīma-nikāya* 27-38.

4 Ibid., The present chapter relies heavily on the exposition of Frauwallner. He has been followed in all sections except that of *Ethical causation*, for which much information was derived from E.J. Thomas's *The History of Buddhist Thought*. However Frauwallner notes a lack of coherence in the doctrine of dependent origination, notably he finds a tension between the concepts of thirst and ignorance (p, 196 ff) In my opinion the two cencepts can easily be harmonized. Therefore in this respect I have departed from Frauwallner. Also in my rendering of the liberating experience. I have simply given my own understanding of the matter, based on various reading. This understanding, I found afterwards, comes close to that of T. Vetter in *The Ideas and Meditative Practices of Early Buddhism*, pp. 3-4.

man condition, seeking the causes of the disease, and prescribing the cure.

> 'These monks are the four noble truths. Which four? Suffering *(duḥkha)*, the origin of suffering, the termination of suffering, and the path that leads to the termination of suffering.
> What, again, is suffering? Birth is suffering, old age is suffering, illness is suffering, death is suffering, to be united with what is not loved is suffering, to be separated from what is loved is suffering; not to obtain what you desire and strive for, that also is suffering. In short, the five groups of attachments: bodily forms, feelings, cognitions, inclinations, perceptions are suffering. This is called suffering.
> What is the origin of suffering? It is thirst *(tṛṣṇā)* that leads to rebirth and that is accompanied by desire and pleasure and finds enjoyment in this or in that. That is called the origin of suffering.
> What is the termination of suffering? It is the rejection without remainder of this thirst leading to rebirth, accompanied by pleasure and desire, and finding enjoyment in this or in that. Its abandonment and suppression; that is the termination of suffering.
> And what is the road that leads to the termination of suffering? It is the noble eightfold path: correct faith, correct thinking, correct speech, correct action, correct livelihood, correct striving, correct attention, and correct concentration. That is called the path leading to the termination of suffering. That, monks, are the four noble truths.'[5]

These four noble truths correspond fairly well with the first four insights that constitute the liberating knowledge in the liberation path described above, viz: 'This is suffering, he acknowledges according to truth. This is the origin of suffering; this the abandoning of suffering, and this the road that leads to the termination of suffering.' The message is clear: life is suffering, and this suffering has its subjective condition in 'thirst.' This, primarily, may be conceived as an inexplicable craving, causing attachments to things in this world of various kinds. It is considered as a sickness, and its remedy is the eightfold path.

The first truth, the characterization of life as suffering, does not deny the existence of the good things in life. It means that life brings

5 Frauwallner, *Indische Philosophie*, vol 1, pp. 183-84, based on *Mahāvagga* 1,6 ff.

either suffering or pleasure, but since all pleasure is by its nature temporal, it necessarily leads to suffering when it is over, for, above all, the transiency of the good things hurts. This makes that life as a whole is nevertheless justifiably characterized as suffering.

The second truth, concerning the origin of suffering, is, that the root of all pain is 'thirst,' and this is taken in the sense of 'longing' or 'desire.' This is not a new concept; already in the old epical literature desire was considered as the cause of the suffering in the circle of rebirth. Only the use of the word 'thirst' is new. But what causes 'thirst'? The answer is, that it comes to be by reason of the contact between the senses and its objects; between the eye and visible forms, the ear and sounds, the nose and smells etc. The contacts are not merely made through the outer senses; Buddhism accepts the thinking organ *(manas)* as a sixth sense, which contacts all objects, whether object of the outer or the inner sense. It is therefore also this contact on a deeper level, that must be considered as the root of 'thirst.' It gives rise to sensory perceptions and feelings, which, in turn, give rise to desires or 'thirst.' Accordingly, when one wants to conquer 'thirst' by means of the eightfold path, one must begin by guarding the senses. When they touch their objects, take heed not to let them nurture any desires.

The third truth merely concerns the eradication of the 'thirst' by means of the *eightfold path*, which is the subject of the fourth truth: *correct faith, correct thinking, correct speech, correct action, correct livelihood, correct striving, correct attention, and correct concentration.* Closer examination reveals, that this eightfold path is nothing else but the liberation path, which we have described above. 'Correct concentration' points to the meditation-stages described; 'correct wakefulness' reminds of the stress on wakefulness characterizing the meditation-path in its first and last stages. 'Correct striving' is the trying to avoid unwholesome phenomena, resulting in contentment and pleasure. 'Correct livelihood' is the begging-life of the wandering monk, taken as a condition for liberation. 'Correct action,' 'speech,' and 'thinking' stand for the ethical attitude that is the prerequisite for the path of meditation; however, 'thinking' also may point to the 'reflection' and 'deliberation' that form the beginning of the first meditation-stage. 'Correct faith,' lastly, denotes the attitude of trust in the master *(guru)*, which is the common characteristic of all classic Indian education systems.[6]

The influence of ignorance.

In the course of the Buddha's life, the contact between the mind and its objects became considered as an insufficient ground for the operating of 'thirst.' It explained how suffering comes to be, but it did not answer the more principal question how it can be. In other words, it gave a genetic explanation of suffering, but it did not explore its transcendental presuppositions. When we remember the Buddha's aversion of metaphysical questions, we can imagine that he was reluctant to treat this topic. But probably discussions with other schools of thought forced him to enter this field.

The result of the inquiry into the presuppositions of suffering can be summarized as follows: in the sermon of Benares we have seen, that the Buddha characterized the so-called five groups of grasping as suffering. These groups were specified as bodily forms, feelings, cognitions, inclinations, and perceptions. Perception – which is here the same as consciousness – and the other phenomena mentioned, form the ultimate constituents of worldly existence. They are phenomena which cannot be reduced to each other, and they also are not aspects of a deeper substratum, like a soul. They are just what they are. But living beings construct out of this raw material of worldly existence a personality, a being in the world. This they do by identifying the ego with a particular body, with certain feelings, cognitions, inclinations, and a conscious and knowing mind. By projecting the unity of an ego on a group of worldly phenomena, the illusion of a mundane personality is created. And only such a mundane personality can be subject to desire. It wants to preserve itself, and to enjoy itself with all the attractions of the world. It wants pleasure and continuity. This very thirst for pleasure and being causes suffering.

As we have seen, the mundane personality rests on a mistake: the phenomena constituting our world are not the ego. Therefore the human condition is ultimately based on the influence of ignorance. When the ignorance is removed, there is no longer a worldly person-

6 Frauwallner, 1, pp. 185-86.

ality thirsting for attractions, pleasures, and a continuing worldly existence, also called in Buddhist terminology 'becoming' *(bhava)*. When the influence of ignorance is overcome, also those of attractions and becoming will become extinct. Then there also will be no more desire for pleasures and existence.

We now can understand why at the end of the description of the path of meditation, when the rise of the liberating insight is touched upon, mention was made of 'subjective' suffering and its origin 'thirst,' and of 'objective' influences, such as that of ignorance. 'Suffering' recalls the sermon of Benares, and summarizes how the human condition arises and how it is to be cured. It reminds one of the practical steps one has to make to obtain liberation. The 'influences,' headed by 'ignorance,' point to the presupposition of the worldly state, and by what insight it can be set aside. Without the right knowledge about the condition of the ego and the world, without keeping before the mind, that the ego is by nature free from every bond with the world, one cannot even prepare to put one's steps on the path towards the realization of this truth.

The final form of the Buddha's lore concerning desire can be formulated thus: desire or thirst only operates under the influence of ignorance. It presupposes an illusory worldly personality, which is by its nature subject to desires of two kinds, the desire for its own continuation and growth, called becoming, and that for sensory enjoyments or attractions. But this desire does not lead to the goal as it is consciously conceived, on the contrary, the reverse is obtained, suffering and death. But when, by great effort, desire is eradicated and ignorance destroyed, there follows liberation from suffering and death, and what is no longer desired is now obtained: the pleasure that is to be found in true freedom and peace, and immortality. Don't try to conservate what is by nature perishable, it is in vain; don't try to enjoy what is by nature painful (the five groups of elementary phenomena), for it hurts.

Dependent origination.

For the Buddha of the sermon in Benares, 'thirst' was the sole origin of the bondage in *saṁsāra*, the circle of rebirth. By mentioning only this subjective cause, the teaching of the Buddha distinguished itself from most other liberation systems, which, as a rule, mention 'ignorance' *(avidyā)* – which was felt as something more objective – as the prime cause of suffering. But although for the Buddha 'thirst' was the origin of bondage, he considered liberation as a form of knowledge. This fact, probably, gave, to the eyes of some of the Buddha's contemporaries, his teaching a lack of symmetry, since one would expect, that, when liberation is a form of knowledge, the cause of bondage should be a form of ignorance. Probably because of the criticism of other systems of thought concerning this point, the topic of the origin of suffering underwent a reformulation, and 'thirst' was brought into a close connection with 'ignorance'. So it came, as we have seen, that the Buddha's mature teaching could put a connection between thirst and the influences of attraction and personality formation (becoming), which both are only possible because of the identification of the subject with the 'groups of grasping': forms, feelings, cognitions, inclinations, and perceptions or consciousness (mind). And this very identification, not being based on the truth, points to the influence of ignorance.

Suffering having now an objective as well as a subjective base, the simplicity of its causation, as put forward by the sermon of Benares was lost. It became replaced by a complex doctrine of causation, which even in the eyes of the Buddha himself was difficult and profound. It was called the 'doctrine of dependent origination' *(pratītya-samutpāda)*, and it may be considered as the final synthesis of the Buddha's thought. At the bottom this doctrine wants to deny that something can come to be out of nothing. Something can appear only in dependence on something else; there are only mutually conditioning phenomena. For instance, there can be no subjective 'thirst' without the 'objective' influence of ignorance. But there is also a dependence in the opposite direction, since 'thirst' is responsible for the preservation of ignorance.

The dependence on one another of the different elements of existence became expressed in a twelve-membered chain of causation, of which every next element is conditioned by the previous. It was described in the following way:

'The inclinations *(saṁskāra)* (2) originate dependent on ignorance *(avidyā)* (1); consciousness *(vijñāna)* (3) originates dependent on the inclinations; name and form *(nāma-rūpa)* (4) originate dependent on consciousness; the six sensory fields *(ṣadāyatana)* (5) originate dependent on name and form; contact *(sparśa)* (6) originates dependent on the six sensory fields; feelings *(vedanā)* (7) originate dependent on contact; thirst *(tṛṣṇā)* (8) originates dependent on feelings; grasping at the five groups [forms, feelings, cognitions, inclinations, and consciousness] *(upadāna)* (9) originates dependent on thirst; becoming *(bhava)* [personality formation] (10) originates dependent on grasping; birth *(jāti)* (11) originates dependent on personality formation; old age, death *(jaramaraṇa)*, complaint, suffering, sadness, and despondence (12) originate dependent on birth.' [7]

Explanation of the chain of dependent origination.

Tradition tells us, that the chain of dependent origination, as given above, represents the working of its diverse elements spreading over three lives. Ignorance (1) and inclinations (2) are said to belong to the former life. Consciousness (perception) (3) until becoming (10) refer to the present life (its conception, development, and the preliminaries for the next life). From birth (11) onwards, the chain points to the next life.

We have seen, that 'thirst' is only possible on the ground of the ego-concept. This concept arises, because people identify themselves with the worldly personality, constituted by forms, feelings, cognitions, inclinations, and consciousness. This identification is mistaken, and points to the influence of ignorance. This intimate relationship between 'thirst' and ignorance, we see reflected in the first two members of the chain of dependent origination; for by 'inclinations' we must understand all conative acts, including those subconscious forces, that impel us to satisfy our needs. They are nothing else but the 'thirst,' which makes us grasp after worldly existence and its attractions. The attachment caused by the grasping for a place in the world, with its inherent desires, leads, in the Buddhist opinion, inevitably to rebirth,

7 Frauwallner, pp. 197-98. F. does not mention the position of this text in the *Tripiṭaka*, but there are many of these lists. H.C. Warren gives a number of them in his *Buddhism in Translations.* He mentions *Saṁyutta Nikāya* 22-90, 22-35, *Mahānidāna Sutta* of the *Dīgha Nikāya*. Significantly in these passages the term *saṁskāra* is replaced by that of *karma*.

which is nothing else but the conjunction of the transmigrating consciousness (i.e. informed consciousness, consciousness with a characteristic habit of perceiving) with a new psychical and physical frame, called 'name and form.' This conjunction of consciousness with the germs of a psycho-physical complex, is indicated by the third and fourth members of the chain: consciousness (3) and 'name and form'.

The chain then goes on to explain 'thirst' in another way. It now does not deal with its presupposition, which is ignorance, but with its temporal antecedents. There is no thirst (8) without a feeling (7) having instigated it, and there is no feeling, when not first a contact has been made between the senses and their objects (the forms, or sensory impressions). The origins of 'thirst,' accordingly, can be depicted in two ways: when we ask for the transcendental condition of thirst, we are led to ignorance, but when we ask for thirst's temporal antecedents, we are led to the contact between the senses and sensory forms. The chain shows, how either way, thirst leads to attachment, the grasping at existence, which leads to a new conjunction with a psycho-physical frame. At the end of the chain, this conjunction is represented by the term 'becoming' (conception) (10), followed by 'birth' (11). The first two rounds of the chain now have instructed us on how 'thirst' can be, and how it comes to be. We know on what it is dependent, and on what conditions it does arise. The last round of the chain then simply ends by stating its unavoidable consequence: 'suffering' (12) in all its different forms, the sickness that is to be cured.

In the three life-cycles of the chain of dependent origination, the same process of the emergence of thirst, with its causes and its consequences, is described from three different angles. The chain gives in the first two members, the first life-cycle, the transcendental causes of suffering, in the members from the third until the tenth, the second life-cycle, its development, and in the third life-cycle its consequence, suffering. But, of course, causes, development, and consequences are present in any life-cycle. Only for the sake of clarity of exposition, the three aspects of the suffering in the circle of rebirth are presented as covering three successive lives.

Elucidation of the separate elements of the chain.

The chain of dependent origination needs some further elucidation. We shall discuss its separate links one by one, beginning with the second: inclinations. The first link, ignorance, and its intimate relation with 'thirst,' will be discussed under a separate heading.

The word 'inclinations' *(saṁskāra)* (2) in Buddhism stands for all volitional and subconscious forces operating in living beings. Since in the early phase of Buddhism no natural causation apart from causation by life-forces is accepted, the 'inclinations' stand for the whole complex of efficient causes, determining reality. What is called 'thirst' is just another name for this complex of factors keeping phenomenal life running. The inclinations or life-forces exhibit a proclivity which moves the mind in a certain direction. Whereas the inclinations constitute the active factors of life, the mind is formed by a series of receptive and cognitive acts, which are the successive perceptions and apprehensions of different objects. It will be evident, that every activity of a living being has consequences for its successive cognition. The mind, being a series of perceptions, conditioned by life-forces, can also be identified with consciousness *(vijñāna)*. Mind, or consciousness, is, by the impetus given to it by the life-forces, led to the fruition or cognition of a certain complex of forms. We can take this as a fact of life. If I want something, e.g. a loaf, I go the baker's, and in going there I see the street, its houses, the trees at the side of the road, and finally I see the baker's shop; I recognize its particular smell, and I hear the voice of the girl asking me what I want to buy. All these facts constitute the forms of my life. But Buddhism goes still further. The series of cognitions does not stop at death. Whereas my desire for bread leads me to the baker's, the desire at the moment of my death, leads the series of cognitions and their perceptions, my consciousness, to the fruition of the forms of a new existence. The desire at the moment of death is determined by the habitual pattern of volition of my whole life. If I had in my life noble aspirations, these may lead me to a birth in heaven, if my intentions were base, they may lead me to hell. This coming to fruition of the series of cognitions in the forms of a new existence, is what is meant, when 'name and form' *(nāmarūpa)* (4) are mentioned as the fourth link of the chain. They constitute the physical and psychical phenomena of a (new) life, to which I have been led by the conscious and subconscious tendencies of my previous life. Form here stands for the 'physical' phenomena, and name for the psychical. More precisely, the 'physical' phenomena are the impressions on the senses such as colours, sounds, odours, tastes, and touch, in short the impressions left on us by the stimuli of the world outside. The psychical phenomena are formed by the impressions of feelings, but also by memories, ideas, imaginations, the subjective elaboration of the sensory material (also called 'cognition'), inclinations, and perceptions.

The following links of the chain are an explication of how name and form develop. The series of cognitions are qualified by the different fields in which they are operative, corresponding with the five senses providing the impressions of the world outside, and with the mind itself, which, as the sixth sense, perceives without mediation the phenomena of inner life. The mind, accordingly, displays a six-fold division, corresponding with the six sensory fields *(ṣadāyatana)* (5) mentioned in the chain. When these fields are filled with their corresponding impressions, this is called contact *(sparśa)*. These impressions are the same as the names and forms contacted by the series of perceptions, mentioned under (3) and from the experience of impressions emerge feelings *(vedanā)*. These, again, motivate the complex of inclinations, presently introduced under the title of 'thirst.' The circle is now closed. For thirst, the complex of inclinations, results in the mind taking up, or grasping (9) at, a new psycho-somatic complex, which consists of the five groups (forms, feelings, cognitions, inclinations, and perceptions), which were earlier summarized under the title of 'name and form,' and are also indicated by the word 'becoming' (10). Becoming, starting with conception, issues in a new birth (11), and ends with old age and death (12). Sadness, complaint, etc. can be conceived as the summary of the suffering implicit in the new life.

Ignorance and thirst.

Ignorance (1) was the (transcendental) presupposition of the inclinations (2), which, to a high degree, can be identified with 'thirst'. But sometimes 'thirst' also was identified with ignorance, as was done by the 5th century Theravāda thinker Buddhaghosa. We need not accept here a real conflict of opinion. The state of bondage, characterized by 'thirst,' is the one that presents alluring objects to the mind, which are not actually there, but which one would like either to have, or to become. These objects make the mind – which becomes inclined to the objects of its desire – move in a certain direction. Now we should know, that it is, according to the early Buddhists, the proper function of the mind to be merely reflective. The presentation of an image of something which is not there, on the contrary, is not a reflective cognition, but a fancy or imagination. It disturbs the pure reflective activity of the mind, and sets it in motion, fills it with unrest. Here we see, how the illusory presentation, the imagination, once conceived, at the same time causes inclination and motion towards itself. For the early Buddhist mind, illusory presentation is nothing else but ignorance. This ignorance, presenting fanciful objects, is inseparable from the volition and motion which it causes. Thirst and ignorance are really two aspects of one and the same process. Therefore they can be identified under certain circumstances. There is a mind which, by not reflecting reality, but by presenting illusions, is in a state of ignorance; it is influenced by ignorance. But what is not there, the object presented by the illusion, attracts the mind. Thus the ignorant mind at the same time is a thirsting mind. The same state of mind is characterized by both, thirst and ignorance. The thirsting state can be called 'ignorant,' and the ignorant one 'thirsting.' The absence of true reflective cognition in the mind can be termed 'ignorance,' but such ignorance is not a mere negation. For the ancient Indian, when something is not knowledge it is not 'not-knowledge,' but something other than knowledge. Other than knowledge – being on the intellective level – is action, change, and what motivates it, thirst, volition, intention, drift – being on the conative plane. These two spheres, the intellective sphere of truth, and the practical or conative sphere of change, form the fundamental contrast in all existence, not only in Buddhism, but in other Indian thought-systems as well. When something is not the one, it is the other. It is the same contrast as between rest (which is quieting and comforting truth) and motion, and as between the permanent (which is abiding truth) and the impermanent (consisting of mere transient phenomena), which is the never ending metamorphosis of temporal reality.

The chain of dependent origination

1) ignorance (avidyā)

2) inclinations (saṁskāra)

3) perceiving (vijñāna)

4) name and form (nāma-rūpa)

5) the six sensory fields (ṣaḍāyatana)

6) contact (sparśa)

7) feeling (vedanā)

8) thirst (tṛṣṇā)

9) grasping (upādāna)

10) becoming (bhava)

11) birth (jāti)

12) old age (jarā), death (maraṇa) … suffering (duḥkha)

The cycle of life.

The fundamental characteristic of the chain of dependent origination is, that it is circular. Ignorance is no absolute beginning, and death is no absolute end. You cannot take one member from the chain and preserve the others. Take out one link, and the whole chain is broken, and when you take one link, you can infer from it all the others. Any single element of the chain functions as the condition for all the next ones. But since the chain is a circle, it means that it also conditions itself. The inclinations reappear in 'thirst,' and, again, they are inherent in suffering. Suffering is nothing else but the separation from the object of your desire, which itself is an illusion impelling the mind to ever recurrent birth.

The point in all this is, that one life-circle can be interpreted as copied in structure from every other one, and that all members in the causal chain can be harmonized in one unifying conception of the development of life.

The five groups of grasping.

In the preceding, repeatedly mention has been made of the five groups of grasping: forms, feelings, cognitions, inclinations, and perceptions (knowledge or consciousness). These groups constitute the elements of all worldly existence, its five irreducible types of phenomena.

The reader will perhaps have noticed, that most of these elements have been considered also in the context of the *Chain of Dependent Origination*. 'Forms' stand for the sense data, caused by the stimuli of the world outside on the senses. These arouse 'feelings' such as pleasure and pain. Impressions and feelings are the starting point of the processes of understanding (intellection) and of action (conation). The impressions together with the evaluation of feeling are apprehended in a definite cognition. The light of consciousness makes that this all is perceived as outer and inner process. The same impressions and feelings also motivate the system of inclinations (conative system) to keep or change its direction.

The inclinations (i.e. subconscious tendencies and conscious volition) constitute the factors which condition the rise of new impressions. They move the conscious system in a certain direction, and in this movement new impressions are received, arousing new feelings. And so the process goes on. Accordingly, we can divide the five elementary phenomena twofold, as receptivity and as activity. Impressions *(rūpa)*, feeling *(vedanā)*, cognition *(saṁjñā)*, and their subsequent perception *(vijñāna)* form the process of receptive apprehension, inclinations, motivating practice, form the active, conative process.

Feelings, positive, negative, and neutral.

Crucial in this whole process is the generally non-neutral character of feeling; it provides us with pleasure and pain. It seems, that instinctively we are endowed with the idea of pleasure, and that every impression is measured by it. We suffer from our present experience proportionally to the pleasures projected by our imagination. And if we are so lucky to experience a moment of pleasure and satisfaction, we become mad in our desire to regain it when it is over. The Buddhists consider this projection to be the root-cause of all trouble. It disturbs the natural tranquillity of the mind, and moves it restlessly to all directions. It makes us strive after the satisfaction of our desires. The proper state of the mind is to be reflective; the cognition, the mental state or content, should simply reflect reality, and not impose upon it its own fancies. Such an imposed fancy is nothing but an illusory cognition, one constituted by the influence of ignorance. Freedom is the abandonment of this fancy of lust. Once it is completely abandoned, all impressions can be accepted in a neutral feeling. This does not any longer spur our desires for a better existence, but enables us quietly to accept the contents of our experience. We are freed from our unrest, and at the same time we see, that it was this unrest alone which caused our pain, and that to be freed from it is true pleasure.

Hope and fear are without any base.

We have seen that only a mundane personality can be subject to desire. Such a person was an illusion created by the projection of the unity of an ego on a group of worldly phenomena. We can put the matter also in a somewhat different way: under the influence of ignorance, the unconditioned reflecting mind identifies itself with the conditioned mind, the mind conceived as a part of the world, which sees in all things objects of desire and fear (or does not see them at all). This conditioned mind considers itself to be a worldly personality, constituted by forms, feelings, cognitions, inclinations, and its perceptions, while in reality the mind is distinct from these constituents of the world. Since these constituents are painful, there is the desire to have – and to be made up of – better constituents, such as do not give pain but pleasure. Or, when the constituents happen to be pleasurable, there is the fear that they may not be permanent. All kinds of dangers may threaten them. But the objects of hope and fear are both projections, illusions inspired by ignorance, not only because they are not there, but also because they have no base, since in reality there is no mundane personality. For when it is the true nature of the mind merely to reflect reality, then it cannot itself be a part of it. For one can only reflect without distortion when not being involved. This being the case, what should the mind want to have, what should it want to become? Its only good, freedom, is already inherent in its own nature.

Ultimate reality.

It is often believed, that the Buddha did not accept the existence of a soul, and that he taught that liberation is a mere extinction. Also the opposite has been defended, that the state of *nirvāṇa* is the entering of this soul into a paradise. Both, the nihilist and the eternalist interpretation, rest on a misunderstanding. These misunderstandings are born from the Buddha's aversion of theoretical questions. He did not want to discuss topics like 'the existence of a soul,' and 'the nature of the ultimate,' since these theoretical discussions do not lead to the goal, viz. the attainment of rest, peace, and freedom. This attitude of the Buddha is clearly displayed in the story about one of his pupils, Māluṅkyaputra, who wants answers to questions like: 'Is the world eternal or not?'; 'Are soul and body distinct, or not?'; 'Does the soul continue to live after death or not?'. To these the Buddha answers:

> 'Did I ever speak to you in the following manner: 'Come Māluṅkyaputra, be my pupil; I want to teach you whether the world is eternal or not,

> whether it is finite or infinite, whether soul and body are akin in nature or not, whether the released continue to live after their death or not?' 'No, Sir.' Or did you ever speak to me: 'I want to be your pupil; teach me whether the world is eternal or not, whether it is finite or infinite, whether the soul is akin in nature to the body, or whether the released continue to live after death?' 'No, Sir.' 'It is also settled, Māluṅkyaputra, that neither I told anything like that to you, nor you to me. What kind of fool you are then, and to whom do you make reproaches?'[8]

Then the Buddha gives a parable: A man is hit by an arrow, and his kinsmen search for a doctor. But the patient says: 'I don't let the arrow be pulled out before I know who shot it, with what type of bow, and how the arrow was made.' The man would die before the doctor could treat him. In the same way it is with pupils who want answers to questions like the above. They will die before they have got an answer. At the same time they will fail to do what is really important: to enter on the path of liberation.

> 'Therefore, Māluṅkyaputra, what I did not preach, let it not be preached, and what I have preached, let it be preached. But what did I preach? 'This is suffering,' did I preach; 'This is the origin of suffering,' did I preach; 'That is the termination of suffering,' did I preach; 'That is the road that leads to the termination of suffering,' so did I preach.'

The subject.

But could it totally be avoided to speak about a subject of bondage and liberation? It seems not. One of the origins of suffering was, according to the Buddha, the believe that the earthly personality, the psycho-physical complex, is the true 'I.' This misconception had to be disposed of, and here it could not be avoided to speak of an 'I.' When, as the Buddha teaches, the five groups of elementary phenomena are not the 'I,' it implies, that there must be an 'I' different from it. What ordinary people call the 'true being' *(sattva)* or 'person' (*pudgala)* is

8 E. Frauwallner, *Indische Philosophie*, vol 1, pp. 219-20; from *Majjhīma Nikāya* 63. The whole story and also the quotation on the next page of the present work are based on this text.

nothing but matter, nothing but 'name and form,' nothing but this complex of the five groups of irreducible phenomena. From these five, knowledge *(vijñāna)*, also identified with 'consciousness' *(citta)* or mind *(manas)*, is most likely to be confounded with the 'I.' But it is impermanent; it dies and is reborn every night and day. Of what is perishable, one cannot say: 'this am I' or 'this is mine.' It is here only the false believe in the earthly personality that is rejected, not subjectivity whatsoever.

But if a subjectivity be accepted, how must it be conceived? It seems that the Buddha made a distinction between the earthly mind, conditioned by forms, feelings, perceptions, and inclinations, and the mind as not conditioned by these phenomena. The conditioned mind is continually changed by its contents. It is nothing but the stream of the awarenesses of one's apprehensions based on impressions, which themselves are conditioned by inclinations. Such a mind is nothing but a series of changing states. It is nothing apart from its content. Therefore it is considered as just a constituent of the world. But mind can also be taken in a different sense, unconditioned by impressions, feelings, and inclinations. And this unconditioned mind may well be the ego as distinct from the worldly personality. Such an ego, however, is not itself a person, transcendental or not, not a permanent substrate of mental states, but the mere function of subjectivity, without a place or identity. It is mere perceptivity, a reflecting of reality without someone who perceives or reflects.

We have already touched upon the problem of the identification of the ego with the worldly personality. Under the influence of ignorance, the pure reflecting mind becomes a projecting mind, creating its own illusions. What happens is, that the mind considers itself as a part of the world, which must be fed with worldly material. It takes the good things and drops the garbage. Worldly life is temporal. Therefore: who's not busy being born is busy dying, and the one that does not grow is bound to decay. The mind that considers itself as part of the world, finds itself continually filled with impressions, feelings, inclinations. It is apprehending these, interpreting them from the angle of its interests. Since the mind identifies itself with the perishable human frame, it is bound to serve its well-being and pleasure. This idea of well-being and pleasure, makes that all things are evaluated in the light of it. These are not like what they would be for a disinterested spectator, but they are qualified by the use I can make of them. When, in my desire to eat bread, I go to the baker's, the stones of the street become a highway to food, the houses and trees on the way become indications of the progress towards the satisfaction of my desire. They are not any longer things for their own sake. They are coloured, even distorted by my aims. They are all involved in the projection of what is not actually there. Their own intrinsic nature is hidden by my intentions. The mind bound to desire by ignorance cannot step out of the net of its own imagined objectives. It is always limited by purposes, which are nothing else but fancies. Every apprehension is focused on something to be expected in the (near) future. And in this apprehension of what is not there, the things of which we presently receive impressions are only subsidiarily apprehended as subservient to the goal, and therefore they are veiled in their proper nature. This makes that the mind appears to be impelled to a certain direction. The unpleasant feeling of hunger conditions the will to go after bread, and this, again, conditions all my subsequent apprehensions.

But such a conditioning of experience is not necessary. Suppose, that by whatever reason I forget my person, then, at the same time, it becomes impossible to mind its interests. The things of the world exist no longer for its sake. Simultaneously, the projection of the person's pleasure and well-being is suspended. But this does not annihilate experience whatsoever; there remains an experiencing subjectivity, but it is not involved; it is as it were an anonymous outsider, a mere spectator, like one looking at a movie. If the man in the movie takes up his gun to shoot in our direction, we do not jump behind our seats. There is nothing to lose, nothing to gain. We are just no part of it, and we see it all in the same perspective. We cannot walk into the movie to see the same occurrences from different angles, let alone that we might be able to choose our own path in that imaginary world.

Let's go back to my hunger and to my intention to buy a loaf . I am on my way to the baker's with bread on my mind, but somehow the thought slips from my brain; I become forgetful of myself, absorbed as I am in the present. The fire of my hunger is quenched. I do not chase any more after the world. But then it offers itself to me. My eyes are opened to see the trees and the stones. I sit down in the middle of the square, watching a sunray filtered by an autumn leaf, which afterwards is abducted by a sudden breeze. Then a feeling creeps up. It is not pleasure, it is not elation, still less exaltation; just a burden is dropped, a pressure taken away. Generally such reflective moods pass as if unnoticed, but they are glances of liberation, although filtered by an autumn leave, which, since long, has withered away without anybody's attention. There was a 'timeless' moment, in the sense that it was not a conditioned phase in the process leading to the fruition of a projected aim, and also in the sense, that for a moment the 'person' and its preservation had fallen into oblivion. There was just a reflection, but it could have been anybody's.

Perhaps there will be someone who is not able to deny and disregard this seed of truth, of which gradually the roots break through the stony cover of his regimented life to demolish its frame. Once, under a roseapple (Jambu) tree on a forgotten spot in a garden, the young prince Siddārtha had a similar experience.[9] It finally uprooted the whole structure of his carefree, superficial upper-class existence, by functioning as a compass in the main decisions of his life. And so he became the Buddha. For if you once have been in touch with truth, you never more can be satisfied with the untruthful.

Although the reflective state of mind may be taken as just one of the phenomena of life, it lacks the characteristics of the normal condi-

9 The oldest description of the experience in the Buddha's youth is given in *Majjhīma Nikāya* 36-1. I quote it here in the rendering of T. Vetter, *Ideas and Meditative Practices of Early Buddhism.*

> Then Aggivessana, I thought: I remember that once my father, the Sakka, was working (in the fields), I was sitting in the cool shadow of a Jambu tree. Separated from objects which awaken desire, separated from harmful qualities, I reached a (state of) joy and happiness *(pīta-sukha)* accompanied by contemplation and reflection which is the first *dhyāna* (meditation) and remained in it for some time. Could it be, perhaps, the way *(magga)* to enlightenment *(bodha)*? After this memory, Aggivessana, I had this knowledge: *this is the way to enlightenment.* [Then] Aggivessana I thought: 'Why should I be afraid of this happiness that has nothiung to do with objects which awaken desire and nothing to do with harmful qualities?'

Both Vetter and J. Moussaief Masson [*The Oceanic Feeling*, Reidel, Dordrecht, p. 73 ff] see in this experience the root of the Buddha's teaching. The situation of the experience in a garden is mentioned in *Lalitavistara* [Masson, p. 74]

tioned existence. In it the volition does not precondition the apprehension, the feeling does not precondition the volition, and the impression does not precondition the feeling, but all these are simultaneously implicit in the momentary cognition. Here is mind not caught up in its objectives, constricted and bound, but mind as such, pouring itself out, reflective, tranquil, and free.

Is this mere extinction? Something has become extinct indeed: the projective activity of the mind. But still there is mind, and even experience. And indeed there is no soul, no permanent subject, with a temporal or even eternal destiny, since nothing is implied beyond the experience itself. But still one may say that there is subjectivity. Is this paradise? Only if you want to call a dirty city square by that name. But one can also say with the Zen masters, that it is just nothing special.

Here there is neither a mortal nor an immortal soul, but the plain experience that can be called 'unconditioned mind.' As such, you cannot ascribe to it a place, nor a path, nor a destiny. But you can say that it is there, positive, and liberating.

The absolute.

For the Buddha, the unconditioned mind, which experiences all without commitment, is the ultimate presupposition and refuge of all living beings. To this mind, not as a substance, but as a way of cognition and experience, the Buddha referred, when he said:

> 'There is, monks, a thing unborn, unbecome, unmade, unformed. If, monks, this unborn, unbecome, unmade, unformed thing would not be there, then there would be no escape for what is born, has become, is made, and formed.'[10]

For an act of mere reflection is not a thing, which develops, decays, and is destroyed. It is not born out of some other thing. It is just there. And it is always there if anything is there. For nothing can be given at all except in the reflection of the mind. The latter can appear conditioned and distorted, but it cannot be destroyed.

10 Frauwallner, *Indische Philosophie,* 1, p. 227, quoting *Udāna* 8-3, *Itivuttaka* 43.

For the Buddha, the unconditioned mind is the basis of all our projections or illusions. There can be no experience, misleading or true, without it. Completely unconditioned, however, it becomes also inconceivable. We tried to describe a liberating experience in life. This we could do, because such a liberation in context can still be contrasted with life as bound, and, somehow, it still rests on the presupposition of such normal life.

But in the Buddha's time the great question was: 'where go the released after death?' The Buddha said, that the senses and the minds of the living cannot follow those beyond the grave, who have gone beyond all lust, and have reached unchangeable bliss. But for the Buddha and his contemporaries, the idea of consciousness, the mind, going on experiencing after death, was very obvious. Mind does not vanish in the hereafter, but how does it exist there? A mind not identified with a history and a destiny can go nowhere. Without eyes, it has no perspective, without feet it has no path. It reflects, but without a mirror. Having no place, it is omnipresent, testifying to the truth of everything. It is twice at the same time, unqualified subjectivity and unqualified freedom. Metaphorically, it can perhaps best be described as light, and when the released die, they go into it, and shine in peace.

Ethical causation.

'*Karma* literally just means 'work,' 'action.' But the word has come to stand for what is called 'ethical causation.' This, again, means, that in whatever way a man acts, be it good or evil, retribution will inevitably follow. This makes man fully responsible for his deeds, not only morally, as in most Western thought on the subject, but in fact. The retribution is not dependent on a judicial instance, be it human or divine, but is given as though it were a natural law. In Buddhism, it seems, that we must interpret it as an inescapable psychological law. But, since Buddhism, as most other Indian thought-systems, accepts the idea of rebirth, retribution need not follow immediately upon the act, or take place in the present life. Such immediate retribution is, in fact, considered to be an exception. The rule is that one's acts in the present life condition the birth in the next, thereby setting the stage for another life on earth, in heaven, or in hell.

All action leads to birth in a certain condition. The murderer e.g. is born in hell. But the expiation of his sins there do not make him fit for heaven, or even for a new human existence. The one fallen into hell has to restart on a lower sport of the evolutionary staircase, for example, as a beast. Good conduct must bring him through many births again at the human or divine level, where again he can become a candidate for liberation, the ultimate aim of existence.

History.

The idea of ethical causation, as described above, is a thought of an early beginning in Indian history. It is absent in the older Vedas, but is already introduced in the early Upaniṣads and the ancient epics. It also was accepted by other liberation systems of the Buddha's time. The idea was probably derived by the Āryan invaders from the indigenous population, which had already developed a high material and spiritual culture. At the time, and in the environment where the Buddha was living, the idea of ethical causation and of rebirth formed already part of the intellectual background; the Buddha simply accepted it, or at most adapted some details.

Retribution.

In the form as it is found in Buddhism, the idea of ethical causation implies retribution of deeds – done on earth – in heaven or hell. No doubt, this idea of heaven and hell, also was no invention of the Buddha, but was borrowed from existing believes among the population.

The rule of ethical causation and rebirth is, that one is reborn in a condition in conformity with the tendencies displayed in the previous life. If a man behaves injurious, he will be reborn in an injurious world, where he experiences injurious impressions, feelings etc. If a man behaves non-injurious, he will be reborn in a non-injurious world, and there he has pleasant impressions and feelings etc. If he behaves in a mixed way, the situation of rebirth also will be mixed. Every kind of deed leads to its proper result. For crimes of violence the award is sickness, for anger ugliness, for pride low birth. These things are so, because, it is said, they are seen to be so by some ascetics of paranormal gifts.

It became accepted that actions have a ripening and a fruit. It seems that the process of ripening can be summarized as *karma* (which generally means merely 'action') in a more specific sense. The action done does not become obliterated when it is over, but it produces a moral quality, which matures and bears fruit according to its merit. The 'moral quality' consists of nothing else but the influences of ignorance, personality formation (becoming), and desire. It can be imagined as a sticky, defiling substance, contaminating the moral purity of the mind. Your deeds influence your moral habitude; they stick to you, and in the end you 'suffer' from them, which means, that you have to face them, and bear their results.

The 'moral quality,' produced by a deed, is in Buddhism said to be of different colours: these are described as 'white' (morally good), 'black' (morally bad), 'mixed' (morally ambivalent), and 'neither white, nor black, nor mixed.' What is here called 'morally good,' is not detached, but aim-directed action, striving after its desires by non offensive means. As such it is still action under the influence of ignorance. Such action leads to rebirth, although of a non-debasing nature. Good (white) *karma* issues in a good result, and bad (black) in a bad one. This result can ripen in the present life, in the case of very heavy crimes, which produce their fruit without delay. Such are: the killing of one or both of the parents, of an arhat, shedding the blood of a Buddha, and causing schism in the community of monks. But usually it ripens and produces its fruit in the following life, be it a next human life, a life as an animal, as a ghost, as a god in heaven, or as a sinner in hell. The true liberating action is that which is accompanied by true insight, and leaves no karmic colouring. It results from the following of the Buddhistic path, including yoga and meditation. It cleanses one from the sticky deposit left by action under the influence of ignorance, and therewith it cancels the results of these actions, it neutralizes them.

To obtain liberation, *karma* must be done away with at all. All action, also ascetic practice, is led by desire, and therefore it leads to rebirth in some form of existence. Since ignorance is the last denominator of all phenomena in the conative sphere, only 'knowledge' can bring the absence of *karma*. When the liberation path, as described in an earlier section, is considered as nothing else but the quest for liberating knowledge, then this can be identified with the collecting of a 'neither black nor white nor mixed *karma*.' This is the *karma* that leads to the destruction of all normal *karma* which is always directed towards a certain object or state.

Retribution as a psychological law.

The 'ripening' of the *karma* is basically nothing else but a conative act striving for its goal, as an arrow shot in a certain direction. But this needs some qualification. If in robbing the bank, I kill an employee, one may expect, that it is my objective to become rich, and to buy a house with a swimming pool in some South American country, for the sake of living in luxury surrounded by sexy ladies, happily ever after. One will not think, that it was my intention to go to hell, while it is this, where the act will lead to, according to the Buddhistic lore. If we want to maintain, that a conative act, like an arrow, is shot to the goal, and does not pause until it hits it, then, at least, we must distinguish different levels in volition. Not without reason we called among the five groups of elementary phenomena the conative ones 'inclinations,' implying therein conscious volitions and subconscious forces. In the act of my robbing the bank, we see that indeed a retribution of the conscious volition may take place. I can get the money and achieve my aims, but I can also fail and be caught by the police. But then one may wonder, whether or not I did build in more or less consciously an omission in my preparations, or whether or not at a time after the robbery I did more or less deliberately give some signs to the inspectors. Anyhow, the act does not only imply the conscious level, but is most of all an expression of subconscious tendencies, which themselves are conditioned by all the actions of my previous births. It may well be, that at the subconscious level I feel in need to be punished, but because of my being under the influence of ignorance, I do not recognize this need on the conscious level, and I project the destructive feelings on a victim, using my desire for wealth as a rational excuse. When we say, that the action strives for its goal, we must not value the action according to its intentional projection, but according to its more objective moral standard, which reflects the inclinations at the deeper levels of psychological reality. At this level the goal cannot be escaped, although one is to a certain extent free to choose the way in which it is realized. A man can make a mistake, repent it, make a confession, and accept punishment; but he can also try to deny the misdeed, banishing it to the subconscious level, while, on the conscious level, his deeds aggravate the situation for him, leading him along the backway to the retribution of his deeds, but now to a worse retribution of worse deeds. In this way the goal is always realized, since the deed determines its own retribution, and inclines the will for so long in its direction until it is achieved. If this interpretation is right, the working of *karma* is evident. For example, someone commits a murder. As Raskolnikow in *Crime and Punishment,* he may at first have thought this to be a righteous thing. But the order of justice is not arbitrary, and after having killed, there is no way of escaping the truth that he is a killer. There is a shadow falling (a black *karma*) that darkens all life to follow. This might, theoretically, just be accepted. But such an acceptance conflicts with human nature, that cannot find peace in a darkened life. This human nature then drives the murderer to the life of suffering that is the expiation of his crime, be it consciously or subconsciously. The working of *karma* is so conceived as a psychological law and not as a law of nature. In the same way, acts of friendliness, directed to the well-being of all creatures, result in the brightening confidence of deserving a good destiny, and they confirm the will to go in that direction. This state of affairs explains why the Buddhists think, that the last wish before death determines the new birth. When the 'karmic' law would have been a natural and not a psychological law, one could free oneself from every sin at death by doing a good wish, and so the idea of the last wish and the law of *karma* would contradict each other. But when the last wish itself is conditioned by this law, no such contradiction needs to occur.

Realms of rebirth.

In Buddhism, human destiny in future life is brought into different schemes. The first scheme is already mentioned. One can be reborn on earth in three forms: as beast, ghost *(preta)*, and man, and besides in heaven or hell. There is also a more philosophical classification of destinies: one can be reborn in the world of desire, the world of form, or in the world without form.[11] In the first abide the beings possessing the five senses. These are: those living in the hells, of which the lowest is the Avīci hell, those living as ghosts, those living as men, and those living in the lower heavens. In the second the senses of touch, taste and smell are absent. This sphere comprises the Brahmā-world and the world of the other higher gods. In this world, by good *karma*, one can be born by simply appearing there. In the third sphere, the formless world, there is only the sense of mind. In it, there are four abodes, which coincide with the stages of the four so-called 'attainments,' corresponding to the perceptions of infinite space, infinite consciousness, nothingness, and of 'neither consciousness nor unconsciousness.' The last attainment reaches to the limit of becoming and of transmigration. To practice friendliness is a means to be reborn in the Brahmā-world, and the practice of the highest contemplations leads to rebirth in the formless world.

The middle way.

The 'median path' forms an important concept in early Buddhism. The basis for this idea was laid, when the Buddha found that one should not fall into the extremes of self-indulgence and self-mortification. The middle way between these extremes is nothing else but the keeping of the noble eightfold path mentioned earlier: correct faith, correct thinking, correct speech, correct action, correct livelihood, correct striving, correct attention, and correct concentration. 'Correct' or 'right' *(saṁyag)* here means simply an avoiding of extremes. This is explained in the example of 'correct thinking.' One should avoid the idea that things have (absolute) being or non-being. The right means here is, that the being of things originates dependent on other things, so that nothing is absolutely existing or non-existent, but only relatively.[12] By always choosing the middle way, one avoids

11 Pāli: *Kāmāvaccara, Rūpāvaccara, Ārūpyāvaccara,* or Sanskrit: *Kāmadhātu, Rūpadhātu, Ārūpyadhātu.*

12 The link between 'the mean' concerning 'being' and 'non-being' and 'dependent origination' is established in *Saṁyutta Nikāya* 22-90, translated in H. C. Warren's *Buddhism in Translations,* p. 165-66.

building a *karma* that leads to rebirth. One creates a neutral *karma* finally leading to ultimate freedom

Stupa Sanchi, from 1st century AD, Wiki Commons

Chapter 2
Early History

Buddhism did not remain a unity. Already in an early stage, it seems, there were tensions between the monks and the laity. As was seen before, only those able to live the life of a wandering monk (or nun) were said to be capable of receiving *nirvāṇa* in this life. Those involved in marriage, householdership, and the practical affairs of the world could only prepare for liberation in a next life. According to a certain tradition, already directly after the death of the Buddha a group of *arhats* (those liberated in life) around the Buddha's pupil Mahākāśyapa established their own canon, while another and greater group, the *Mahāsaṁghikas*, did the same. This tradition does not refer to doctrinal differences, but points to the creation of an elite within the community. Most sources mention a real schism under the government of Aśoka, in the middle of the third century BCE. According to the Singhalese tradition, this schism took place after the council of Pāṭaliputra. And whether or not there did already exist at the time a group of Buddhists bearing the name of 'the greater community' *(Mahāsaṁgha)*, here a group under this name separated itself from the Buddhist elite (the *Sthaviras*, the elders).

Again, the issue was not about doctrinal differences, but about the prerogatives of the so-called *arhats* (holy ones), who claimed special authority and advantages. The others, the lower monks and the laity, were put at a lower level, in a subservient role. The well educated laity, and the studied monks, who, although having entered the community, were as yet not qualified as 'holy ones,' understood, that not all who called themselves 'arhats' were so indeed. What was the case? Under the rule of Aśoka religious life, and that of Buddhism in particular, was fostered. Many donations were given to the convents, providing the community a state of welfare. No doubt under these conditions not only seekers of truth, but also aspirants for an easy life were driven to take on the yellow robe. And although never was every monk considered to be an *arhat*, it now could become advantageous to be considered as such, because these holy ones especially were benefitted.

The five heretical theses.

Under these circumstances there came to circulate five 'heretical' theses, so-called, anyhow, by the group of *arhats*, and their supporters *(Sthaviras)*, against whom they were directed. Some sources ascribe these theses to a certain Mahādeva, who was accused by his opponents of every possible crime. Besides being the maker of schism, probably the only true accusation, they say that he had a sexual relation with his mother, killed his father, and after discovering that she deceived him, his mother as well. Besides he killed an *arhat*. After being rejected by a woman, he took on the saffron robe, and started to teach his own ideas, which came to be formulated in the five 'heretical' theses.

These theses are the following:

1) *Arhats* can be seduced, and have nightly emissions of semen, under the influence of erotic dreams, caused by the gods, adopting female forms.
2) *Arhats* still suffer from ignorance, not the most severe form of it, but the so-called unsoiled ignorance. And they carry the residues of their old passions. They can get lost, forget the names of trees etc.
3) *Arhats* still know doubt.
4) *Arhats* can be taught by others.
5) The entrance to the path of Buddhism can be accompanied by an exclamation: 'o pain!,' after reaching the first stage of meditation.

Although the last thesis may be unclear, the purport of the first four seems lucid enough. Far from being doctrinal, and therefore 'heretical,' they obviously try to force the so-called *arhats* either to admit, that they are not arhats at all – since the theses all formulate easily demonstrable situations, which were evidently known to be facts – or to maintain the arhatship, in which case they had to accept the theses as true. In either case the outcome would be, that the difference between the arhats and the lower monks and laity is, after all, not so great. The clever Mahādeva had trapped the arhats. It seems that much discussion, votings, and possibly a council resulted. It is said that Aśoka, after a majority decision in favour of the Great Community of Mahādeva, took the side of the latter and sent the *arhats*, the *Sthaviras*, sticking to their old opinions, in a sinking ship midway the Ganges. There they used their magical powers and flew, changed into birds to Cashmere, where they established new convents. After some time Aśoka, seeing he was wrong, asked them to return, but they refused.

If there is some truth in this story, we might interpret it as follows. Aśoka's intention was to maintain the unity in the order. The Buddhist rule was, that in case of differing opinions, majority voting gives decision. After such a voting, the *arhats* should have abandoned their stubborn position, and it is not impossible that Aśoka has made that clear to them. But there was one thing in which *arhats* were believed to distinguish themselves from all normal people, their supernal powers. The story of the sinking ship might be the relating of a challenge to the *arhats*. Unless one really wants to believe that the *arhats* met this challenge by becoming birds, one should interpret it as the beginning of a disgraceful banishment to Cashmere. There the old school of *Sthaviras* obviously did very well, since the important subschool of the *Sarvāstivādins*[13] seems to have matured here. Being respected again as Sthaviras, as orthodox school, the temporary disgrace was blotted out by giving history a facelift. In fact it seems that only a disgraceful treatment can explain the resentment leading to the slanderous story about Mahādeva. However, since it formed part of the very influential *Vibhāṣa* (The commentary), work of the Sarvāstivādins of Cashmere,

13 The Sarvāstivāda is often seen as a school of absolute realism, which states that everything *(sarva)* is *(asti)*. The school was important about 200 AD in North India, but must have originated centuries earlier.

the story was adopted, even by many Mahāyānists, who are themselves said to be an offshoot of the Mahāsaṁghika initiated by Mahādeva. Only for the sceptical attitude of the Chinese it becomes suspect. Xuánzàng, around 600 AD keeps silent about the capital crimes of Mahādeva, although he must have been aware of the story. But his pupil probably expresses his master's conviction when he says about Mahādeva:

> 'High was his reputation, great his virtue. In spite of his youth, he had tasted the fruit; he was respected by kings and nobles and adored by monks. And that's why they accused him of the three sins that lead to retribution in the present life, to which they added the five theses.'[14]

It is difficult to make conclusions about the above. We should not beforehand choose for the interpretation of a conflict between some old stubborn potentates, thinking themselves better than others, and a young generation, defending its rightful claims. Both parties may be suspected of trying to serve their own interest rather than truth. The *arhats* and their supporters, the Sthaviras, may not have been able to justify their eminent position; but to launch an attack against which there can be no defense, is also suspect. There was not only a profit to lose but also one to win.

The result, anyhow, was, that from the time of Aśoka, or thereabout, there exist two schools of Buddhism, those of the Great Community *(Mahāsaṁghika)* and of the old 'orthodox' school, the Sthaviras. Both schools will soon become divided in themselves; a large quantity of sects develops.

T*HE SECTS.* The schools of the Sthaviras and of the Mahāsaṁghikas both developed into a variety of sects. At first there was not so much difference in doctrinal opinions. All schools kept themselves to the basic doctrines of the Buddha, even to that of 'dependent origination.' Differences were mainly to be found in the field of discipline. Besides, the differences could, because of the wandering life of the monks, never become so severe. In the first stages of Buddhism there has been

14 In Étienne Lamotte's *Histoire du Bouddhisme Indien*, p. 307. It was Kēguī [?] (632-682 AD who uttered the quoted rehabilitation.

something like hostels for monks, where these could find a refuge on their travels. Although the different convents were claimed by some sect or another, any monk, also of other sects, could stay there. In one convent, accordingly, were lodged monks of a variety of schools, who could easily exchange ideas with one another. There is evidence that in this situation many monks, to what community they ever officially belonged, built their private opinions. A monk belonging to one sect, might hold opinions leaning heavily on those of another. As long as not at least nine monks would subscribe to the same opinions, and start celebrating the ceremonies among themselves, in separation from the others, the unity of the sect was not considered to be broken. The greater masters developed their thought in complete freedom. Instead of explicating the doctrine of the sect, they continually remodelled it. Vasubandhu, for example, who has offered us an invaluable commentary on the *Sarvāstivāda Abhidharma*, displays in his thinking many characteristics of the rivalling sect of the Sautrāntikas – who reject the reality of 'nominal entities' –, and can even be considered as sympathetic towards the Yogācārins or Idealists.[15]

Most schools developed in the second and third centuries BCE, from the time of Aśoka in the middle of the third century onwards. The oldest information we have on the separation of the schools is derived from a work of a certain Vasumitra, the Treatise on the Sects. This work is probably from the second century AD, and from the hand of a North-Indian Sarvāstivādin. A plausible list based on this work, of the early ramification of Buddhism at the end of the third century BCE would look as follows:[16]

15 I am presently studying the idealistic tendencies in the *Abhidharmakośa* of Vasubandhu and I am inclined to the conclusion that the author of this work is the same as the Vasubandhu who wrote 'idealistic' works. In fact it seems to me that the nature of all the works attributed to Vasubandhu belongs to a tradition that later weas called *Yogācāra Sautrāntika* and to which are reckoned among others Dignāga, Dharmapāla and Dharmakīrti, and of which the said Vasubandhu is probably the founder. Compare also what Stafan Anacker has to say in his introduction to *Seven Works of Vasubandhu* (Motilal, Delhi, 1984, 86, pp. 7-24.) See also note 87 of the chapter in the present work on *Buddhist Idealism*.

16 Based on É. Lamotte, *L'Histoire du Bouddhisme Indien*, p. 579, 585 (Mahāsaṁgha, following Tāranātha) The schematic presentation on p.. 69 supra is based on p. 586 of the same work. Most information in this chapter is derived from this work. The latter diagram is fiollowing Xuánzàng.

The Sects

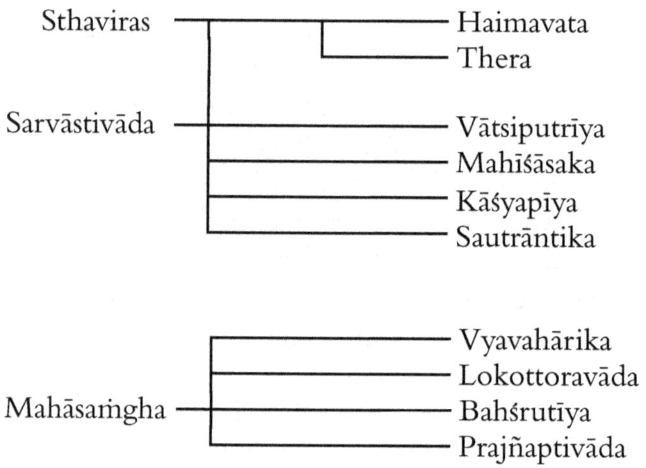
Sthaviras
Haimavata
Thera
Sarvāstivāda
Vātsiputrīya
Mahīśāsaka
Kāśyapīya
Sautrāntika
Vyavahārika
Lokottoravāda
Mahāsaṁgha
Bahśrutīya
Prajñaptivāda

Sthaviras.

The Sthaviras are the stern defenders of arhatship, wanting to stand close to the original lore of the Buddha. They are the traditionalists. As their name already indicates, the Theras of Sri Lanka – 'Thera' being just the Pāli equivalent of the Sanskrit word 'Sthavira' – are closely connected with them. The Haimavatas seem to be of the same group, deriving their name from the snow-clad *(haimavata)* mountains of the Himalayas, where a part of the Sthaviras seems to have taken refuge. The *Sarvāstivādins* form a very important school of pluralistic realism. They have been very influential in the north, e.g. in Cashmere, but also in other places. We shall come to speak of them again in the section on 'Abhidharma.' Of the branches of this sect, something more is known about the Vātsiputrīyas and the Sautrāntikas. In the tradition the Vātsiputrīyas are mentioned for their laxist attitude concerning the order rules. They accepted gifts of money, which were not allowed by the severe Sthavira rules, and they also had more liberal eating and drinking habits than other sects. Philosophically they are known for letting room for the existence of some kind of individual soul *(pudgala),* although this must be stated with reservation. All other schools denied such an existence. The Sautrāntikas are known for combatting the nominal existences of the traditional Sarvāstivādins. The Sarvāstivādins e.g. held the view, that past and future have a real existence, an entity passing from past to future only changes its mode, but does not come into existence or ceases to be.

The Sautrāntikas retorted that entities should not be multiplied here without necessity, and kept to the common sense view, that the past is that which did exist, but does not exist now anymore, and the future that which does not yet exist, but will exist in the future. They also denied the existence of *nirvāṇa* as a separate state, defended by the Sarvāstivādins, saying that the end of something existing, viz. the suffering in the circle of rebirth, is not itself an existence, but simply the end of an existence.

Mahāsaṁghikas.

Of the schools of the *Mahāsaṁghika* little is known. As a whole they are believed to be the precursors of Mahāyānism. Judging from the names of the different sects, the *Vyāvahārikas* stood in opposition to the *Lokottaras*, since *'vyāvahāra'* means 'the world of earthly experience' and *'lokottara'* denotes 'a place beyond the world.' Probably the former school expected salvation in this life, and the latter beyond life and the world. From the term '*Bahuśrutīya*' one might deduce that it was a school of theoretical learning. The *Prajñaptivādins* may have been a school of nominalism, since *'prajñapti'* stands for a mere denotation by convention. Although there is known an extant Mahāsaṁghika compilation of order rules, we are constrained, in describing the thoughts of the ancient schools, to confine ourselves to the Theravādins of Sri Lanka and the Sarvāstivādins and some of their developments, since only of these something more is known.

To complete this exposition of the *Mahāsaṁgha,* we mention some more divisions, known from the second century BCE. A century after the schism under Aśoka, there again is made mention of a certain Mahādeva, who, according to the Sarvāstivāda sources, is now seen as a reformer. He is the founder of the sect of the *Caitikas*, splitting soon in *Pūrva-* and *Apara-śaila.*

Vātsiputrīyas and Dharmaguptakas.

The *Vātsiputrīyas* have once been a wide spread sect. It was the latest Hīnayāna sect being influential on the Indian continent. They were split up in Dharmottarīyas, Bhadrāyanīyas, Saṁmatīyas, and Ṣaṇṇagarikas. Of these the *Saṁmatīyas* have been important. The *Dharmaguptakas* are mentioned as a development of the Mahīśāsaka, another branch of the Sarvāstivāda, and have been influential especially in China. Their teaching was studied by the erudite Sēngyòu.

More and other subdivisions have been made, but the above will do to give a birdseye view on the tissue of Buddhism in the centuries before the Christian era.

Later developments of the Mahāsaṁghika and Sarvāstivāda

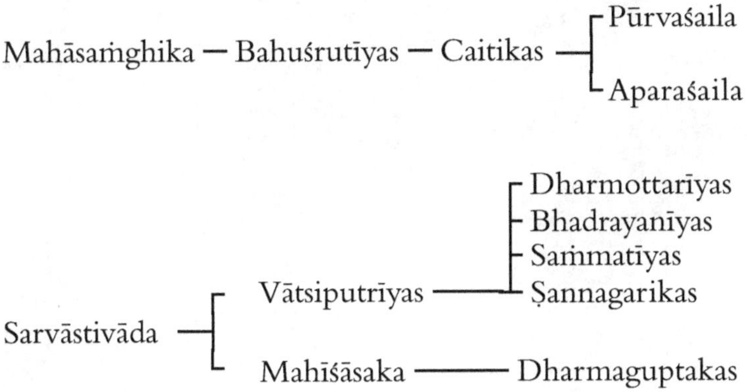

Kanheri, Main Vihara, 2nd century, Wiki Commons

Chapter 3
Abhidharma

What has come to us under the name of 'abhidharma,' or in Pāli, 'abhidhamma,' is a detailed systematization of the teaching of the *sūtras*. It contains classifications, enumerations, controversies, and 'questions and answers.' As was stated already, the development of this corpus of scriptures is of later date than that of the *Sūtras* and the *Vinaya* (order rules). While the latter are much the same in all schools, the different *Abhidharma* scriptures do not contain the same materials, and are characteristic of certain schools. It is especially in these scriptures that the roots of philosophical speculation are found. The term 'abhidharma' itself was coined at a later date; the canonical texts refer only to 'catechism' *(mātṛka)*. By 'abhidharma' is meant the 'dharma' as expounded by the *sūtras*, but 'nude' as it were, without literary embellishments and without putting it into scene. It is the teaching without teacher and without pupils.[17]

The development of the Abhidharma must have taken place – roughly speaking – between the beginning of the third century BC and the end of the first century AD.

The catechism, that later in the chronicles and commentaries was called 'abhidharma' is said to have been started by the direct pupils of the Buddha. In this context the names of Kāśyapa, Katyāyana, Ānanda, and Śāriputra are mentioned.

17 É. Lamotte, *L'Histoire du Bouddhisme Indien*, p. 197–8.

There have been known Abhidharmas of the Sthaviras (Theras), Mahāsaṁghikas, Saṁmatīyas, Kāśyapīyas, Dharmaguptakas, and Sarvāstivādins.[18]

Most of these schools consider their Abhidharma as the genuine word of the Buddha, although given in the rendering of his direct pupils. Only the Sarvāstivādins frankly admit that theirs was composed by a variety of authors. But they maintain that these authors were genuinely inspired by the Buddha, and therefore, they hold, the work must, despite of its late composition, be considered as authoritative.

There are four Abhidharmas that have come to us in a more or less integral state:

1) the Peṭakopadesa
2) the Śāriputrābhidharmaśāstra
3) the Abhidhamma of the Theras of Sri Lanka
4) the Abhidharma of the Sarvāstivādins

The first and the third are preserved in Pāli, the second and the last in Chinese. The *Peṭakopadesa* is cited by Buddhaghosa, the systematizer of the Thera-canon of Sri Lanka in the 5th century AD. The Burmese Thera-Buddhists consider it as a part of their Khuddakanikāya. But the work is really distinct from the Thera-tradition. It is said to have been compiled by Kātyāyana, the pupil of the Buddha, in Avanti, which, if Lamotte is right in considering the Pāli as the dialect of Avanti, would explain its preservation in that language. The Prajñaptivādins seem to have given credence to this Abhidharma, which might mean we have here an Abhidharma of the Mahāsaṁghikas.[19]

18 The affiliation of the *Peṭakopadesa* with the Mahāsaṁgha – in particular with the Prajñaptivādins – is found in Lamotte's *L'Histoire*, pp. 208 & 210, and also in A.K. Warder, *Indian Buddhism*, p. 223 (revised ed. Delhi, 1980. The *Śāriputrābhidharmaśāstra* must have been a work honoured by the Dharmaguptakas (Lamotte, p. 208, Nakamura, Indian Buddhism, p. 108. The Vātsiputrīyas and Saṁmatīyas possibly also had a work listening to the same name, but having in all probability a different content (Lamotte, p. 209). Reference to the Abhidharma of the Kāśyapīyas is made by Warder (p. 220/1), the same author mentions a work, the *Āśrayaprajñaptiśāstra* of the Saṁmatīyas (p, 295), even translated into English (by K. Venkataramanan in Viśvabhārati Annals, vol. v, 1953).

19 Warder, *Indian Buddhism*, p.223, Lamotte, *L'Histoire du Bouddhisme Indien*, pp. 208 & 210.

The *Śāriputrābhidharmaśāstra* is the Abhidharma of the Dharmaguptakas, and was translated into Chinese by Dharmagupta and Dharmayaśas. The Dharmaguptakas were influential in China, and they seem to derive their name from the one of the translator. According to Kumārajīva, another important Indian missionary in China, the same Abhidharma was used by the Vātsiputrīyas. But this is doubtful, since the text that is preserved accepts the doctrine that denies a substantial soul (as most sects do) and does not teach the existence of an unspeakable soul *(pudgalavāda)*, which doctrine is ascribed to the Vātsiputrīyas.[20]

Theras and Sarvāstivādins.

The most complete and elaborate Abhidharmas are those of the Theras of Sri Lanka, and of the Sarvāstivādins of North India. With these exclusively we shall deal in the following. The Theras have an *Abhidharmapiṭaka* (basket of Abhidharma) consisting of seven books:

1) *Dhammasaṅgaṇī* (enumeration of the 'dharmas')
2) *Vibhaṅga* (analysis)
3) *Dhātukathā* (discourse on the elements)
4) *Puggalapaññatti* (description of personalities)
5) *Kathāvatthu* (controversial. issues)
6) *Yamaka* (coupled problems)
7) *Paṭṭhāna* (conditional relations)

This Abhidharma has many similarities with the cathegetical *sūtras*, as e.g. found in the *Aṅguttara-nikāya.* It has something of an unfinished work. The most metaphysical of these works are the Enumeration, the Analysis, and the Conditional Relations. Together with the Discourse on the Elements they form a systematic unity. The ideas contained in it are defended against other sects by Moggaliputta Tissa in his Controversial Issues. Therefore the latter work must be of a more recent date than the others. This Moggaliputta Tissa is believed to have lived in the middle of the third century BC. If this is true, the basic ideas of the other Abhidharma works must be older than that, and can hardly

20 Ibid. p. 209.

be of a later date than 300 BC. When we accept the short chronology, this would imply, that there may be truth in the tradition which traces the Abhidharma back to the Buddha's direct pupils. However, if Moggaliputta Tissa lived later than tradition wants to have it, the whole Abhidharma may have been created in later times.

The *Enumeration of the Dharmas* is a classification of psychic phenomena. The *Analysis* seems in many respects a repetition of, and an extension to, the *Enumeration*. The *Discourse* is an inquiry into the constituents of the phenomenal world, i.e. the world of forms *(rūpa)*. The *Conditional Relations* analyses the dynamic relations between the phenomena classified in the preceding works. It is considered as the zenith of Abhidharmic thought. The *Issues* contains the repudiation of the heretical theses of 26 different schools. The Thera Abhidhamma was commented upon and further systematized by Buddhaghosa (5th century AD) in his different works, most notably in his *Atthasālinī* (exegesis).

The Abhidharma of the Sarvāstivādins also consists of seven books, but it is called, remarkably enough, the 'Ṣadpādābhidharma' (the Abhidharma in six books). It consists of the following works:

1) *Saṅgītiparyāya* (commentary on the Saṅgīti-sūtra)
2) *Dharmaskandha* (groups of dharmas)
3) *Dhātukāya* (classes of elements)
4) *Vijñānakāya* (classes of consciousness)
5) *Prajñaptiśāstra* (treatise on conventional denotation, i.e. the world)
6) *Jñānaprasthāna* or *Aṣṭagrantha* (method for [acquiring] knowledge)
7) *Prakaraṇapāda* (discussion section)

The reason that is spoken of only six books may be, that at the time when the reference was made, the last book had not yet come into existence, or was not yet considered as part of the Abhidharma. The first work is certainly the most primitive and looks like a less elaborate version of the Pāli Enumeration. It is really a commentary on the *Saṅgīti-sūtra*, consisting in a schematic arrangement of topics (the *mātṛka* proper). Significantly it is ascribed to Śāriputra, a direct pupil of the Buddha. The same can be said of the Groups of Dharmas, which has some affinities with the Pāli work *Analysis*. The works on the elements and on consciousness contain older and newer parts, corresponding in theme with parts of the Pāli *Discourse on the Elements* and *Conditional Relations*. The works were possibly enlarged by respectively Vasumitra and Devaśarman. Since the last author seems to refer to the *Kathāvatthu* of Moggaliputta Tissa, the *Classes of Consciousness* in its extension must be somewhat later. If tradition is right in placing Moggaliputta Tissa around the middle of the third century BC, the third and fourth work of the Sarvāstivāda Abhidharma may be situated slightly after this time. The *Prajñaptiśāstra* will not be much later. It deals with cosmological concepts and the problem of free will. The great work of the sect is the *Method of Knowledge*, ascribed to a certain Kātyāyanīputra; it contains the typical doctrines of the Sarvāstivāda. Its date is usually settled at about 200 BC. The last work of the Abhidharma is possibly some addition composed in the two following centuries. In all this we must keep in mind that research is only beginning, and that as yet nothing can be said that may claim certainty.[21]

Around 100 AD, it is said, there was held a council under the government of King Kaṇiṣka in Puruṣapura near present day Rawalpindi. On that occasion a huge commentary *(Vibhāṣa)* was composed on the Abhidharma, preserved only in Chinese through the translations of the group around Xuánzàng. Like the books of the Abhidharma itself, also this work is virtually unknown in the western world. But the latter work again formed the basis of the *Abhidharmakośa* (Treasury of the Abhidharma) by Vasubandhu (4th or 5th century AD), a work translated into French by Louis de la Vallée Poussin.

Most of our knowledge in the West of the work of the Sarvāstivādins has come to us through the mediation of this book.

Nature of the Abhidharma.

As was already said, the Abhidharma does not present a totally new development. It is the explanation and interpretation.of the teaching of the *sūtras*. But this interpretation proceeds from a central perspective, perhaps the perspective that was from the beginning presupposed

21 The chronological order is mainly based on data provided by Warder *(Indian Buddhism*, p. 342ff), but also Lamotte's opinion has been taken into consideration (p.205/6). These two authorities being not in complete agreement, I made my own decisions as to what is the most likely chronology.

in the teaching of the *sūtras*. The whole of reality is caught under one common denominator, viz., that of *dharma*. Everything that in any way can be an object for awareness is called *dharma*, and that comprises everything that can be perceived. We may perhaps translate the word 'dharma' with 'phenomenon.' As is often the case with translations from Indian languages, this word is chosen for want of a better. We have chosen this word, because in German phenomenology, especially in the work of Edmund Husserl, the word 'phenomenon' is used in a manner much similar to the use of the word 'dharma' in Buddhism. The word 'phenomenon' here stands for the object, whatever it is, given as it is in relation to consciousness. It does not stand for a thing as something existing in itself, but for a thing only insofar as it is given to consciousness. The phenomenon, accordingly, only exists as a correlate of consciousness. It can never exist outside its being perceived and conceived. In a sense this can even be stated for consciousness itself; it can only be given insofar as it is perceived.

This being given exclusively as a correlate of consciousness or mind (manas) – and also as a correlate of all other phenomena – is exactly what the early Buddhists meant by 'dharma,' although in the Sarvāstivāda the word may have a slightly more realistic or materialistic meaning. 'Dharmas' can be named 'things,' but they are not things existing in themselves. They are not substantial, but inseparable from consciousness, and they only exist in their 'givenness' and correlation. Besides, there are some traditional connotations, which also may have been felt in the word *dharma*. The word is etymologically related to the English word 'firm,' and traditionally it stands for something 'firmly' established, like e.g. the law-like movement at the firmament. From here the word 'dharma' can take on the meaning of 'law.' The word stands also for what is in conformity with the law, e.g. good (ethical) qualities. But the range of meanings of the word can even reach to 'positive quality.' In Buddhism we find the word 'dharma' also used to denote the ethical Law governing all life and existence, forming the core of the Buddhist teaching. The use of the word 'dharma' for all perceptible phenomena, might have been derived from the idea that nothing can escape being in conformity with this Law. Everything within the field of the Law conforms to the Law, and conforming transmits the Law, just as iron in a magnetic field becomes magnetic itself. Seen in the light of the general meaning of the word, in the Buddhist meaning of the word 'dharma' can be felt something that is objectively lawful, like an objective order, a pattern. Later in the waning of the Abhidharmic period, the meaning can even shift to 'essence.' But all these meanings must be considered as subordinate to the central connotation of 'phenomenon,' as we have explained above.

All things are related, and exist in relation to the mind. One may say that phenomena can be present only as states of the mind (considered as pure consciousness). In this way one may interpret the famous lines of the *Dhammapāda*: 'All phenomena have mind as their presupposition, are dependent on mind, and are made of it.'[22]

But this cannot be taken in the sense, that all phenomena are without remainder reducible to mind. Mind in itself is empty, and the different patterns of life and existence appearing in it, cannot, accordingly, be derived from it; true as it may be, that they cannot be without mind. They exist as they are under the law of their mutual conditioning, which law forbids that one *dharma* should exist alone for itself. This whole system of the interdependence of consciousness, life and existence revolves in circles from birth to death, and ever again. There is only one way out, the escape into the unconditioned: liberation, *nirvāṇa*.

T*HE THERA ABHIDHAMMA*. What has been said sofar, is common to both, the Theravādins of Sri Lanka and the Sarvāstivādins of the north. We now start a separate treatment of their respective Abhidharmas.

The Abhidharma of the Theras is essentially a classification of all the different types of *dharmas* and an indication of the way in which they are interrelated. The work of classification is mainly to be found in the *Dhammasaṅgaṇī*, the analysis of the interrelationship in the *Paṭṭhāna*. The Thera Abhidhamma (Pāli for 'Abhidharma') distinguishes 82 *dhammas* (dharmas). We shall try to sketch their basic structure and relatedness. This we shall do analytically, starting from the most central

22 *Dhammapāda*, vs. 1.13.3, quoted in A. Piatigorsky. *The Buddhist Philosophy of Thought* (Totowa, 1984), p. ix.

notion and going down to the differences and varieties that constitute reality.

Freedom and bondage.

The most fundamental distinction made in Buddhism, and also in the Abhidhamma, is that between the freedom of liberation and the bondage in a conditioned state. Correspondingly, the Theras make a basic distinction between the one unconditioned 'dharma' of freedom *(nirvāṇa)* and the 81 types of conditioned *dharmas*. The 'dharma' of liberation here, is really not a 'dharma' at all in the sense as described above. There can be no adequate objectivation of liberation. It cannot be fully described or conceived; it can be attained, but it cannot be exhausted by thought. And to be a *dharma* was to be an object for thought. That liberation is here introduced under the heading of 'dharma,' cannot be but to provide a base, boundery, and shelter for the whole system, that otherwise would be pending in plain air. The sphere of liberation presents that what is uncompounded, simple, eternal, and unconstituted, and this forms, as we have seen, the presupposition of all that is compound, perishable and constituted. It is that without which thinking, and the whole reality depending thereon, cannot be.

Mind and 'saṅkhāra.'

Excepting the unconditioned, all other *dharmas* are comprised in one, that of mind *(mano, citta, viññāna)*. This mind must be conceived as pure consciousness, the medium in which only a thing *(dharma)* can be given, if it is to be given at all. All phenomena are formed or constituted *(saṅkhata)* in this consciousness, which is even considered as itself constituted for itself. As all phenomena are constituted (*saṅkhata* or S. *saṁskṛta*), the concept of 'phenomenon' *(dhamma, dharma)* seems to be the correlate of the idea of *saṅkhāra* (S. *saṁskāra*). While *dharma* stands for all that can be given to thought or the mind, *saṅkhāra* stands for the whole system of stimuli – which rise out of the mind itself – that lead to the givenness of a *dharma*. When we call a *dharma* something constituted by mind, then we may call *saṅkhāra* a constituting activity of the mind. To understand this activity, we must look briefly to the conditioning function of consciousness. When something is apprehended, this is a conscious experience which leaves behind a trace in the subconscious, or, formulated in another way, this apprehension, after vanishing from the presence, disappears to the background of consciousness. There it remains operative in a variety of ways. One is, that it is always at hand to be consciously re-enacted by memory. But more important is, that such subconscious apprehension – which is nothing else but a past apprehension – after having vanished from the presence, conditions all future conscious experience. When, for example, our mother told us in our youth, that such and such a bird is called a 'swallow,' then on future occasions our apprehensive faculty is 'formed' to see at the appearance of a similar outline a swallow, and not just a bird or some other bird. Such 'formation' of the apperceptive system remains until it is adapted or modified by another conscious experience. The subconscious experience is thus active as a disposition or habitual tendency. It makes us see and do the things which we have learned, and to ignore the things outside our scope. In short, it sets the stage of our world, and determines the direction in which our experience is to develop. Our information limits the field of our apprehension. Of crucial importance is here that information which guides us with respect to our ultimate destiny: beauty, peace, and understanding wisdom, in short *nirvāṇa*. By wrong information we are led astray, and start to act in a wrong direction. Finally one's initial information is refuted by circumstances when it results in misery. This is called the 'fruit' of action (or of apprehension), and this is, generally speaking, the fruit of the use of one's freedom. By going, on the contrary, consistently in the right direction by following the Buddhist path, the ultimate aim, *nirvāṇa*, itself is attained as the 'reward.'

It is a characteristic of the Buddhist idea of 'saṁskāra,' that this notion presents the unity of tendency and information. It is, as one may say, directed information. It makes that everything newly experienced is conceived in a conditioned conceptual form. Accordingly, the *saṅkhāra* conditions the intentional hold on any phenomenon in every perceptive or apprehensive (apperceptive) act. As we keep in mind that there is nothing in an object, except truth or *nirvāṇa*, that is not conditioned by the intentional grip, it follows that all our experience, insofar as it is limited experience, is the result of former apprehensive and practical acts. In the light of the idea of rebirth, the causes of our present experiences can date back to the most remote past. One is equipped with information-based tendencies accumulated in innumerable lives, and one can be confronted in this life with faults from previous ones. This also makes that actual behaviour which fails to become corrected in the present life, will – in the form of initial information – be transmitted to the next, waiting there for expiation. The idea that any conscious experience vanishes with the lapse of time to the background of consciousness, and the correlated idea, that any activity based on wrong information cannot fail to be corrected, explain the origin of a difference of opinion between the early Abhidharmists, notably between the Theras and the Sarvāstivādins. The Sarvāstivādins taught, that *dharmas* exist in the three periods of time: present, past, and future – since its information is retained in the past and its impetus transmitted to the future. It is the nature of the 'dharma' that persists through all time, while only its temporal condition is changed. This is a rather ontological view. The Theras stick to a soteriological approach, and teach that only the present and that part of the past, which has not yet resulted in its fruit, is real. Or, what is practically the same, one's reality or world holds until it is corrected; a notion until it is refuted, a deed until it is retributed.

Buddhism rejects the existence of substantial entities. Also the mind is not a substance that continues its identity in time, but it is in a literal sense a contingency *(saṁtāna)*, by which the Abhidarmists mean, that the consciousness that I have now is not the same as the consciousness 'I' had a moment ago. Its existence does not reach beyond the actual event or occasion *(samaya)*. 'Its' next moment is the rebirth of consciousness conditioned by the series of similar previous consciousness-events. This adjection of new consciousness-events *(citta-vīthi)*, creates the idea of a continuous consciousness. But really, discontinuous events are placed together. That the next event is conditioned by the previous series and is not introduced at random, needs not even to be explained out of some inner connection, because when the next moment would not be the one conditioned by the previous one, no continuity would be conceived of. Since mind is essentially not conceived as an object in space and time, there is no other way of conceiving continuity than by the conditioned series itself. Let's make ourselves clear. If there are nothing but discontinuous events, I can sit here near the window, looking at the cars passing by, believing myself to be this selfsame person, born from this particular family. Nothing can exclude principally that in the next moment I consider myself a person of different sex, race and family in the midst of say a guerilla-war, trying to find refuge for myself and my suckling child. But it is impossible to melt these two lives together in a continuity of apperception, anyhow unless again certain conditions are satisfied. One life is a conditioned series; when the conditioning breaks down, the life breaks down, since a randomized series is in fact no series at all.

Let's accept for the moment that the mind is the collection of all factual and possible events, and let's imagine that someone could see from the outside into this mind, he might see then all events thrown together in a total disorder, like the pieces of a jigsaw puzzle. But if he would make for himself the resolve: 'I want to cross this mind,' he could only do so by jumping from event to event in a conditioned order; he would have to search the fitting pieces together, thus finding a passway through mind, worth to be called a life. Seen in this light, it is the meaningful picture itself that selects its own constituents, instead of one's identity being the result of objective circumstances.

What is important in the excursion above is the conception of mind not as an individual faculty, but as a universal mode of being that is the presupposition for anything to appear. What can be said of a life-constituting conditioned series in mind, can also be said of anything that, as a certain entity, is constituted in life. It is only constituted as a conditioned series of events. Mind is the consciousness-form in which all is apprehended, and the *dharmas (dhammā)* are the phenomena which are so apprehended in consciousness. They too are constituted as a conditioned series of events. Besides the consciousness-*dharma* of mind itself, two kinds of *dharmas* are distinguished, those that are object for sensory awareness and also those that are object for the inner reflection and feeling.

As may be clear from what has been said, mind, in normal circumstances, never appears devoid of its content. It is always characterized either by its conscious apperceptions, or by its unconscious dispositions. All these make that mind is always in a certain state, corresponding with the present apperception or with a disposition below the conscious level. To start with apperception: it can be directed, as stated, towards some object of the outer sense, but also towards phenomena of psychic life. Such apperception, considered as a state of mind, is called a *citta*, which literally means nothing else but 'mind.' The word 'mind' here can be used in plural *cittāni* to denote 'mind' in all the possible forms it can assume (but not to indicate different personal identities). 'Mind' in general is a possibility for all forms or contents, but the factual 'minds' are always determined by some particular content. The use of the plural to denote states of mind, even of one individual, displays clearly that mind is not seen as some persisting entity, but as something that is new at every apperception. What makes mind to mind is not its persistence, but its sameness of function. This function is that it reveals its content, be it some psychical factor *(cetāsika)*, or some sensory form *(rūpa)* to which it is directed, and which it holds. These psychical factors and sensory forms are classified under different categories. Many descriptions try to render the categories of sensory form, and become weary as it comes to the psychical factors. But especially these are important in Abhidarmic Buddhism, since it is the inner life that directs the steps to, and indicates the progression on the liberation-path.

Consciousness and rebirth.

There are two notions of importance in early Buddhism: that of individual life as a conditioned series of occasions of consciousness, and that of rebirth *(saṁsāra)* as a conditioned series of individual lives.

Just as the individual consciousness forms a collection of separate events, the string of *saṁsāra* forms a collection of these collections. This collection is not disorderly, but its members form series. The first and the last elements of the life-series at the same time constitute the decisive elements in the *saṁsāra*-series.

The last event of life, the decay *(cuti)* is the net karmic result of a life-series. It is what comes out after making up the balance of a life's merit, the apperception of one's desert. It is the life that starts with exactly that karmic balance with which another ended that is considered as the 'rebirth' of that other previous life. Although the continuity of physical apperceptions here is broken, their information, impetus, and direction continue. They become reunited with a new life stream at conception, just as the impulse of a billiard-ball is transmitted to another in contacting it, without mingling or exchanging any matter. The initial phase of new life-consciousness, with its inherited disposition, but as yet without any conscious experience is called *paṭisandhi* (reunion). It is the beginning of a new stream of background consciousness *(bhavāṅga)*, which is the dispositionally coloured, ever renewed canvas on which any conscious experience may be depicted. It can be changed by conscious experience insofar as this leaves behind a karmic colouring of a certain moral value.[23] At the end of a life the background consciousness closes with presenting a new 'balance.'

The process of conscious apperception.

The background consciousness can be compared to a river. It flows quietly down as long as it does not meet with resistence. It does not become conscious of itself unless it becomes activated by finding some obstacle, i.e. object on its way. Then it reveals both, the object and its own conscious nature, like an electric current which can be manifested only when it produces heat or light or movement when passing resistent material. An object obstructs the stream by entering through one of the six doors *(dvāra)*, five – those of the sensory organs – presenting outwardly perceptible objects, and one – that of mind – presenting objects of inner life. Because of that, the flow is cut off *(uppaccheda)* and is set into vibration *(calana)*. Thus the process of conscious apperception starts. Firstly the mind comes into a state of alertness *(āvajjana)*. Then, in the case of an external object, follow one or more perceptions by one or more of the sense organs, resulting in seeing, hearing, smelling, tasting, or touching. After that (in the case of sense perception), or directly after the phase of alertness (in the case of inner perception) follows the reception of the object *(sampaṭicchana)*. Following comes a phase of investigation or scrutinizing *(santiraṇa)*, and one of determination *(voṭṭhappana)*. Only then full cognition or conscious apperception *(javana)* takes place. Determination and apperception (apprehension) are free synthetic acts *(samūhaggaṇa)*, which

23 Cf. supra p. 58.

Apperception

1) vibration of background consciousness (calana)

2) being alerted (āvajjana)

3) sight etc. (dassana)

4) reception (sampaṭicchana)

5) scrutinizing (santiraṇa)

6) determination (voṭṭhappana)

7) appercdeptiom (javana)

8) appropriation / identification (tadārammaṇa)

involve a judgment that can be true or false. Such judgment in apperception may be merely occasionally, lacking the force to change the subconscious disposition. But when such a judgment is appropriated, it leaves behind a karmic trace. This means, that such apperception modifies the information which lies in the background consciousness, and changes the apperceptive inclinations on future occasions; it is counted on life's balance. One has learned something about the meaning and value of life. In the future similar cognitions may become automatized. The judgment phase of apperception is then changed for one of automatic identification; the object is taken as such. The phase of appropriation of the apperception, and the re-enactment of this appropriation in passive identification, is called *tad-ārammaṇa* (the taking as such). In the case of passive identification it consists in the projection of the subconscious habit on the object presented. [24]

The process of apperception can be analyzed in more detail than is done above. Actually it is based on a large amount of separate perceptions *(pañca-dvāra-vīthi)*. These are continually intersected by reproductive acts, linking together the different aspects of the perceived object) and recollective acts, linking the perceived object with similar, formerly perceived objects *(tad-anuvatthuka-mano-dvāra-vīthi)*. Then follows the grasping of the name *(nāma-paññatti-vīthi)*, and the grasping of the meaning *(attha-paññatti-vīthi)*.

That apperception may have karmic result, based on its freedom of judgment, may appear from the following story:

A Dutch woman goes shopping in a rural village in the United States. She asks the shopkeeper for 'maize,' but pronounces this word in the Dutch way, which makes it sound like 'mice.' This misjudgment made in the 'grasping of the name,' results in the shopkeeper (who anyhow is more accustomed to the word 'corn') believing the woman not to be quite sane. And the woman fails to obtain the desired food.

Psychical factors.

For the Abhidharmic thinker, there really is nothing but actual and 'background' consciousness. There is a continuous succession of actual

24 Cf. Anagarika Govinda, *The Psychological Attitude of Early Buddhist Philosophy* (London 1961), pp. 132-137.

moments of consciousness, but these are conditioned by subconscious forces, which themselves are the outcome, the residue, of former conscious acts, existing as the dim presence, in the form of faint reminiscenses, of past deeds and experience that contributed to the shaping of a character. To the dim but effective background consciousness also may be reckoned the anticipations of the future that dye the present acts of perception, and which consist of so many implicit expectations projected by the imagination. All those perceptive or conscious acts, with their implied echo's of the past and anticipations of what is to come, have a formal constitution, but also a moral value. The constitutive factors of a conscious act, as such, are morally neutral *(avyakata)*, i.e., they do not indicate progress or regress on the path towards liberation. As constitutive factors they are part of each conscious or perceptive act. The typically moral factors are spicing these acts with different flavours. They are not constitutive elements, but regulative components of conscious life. Only these can be termed morally wholesome *(kusala)* or bad *(akusala)*. They lead life either to peace or to distress. It is these which condition *karma*, and the development of the cycle of rebirth. Together, all these constitutive elements and regulative factors of conscious life are termed *cetāsika*. In their conjoined appearance they constitute any conscious act qua shape and content, and thus they give shape and direction to all intellectual and practical life.

The factors just mentioned are decisive in the development of conscious life. The mind becomes aware of them through self-reflection. The Theras have analyzed them, and have ordered them in a system. They made the basic distinction between the factors determining moral debasement or emancipation and those not doing so. The first are karmically wholesome or noxious, because they influence the processes of rebirth and liberation, the latter are neutral in this respect. As was already said, the neutral psychical factors or mental faculties are those factors that enable intellective and practical life. In itself they are neither wholesome nor unwholesome. Their karmic value is determined not by their own merit but by that of the activity in which they are involved. The following seven are faculties or factors which are involved in every mental perception:[25]

25 Ibid., p. 115

1) *phassa* (contact, the activation of the senses by an object [S. *sparśa*].
2) *vedanā* (feeling)
3) *saññā* (cognition, apprehension [S. *saṁjñā*].
4) *cetanā* (volition, responsivity).
5) *ekaggatā* (one-pointedness [S. *ekāgratā*].
6) *jīvitindriya* (psychic vitality)
7) *manasikāra* (spontaneous attention [S. *manaskāra*].

Here, again, we find in the enumeration of the Abhidharma an indication of the five types of elementary phenomena, which by the early Buddhists were held to be constitutive of conscious life. Two factors, 'feeling' *(vedanā)* and 'cognition' or 'apperception' (*saññā*, S. *saṁjñā*), are mentioned by the same name, two, 'contact' or 'impression' (*phassa*, S. *sparśa*) and 'volition' *(cetanā)* are closely connected with respectively 'sense data' *(rūpa)* and *'saṁskāra'* (will, disposition). But in Abhidharmic thought they are, nevertheless, not completely synonymous with these older concepts. Firstly, *'rūpa'* is now felt as a more objective outward shape, that becomes actualized in a more subjective impression. This means, that the outward shape and its sensory reception become distinguished, although they still seem to be considered as correlative factors, and not as distinct and independent entities. The origin of this distinction lies in the absence of 'sense data,' and the presence of 'impression' on the list of the chain of dependent origination. This fact required the establishment of the relationship between the two key-concepts. In the Abhidharmic list the word 'volition' *(cetanā)* replaces the older concept of 'disposition' *(saṁskāra)*, because in the Abhidharmic thought the concept of *'saṁskāra'* covers, apart from mere volition, the whole range of dispositions of character, which now are enumerated one by one as karmically wholesome and unwholesome mental factors. In other words, the Abhidharma now makes the distinction between volition proper and the disposition by which this volition is conditioned, two ideas which formerly were combined in one concept. Together, the four elements, mentioned until now, constitute the more objective elements in any conscious act *(citta)*, the other three elements form the more subjective side of the perceptive act. 'Spontaneous attention' *(manasikāra)* and 'one pointedness' or 'concentration' are two subjective phases in the seizing of the more objective conscious *(noematic)* datum, while the element of psychic vitality is indicative of the intensity of the perceptive process.

If the above is too abstract, let's make it concrete. If a sense datum appears it is made conscious to the mind in an impression. For instance, I become aware of a 'red' impression. Such particular 'red' is associated with a particular 'feeling'– e.g. a feeling of the nearing satisfaction of hunger. And this feeling, again, leads to the recognition' of the 'red'-impression as 'tomato soup.' From the beginning this whole cognitive process was already animated by a 'hungry' intentionality, always more or less vaguely present, standing in the service of self-preservation. 'Spontaneous attention' and 'concentration' are two subjective *(noetic)* and temporal phases of this process, corresponding to the succession of the more objective givenness of impression, feeling, and cognition. The attention directs itself towards the impression, and, after reaching a certain intensity of concentration, it issues in the grasp of a definite cognition.

The whole process of the hungry man becoming aware of the soup may occur with more or less fervour, in accordance with the intensity of the feeling of hunger and the general condition of his vitality.

According to the feeling accompanying the perceptive act, the whole conscious process may be pleasant *(sukha)* or unpleasant *(duḥkha)*, or – as in the case of a disinterested contemplative act – it may be emotionally neutral *(upekkha)*.

Additional to the neutral mental factors that accompany any apperception, there are six other karmically neutral mental faculties. These only accompany some apperceptive processes.[26]

1) *vitakka* [S. *vitarka*] deliberative [logical] thinking).
2) *vicāra* (reflection, pondering).
3) *adhimokkha* [S. *adhimokṣa*], decision.
4) *viriya* [S. *vīrya*] effort, strength).
5) *pīti* [S. *prīti*] interest, zest, rapture [according to intensity]).
6) *chanda* (desire to act, will to accomplish).

The first group of mental faculties were those enabling apperception. They result in an assault of wakefulness (attention) in consequence of a

26 Govinda. Ibid., p. 119.

response-reaction to a stimulus. In this wakefulness itself the apperceptive functions of consciousness are actualized which were described in the previous section: becoming aware, seeing, hearing etc., followed by reception, investigation, determination, apperception, and (in some cases) appropriation. The faculties with which we are dealing now display some analogies with the functions that come after 'seeing' etc., mentioned when we treated the process of conscious apperception (compare p. 87 ff). Thinking in its initial deliberative phase stands beside reception, pondering beside investigation, decision beside determination, but then the difference becomes clear. The apperceptive functions work together to constitute knowledge, but the present group of faculties work in a practical direction. This at the same time indicates, why they are not necessarily involved in every act of apperception. Apperception is an intellective process which is set in motion by external stimuli. It can be absent, but then consciousness itself is dormant. Since a dormant consciousness cannot arouse itself, the process of apperception is – at least in its initial phase – not voluntary. Only in the higher strata of the apperception, from determination onwards, a voluntary element creeps in. This is from the moment in which one can decide to abandon the stimulus, and notably in the act of full apperception *(javana)*. The active processes, on the contrary, do – insofar as they are not automatic vital processes (i.e. from *vitakka* onwards) – arise voluntarily. This implies that they always start on a conscious base, take their departure from an apperception. On this base they can be accomplished, but they do not need to be so. The faculties in question, now are necessarily involved in action, but not in every conscious act, since a conscious act does not necessarily imply action. In short the second group of neutral faculties enables the working of the practical reason. It is not necessarily active since it is based on practical freedom. All faculties are here subordinate to free will *(chanda),* which is called neutral precisely because it is free to choose for the right or for the wrong. When it chooses for the wrong, it chooses the easy way of going down the stream, and articulates itself as *kāmachanda*, the resolve to plunge into worldly desire, which is 'thirst' *(taṇhā)*; when it chooses the right, it chooses the difficult way of 'entering the stream' in the sense of wrestling oneself to the source.

The will then articulates itself as *dhammachanda*, the resolve to attain liberation.

Wholesome and unwholesome mental factors.

The so-called wholesome and unwholesome mental factors are those which are decisive as regards one's progression or retrogression on the path of liberation. Of these, two groups of three are basic for one's movement on the Path: the unwholesome root causes: greed *(lobha)*, hate or aversion *(dosa, S. dveṣa)* and infatuation *(moha)* which are the three forms of ignorance (*avijjā*, S. *avidyā*), and the wholesome root causes which consist in the mere absence of the aforementioned unwholesome causes: *alobha* (absence of greed), *adosa* (absence of hate) and *amoha* (absence of infatuation), which three are based on knowledge or insight. The root-causes are so called, because they form the basis of all other wholesome or unwholesome psychical factors or mental faculties. Based on the unwholesome causes are eleven other mental objects. Based on infatuation are shamelessness *(ahirika),* unscrupulousness *(anottappa)*, and restlessness *(udhacca)*; based on greed are (false) opinion *(diṭṭhi),* and self-conceit *(māna)*; based on hate: envy *(issā)*, egotism *(macchariya)* and worry *(kukkucca)*. Added to these unwholesome mental possibilities are the negative ones of sloth *(thīna)* and torpor *(middha)*. The group is closed by 'doubt' *(vicikicchā)*, which is linked correlatively to the first quality of the wholesome group: faith.

We thus find the following group 'of unwholesome factors:[27]

1) infatuation *(moha)*.
2) shamelesness *(ahirika)*.
3) unscrupulousness *(anottapa)*.
4) restlessness *(uddhacca)*.
5) greed *(lobha)*.
6) erroneous views *(diṭṭhi)*.
7) self-conceit *(māna)*.
8) hate *(dosa)*.
9) envy *(issā)*.

27 Govinda, Ibid. p. 120.

10) egotism *(macchariya).*
11) worry *(kukkuccha).*
12) sloth *(thīna).*
13) torpor *(middha).*
14) doubt *(vicikicchā).*

The wholesome objects are divided differently; they are really not following out of three different roots, since they are essentially a unity for which space is created by the absence of the three basic vices. In their most general form they are characterized by faith or confidence (*saddhā*, S. *śraddhā*). Connected with this are a great number of mental qualities (objects) or 'ideas,' that always go together with confidence. These qualities together form a group of mental factors that combine in characterizing the state of mind that is the prerequisite for entering upon the liberation-path. These qualities form a first group (i) of mental factors. Such factors are e.g. mindfulness (*sati*, S. *smṛti*), balance of mind *(tatramajjhatatā),* tranquillity, suppleness, flexibility and agility, to mention a few. This group of qualities characterizes every wholesome state of mind. Besides there are the (ii) 'abstinences,' already mentioned in the description of the liberation-path: right speech, right action, right livelihood; (iii) the so-called boundless qualities: compassion *(karuṇā)*, sympathy or joy *(muditā)*. Lastly there is (iv) reason (paññindriya), the organ of wisdom or reflective understanding. Understanding wisdom or insight (*paññā*, S. *prajñā*) is the ultimate aim of the Path, coinciding with the complete disappearance of 'thirst.' And reason is the faculty which enables this wisdom.

The qualities numbered after ii, iii and iv correspond with the three fields of a basic distinction concerning the Buddhistic path: between the practical field of ethics (*sīla*, S. *śīla*), the 'tensional' field of meditative absorption *(samādhi)*, and the intellective field of understanding (wisdom [*paññā*, S. *prajñā*]). One may compare these respective fields to the striking, the tuning, and the hearing of a guitar-string.

A list of the wholesome factors, divided over their four groups, looks as follows: [28]

1) faith, confidence (*saddhā*, S. *śraddhā*).

28 Govinda, ibid., p. 121.

2) mindfulness (*sati*, S. *smṛti*).
3) shame *(hiri).*
4) scrupulousness *(ottapa).*
5) greedlessness *(alobha).*
6) hatelessness *(adosa).*
7) balance of mind *(tatramajjhatatā).*
8) inner tranquillity based on physical balance *(kāyapassaddhi)*
9) tranquillity based on (7) the mind *(cittapassaddhi)*.
10) inner agility based on (8) the body *(kāyalahutā).*
11) agility based on (9) the mind *(cittalahutā).*
12) inner flexibility based on (10) the body *(kāyamudutā).*
13) flexibility of the mind, based on (11) *(cittamudutā).*
14) adaptability of the body based on (12) *(kāyakammaññatā*
15) adaptability of mind, based on (13) *(cittakammaññatā).*
16) proficiency based on (14) of body *(kāyaguññatā)*
17) proficiency of mind, based on (15) *(cittaguññatā).*
18) rectitude of body, based on (16) *(kāyujjukatā).*
19) rectitude of mind, based on (17) *(cittujjukatā).*

ii

20)· right speech
21) right action
22) right livelihood

iii

23) compassion *(karuṇā).*
24) sympathy *(muditā).*

iv

25) The faculty or field of understanding *(paññindriya)*

States of mind.

The elaboration of a system of states of mind is the most scholastic aspect of the Abhidhamma. In a conscious state of mind the actuality of some of the possible objects of the mind, and some of the mental factors are realized. In a fully conscious state of mind all mental factors that are not mutually exclusive may combine. Besides, there is a whole range of states between background consciousness and full consciousness. As we have seen, there were seven factors or faculties active in each conscious act, and accordingly in every conscious state of mind. The other factors may be present in several possible combinations. It will be clear that the sum total of all possible states of mind is infinite. Nevertheless the authors of the Abhidharma have felt the need for at least some systematization. They created a list of types of consciousness by classifying conscious states *(cittāni)* according to certain criteria.

In the first place they made a distinction between conditioned and unconditioned states of mind. By a conditioned *(sahetuka)* state of mind they meant a state of mind being significant for one's progress on the liberation-path, viz. a state of mind bearing a karmic value conditioned by the root-causes, the wholesome or unwholesome basic mental factors that were already mentioned earlier: greed, hate, and infatuation as the karmically negative factors, and the absence of these as positive factors. Another criterion for classifying mental states was the distinction between states not leading to karmic results, those leading to karmic results, and states that are themselves fruit of *karma (vipāka)*. Again mental states are divided according to the pleasure or pain feelings, cheerful and gloomy feelings, or indifferent *(upekkha)* feelings involved in them. Besides, states are distinguished on the ground of their being connected with knowledge *(ñāna)* or not, or with erroneous views, and also on the ground of their whether or not being determined by subconscious tendencies *(saṅkhārā)*. Lastly, states are distinguished according to the world (*āvaccana*, S. *dhātu*) to which they belong, viz. that of desire, that of pure form, or that without form. Finally also the states of supramundane meditation are enumerated as special types of consciousness. In total 121 types of mental states are counted. It is of no use here to enumerate them all. The general distinction is between the unwholesome states (conditioned by the three unwholesome root-causes *(akusala cittāni)*, unconditioned states *(ahetuka-cittāni)*, and conditioned states [by wholesome root-causes] *(sahetukacittāni)*. This basic distinction determines the direction of further specification. An unwholesome state e.g. can never be combined with knowledge, and an unconditioned state can never be determined by subconscious tendencies, and the higher states of consciousness are never devoid of understanding. To give an example of how such classification works, we give below a diagram of greed-conditioned consciousness. Such consciousness can never be combined with an unpleasant feeling, since such a feeling would counteract greed. Furthermore it cannot be combined with knowledge, but only with false views or no view. Then the following possibilities present themselves:

- cheerful
  - erroneous
    - subconscious tendencies
    - no subconscious tendencies
  - unknowing
    - subconscious tendencies
    - no subconscious tendencies
- indifferent
  - erroneous
    - subconscious tendencies
    - no subconscious tendencies
  - unknowing
    - subconscious tendencies
    - no subconscious tendencies

Matter.

Matter in Theravāda is not considered as some mathematical entity existing in itself as is the case in the Western scientific tradition, but just as the mental factors and faculties, it is considered as a correlate of consciousness. The general term used to indicate matter is *'rūpa'* (form). All form is represented by the senses and is based on the primary elements *(dhātu)*: earth *(paṭhavī)*, water *(apo)*, fire *(tejo)*, and wind *(vayo)*, which are formed of quantities of very short living atoms, or better 'events.' These primary elements are the objects of the different sensations of touch. Besides, the concrete sense-objects of the senses other than touch are, as separate *dharmas* of a more subtle matter, distinguished from the primary elements These are sound, corresponding to hearing, form or apparition, corresponding to sight, savour, corresponding to taste, and odour, corresponding to smell. Also these consist of evanescent events.

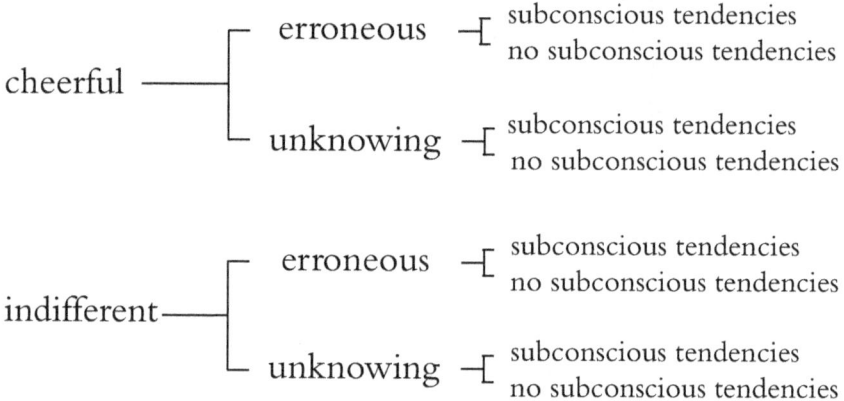

As further formations of form are mentioned: manliness and femi-nineness, the heart as physical base of mental life, the notifications (vocal or bodily signs), bodily vitality, the three bodily properties: agility, flexibility, and adaptability. As separate *dharmas* are furthermore counted the three phases of development: growth or rising *(upaccaya)*, duration *(saṁtati)* and decay *(jarā-aniccattā)*. Also the taking of food *(āhāra)* is counted separately.

'Space' occupies a special position in the lists of the Abhidhamma. In contradistinction to the general tenor of classical Indian philosophy, which takes space as a positive entity, it seems here to be considered as a limiting principle of the other elements. Here below follows a list of all the material *dharmas*: [29]

1-4	earth, water, fire and wind *(paṭhavi, āpo, tejo, vāyo)*
5-9	sense-organs *(indriya)*
10-14	sense-objects *(visaya)*
15-16	virility and femininity *(itthi-purisa-indriya)*
17	the heart *(hadayavatthu)*
18-19	signs (*viññapti* [vocal or corporeal])
20	bodily vitality *(rūpajīvita)*
21	space *(ākāsa)*
22-24	the three properties of the body (agility *[lahutā]*, flexibility *[mudutā]*, adaptability *[kammaññatā]*
25-28	the three characteristics of constituted phenomena *(dharmas)*: rise *(upaccaya)*, duration *(saṁtati)*, old age and impermanence *(jarā-aniccattā)*

Time.

For the Thera-abhidharmist time manifests itself as a consequence of the difference in speed between thought and the objects of sensory awareness. The fast movement of thought explains why sense-objects appear relatively stable and enduring. Seventeen events of thought cover the time of one smallest event of form-*dharma*. These seventeen events are the smallest time needed for one complete apperception. And the acceptance of the 17 to 1 rate is, accordingly, prescribed by

29 É. Lamotte, *L'Histoire du Bouddhisme Indien*, p. 609.

the need to avoid the introduction of unknowable phenomena, which would be a nonsense. It is here the apperceptive process which prescribes what is the smallest knowable entity. One moment is needed for blocking the background consciousness; two for setting it into vibration; one for alerting consciousness; one for sensory perception; one for reception; one for scrutinizing; one for determination; seven for full apperception, and two for appropriation.

General characteristics and interpretation.

It is often stated, that the Abhidharmic approach of the world is a realistic and pluralistic one, which would set it apart from later idealistic developments of Buddhism. But this is true only relatively, and less so for the Theras than for the Sarvāstivādins. To the Thera the process of suffering and liberation is real indeed, but he does not accept a being in itself, independent of the mind. All being is conditioned by mental factors, excepting only *nirvāṇa.* This confronts us with a central question: every conscious act begins with a blocking and subsequent vibration of the subconscious series of background consciousness, containing information and tendencies, which under normal circumstances become renewed constantly; there is nothing outside this subconscious stream or 'continuum' *(saṁtāna),* so whence comes its blocking? The answer can only be that it must be the consequence, the result of the ripening *(vipāka)* of a former act in the present or in a previous life. All experience, insofar as it is passive, is the outcome of former experience. Only conscious activity insofar as involving judgment and free will creates something new. The complexity of our present world is the product of innumerable former acts of freedom. This complexity is transmitted through the continuum of subconscious life by being ever re-embodied in the next event, like the ripples caused by a stone move through the pond until they are obstructed. Each tendency maintains its momentum until it is counteracted by a momentum of contrary direction. But what can counteract a 'protending pattern'?

Here we must remind the liberation-context of Buddhist thinking. Life is suffering and there is but one way out. There is but one direction without a dead end, the direction given by understanding, wisdom, and truth. Progression in any other direction strands on its limits. It sails out of the medium of truth – in which momentum can be transmitted indefinitely, into the muddy shores. To put it differently: Buddhism accepted two forms of 'thirst,' one for sensory enjoyment, and one for individual being *(kāmatṛṣṇā, bhavatṛṣṇā)*. But the fact is that extreme desire for sensory enjoyment leads to suffering and desire for individual being leads to destruction, since by these tendencies the continual replenishing of life, which requires the non-fixed state of openness, is obstructed. The tendencies, accordingly, evoke their refutation precisely by obstructing the renewal of the subconscious stream. And, as we saw, such obstruction causes the vibration of the stream, and sets in motion the apperceptive process, which provides one with the second chance liberty to remove (or avoid) the obstruction by choosing the direction of truth. In the context of the Abhidharma the root-causes, beginning with greed, present the systematized form of 'thirst.' They, in the end, cause the blocking of the continuum by their gradually starting to display their intrinsic contradiction.

The development of life in this way becomes characterized by learning of one's faults, in the process of which the pernicious root-tendencies should become gradually eliminated. This elimination is the extinction of 'thirst' *(nirvāṇa)*. But this is only the extinction of the unwholesome root-tendencies. What is not 'repulsive' is quietly transmitted in the refreshing of the stream. The stream of 'protending patterns' now has become a stream of knowledge (*ñāna*, S. *jñāna*). There is nothing left in it to be refuted. Being thus, it has left behind its individual limitations, carrying with it the whole world, even the wrong, but recognized as such. This stream of knowledge does not know anymore of the distinction between apperceptive and background consciousness, since the causes for the obstruction lying at the base of any particular conscious apperception are no more active. It may then be assumed that the background itself becomes foreground in an extremely intensified and magnified form of consciousness, which does not contain confronting but 'sympathetic' apperceptions. Such apperceptions differ from the apperceptions that need an obstruction as an occasion to realize its freedom; it is the free unhampered flow of true knowledge itself, the ultimate presupposition of all occasioned acts of freedom. This apperception is one of beauty insofar as it is made possible by right behaviour *(sīla)*, of peace, insofar as it is the end of right concentration *(samādhi)*, and of truth, insofar as it is the refuge of wisdom (*paññā*, S. *prajñā*).

T*HE SARVĀSTIVĀDA ABHIDHARMA*. The name 'Sarvāstivāda,' which means 'the lore that everything exists,' denotes a school of Buddhist realism. The extant Chinese translation of the Abhidharma of this school has not yet been explored sufficiently. That is why our exposition of it is based on a late commentary, the 'Abhidharmakośa' (treasury of the Abhidharma) of Vasubandhu (4th or 5th century AD). This gives an interpretation of the *Vibhāṣa*' (commentary from the end of the 2nd century AD), which, again, interprets the Abhidharma itself. Such an indirect rendering has dangers of misrepresentation. But as we may believe authorities on this point, Vasubandhu's rendering seems to be reliable.

Although in general outline the Sarvāstivāda Abhidharma does resemble that of the Theras, the central issue being a classification of the *dharmas* (the phenomena that form the ultimate building bricks of our world), there is an important difference; unlike that of the Theras, the system of the Sarvāstivādins has a dualistic character. Like that of the Theras it makes a distinction between a conditioned and an unconditioned realm. The sphere of the conditioned phenomena contains the familiar types of *dharmas*, the mind, its faculties, and its objects, which are all considered as separate though momentary entities. But on the level of the unconditioned there are found two fundamentally different principles, not only *nirvāṇa* (liberation), but also 'space' *(ākāśa)*, accordingly, there are two different ultimate principles.

The conception of personality of the Sarvāstivādins is basically the same as that of the Theras. The person is formed by a series of events, succeeding each other in a conditioned order. The mind, called by the terms '*manas*,' '*citta*,' or '*vijñāna*,' is the most important constituent of the personality. It is formed by a series of special consciousness-events, always appearing in direct association with those of the mental faculties *(caittā)*, which on the one hand are identified with separate *dharmas* (phenomena), but on the other hand can only be given by a consciousness manifesting them. The mental faculties are of two kinds, those facilitating actual intelligence or perceptiveness, and those facilitating activity. The active powers fall under the heading of 'force' *(saṁskāra)*, the receptive under those of 'sense data' *(rūpa)*, 'feeling' *(vedanā)* and 'cognition' [or apprehension, apperception] *(saṁjñā)*.

The stream of mind-events, accompanied by the streams of the events of the mental faculties, and of those of their objects, is called '*saṁtāna*' or '*saṁtati*.' It is this series of discontinuous appearances, that constitutes the personality, and not some persisting substantive entity, like a soul. Men, and things in general, are nothing beyond what is so given. They are a series of distinct phenomena *(dharma)*, and have no stable nature of their own. The identity of a living being is comparable to that of a fire consuming a forest, which can be denoted as one fire, but in fact the flames renew themselves constantly, and no one of them subsists even for the shortest time.

For the Sarvāstivādin, like for most early Buddhists, the *dharmas* appear conditioned, but spontaneously. A *dharma* can only emerge when its conditions are given. These conditions are nothing else but the complex of *dharmas* which was in actuality the preceding moment. Since in any preceding moment a certain configuration of such phenomena is given, on its base only such and such can arise. When *such* is the case, *this* will follow. However, there is an important difference with e.g. the Theras. For the Sarvāstivāda a '*dharma*' is not just a fleeting existence, it has a momentary appearance, but a lasting nature, which at the same time is its real being. The fleeting appearance is only a momentary state of this enduring nature. One might call this nature also the information or 'truth' transmitted by the event. It seems that it comprises the whole of the possibilities of a *dharma*, in practice its past and future occurrences. But beyond that, it is considered as something 'deep' and mysterious, not to be fathomed by rational thought. It is a permanent essence.

The Sarvāstivādins consider the phenomena falling under the heading of 'force' – the active powers – to be of central importance. The *sūtras* tend to identify the forces *(saṁskāras)* with volition *(cetanā)*, which is considered as the ultimate moulder of the world. There is nothing which does not result from action, and the beginning of all action *(karma)* is volition. But by the Sarvāstivādins volition is not conceived as something so universal. Apart from volition, they also assume natural forces *(viprayukta saṁskāra)* to explain the world's processes. These forces are in the first place those of birth, growth, decay, and destruction, but they also contain all those forces, somehow connected with the personality, but not actually being part of it; such as those forces operating in the domain of language concerning the transmission of meaning, the life forces controlling, what we would call the autonomous nerve-system, the forces regulating sleep and dream, and those active in the unconscious and semi-conscious trances. In short everything not being matter, but nevertheless beyond the power of the will was brought under this denominator. Most characteristic of the Sarvāstivādins in this respect are the phenomena of 'appropriation' *(prāpti)* and 'immunity' *(aprāpti)*.

Retribution.

To elucidate these concepts, we will describe their function in the explanation of retribution. We shall then at the same time learn how volition and the natural forces are interconnected.

Visible deed and invisible result. Retribution is the fruition of the results of a deed set in motion by the will. It is accomplished in the following way. From the actual volition, which is something purely mental, issue two types of acts in the current world; in the first place there is the bodily or vocal behaviour, that is the direct expression of the will, and which is at once, the performance *in re* of the deed and its communication to the world. For example, in the case of a murder it is the actual stabbing of the victim. This physical expression is called the 'notification' or 'sign' [of the will] *(vijñapti)*. But at the selfsame time at which the notable act is performed, another imperceptible act is effectuated, which may be compared to the laying of an invisible egg. This egg or seed is of a kind of subtle, or implicated matter. It yet does not have the characteristics of perceptible matter. As a seed it has no extension, but it has the intrinsic ability to materialize in space. This materialization is the matured retribution of the initial act. The egg, accordingly, is a force which automatically procures the retribution of the act. It is called '*avijñapti*,' and it is considered as a separate *dharma* in the material realm. A physical deed causes an '*avijñapti*,' which grows and ripens in conformity with its own laws, and finally evokes its own neutralization or retribution.[30]

Whose is the deed? But this materialistic interpretation of the process of retribution raises an important question: in what way is the act, its egg, and its little chicken connected with the one responsible? The very autonomy of the process renders it possible that the act is retributed in quite another psychic stream as the one out of which it came. In other words, what makes the egg a satellite of this stream and not of another? The Sarvāstivādins found for this problem the following solution. At the moment the act is completed and 'projected' it creates in the personal series to which it belongs its 'appropriation' *(prāpti)*. This is a *dharma* belonging to the group regulating the autonomous vital processes. It continues to be renewed until the moment the 'fruit' is ripe, i.e. when the deed hits its goal. At that moment the incessant regeneration of the 'appropriation' is interrupted, and from that moment the act is retributed, precisely from the perspective of the one who performed it. For it is 'his' stream which is now freed from it.[31]

Two *dharmas*, therefore, are operative in the process of retribution, (1) the '*avijnapti*' created by an act of volition combined with a physical deed, which governs the retribution as such, and (2) the glue of the 'appropriation' *(prāpti)*, which makes this unnoticeable 'egg' stick to the stream of events from which it came until the time of breaking apart and freeing its 'chicken.' Besides the 'appropriation' of retribution, the Sarvāstivādins also mention its opposite, '*aprāpti*,' which we will translate as 'immunity.' This concept is particularly relevant for those having reached the higher stages of the Buddhistic path. Their wealth of accumulated good works can render them immune to the results of evil ones, if they might happen to commit these. It seems justified to relate in this connection the story of the Sthavira Chakkhupāla, who was blind. One evening he went for his walk, but since at the time many little insects populated the ground under his feet, he killed these in great numbers. The other monks complained to the Buddha, but the latter explained, that because of the elder being deprived of the sense of sight, he invoked no guilt by the act of killing.

30 Cf. É. Lamotte, *L'Histoire du Bouddhisme Indien*, p. 662.

31 Ibid. cf. p. 672.

Although here is a physical deed, which according to the Sarvāstivāda lore must have created an '*avijnapti*' of killing, nevertheless there was no 'appropriation' *(prāpti)* of it, since Chakkhupāla's state of arhatship precluded any thought or intention of death, he was immune to the deed of killing.

Further reflection on the matter may help to elucidate more of the structure of Sarvāstivāda thinking. It will thereby be helpful to look at the matter from three angles: (1) that of volition and fruition, (2) that of the five substrates (or groups of grasping), (3) that of will and space.

1) volition and fruition. When we read again the above, we find that action starts with a volition, which expresses itself in perceptible matter. For a brute materialist this would be the whole story, but Buddhism adds something to this. An action has a moral value, and when it is called into existence, it produces a special force, which by the Sarvāstivādins is interpreted as the seed or subtle existence of a certain phenomenon in the material world. In due time the seed will yield its fruit, and the instigator of the deed will be the one to harvest it.

This reaping of the fruit may be called 'experience' (or fruition). It is nothing but the reception of the results of former deeds.

We have found a simple scheme: there are the conative acts, which generate processes that finally are received by fruitive experiences. These may be interpreted as intellective acts. Man's activity conditions his experience and understanding.

2) five substrates. We have seen that Buddhism recognized five types of irreducible phenomena: inclinations (volitions), forms, feelings, apprehensions, and conscious perceptions. The whole universe was composed out of these five elementary 'substrates'; Apart from it there were no other constituents of life and the world. Volition was the beginning of action and this action conditioned further experience in the form of sensory impressions, arousing feelings and being interpreted by apprehensions. The experience was simply the retribution of the volition. The relation between de deed and its 'fruition' lay in the nature of experience itself. Nothing external was required to explain its operation. But now the Sarvāstivādin poses something between the deed and its retribution by experience. It accepts a non-phenomenal existence to account for the connection between the deed and its retribution, between volition and experience. This non-phenomenal existence is a kind of natural force.

3) will and space. For the Sarvāstivādins the group of 'inclinations' *(saṁskāra)* contains more than only conative acts. It encompasses all that generates processes whatsoever. Therefore, in speaking about the Sarvāstivāda, we have chosen for the word 'force' as translation of '*saṁskāra*' rather than for 'volition' or 'inclination.' Not everything is here a function of volition. The generative, conative act provides the information of any process, it determines what is to be the subject of development, but this evolution itself, the growth, stabilizing, maturing, decay, destruction, holding together of its subject matter, and the keeping in abeyance of what presently does not fit in with it, is ruled by autonomous or natural forces. From where that autonomy?

All natural forces regulate what may be called, the definition of the will in space (the container of form and matter). The will formats the principle *(avijñapti)*, which thus informed develops into a spatial manifestation. For the Sarvāstivāda space is an unconditioned *dharma*, something infinite. This infinity stands in a striking contrast to the finitude of a principle (in which is laid down the information produced by a deed). Now the path from finitude to infinitude is that of growth, the path in the other direction is that of decay. The other natural forces too have something to do with positioning in space. May we then suppose, that the natural forces are somehow an outcome of the nature of space itself and of its material contents, which tend to give everything a momentum of expansion or diminution? It may very well be the lure of infinity itself that is responsible for this. And since space for the Sarvāstivādins is not a function of the will or of the mind, this would explain why the functions based on it are autonomous. Space is dragging and inflating our intentions once they are exposed to it, and when they cannot stand the light, they may even damage or obliterate our own spatial existence.

Death and after.

The cycle of '*karma*,' action and retribution, is by the Sarvāstivādins conceived in the same way as among most Buddhists; one's last thought presents the moral result of one's life and determines the setting of a future birth. But there are some particularities. Between death and birth the mind-series wanders through an intermediary life, conceived in order to bridge the assumed time-gap between death and a new birth. In this intermediary existence the mind assumes the faculties of a Gandharva, a being sometimes thought of as a heavenly minstrel, but here it is conceived as a being feeding itself solely with odours.

Knowledge and volition

The Theras had definite thoughts about how a stimulus of the subconscious (the body of habits and dispositions) could develop into a conscious apperception. The conscious apperception itself involved free judgment, and the freedom of action seemed to depend upon the freedom of the judgment implied in it. This concept of free judgment provides a base for the moral responsibility which is a presupposition of the Buddhistic path. The doctrine of the Sarvāstivādins lacks such systematic base of freedom. It sees freedom not as anchored in judgment but in volition. And unlike judgment, volition, and the resulting action, is not a function of consciousness, but a *dharma* apart, functioning only in conjunction with consciousness. Since there is really no causal connection between the two, there can be nothing that motivates volitional events, but antecedent events, and such motivation is actually merely a conditioning. The will follows upon events of such and such a kind, and these again follow upon certain volitions. Volition here becomes a response to conditions. This seems to be considered as a free activity. Although the Theras also took volition as a response to conditions, they looked upon freedom as the free judgment implicit in the act of apperception from which the deed springs, and not as the deed itself. And, although the will for them is not free, the moment of actual apperception, preceding it, is. But apperception does not play a significant role in the thought of the Sarvāstivādins.

Free judgment is not the root of action; the conative domain here seems to be regarded as more autonomous.

We here touch upon a fundamental difference between the Theras and the Sarvāstivādins. The position of the Theras is predominantly intellectual, whereas that of the Sarvāstivādins is voluntaristic or practical. For the Theras it is the essence of temporal life that apperceptive moments succeed one another in an order that is admittedly conditioned, but leaving room for the operation of freedom. Each moment of time can be an occasion of freedom. The forming of an apperception is a temporal process. While one apperception arises, another merges in the background-consciousness or 'bhavāṅga,' which is a kind of subliminal consciousness, in which all relevant knowledge is stored. For the Sarvāstivādins consciousness is not primarily directed at apperceptions but at action. And more stress is laid on the fact that in itself consciousness is an undifferentiated light, revealing anything that comes into its vicinity. This makes that it is not really conditioned by its own former states. Although consciousness in itself is a series of light-moments, and not a persisting entity, the uniformity of its nature makes its evanescent character practically irrelevant. The changes of time lay outside its proper domain. Knowledge, accordingly, here cannot consist in the rising of a moment of truth, and so be a fact in the development of time, but must, on the contrary, be conceived as a corollary of space. It is the close vicinity of some object to the light-stream that makes it manifest. Since consciousness in itself is unqualified, the whole dynamics that constitutes knowledge derives from the objects and the independent mental faculties.

Knowledge then depends upon the changing of the coordinates of the *dharmas* in absolute space. In fact all change is nothing but a movement of place. In this scheme the idea of a subliminal consciousness, storing past apperceptions, is superfluous. What is retained from the past is not primarily conceived as something intellective, but as stored action, working as a force in actual life. Present action transforms into force, and this force again is at work in action, as if human endeavour is subject to a kind of natural law.

Here the forming of knowledge is not really the sudden rise of insight, conditions being fulfilled. There is no truth in this sense, but only a greater or lesser clarity, depending on the distance to the light-source. Wisdom itself is not conceived as a state of mind but as its object, which, by the way, is a reason why ultimate liberation or *nirvāṇa* here cannot be conceived as a destiny of the intellect, but must be seen as a result of birth-suppressing effort and action. The actual process of cognition is described by Stcherbatsky as follows:[32]

> 'A moment of colour [or form] *(rūpa)*, a moment of sense-vision-matter *(cakṣus)* and a moment of pure consciousness *(citta)* arising simultaneously in close contiguity, constitute what is called a sensation [or 'contact'] of colour [or form] ... although there is no real coming in contact between elements, no grasping of the objective element by the intellect, nevertheless the three elements do not appear on terms of absolute equality; there is between two of them – consciousness and object [form] – a special relation which might be termed 'coordination' [conformity] *(sarūpya)*, a relation which makes it possible that the complex phenomenon – the resulting cognition – is a cognition of colour [form] and not of the visual sense.'

The central idea is here, that knowledge is basically a relation between subject (consciousness) and object (form), both occurring in space. The senses are just the doors that let through (or cut off) the light of the mind to illuminate its object. This suggests a real contact between the light and that on which it falls. But such real contact is impossible, because a real contact presupposes a being in contact for a while, and such enduring touch is impossible in the light of the momentariness of the phenomena. To overcome this problem the Sarvastivada accepted, that the light somehow takes on the form of its object. It follows its shape. The concept of 'conformity' expresses this idea.

Mental faculties.

Like the Theras, the Sarvāstivādins accept the triple distinction of consciousness, the mental faculties, and the sensory realm. Consciousness is that which, by shining upon them, reveals the other two. 'Consciousness is the awareness in every single case,'[33] which seems to mean,

32 Th. Stcherbatsky, *The Central Conception of Buddhism*, p. 46-47 (London 1923, Calcutta, 1956, '61, Susil Gupta. Text between [] added.

33 Ibid., p.16

that it just witnesses whatever may be given at a certain moment. But there is no witnessing without mental faculties being involved. As was the case with the Theras, the faculties involved make of the witnessing a concrete act, which may or may not have a moral value, since the faculties involved may be wholesome *(kuśala)*, unwholesome *(akuśala)* or neutral *(avyākṛta)*. Ten neutral faculties *(citta-mahābhūmika dharma)* are involved in every mental act. These correspond to a certain degree with the seven which the Theras found as being involved in every mental apperception, although there is a difference, as we shall see. These ten are:[34]

1) *vedanā* (feeling)
2) *saṁjñā* (apprehension, understanding, cognition)
3) *cetanā* (responsivity, effort)
4) *sparśa* (being in 'touch' with an object, mere sensation)
5) *chanda* (will or desire to act, intention)
6) *prajñā* (right understanding, wisdom)
7) *smṛti* (mindfulness, memory)
8) *manaskāra* (attention)
9) *adhimokṣa*
10) *samādhi* (concentration)

Of these (1), (2), (3), (4) and (8) correspond to the same faculties mentioned by the Theras. '*Samādhi*' or concentration fairly well corresponds to the Thera-faculty of one-pointedness *(ekaggatā)*. The other faculties indicate the differences between Sarvāstivādins and Theras. The faculty of psychic vitality, mentioned in this connection by the Theras, is not found on the Sarvāstivāda list, since this factor is not considered as mental but as material. But the other differences are more significant. *Chanda*, *prajñā*, *smṛti* (P. *sati*), and *adhimokṣa* (will, wisdom, mindfulness and decision) are mentioned by the Theras, but not as factors belonging to every mental act. Decision and will were mentioned as karmically neutral faculties, but not as belonging to every act, but only to the practical ones. Wisdom and mindfulness, moreover, were not considered as neutral but as wholesome or 'good' *(kusala)*. What does this difference mean? It seems that the Sarvāstivādins do not want to make a clear separation between the active and the

34 Ibid., p. 86.

intellective sphere, and besides, they do not subscribe to a primacy of the intellective as the Theras do. For the latter the intellective is basic, since every act implies intellection, but not every act is practical. The Sarvāstivādins, on the contrary, seem to consider every act as basically practical and take the intellective aspects only as something belonging to it. This contrast is even more emphasized by taking mindfulness (or memory) and wisdom as neutral factors instead of wholesome ones, as do the Theras. It seems clear that the Theras consider liberation as characterized by insight, as it seems to have been in original Buddhism. But the Sarvāstivādins interpret mindfulness, which for the Theras characterizes every wholesome act, as a peculiarity of every act per se, also bad ones, and the same they do with wisdom, which for the Theras was the highest of the good factors standing closest to liberation. Therein lies clearly a depreciation of the intellect, as something not helping very much, or at most – if well used – as an aid, on the path of liberation. Vasubandhu even suggests that agility of mind can be a handicap rather than an advantage in the realization of the more important stages of meditation.

Like the Theras the Sarvāstivādins also accept some neutral faculties that may, but need not, accompany (mental) acts. Only two of those correspond with those of the Theras, viz. '*vitarka*' (deliberative thinking) and '*vicāra*' (pondering). The whole list is:[35]

1) *kaukṛtya* (worry, P. *kukucca*)
2) *middha* (absentmindedness)
3) *vitarka* (deliberative thinking)
4) *vicāra* (pondering)
5) *rāga* (desire)
6) *dveṣa*
7) *māna* (self esteem)
8} *vicikitsā* (doubt)

Excepting deliberation and pondering, the Theras reckon all these to the unwholesome factors. Again we must assume for this the same reason, the high value they put on the intellect. This is clear in the cases of worry, absentmindedness, self-esteem (conceit) and doubt. These

35 Ibid., pp. 88-89.

factors all trouble insight, which the Theras consider to be the highest. It therefore counteracts the wholesome and is therefore unwholesome. But when extinction of birth is the highest, and the faculty of understanding *(prajñā)* leading to insight is indifferent in that respect, then also the mental trouble disturbing understanding becomes indifferent). Remains to explain the occurrence of desire and aversion in this list. For the Theras these were even root-causes of evil. For the intellectual to whom, for the realization of insight, the abandonment of the active life itself is enjoined, its incentives fall under a verdict. But for the voluntarist desire for the good and aversion of evil are potent factors in the progress on the path. They cannot be abandoned, since there is no realm beyond action, except its suppression, which, however, itself is an outcome of action.

Summarizing we may say, that the most important difference between Theras and Sarvāstivādins is, as far as we can conclude now, that for the Theras the faculties of action are not necessarily involved in every conscious act. For the Sarvāstivādins, on the contrary, every act implies activity, but not necessarily intellectual effort, although some moment of discrimination is always implied. But this discrimination is not acquired by the effort of inquisitive thinking and pondering, but one should see it rather as the automatic result of the shining of the conscious light in every act, revealing existing distinctions by its very nature.

Connected with this distinction is for the Theras the contrast between a conscious and a pre-conscious (or subconscious) realm. Activity is based on the workings of the subconscious, which can only be modified by gaining the knowledge that changes its nature or disposition. It is this disposition which determines practical behaviour, not the conscious intention, which, on the contrary, is itself determined by the disposition. Real progress is not made on the path of action but on that of knowledge and insight, which tends to make the subconscious realm of dispositions transparant in the end. It is like the bubble in the water finally dissipating in the air above. But the Sarvāstivādins do not admit such a pre- or subconscious realm. For them there seems to be nothing between the conscious and the unconscious. Accordingly, for them it cannot be the gaining of knowledge that is in the focus of the liberation process. It is the suppressive effort and activity that forms the central issue here. Knowledge here is only a means; it is the light by which you can act.

Wholesome and unwholesome mental faculties. The Sarvāstivādins make a distinction between defiling *(kleśa)*, unwholesome and wholesome mental faculties. The defiling and unwholesome factors generally belong to the same class, but it seems that only the latter are morally bad in a strict sense. Besides, some faculties, which one would expect to be characterized as 'unwholesome,' like desire, hate, and doubt are put in an indifferent class, as we have seen. The thought behind this classification is, that a distinction is made between attachment to the world of (objects of) desire (the normal world of men and animals, and lower heavenly and hellish beings) and attachment to that of form, or of existence. These latter worlds are extremely pure. They are realized in meditation, and by extreme good '*karma*' one can be reborn in them. Attachment to these higher worlds cannot be termed 'bad' or unwholesome, but such ties are nevertheless defiling, they hinder the aspirant for liberation. The general characteristic of 'defilement' is that it obscures the light of consciousness, so that it cannot provide sufficient light for (good) action. The obscuring is due to mental perplexity *(moha)* identified to a high degree with ignorance. This perplexity is the root-cause of all the other 'defilers.' At the least it inspires the believe in a permanent personality, denied by all Buddhists. Six of these defilers are present in every obscured act:[36]

1) *moha* (perplexity)
2) *pramada* (heedlessness)
3) *kausīdya* (mental heaviness)
4) *aśraddhā* (lack of faith)
5) *styāna* (sloth)
6) *auddhatya* (restlessness)

One might expect, that while attachment to existence as such is inspired by '*moha*,' attachment to the normal sense-world, the world of desire, is inspired by (what else but) desire, and its negative counterpart, hate. But we have seen that such is not the case. The reasons for

36 Ibid., p. 87.

this are not fully clear, but as we have suggested, the Sarvāstivādins did not accept the superiority of the intellective or contemplative life, and so also the usual abandonment of activity implied in the ideal of contemplation could not be accepted. But this being the case, some positive role for desire and hate could not be denied. How should the good motivate you, if you do not desire it, and how can you avoid the bad if you do not loath it? And is not desire indispensable for the maintenance of existence? The point becomes clearer by examining the only two factors that are universally present in every bad or unwholesome act. These are:[37]

1) irreverence *(ahrīkya)* and
2) unscrupulousness *(anapatrapya)*

'Unscrupulousness' is really the not becoming indignant on seeing offences done by others. Now it seems that irreverence implies a lack of care, which care is based to a certain extent on desire. But as concerns the lack of indignance, it must be admitted that this implies a lack of hate. Besides these defiling and universally bad factors, there are ten bad factors, that may or may not occur in any bad act: [38]

1) *krodha* (violent anger)
2) *markṣa* (hypocrisy)
3) *matsarya* (envy)
4) *īrṣyā* (jealousy)
5) *pradāsa* (approving objectionable things)
6) *vihiṁsā* (causing harm, menacing)
7) *upanāha* (breaking friendship)
8) *māyā* (cheating}
9) *catya* {trickery)
10) *mada* (complacency)

If we compare all these lists with the list of unwholesome factors of the Theras, the missing factors in the Sarvāstivāda list are much more significant than the added ones. Besides the fact that hate, desire ('greed'

37 Ibid., p. 87-88.
38 Ibid., p. 86-89.

in the Thera-list), and doubt, which we have already found in an 'indifferent' list, are not mentioned here, the omission of 'erroneous views' must be noted. It points again to the low importance attached to intellectual issues.

Like the Theras, the Sarvāstivādins also have a list of 'good' or wholesome factors. Typical of these factors is, that they all imply each other. All of the ten following factors are present in every good act:[38]

1) *śraddhā* (faith)
2) *viryā* (virtuous courage)
3) *upekṣa* (equanimity, placidness))
4) *hrī* (modesty, humility)
5) *apatrapya* (aversion of things objectionable)
6) *alobha* (absence of desire)
7) *adveṣa* (absence of aversion or hate)
8) *ahiṁsā* (non-violence [-killing])
9) *praśrabdhi* (mental dexterity)
10) *apramada* (care, tending the good)

The presence of 'absence of desire and hate' in this list might seem inconsistent, since desire and hate are not classified as 'bad,' and (5) 'aversion of objectionable things' seems to imply some kind of hate. But evidently systematization was not put that far. It was believed either, that desire and hate could be indifferent (occasionally good), but as a habit never good, or one has not dared to wipe 'absence of desire and hate' from the list, since its presence there was of respected antiquity. Noteworthy again is 'virtuous courage' on the second place instead of the 'mindfulness' of the Theras, again an indication of the primacy of practice.

Matter.

The Sarvāstivāda recognizes four so-called 'great elements' *(mahābhūtāni)*, earth, water, fire, and wind. These have as common characteristic mutual impenetrability; the space occupied by one cannot at the same time be occupied by another. This relationship with space points to the great elements being a kind of conditioned space. They cannot exist apart from it. But at the same time this characteristic of impenetrability makes them object for the sense of touch. Their impenetrability makes them tangible. This tangibility can be manifested in four ways, as movement, heat, attraction, and hardness. And it is just because of these four manifestations of tangibility that the elements are distinguished from each other: what is experienced as movement is called 'wind,' heat is called 'fire,' the quality that makes a liquid stick to the skin, which is the same that makes it form drops, viz. cohesion and adhesion, is called 'water' (or liquid), and the hardness of solid matter is called earth. All things of the sensible world are composed of all these four elements; the concrete water, and the concrete fire contain the other elements as well, even in equal proportion. It is only the intensity of the respective elements in each thing that makes one thing appear as fiery and the other as wet.

All matter is composed of atoms, which, according to the Buddhistic fashion, are not permanent but momentary entities. An atom appears, and vanishes the next moment, but another will reappear in the same manner if nothing comes in between. It is a flashing of a point in space to be noticed by touch, a flashing conditioned by other similar flashes, for it never appears without a cause. The flashing, however, is only its appearance, and not its nature, for that is considered to be permanent. One might say, the truth of its having appeared in all its impermanence in such or such nature, is itself lasting.

The atoms of the great elements are accompanied by other atoms of a more subtle character. These are the atoms that form the basis of sensory awareness through the senses other than that of touch, the atoms of visible matter, audible, smellable, and tasteable matter. They are connected to the basic elements, and are perceived by the mind through the medium of a translucent matter constituted by similar atoms. It is this translucent matter that forms the sensing stuff attached to the tangible (for composed out of the 'great elements') sense organs.

One can differ in opinion concerning the question whether all these atoms should be considered as entities in itself (although impermanent) or simply as entities for consciousness. The momentary flashes do not seem to exist apart from their being perceptible to touch. But does this mean that they do not exist untouched? Besides, the Sarvāstivādins consider space as an absolute reality. This suggests that the atoms will be at least as dependent on space as on consciousness or mind. And such dependency on space, as an absolute entity, may at the same time be interpreted as a relative independence with respect to the mind, which unlike space, is itself only a conditioned phenomenon. Considered as functions of absolute space, the atoms – and all things as far as constituted by atoms – may well be thought of as independent of mind. As functions of perception, however, they may be mind-dependent. There can, to put it in a different way, be made a distinction between primary and secondary qualities of things, of which the first are ultimately real, and the second only subjectively.

Perception.

On the basis of the atom-theory the theory of perception is built. Perception has two material bases, an external *(bāhya-āyatana)* and an internal *(adhyātma-āyatana):* formed by the tactile and subtle matter mentioned above). These again are each divided sixfold in the following manner:[39]

internal base	*external base*
1) sense of vision	7) colour and shape
2) sense of hearing	8) sound
3) sense of smell	9) odour
4) sense of taste	10) taste
5) sense of touch	11) tangability
6) mind	12) mental objercts

Only the mental objects and sense have no material base. Together they form the four mental 'groups' *(skandha)*, feelings, apprehensions, forces (responsivity), and mind itself. The other five senses and their objects belong to the group of 'form,' which comprises all the nor-

39 Ibid., p. 6-7; The Sanskrit names of the internal and external bases are in the numbering as given in the text: (1) *cakṣurindriyāyatana,* (2) *śrotrendriyāyatana,* (3) *ghranendriyāyatana,* (4) *jihvendriyāyatana,* (5) *kāyendriyāyatana,* (6) *mana-indriyāyatana,* (7) *rūpāyatana,* (8) *śabdāyatana,* (9) *gandhāyatana,* (10) *rasāyatana,* (11) *spraṣṭavyāyatana,* (12) *dharmāyatana.*

mal senses and their objects. The sense of touch is based on the 'great elements,' the others on the subtle elements that constitute the higher senses and their respective objects. These bases given, perceptive consciousness *(vijñāna)* can be realized in six different corresponding modes: visual, auditory, olfactory, gustatory, tactile, and non-sensory or purely mental perception. Together with the twelve bases mentioned above, these six forms of perceptive consciousness form the so-called eighteen '*dhātus*' (bases).

Stcherbatsky compares these to mines of various metals. 'Just as different metals might be extracted from a mine, just so does the stream of individual life reveal elements of 18 different kinds.'[40]

In the above scheme, mind itself is enumerated in three different places: (1) as the consciousness of the perceptive act itself, (2) as the faculty or sense enabling this consciousness, and (3) as the object of this consciousness, since mind is able to apprehend itself. In a pure reflective act (2) and (3) are nothing else but preceding moments of the same stream of consciousness. One can see a previous moment of thought through the medium of the moments lying between that past moment and the present moment of vision.

Time.

The Sarvāstivādins differed in their concept of time from most other Buddhists. Most ancient Buddhists were so-called '*vibhajyavādins*,' those who affirm that only the present, and that part of the past which has not yet ripened is real, but deny the reality of the future and of the perfect tense. The Sarvāstivādins taught the reality of all three times, past, present and future. The nature *(svabhāva)* of a thing is fixed and does not change in time. It only changes its appearance *(lakṣaṇa)* or its conditions *(avastha)* (according to different teachers). This idea conflicts obviously with the momentariness of things generally accepted in Buddhism, the more so, since it is stated that the being of a phenomenon does not differ from its nature. The idea, that change is but a change of the condition of the essence, seems to be adopted from the transformation-lore of the Sāṁkhyas. However, the Sarvāstivādins did not apply it to reality as a whole, but to each phenomenon *(dharma)*

40 Ibid., p. 8, with reference to *Abhidharmakośa*, I, 20

apart. In doing so, they maintained the pluralism of Buddhism, but they flatly contradicted its general idea that change is a serial succession of separate moments, an idea to which they themselves subscribed as far as appearances are concerned. But beyond this phenomenal realm they accepted a world of unchangeable, deep essences, unfathomable by rational thought. It is not surprising that this combination of mutually conflicting thoughts became the target of the severe criticism of other Buddhistic schools. Among the critics, the Sautrāntikas – about whom we shall come to speak – are most prominent.

The concept of Nirvāṇa

One aim of the Buddhistic path is to counteract attachment by detachment. On this ethical field the role of volition is evident, since it is the will that either yields to desire and binds itself to the world, or commits itself to the Buddhistic path which in the end leads to detachment and liberation. But volition even has a role to play in the suppression of the natural processes. We have seen, that, unlike the Theras, the Sarvāstivādins did not include the natural processes into the ethical realm. For the Sarvāstivāda, nature (in the Western sense), although not absolutely independent of the will, is so to a certain extent. Mere good action cannot suppress this nature, but still it was believed that the suppression or termination of nature is required to attain *nirvāṇa*. In fact the Sarvāstivādins dintinguished two kinds of *nirvāṇa*. The first kind of *nirvāṇa (pratisaṁkhyanirodha)* was due to the rising of the insight into the Buddhistic truths, concerning suffering, its origin, and its termination. For early Buddhism, and for the Theras, liberation simply followed as the outcome of this insight, and it was the Buddhistic path that brought this vision. Meditation and practice led to a gradual growth of wisdom until the final truth was clearly seen. By this insight worldly existence itself was dissolved. But for the Sarvāstivādin, the truth does not set aside worldly existence without remainder. For although the volitional life may be purified, its existence in space is still there. Because existence (in space) is a reality depending on an absolute (space), it cannot be dissolved by good behaviour or insight. To overcome the last remainder of existence, intelligence and insight are of no avail, in fact they may even be an obstacle. The highest meditative act here is not intellectual, but volitional. It does nothing else but suppressing mind and intelligence itself, until the state of catalepsy is reached. This is the second and highest type of *nirvāṇa (apratisaṁkhyanirodha).*

It has often been said that the Sarvāstivāda concept of liberation *(nirvāṇa)* is a purely lifeless one, a kind of eternal death. This e.g. is the opinion of Stcherbatsky[41] and it may also be concluded from what is said above about *nirvāṇa* as a kind of catalepsy. Now what we can conclude with certainty is, that *nirvāṇa* is a state in which the seeds of birth are eradicated, and where, accordingly, is no more birth or death. Then it seems that life and death are equally absent from liberation, which makes that the qualification 'eternal death' should better be avoided. *nirvāṇa* is a real existent, it is not a nought. According to the descriptions one is led to equate liberation with that deep eternal essence that lies at the base of all phenomenal change. To call this essence 'materialistic,' as is sometimes done, is not warranted. There are not only essences of the material, but also of the mental realm. These essences form the abode of rest of whatever is. This realm of essence is presupposed in all practical life and in all appearance. Now in the final tranquillity this realm is freed from life and appearance. But what is tranquillity if it is not somehow experienced? If liberation is not somehow the coming to rest of the mind, what is left of the soteriological character of Buddhism; what sense is left in the metaphor of final quiescence? The solution probably is, that the end of all turbulence of life, and of the mind's activities, does not preclude the continuance of a still, pure spiritual light as the eternal essence of the mind, a light that can, admittedly, not be reborn every new moment of existence in *nirvāṇa*, but also it does not die every moment, as in normal existence. It just shines in the deep, without obstruction filling the (w)hole of space.

41 Th. Stcherbatsky, *The Conception of Buddhist Nirvāṇa*, p. 27 (Leningrad 1927)

Chapter 4
Sautrāntikas

The Sautrāntikas derive their name from the fact that they reject the authority of the Abhidharma, and accept only the *sūtras* as the word of the Buddha. Their thought developed in the same time as that of the Sarvāstivādins, although its beginning is probably later. It can be traced to the 2nd century AD. It seems that they are not really an independent school with own cloisters, order-rules and the like. They are rather a group of thinkers having come to disagree on intellectual issues with the Sarvāstivāda, with which they were in close contact. They are likely to have assimilated some ideas from the Mahāsaṁghikas and from Mahāyāna. They must be counted among the Hīnayāna schools, because they accept the reality of the temporal world, and share the essentials of the *dharma*-theory with the Theras and the Sarvāstivādins. Our source of knowledge of Sautrāntika thinking is the same as that of the Sarvāstivāda, the *Abhidharmakośa* of Vasubandhu, dating from the 5th century AD. The Sautrāntikas stood in a dialogue with the Sarvāstivādins, and they may, because of that, most fruitfully be compared with them, rather than with the Theras. In the following, we shall be content to note the differences with the schools already spoken of. We shall not repeat indefinitely the things common to all Hīnayāna schools, or try to describe a finished system.

The stream of mind.

The Sautrāntikas reject the reality of many mental faculties, and also of the forces 'dissociated from thought' such as the forces of origination, growth, decay, and destruction, which the Sarvāstivādins regarded as separate essences.

Important is the conception of consciousness. For the Sautrāntika consciousness is not an undifferentiated light, but something that ever assumes the characteristics of its object. It is itself coloured by the variety of the phenomena, which it represents. In this light it is doubtful, whether for them mental faculties are irreducible phenomena, as in Thera and Sarvāstivāda thinking, or just possibilities of the mind.

Just as for other early Buddhists, also for the Sautrāntika a living being is conceived as a stream of momentary events. It is a series of consciousness moments of which each for itself lasts only an infinitely short time. Each of these moments is conditioned by the previous ones, and by the series of moments of its objects. They appear and disappear spontaneously, but they are ever reproduced in the same way if nothing prevents it. What prevents this reproduction is called a cause, occasioned by volition and action. But this is nothing else but some earlier moment of the same stream, which is itself conditioned by other volitions and actions.

Action and fruit.

As in the preceding two forms of early Buddhism, the whole conditioning of the stream is the result of the interplay between the action and its fruit. Both, cause and effect, are momentary events, and their connection may be compared to the arms of a balance; when one goes down the other goes up. The beginning of a deed is constituted by a particular volition, and the end is its retribution according to its merit. But the operating of this retribution is not proceeding as with the Theras or the Sarvāstivādins. For the Sarvāstivādins a volition issues in a physical and psychical act, which both have a manifest and an unmanifest moment. The manifest bodily and vocal actions were called 'signs' *(vijñapti)*. But at the same time an invisible but material string of events was created, made of the great elements, which remains in existence and ripens. It constitutes a state of being retributable called *avijñapti*. The same was the case in the mental field. When an act is completed it creates in the series of which it is a part the 'appropriation' of it *(prāpti)*. This transitory phenomenon is ever reproduced in the series until it has ripened and the time has come for its retribution.[42] The idea behind this all is, that a deed directly creates some force or seed, which follows its own development, and yields its fruit autonomously when the time has matured. This thought of an autonomous maturing of the deed in a separate *dharma* (expressed by the concepts of *avijñapti* and *prapti*), apart from the normal development of consciousness, is rejected by the Sautrāntikas. For them the fruit does not emerge directly from the past act, the only direct result of an event being the next event. The deed does not cause its result without a go-between. The ripening of some action is occasioned immediately only by the moment just preceding it. Accordingly, a deed is not stored away only to reappear when it is to be counteracted, but it affects the whole series that lies between itself and its retribution. It is not hidden in a box of its own, but tinges all subsequent mental and physical phenomena. These phenomena of life themselves undergo an evolution, which finally ends in the retribution of the initial deed.

Forms, volitions, mind.

The Sautrāntikas tend to reduce the range of phenomena *(dharma)* to three main types: forms (sense data), volitions, and consciousness or mind. Strings of living beings are composed of these. For the development of the world, the first two are most important. Volition leads to the obtainment of sense data (including feelings and awareness) of a certain kind; volition leads to activity, activity to change, and change to the fruition of a certain type of sensory forms, accompanied by feelings. The volitions and their suite appear spontaneously on the conditions that are required for them. These active and fruitive events are presented by consciousness, which moulds itself into their forms. All these events in the series between cause and effect are instantaneous; furthermore they have no nature beyond their appearance. The Sarvāstivāda idea of a lasting nature is rejected. Volitions, forms and thoughts are nothing but momentary flashes.

42 É. Lamotte, *L'Histoire du Bouddhisme Indien,* pp. 662, 672.

Subtle consciousness.

Some Sautrāntikas accept the existence of a subtle consciousness, which is the subject of transmigration. In doing so they accept a thought that is widespread in Indian thinking as a whole, but which is absent in some forms of the early Buddhism of which we have knowledge. This subtle consciousness is, according to the general Buddhist believe, not conceived of as a lasting substance, but as a string of momentary events. But since a momentary entity is born in a similar state as the preceding one, when nothing prevents it, practically spoken it is a continuous existence lasting through all time. This subtle consciousness is like a seed, out of which develops the whole temporal world. All perishable things are but a manifestation of it. The subtle consciousness is something impersonal and universal. It must be distinguished from the balance of merit that concludes the death of each individual. It is not the blue-print of a particular type of life to come in a new birth, but a possibility for everything. It is therefore the principle of spiritual growth, the potentiality of Buddhahood in everyone. This idea of a subtle transmigrating consciousness is closely connected with that of the '*dharma*-body' *(dharmakāya)*. One might say, that the latter is the whole world as given to the Buddha. It is nothing else but the actuality of the powers contained in the seed of subtle consciousness. Here neither the world nor consciousness are deemed incompatible with Buddhahood, which becomes equated with an omniscient and omnipotent principle, seeking to free itself from all conditioned existence. These thoughts have much in common with the ideas of Mahāyāna Buddhism, of which we shall come to speak in the next section. The Sautrāntikas, however, do not accept the illusory character of the world as does Mahāyānism, but accept the events of existence as momentary but real. Later Sautrāntikas gave up the idea of the subtle transmigrating consciousness, probably because they did not want to become associated with Mahāyāna idealism.

Knowledge.

The theory of knowledge of the Sautrāntikas must be seen against the background of that of the Sarvāstivādins. For the latter knowledge consists in the flashing together, in close vicinity, of the *dharmas* of form, sense, faculties, and mind. In the case of a perception, a flashing of the material object (form-colour), of vision, the sense organ, and of consciousness appear together in close connection to produce the knowledge of a certain object. But there was also the idea, that basically the relation of knowledge is that between consciousness and object only, the sense organ being only the condition of its possibility. Between the consciousness and the object there was a 'conformity,' which means that consciousness contains a knowledge of the thing. The Sautrāntikas present a further reflection on the subject. They see in the object a pattern constituted by a series of infinitesimal flashes, and in consciousness they see another of such series. The function of consciousness is to form images *(ākāra)* of its objects. Knowledge begins with copying the properties of the world outside to the world inside. It is based on a series of representations in the thought-stream of the objective events. Consciousness is filled with such representations, and, in normal circumstances, is never without them.

For the Sautrāntikas the objects of the surrounding world are primarily conceived as sense data. As far as the organ of vision is concerned, only colours are real. Shapes *(saṁsthāna)* are constructions of the mind, projected upon it.[43]

This clearly indicates that the idea of absolute space here is not accepted. Space rather is conceived as a form of consciousness; and if space is, the more so anything else that can be considered as intelligible. Matter is solely constituted by the elementary forces, which form the possibilities of touch, and the more subtle forces of the other sense organs, constituting colours, sounds, tastes, and odours. On its frame the mind weaves its web of meanings. Except the elementary data that form the condition of thought, everything is then a product of the mind's spontaneity. The mind imposes its enduring and changing patterns on the sense-moments. This comes close indeed to idealism. This idealism appears the stronger, since sense data have no temporal extension, being gone immediately after they have come into existence.

43 Th. Stcherbatsky, *The Central Conception of Buddhism*, p. 10.

Time versus space.

The Sautrāntikas abandoned the notion of contemporaneousness, based on the possibility of events appearing together in absolute space. They reverted to the original Buddhistic notion of reality as a temporal succession and conditioning. Knowledge then, cannot be an appearing together of thought and object, but is something conditioned by its object. It succeeds its object. Accordingly, when in thought the image of an object appears, the conditioning events themselves have already vanished. Knowledge at best renders the recent past. We find here the beginning of a consideration of the facts from the phenomenalist perspective. When there are no things in themselves, they cannot be posited in an absolute space, but can only appear as a particular experience in a stream of other experiences. Knowledge does not provide insight into the hidden nature of things, but is just a phenomenon conditioned by other phenomena which are part of its 'history.' The conception of these antecedents as something which was 'outside' before it came to be known, clearly seems to be a remnant of the Sarvāstivāda idea of absolute space. We shall meet with a more rigid solution of the problem of knowledge in a following section, when dealing with the idealism of the Yogācāra school,

Development in time.

The Sarvāstivādins contended that the nature of a *dharma* lasts through all three times: past, present, and future. This means that past and future are somehow contained in the present, since they are present in the *dharma* now given. Past, present, and future all exist. The Theras, in principle, wanted to accept only the given, i.e. the present, but they had to allow for the efficacy of the past act, which has not yet given its fruit. Therefore they had to admit the reality of the present and of that part of the past which has not yet come to fruition. In other words, they accepted the present and the imperfect, but not the future and the perfect tense. They abandoned what could be dispensed with. The Sautrāntikas went even further. For them only the present was real, and they criticized the Sarvāstivādins for their inconsistencies: 'According to you the nature (of the *dharma*) exists always, but you want to admit neither that being is eternal nor that being is different from nature; that's clearly acting in the way of the prince (i.e. without justification).'[44] For the Sautrāntika the present only is what exists, the past what did exist, and the future what shall exist in the future, when its conditions are given. Being is but a chain of moments the one following after the other. The Sautrāntikas also denied the existence of a past which is still to yield its fruit, and they do not admit that the fruit springs directly from the past act, for that does not exist anymore. The fruit springs from a certain moment in the series following the act (which is a 'strong fact,' capable of bringing a change in the series of sense data, feelings, volitions, and thoughts). 'On the moment the act is completed, it transforms the series, and this transformation determines an evolution *(pariṇāma)*. The last moment of this evolution has a special or culminating efficacy, the capacity to produce the fruit directly.'[45] This moment is called the 'distinguishing moment' *(viśeṣa)*. In the same way, in nature, the seed does not yield the fruit immediately, but only after a process of long development. First there is a sprout, the stalk, leaves, flower, and only finally the fruit.

Nirvāṇa.

Another major discrepancy with previous forms of Buddhism presents the conception of *nirvāṇa*. In their concept of it, the Sautrāntikas come close to the Mahāyāna. *Nirvāṇa* is not the entity described in negative terms that it was for the early Buddhists. In fact it is not an entity in itself, but just the end of suffering. It is not something apart from temporal existence, but this world itself attaining eternal life. The Buddha, having entered *nirvāṇa*, begot a glorious body, the realization of all the seeds of subtle consciousness. It was called *dharmakāya* (*dharma*-body). It is on the one hand an idealistic absolute, but, on the other, at the same time the living world itself, which – as the conditioning factor of consciousness – is still ·conceived as something real.'

44 *Abhidharmakośa*, v, p. 58, É. Lamotte, *L'Histoire*, p. 668.
45 Lamotte, *L'Histoire*, p. 673.

Buddha flanked by bodhisattvas, Ajanta, 4th century, Wiki Commons

Chapter 5
Mahāyāna

The change from the early Buddhist phase, mainly characterized by the elaboration of the Abhidharma, to the later phase, called 'Mahāyāna,' has two aspects, a religious and a philosophical, which should not be confounded. Its religious aspect is characterized by the gradual change in the conception of the nature of the Buddha. Buddha at first was a noble but merely human sage, but in Mahāyāna he loses more and more of his human aspects and assumes divine ones, like omniscience and omnipotence. At the same time the idea of the Buddha becomes disconnected from that of Śākyamuni, the particular person at a particular time that the historical Buddha was. In the second place the religious change is characterized by the cult of the *bodhisattvas* (those destined to become Buddhas). For the early community the Buddha was a unique personality. He was the one who found by his own effort the access to the redeeming knowledge, which he communicated to others not able to find it on their own. This, from the outset, created a difference between the master and the followers. To find the liberating knowledge the disciples were dependent on the teaching of the Buddha. Only through the latter's compassion they could find the calm and peace, the state of being disconnected from this world, that is *nirvāṇa.* And although this state of calm was of the same nature as that of the master, the liberated followers remained different from him in the extent of the penetration of their insight and of their powers. That's why they were called *arhats* (holy ones) and not 'Buddhas' (enlightened ones). In the early community a Buddha was considered to be a rare figure, appearing only once in an epoch.

And just as there could be only one universal ruler in a certain time to wield political power over the whole world, so there could also be only one Buddha in a period to wield spiritual power over the realm of mind. Mahāyānism, now, tries to bridge the gap between the epochal figure of the Buddha and the community of *arhats* dependent on him. Every being carries deep in itself the Buddha-nature, and is because of that, destined once to become a Buddha itself. From the moment that someone has taken the firm resolve to become a Buddha, and has made the vow to free all beings from suffering, he becomes a so-called *bodhisattva*, a being striving for '*bodhi*' or 'illumination.' His destiny is now not merely to acquire the perfect calm that is equivalent to the state of liberation, but to penetrate the universe by power and insight, i.e. to become a Buddha himself. These *bodhisattvas* became a cult-object in Mahāyāna. Many stories circulated about the *bodhisattva*-stages of Buddhas from past epochs. These are similar in nature to the Jataka-stories about the past lives of the Buddha Śākyamuni found in the Tripiṭaka (three baskets), the canonical works of early Buddhism, but less attention is paid to the former lives of the historical preacher, and much more space is reserved for all kinds of *bodhisattva* lives of imagined Buddhas of the far past. There also developed the messianic cult of the *bodhisattva* Maitreya, the future Buddha. Probably this idea of the saviour, who in the last of days will gather the forces of light to beat those of darkness, was derived from Zoroastrianism.

One can discover in this shift of the attention away from the historical Buddha, a tendency to universalize the idea of Buddhahood in an archetype. This may have been part of a process to make Buddhism acceptable to converts from different creeds. Being of flesh and blood, it is difficult to submit to the superiority of one who is also made of the same stuff, but it is easy to venerate the principle behind him, especially when this can be identified with a principle held in honour already from ancient times. On the other hand, the *bodhisattva* principle made it easy to incorporate local deities into the Buddhist pantheon, so that no one had to be forced to give up cherished believes completely. Mahāyāna, in this light, can be conceived as the outcome of a strong missionary movement, going even beyond the borders of the Indian continent, probably following the period of the great migrations of peoples on the Central Asian continent, starting from a few centuries before the beginnings of the Christian era. In such process foreign elements were adapted to the original Buddhistic lore. Lamotte, for example, sees in the Mahāyāna figure of the Buddha Amitābha an echo of an Iranian solar god, and he also finds notable analogies between the *bodhisattvas* of Mahāyāna and the Ameshapenta of Zoroastrianism.[46] But it certainly does not seem correct to explain Mahāyānism solely by Iranian influence. In many respects the similarities with Vaiṣṇavism (Viṣṇuism) are even more striking. Vaiṣṇava influence is easily accounted for by the long coexistence of Hindus and Buddhists in the same territories, where members of the same families adopted the respective religions or sometimes even the same persons both. The intermingling of the two creeds is e.g. seen in Vasubandhu's *Kośa*, when the omnipotence of the Buddha is identified with the force Nārāyaṇa, which is, as may be known, a name for the absolute God of the Vaiṣṇavas. By the way, here we note one of the Mahāyānic traits in Vasubandhu, genereally known as a Sautrāntika.

The transformation of the human Buddha into a divine (or superdivine) one, finds its correlate in a shift from a moral to a religious attitude in Buddhist life. Śākyamuni taught a way of life, which, if practised with discipline, will result in a liberation from suffering. The monk or lay adherent had his destiny in his own hands. If he succeeded it was his own merit, and if he didn't, he was himself to blame. There was nothing supernatural to interfere with all this. The Law of *karma*, although profound, did not hide any mysteries. But in Mahāyāna there emerges a quite different, more religious feeling. The Buddha now is less of a teacher, and is more like a transcendent father beyond heaven. It seems that man has lost faith in himself, and has become like the wretched child in need of the mercy of a loving father, who by all means trying to save his beloved but unmature children, lures them from the fire of the world with toys, instead of warning them as adults (since they would not listen to that). Although for the Buddha the intention had been the decisive moral factor from the beginning – and not the patent act – still moral discipline had been in the centre of the Buddhist way. But in Mahāyāna religious categories like repentence and mercy, and the deep desire for relieve become of central importance. The Mahāyānist cannot do only with good

46 É. Lamotte, *L'Histoire du Bouddhisme Indien*, pp. 550-5.

advice, he must be brought home at the hand. When he is lost, he does not contrive a method to find his way out (for instance by using a map), but starts crying until someone finds him. There is here the basic feeling of complete dependence and surrender, and of humility. The counterpart of such a believer is the *bodhisattva*, who leads him, and takes over his suffering, since vicarious atonement on the part of the *bodhisattva* is also a characteristic of Mahāyāna.

Since liberation is not any more dependent on mere human discipline, but on salvation coming from above, the religious reward is conceived to be so much greater than before, because the limits of the merely human now can be transgressed. The final end of every craver is not any more the calm and peace resulting from the abandonment of the world, but nothing less than a kind of *theosis*. One is to become a Buddha beyond the highest sphere, and there participation in omniscience and almightiness is achieved. But such a state you cannot make by yourself, it is given. Although also in the Three Baskets mention is made of all kinds of remarkable powers acquired by the monk in meditation, many of them corresponding with what is believed in in Mahāyāna, it remains that the feeling is different. What for the early Buddhists is an extraordinary but nevertheless natural thing, in Mahāyāna becomes something supernatural, some kind of marvel. And devotive veneration before it is more befitting than mere moral discipline. In this respect Mahāyāna seems to reflect a tendency generally found in the Indian culture of the time, also in Brahmanism, not to speak about contemporaneous developments in the Occident.

Corresponding with the change from the practice of self-perfection in early Buddhism to 'divine' guidance and dependence on mercy in Mahāyāna, is a weakening of the emphasis on monastic life. In the opinion of the early Buddhists only a monk can attain salvation, but in Mahāyāna the laity is emancipated. As ordinary people too have Buddha nature, they also can adopt *bodhisattva*hood, and can realize final liberation. The life of a monk is no longer a necessary condition of *nirvāṇa*.

Mahāyāna as philosophy.

Early Buddhism denied the reality of composite and permanent things. It denied the existence of a permanent entity like the soul, and also the substantiality of all enduring things of experience. But it did not deny the existence of the '*dharmas*,' of which it distinguished the eternal one, *nirvāṇa*, and the momentary ones, of which there were five types, the irreducible phenomena of form, feeling, apprehension, volition (or force), and mind (conscious perception). All these phenomena were constituted by evanescent flashings ordered in series giving the suggestion of permanent entities. One flashing does not influence another one, i.e., it does not interfere with its nature, but it does condition it, i.e. no *dharma* will be present if not certain others also are given. The conclusion of all this was, that although most things as we conceive them do not really exist (as e.g. the soul), there are some phenomena that we must consider as real, viz. forms, feelings, apprehensions, volitions, perceptions, and liberation. These constitute the real base of all existence out of which all apparent entities are composed.

Now we have already noticed, that nevertheless some questions about the reality of these elementary *dharmas* may be asked. If they are entities existing in themselves, how can it be that they are not permanent? For the Sarvāstivādins this question led to the acceptance of a distinction between the appearance and the nature of a *dharma*. Evidently an appearance cannot exist in itself. It needs two, an object of which it is the appearance (the permanent nature) and a subject to which it appears. The idea of a plurality of independent momentary entities here becomes a problem. It seems that the momentary can exist only in relativity, and that because of that it is not something existing in itself. But may it then be said that it exists at all?

The dharmas are without a self

All these problems could arise before the ontological reflections of the Sarvāstivādins. For the Buddha and his early community such problems did not exist, because of the absence of such ontological reflection. Their problem was the suffering of mankind and how this was to be overcome, this being the only thing important. But the Mahāyānists start to take the ontological reflections of the Sarvāstivādins seriously, and connect with it some radical conclusions. Since they do not want to accept a plurality of eternal essences, their first conclusion is, that not only there is no permanent entity like a soul, and no substantiality in composite things, but that the *dharmas* themselves are without self, being like a mirage, or being just a projection of the imagination. By coming to this conclusion, whatever may have been realistic in Buddhism came to an end. The ultimate constituents (the *dharmas*) being no longer ultimate, Buddhism now had become baseless, and was in need of a new ultimate. In the quest for this new absolute, the speculations of the Sarvāstivādins about the eternal nature of the *dharmas* probably formed a starting point. This nature had been described as something deep and inexpressible. The Mahāyānists accepted something of that kind, but they could not accept a plurality of eternal essences. Since all plurality is relative and momentary, the ultimate principle should be found in the unbreakable tie that prevents anything particular to escape from relativity. This tie is not the particularity of things or *dharmas*, or even their particular nature, but the nature of their being a *dharma* itself, their dharmahood *(dharmatā)*, also called *tathatā* (truth). 'this also can be identified with the whole of all *dharmas*, the dharmabody *(dharmakāya)*. This absolute is, accordingly, not something different from the beings of the universe. It fills all space, and it is the basis of all that can be given. It cannot appear in its own nature or unfold itself. It is without any finite form or finite mind. It is the unity beyond which there can be nothing else; it is the only reality, everything else being only mirage, magical illusion, or dream. It even transcends the individual Buddhas; these all have but one *dharmakāya* as their base; and all live out of one Truth. This Truth is unknowable, but can be met with in oneself. That's why it is also called *svabhāvikakāya*, the body of one's own nature. It is the essence of all things, and this ultimate essence is in all things the same, and at the same time it comprises all; all things are in it.

The truth and the illusive power.

Although the terms used are different, this ultimate has much of the characteristics of the Vedāntic absolute. It is the ultimate Truth *(paramārthasatya)* at the base of all appearances, the sameness in all things as e.g. the Bhagavad Gīta of the Vaiṣṇavas teaches. That there is an influence here becomes clear, when we compare the 'Lord' of the Gītā with the Buddha conception of Mahāyāna. In the Gītā Kṛṣṇa teaches the essential sameness of all things, which coincides with his own nature. The diversity of the world is explained by his creative power, his dynamic nature *(prakṛti)* or *māyā*, the power of creating illusions. Now, in Mahāyāna the diversity of the world is explained in a similar manner. There is a penultimate form of the *dharmakāya*. It is really a body, but of a very subtle material. It is the refulgent body, which the Buddhas adopt on the highest plain of existence, and which is different from epoch to epoch. By reason of such a body, Buddha can also be called Viṣṇu (!) Īśvara (Lord!), *pradhāna* (=*prakṛti*) etc., all names one would expect in connection with Vaiṣṇavism. From this body emanates all phenomenal existence from the highest plain of being to the lowest. This body, in fact the highest form of illusion, is called by different names; sometimes it is simply called *dharmakāya*, sometimes *svasambhogakāya*, but it is also called *prakṛtyātmābhāva*, and thus it can be put on one line with the creative nature of the Gītā. The world has one ultimate nature, and a penultimate one to account for the existence of the illusory appearances that constitute this manifold world. Here we meet with a theory of emanation that is proper to the Gītā or to the later theistic Upaniṣads.[47] It admits of a creation, although be it an illusive one, and this has departed far indeed from the original Buddhistic lore, which only admits the irreducible phenomena as they are, recognizing their nature, but refusing to inquire into their origin and destiny. Paradoxically, the denial of the being *per se* of the *dharmas*, their being deprived of ontological reality, led to the demand for their explanation. If they were not really there, why were they given at all? The denial of phenomenal existence as existence, led to the acceptance of a non-phenomenal, ontological existence, although it was preferred not to speak about 'existence.' And was this not precisely the kind of existence the Buddha refused to speak of, since it was useless for salvation?

Scriptures.

The tenets of Mahāyāna could not be defended solely on the base of the classical canonical scriptures; new ones were 'discovered' to provide an authoritative base for the new conceptions. These scriptures again were in the form of *sūtras*, presenting the Buddha in discussion with his pupils, gods or other beings. They had the force of being spoken by the master, but why did no one hear of them before? Well,

47 N. Dutt, *Mahāyāna Buddhism*. pp. 158, 161, 162, Delhi Motilal, 1978.

in the time of the Buddha's life the ears were not fit to understand the message, and therefore the true meaning of the lore had not been given to the great public. It was only transmitted to some disciples being able to understand it, and who kept it secret until the time was ripe to make it known. It was also told that the new *sūtras* were guarded for centuries by the dragons. Finally, at the appropriate time, the gods made known to the able listener what they once heard from the mouth of the Buddha. In spite of the fact that the Buddha told that he never preached anything in secret, such stories seem to indicate a secret tradition in which ideas had a long development before finally they were put to writing during the first two centuries AD. The new *sūtras* were written in a hybrid Sanskrit, which indicates Brahminical influence, easily to be explained from the fact that many Buddhist intellectuals (mastering the art of writing) were of Brahmin origin. And this, at the same time, accounts for the introduction of new ideas. The oldest parts of the writings are often in verse, and these display strong characteristics of the vernacular, or at any rate of an Indian language other than Sanskrit. These older parts are embedded in prose of more regular Sanskrit, obviously of a later date. As a rule the new *sūtras* are much longer than those of the old canon.

The oldest, and best known, new *sūtras* are the so-called *Prajñāpāramitās* (*sūtras* of perfection in wisdom). Their origin may date back to before the Christian era. Of these *sūtras* there are several collections, arranged (although for the greater part written in prose) according to their length in stanza units (a length of 32 syllabes). There is the collection of 100,000, 25,000, 18,000, 10,000, and of eight thousand units. This last one especially is held much in honour by the Mahāyānists. Besides there is also a synopsis, the *Essence of the Perfection in Wisdom*. Mahāyāna has no official canon, but besides the *Prajñāpāramitā* of the eight-thousand, there are eight other works, meeting with so much respect, that they can be accepted as authoritative works. These *sūtras* are: *The Lotus of the Good Law, The Detailed Account of Buddha's Charm, The Descent on (Sri) Lanka, The Golden Radiance, The Order of the Double Meaning* (part of *Garland-sūtra), Buddha's Secret, The King of Absorption,* and *The Lord of the Ten Stages*. To this list can be added the two versions of the *Description of* (the paradise) *Sukhavatī* (also called *Amitabhā-sūtra*). Besides mention must be made of the *Pearl-* or *Jewel-peak-collection*,

'Jewel-peak' being an epitheton of the Buddha). Its oldest parts are mainly concerned with the *bodhisattva.* and his training, and it may contain genuine parts of the *bodhisattvapiṭaka* of the Mahāsaṁghikas, and so be the missing link between the old Mahāsaṁghika school and Mahāyāna. For the usually untranslated Sanskrit names of these *sūtras*, have a look at the following table.

Mahāyāna·sūtras

1) *Ratnakūṭa-collection* (Pearl-peak).
2) *Prajñāpāramitā-sūtras* (Perfection of Wisdom), to which belong the collection of:
   100,000 *(śatasāhasrika)*
   25,000 *(pañcaviṁśatisāhasrika)*
   18,000 *(aṣṭadaśasāhasrika)*
   10,000 *(daśasāhasrika)*
   8,000 *(aṣṭasāhasrika).*
   Prajñāpāramitā-hṛdaya-sūtra (Essence of the Perfection of Wisdom).
   Also small works as the well-known *Vajracchedika* (Diamond Cutter *Sūtra*) must be associated with these collections.
3) *Saddharmapuṇḍarika* (Lotus of the Good Law).
4) *Laṅkāvatāra-sūtra* (Descent on Lanka).
5) *Lalitavistara* (Detailed Account of (Buddha's) Charm (naturalness).
6) *Suvarṇaprabhāṣa* (Golden Radiance *Sūtra*).
7) *Gaṇḍavyūha* (Order of the Double Meaning), part of Avataṁsaka (Garland-*sūtra*).
8) *Tathāgataguhya* (Sūtra of Buddha's Secret).
9) *Samādhirāja* (King of Samādhi *sūtra*).
10 *Daśabhimīśvara* (Lord of the ten Stages *Sūtra*; constitutes with *Gaṇḍavyūha* the 'Garland-' or *Avataṁsaka-sūtra*).
11) *Sukhavatīvyūha* (or *Āmitabhā-sūtra*) (Description of *Sukhavatī*).
12 *Rāṣṭrapālaparipṛccha*

Origin.

It is often believed, that Mahāyāna had its origin in the territory south of theVindhya range. The *sūtras* themselves suggest the idea that they were first known in the south, and spread afterwards to other parts of India. Especially the later *sūtras* like the *Laṅkāvatāra* and the *Gaṇḍavyūha* are located in the south. By many Mahāyāna thinkers the Mahāsaṁghikas were considered as forerunners. In the first centuries AD, when Mahāyāna became prominent, the most active sect of the Mahāsaṁghikas, those of the Caitikas (divided in Pūrva- and Aparaśaila) was strong in Andhra Pradesh. Some verses of the Tripiṭaka of the Pūrvaśaila are quoted by Candrakīrti (the great Mādhyamika commentator) as authoritative, and endorsing the selflessness of the *dharmas*. But not denying the influence of the Mahāsaṁghika, and the southern origin of many Mahāyāna scriptures, we cannot be blind to the fact, that also in Sarvāstivāda (and Sautrāntika) circles many typical Mahāyāna ideas were known, and that these circles produced scriptures being on the borderline of Mahāyāna-thinking, of which the Lalitavistara (Account of Buddha's Charm) is an outstanding example. Besides, Mahāyāna-criticism against Lesser Vehicle conceptions is mainly directed against the Sarvāstivāda, which indicates, that early Mahāyāna stood in close contact with this school. This, of course, does not deny, that important ideas and scriptures came from the south – maybe even the Sarvāstivādins themselves adopted ideas from the south –, but it may well be that Mahāyānic ideas already in an early period spread much wider than only in the south. Anyhow the spread of Mahāyāna to Central Asia went through the north. And if Lamotte is right in assuming Persian influence, then there must have been Mahāyānic centres in the north. If we are right in seeing Mahāyāna as the outcome of a missionary zeal, then we may expect adaptations to local creeds in which there may have occurred incorporation of *bodhisattvas* from Iranian religion, or of elements of Śaivism in the north, and also adoption of the divine characteristics of the Buddha from the Vaiṣṇavism of the Andhra territory. Later all theser elements may have been mixed up to form a universal religion.[48]

48 Cf. A. K. Warder, *Indian Buddhism*, pp. 352-355, Delhi 1970 [Motilal], also H. Nakamura, *Indian Buddhism*, pp.159-160, De;hi, Motilal, 1989.

HISTORY. The destiny of religions in India seems much influenced by that of the political powers. Since the decline of the Mauryan empire, India has been the battlefield of a continuous war between local royal houses. Each of these houses favoured one or more religions or was especially disinclined towards some. The map of ancient India, accordingly, was blotted with local centres of religion. One kingdom could be mainly inclined to Buddhism, while another, not far off, could be Vaiṣṇava, Jain or Śaiva. E.g., while at a certain date the whole of South-, Central- and East-Asia had underwent the influence of Buddhism, there never had been any significant Buddhist activity in Rajasthan near he Thar desert. When one of the local monarchies became a regional or national power, because of success in war, traditional religions in the conquered territories could easily be influenced by the religion of the victorious nation. Sometimes it even came to severe persecutions of subjugated faiths.

Kāṇvas and Śuṅgas.
After the fall of the Mauryan empire about 185 BCE, power in central northern India was wielded by the Kāṇva and Śuṅga houses. They had their centre of power in Vidiśa, and were followers of Brahmanism and mainly benefactors of the Bhāgavata cult. In the period of their reign, until about 40 BC, the roots of Mahāyānism must have been laid. And this can partly be explained from the impact the Vaiṣṇavism of the Bhāgavatas had on Buddhism.

The power of the Śuṅgas extended over a large part of central and northern India, but was by no means everywhere firmly established. They were no absolute monarchs over the territories under their influence, but reigned by means of a kind of feudal system, which is always unstable. The south had always remained independent, and many parts of western and northern India fell outside their dominion. In the north Gandhāra had remained under Greek influence. There Buddhism was favoured, while in neighbouring Cashmere Śaivism was strong, and developed side by side with Buddhism, mainly of the Sarvāstivāda sect.

Scyths.

In the north, from about 140 BC, the Śakas (Scyths) invaded. They passed along the leftovers of the Greek dominion, and ended by settling in Sindh, Kāthiawār, Gujarāt, and Avanti. They started to dominate the north-west from 110 BC, and they stayed there until about 60 AD. In that time they uprooted the remnants of the Greek rule. But they in turn were beaten by the Kuṣāṇas, called Yuèzhí by the Chinese, Tokharoi by the Greeks, and sometimes also Turuṣkas by the Indians, and maybe they should be identified with the early Turcs. The Śakas, however, remained – with some interruptions – in power in the region of Kāthiawār and Avanti until the end of the 4th century AD. During most of their reign they were religiously tolerant, and they favoured Buddhism.

As we know that Avanti was a centre of the Sthaviras, it seems that these especially were benefitted by their protection; but during the Śaka-reign in the north, also the Sarvāstivādins were favoured.

Kuṣāṇas

The Kuṣāṇas, or in Chinese 'Yuèzhí,' migrated from east of the Tarim Basin to the west. By passing the mountains forming the borderline between the higher Central Asian plains and the lower ones of present day Uzbekistan, they came into Scythian territory, driving the Śakas to the south, who, in consequence of that, occupied large parts of northern India. The Kuṣāṇas, originally probably speaking some Mongolian or Turkish language, finally themselves entered India, in the trail of the Śakas, and they occupied the territories that not long before had belonged to the Greeks. About 60 AD they had robbed the Scyths of their recently gained territories in the north, Gandhāra and Cashmere. The rulers who won these conquests soon adopted the Buddhist faith and perhaps had accepted the Parthian as a court-language. In this they seem to have followed the Śakas. The Kuṣāṇas in general did much to foster Buddhism, although some of their rulers were inclined to Śaivism. The Kuṣāṇa ruler Kaṇiṣka probably lived in the first part of the second century AD. He has gained fame for being one of the greatest protectors of Buddhism in his time. As the Sarvāstivāda was the dominant sect in his northern territories, he did much to its benefit, but since the conquest of Magadha also important centres of the Mahāsaṁghika were added to his power, and he also bestowed favours on them. Of Kaṇiṣka it is said that he organized the fourth Buddhist council, in which an attempt was undertaken to reconcile the divergent opinions of the different sects. The outcome was that all current *piṭaka* texts were recognized as the genuine word of the Buddha. As a result of this council, it is said, that several commentaries on the Tripiṭaka were composed, which were called Upadeśa- and Vibhāṣa-śāstras. One of them is the Abhidharma-interpretation on which Vasubandhu wrote his commentary.

Under Kaṇiṣka the north became a centre of Buddhist learning, attracting Buddhist scholars from all territories. It seems likely that during the reign of the Kuṣānas, the Buddhist mission to Central Asia and China was undertaken, since the route of the missionaries went along the same track as the Kuṣāṇas had travelled. It was the transmission to the Mongolian homeland, and beyond, of the newly discovered faith.

Cedi and Sātavāhanas.

Approximately about the beginning of the Christian era, the Cedi of Kaliṅga under their king Khāravela became powerful for a short while. Their dominions covered the east-coast of India and stretched to the north and the south. They mainly fostered Jainism. Of decisive importance for the development of early Mahāyāna Buddhism was the reign of the Sātavāhanas in the upper Dekhan. Their power originated from the centre of Pratiṣṭhāna (Paithan) in Mahārāṣṭra from about 60 BC. At that time their king Simuka founded the dynasty, of which the territory gradually spread over the whole of Central India, subjugating parts of the north and the south. They later had an eastern capital at Dhānyakaṭaka.

Although the rulers themselves mainly seem to have been adherents of Brahmanism, more specifically Vaiṣṇavism, they also were friendly toward the Buddhist community, and so they created a climate for a mutual osmosis of the two creeds. Especially Gautamiputra Śatakarṇi (106-130 AD.) was a great patron of Buddhism, and may have been a Buddhist himself. Nāgārjuna, the founder of the Madhyamaka philosophy, lived during his reign, and is said to have been his friend. He adressed to him a famous epistle. The Sātavāhanas remained in power until about 270 AD.

The Sātavāhana empire formed a centre of trade and culture. The finest specimens of Buddhist art were created under it. It saw the completion of the *stūpa* of Sāñci. We also find here the beginning of the building of the famous rock-temples near the coast of Mahārāṣṭra, e.g. those of Kaṇheri, Kārli, and others. Probably the sects of the Caitikas, those of Pūrva- and Apara-śaila, were named after these temples, since the word 'Caitika' is derived from *caitya* (temple) and *śaila* means something like 'hewn out of the rock.' And so, it seems, here at the west-coast we must search for the origin of these sects. When the centre of gravity of the empire shifted to the east, also these sects migrated, settling in Andhra territory and creating the *stūpas* of Amarāvati and Nāgārjunikoṇḍa. Meanwhile they had assimilated Vaiṣṇava ideas and were developing into Mahāyānism. It is possible that the region of Avanti here was of crucial importance, for it lay on the borderline between the Śaka- and Sātavāhana rule. As we know that Avanti was traditionally a seat of the Sthaviras, we find here a meeting place of at least three distinct traditions. Here a nascent Mahāyānism may have adopted the intellectual attitude from the Sthaviras, the *bodhisattva* and Maitreya cult from the Śakas, who were strongly influenced by Persian culture, and current Vaiṣṇava ideas about the absolute from the Dekhan ruled by the Sātavāhanas.

The Guptas.

Towards the end of the third century AD, when the powers of the Śakas, Kuṣāṇas and Sātavāhanas declined, in old Magadha, once the centre of the Mauryan empire, a new dynasty arose. Its first ruler was possibly a certain Śrīgupta, but more is known about Candragupta I (not to be confused with the old Mauryan king). His reign falls in the first quarter of the fourth century, and he established his grip on Magadha and the surrounding territories. His son Samudragupta (328-380 AD) added the whole of North-East India to his reign, and made the whole of India, with the exception of the Śaka territories in the west, and the traditionally independent south, tributary. In the territories under direct control the feudal system was abolished and replaced by a system of appointed officials. Candragupta II (380-415) beated the Śakas in the west, and became sovereign of the whole of northern India, while in large parts of the south his influence was important. About 450 AD the stability of the Gupta empire was disturbed by raids of the Hūṇas (Huns). Skandhagupta (about 460) succeeded in saving the empire, but at the end of the century the Huns attacked again under their leaders Toramāṇa and Mihirakula. They affirmed their power in the north-west for some thirty years, while in the east the Gupta empire disintegrated and subsequently vanished about 550. The last important Gupta was Narasiṁha, who defeated Mihirakula (who was a cruel persecutor of the Buddhist community) and favoured Buddhism. It is said that the great Buddhist teacher Vasubandhu (author of the *Kośa*) has been his tutor. This places the latter in the middle of the fifth century, if it is true, as we think it is, since it fits all other data. His important pupil Dignāga may then be situated in the late Gupta period.

The Guptas were Vaiṣṇavas; they exercised a mild administration and were religiously tolerant. Although they had a stimulating effect on the development of Vaiṣṇavism, they did not hinder the stabilization of Buddhism. What was said about the climate of mutual osmosis between Vaiṣṇavism and Buddhism under the Sātavāhanas may, mutatis mutandis, also be said to characterize the situation under the Guptas. Under their reign Mahāyāna seems to have clearly distinguished itself from the older Mahāsaṁghika schools, which distinction was perhaps not so clear under the earlier rule of the Sātavāhanas.

Puṣpabhūtis and other houses.

After the breakdown of the Gupta empire, northern India fell apart. About 600 AD in Bengal king Śaśāṅka had come to power. At the same time Assam (Kāmarūpa) was ruled by the Maukhari king Bhāskaravarman, and a relative of him ruled in Uttar Pradesh with as centre the city of Kānyakubja (modern Kanauj). In Thanesar, between the Satlaj and the Jumna (Yamunā), the Puṣpabhūtis came to power.

King Harṣa of this family brought large parts of northern India under his influence. It seems that during his reign the good tides of the Gupta period returned for a while. But his rule was not so strong, that he could dispense with the feudal system. Nevertheless Kānyakubja (capital of Harṣa after the death of its Maukhari ruler), grew to the format of a great national and cultural centre. Harṣa died in 643 without children, and his territories fell apart. 'He had not only been a politician but also a man of learning and of artistic feeling. A few plays are handed down under his name.

The Puṣpabhūti family seems to have been dedicated to sun worship. This might indicate that it had been under Parthian influence, but Harṣa himself was probably converted to Buddhism. Anyhow it is said by the poet Bāṇa that his sister became a Buddhist nun, and certainly Buddhism was protected under his reign. In the Assam of his friend Bhāskaravarman, however, Buddhism never held a footing, and in the Bengal of Śasāṅka, although there was a large Buddhist community, it became severely persecuted. Perhaps here a number of Buddhists converted pro forma to Hinduism, and laid the foundation of later Advaita Vedānta. In the time of Harṣa we also hear of the growth of tantric practices.

About the time of Harṣa two of the greatest Buddhist scholars must have been working, Candrakīrti, the Mādhyamika, and Dharmakīrti the Vijnānavādin (or epistemologist), both being born in the south.

Cashmere and Gandhāra.

Since early times Buddhism was strong in Gandhāra and Cashmere. This was so since the time of Aśoka and of the Greek occupation. The situation did not change much under the Śakas and Kuṣāṇas. Especially the Sarvāstivādins had a wide dissemination. But not only Buddhism was of importance, especially in Cashmere also Śaivism was widespread. But generally speaking the two creeds could coexist happily together. The Hūṇa invader Mihirakula (who probably was ethnically akin to the Kuṣāṇas, and probably one of the leaders of a tribe of Turco-Mongolian peoples) changed this idyllic situation and confronted the Buddhists with persecution. But at the end of his life he became milder and was converted to Śaivism. His son, again, became a normal patron of Buddhism.

Now it seems, that since the Hūṇa invasion Gandhāra and Cashmere were ruled by different houses, Cashmere by descendents of the Hūṇas, who now also are called Turuṣkas, znd Gandhāra by the Turkisāhis who may have been the descendants of the older Kuṣāṇas. In later time we also hear of a tribe called 'Daradas' (perhaps Tatars?). Although in both territories Śaivism and Buddhism existed side by side, it seems that Buddhism remained predominant in Gandhāra and

Śaivism in Cashmere. Sometimes Buddhism in Cashmere was reinforced, as when e.g. at 700 AD a prince from Gandhāra, Meghavāhana, ascends the throne. One of his followers, Jayapīḍa was an important patron of Buddhism. We should place him in the middle of the 8th century. He invited Dharmottara to Cashmere, and in this way introduced the school of critical idealism in the line of Dharmakīrti into that region. In this time we find also kings with Vaiṣṇava leanings. A situation emerges in which Vaiṣṇavism, Śaivism and Buddhism seem to mingle. In post Kūṣāṇa time Mahāyāna became more and more important. From the eight century onward also tantric type of Buddhism (and of Śaivism) becomes significant.

In 939 the Brahmin Yaśasākara ascended the throne of Cashmere, and afterwards a less favourable climate for Buddhism developed. Circa 950 Kṣemagupta burnt down the Jayendravihāra (monastery). Under king Harṣa (not the Puṣpabhūti) there was again patronizing of learning, almost at the same time we hear that this Harṣa was a 'mleccha', a heathen (but of course from Indian not from Christian perspective), since he destroyed Buddhist and Hindu temples. One might wonder whether this perhaps points to the fact that he was a moslim. Nevertheless, under his rule lived Yaśomitra, the famous commentator of Vasubhandhu's *Kośa*. We find a last revival of Buddhism in Cashmere under the reign of Jayasiṁha (1128-1149).

Decline of Buddhism in India.

It is difficult to sketch a full picture of the development and spread of Buddhism in India. It seems that from the seventh century onwards in Central India Buddhism progressively disappears. There are still important thinkers – do not the owls of Minerva fly in the twilight? – but religiously the battle is lost against devotional Hinduism of both the Śaiva and the Vaiṣṇava, and philosophically it is lost against the Vedānta (especially Advaita). Only on the outskirts, Sri Lanka in the south, Cashmere-Gandhāra, Nepāl, and Bengal in the north, Buddhism lingered. Again, the decline of Buddhism may be due to the political situation. The time of the great empires with their intensive city life and mercantile class was over. And especially among the bourgeoisie such creeds as Buddhism and Jainism selected their followers. When India in the Middle Ages again became a rural society, centred around the village more than being located in a city, the Brahmanism, that always had been predominant there, became the only way of life. In the south and the east the devotional Hinduism especially became very important. And when in the north-west nevertheless much remained of the old Buddhism, this in time was overrun by the Islam, entering from that direction, destroying monasteries and books. The development of Buddhism continued in other countries, Hīnayāna in Sri Lanka, Thailand, Burma, and Indo China, Mahāyāna yet for a little while on Java (where afterwards it coalesced with Hinduism), and in Tibet, China, and Japan. In our own time Buddhism seems to be in the lift again in India. Many people in India, who by traditional Hinduism are considered as outcasts, in spite even of their economic or social (in the Western sense) status, conclude that it is foolish to adopt a creed that degrades you as a human being, and adopt the old faith that accepted followers without distinction of caste.

Magadha as the melting pot of ideas.

In the above we have endeavoured to sketch a regional development of Buddhism, but to be sure Buddhism was far from provincial. As it may be true that many schools had their main centre in a certain region, which was as the soil on which certain ideas might germinate and develop, there always came a point, that these ideas having matured, had to go out into the open to defend their claims against all rival ones. The greatest masters did not live as recluses in some forgotten forest, or if they did, no one nowadays knows of them, but they travelled through the whole of India, lecturing everywhere, being continuously engaged in public debates, and not only with Buddhists. And they wrote books which spread all over the country and beyond. The old Magadha, where it all began, was the place where all new developments were brought home again. Buddhists from all signatures came here to advocate their ideas. The monastary of Nālanda became like a university, similar to the Sorbonne of Paris in the European Middle Ages, where scholars of all sects flocked together, and assimilated each other's ideas. When here appeared something new, no one could ignore it. The very subtle speculative and epistemological philosophy that was thus developed, was more or less respected by all schools. The masters that we in the West like to consider as exponents of e.g.

the Yogācāra or the Mādhyamika, idealism or illusionism, respectively Dharmakīrti and Candrakīrti, in their own time probably were more considered as specialists in their respective fields of thinking, epistemology and metaphysics. Few people really understood what they meant, and only those of their own standard of learning and penetrative insight were able to criticize their views. In a certain way they were above all parties, instead of being their exponents.

It is said of Nāgārjuna that he brought with him from the south (probably Dhānyakaṭaka), where he came from, to Magadha some of the Prājñāpāramitās, which he utilized in his new interpretation of the classical Buddhist doctrine. This is something very different from simply expressing the ideas of a certain school. Here we do not meet with the attitude of the missionary but with that of the hermeneutic, having discovered·some new material shedding a new light on old data, or with that of the theologian, who is a believer himself, but is nevertheless committed to scientific method.[49]

T*HE PATH OF THE BODHISATIVA*. The way of Mahāyāna is that of the *bodhisattva*, the person, mostly a monk, who by leading living beings to Buddhahood, finally thereby becomes a Buddha himself.

To become a bodhisattva, first, certain conditions should be fulfilled. By good works in previous lives one should be born in a noble family, and be endowed with a natural inclination towards the good; one should find delight in hearing good words, stories about the Buddha etc., and abhor the contrary. When these conditions are fulfilled, one is born, as it were, in the Bodhisattva-family.

But the conditions fulfilled, still Buddhahood does not automatically follow. One can fall back. If someone wants to proceed, he should fill himself with true aspiration *(adhimukti)* to become a Buddha. Thus are the two preliminary stages for becoming a *bodhisattva.* The veritable entering on the path takes place, when the aspirant realizes '*bodhicitta*,' i.e. when he in all earnest fixes his mind on becoming a Buddha, which happens in the form of a vow. He pledges from now on to work unceasingly to lead all beings to Buddhahood. This implies amongst

49 N. Dutt, *Mahāyāna Buddhism*, most information in this section is derived from pp. 1-70.

others the following duties:

- the relentless service to all Buddhas and *bodhisattvas*.
- to make all beings ripen, and help them to attain omniscience.
- to work for comprehending the endless distinctions of the world.
- to be righteous by body, speech and mind, gaining superior health, and becoming of speech that is never fruitless.

Thus the first step is made on a path progressing through ten stages *(bhūmi)*, ending in the theosis which is the realization of Buddhahood.

The ten stages.
The first stage on the path to Buddhahood is called the joyous *(pramuditā)* [following the *Daśabhūmīśvara*]. It is based on the great renunciation that is the abandonment of the world. But in Mahāyāna this does not necessarily imply the state of a (wandering) monk. The renunciation may be merely spiritual in the midst of practical life. The quality of not being attached to possessions or the ego, makes of the *bodhisattva* in the first stage a great benefactor. He realizes the first perfection *(pāramitā)*, that of charity, of giving *(dāna)*.

Connected with this realization is the acquisition of the qualities of faith, compassion, love, modesty, steadiness, humility, patience in trouble, insight into what is beneficial for people, and knowledge of scriptures. The most salient experience in this stage is that of joy and pleasure, but one also feels elation, exaltation, fragrance, and energy, and becomes devoid of pride, malice, and anger. The *bodhisattva* also becomes free from fear, since he is no longer attached to the self and to things; and he knows that when he is death he will be in the company of Buddhas and *bodhisattvas*. He can no longer fall back in lower forms of existence or in hell.[50]

The second stage is called the immaculate *(vimalā)* or the one pertaining to good conduct *(adhiśīla)*. As is already implied in the second name, the perfection to be realized at this stage is that of conduct *(śīlapāramitā)*. One can recognize a stage by the mental characteristics displayed by the one who abides in it. These characteristics are conceived

50 Dutt, pp. 102-105.

as 'resting-places *(āśayas)*, named after their quality. With respect to the present stage these are amongst others those of softness, pliability, submissiveness, beneficiality, and magnanimity. From the possession of these characteristics the observance of the Buddhist rules quite naturally follows. A person with these qualities does not take life, steal, lie, or is given to sexual misconduct; he does not indulge in slander, rough or idle language. He becomes non-avaricious, devoid of ill-will, and endowed with the right opinions. As also in other stages, here the bodhisattva diagnoses the sickness of living beings as the absence of those perfections which he has reached at the stage of his progress, and he tries to help and cure people by sharing with them his own realizations in knowledge and practice. At the present stage, accordingly, he tries to educate them in morality or ethics, while at the same time by living thus in the proper way, he purifies himself. Compassionate and loving, he guides the beings from their wrong opinions and manners, thereby freeing mankind from anger, avarice, desire, hatred, and delusion etc., caused by the attachment to pleasures and existence, and by ignorance, which operates under the influence of possessiveness and the idea of egoity.[51]

At the third stage, called the shining *(prabhākarī)*, which is the one pertaining to meditation as a training of the will *(adhicitta)*, and in which the perfection of forbearance *(kṣānti)* is realized in addition to the 'resting places of the previous stage, there are found those of pureness, firmness, strength, energy, introversion, and others. These are the qualities of a mind striving after the Buddha-knowledge, the *Dharma*, which is unthinkable, immeasurable, and above all misery and despair. The path is followed with perseverance and forbearance. It demands sacrifice of wealth and enjoyment; it leads through suffering for the sake of the goal to the understanding of the Teaching, which, once understood, is explained also to others. The *bodhisattva* becomes rocksteady in absorption, in which he realizes successively love, compassion, gladness, and equanimity, after which he becomes endowed with paranormal gifts *(abhijñā)*: those of miracle performance, divine ear, thought reading, remembering former lives, and clairvoyance. He comprehends the momentary nature of the '*dharmas*,' which are without any permanence and are only subject to conditioning. The fetters

51 Ibid., pp. 106-111

of the pleasures (*kāma*), form (*rūpa*), existence (*bhava*), and ignorance become weak, part of them (those due to wrong views) having been destroyed already in earlier stages. The *bodhisattva* becomes forbearing, mild tempered, and free from elating and depressing moods, and he works without any selfinterest.[52]

The fourth, fifth, and sixth stages are concerned with the rise of wisdom *(prajñā)*. In the fourth, the radiant *(arcismatī)*, the perfection of energy *(vīrya)* is realized. This energy ultimately leads to illumination *(bodhi)*. At the same time this energy, which overcomes all doubt, is the fruit of the preceding meditation; it dispels the believe in a permanent body *(satkāyadṛṣṭi)*, leaving one with a feeling of sameness in everything.

The fifth stage, called hard to conquer *(sudurjayā)*, brings the clear insight into the four noble truths. The *bodhisattva* in it also becomes aware of the distinction between worldly *(saṁvṛti)* and highest *(paramārtha)* truth. From the standpoint of the highest or transcendental truth he sees that all constituted and relative things lack a real base, are 'void' *(śūnya)*. This insight he wants to transmit to other beings to guide them out of their worldly or relative truth. The perfection realized at this stage is that of meditation *(dhyāna)*.

The sixth stage is called turned towards illumination *(abhimukhī)*. here the chain of dependent origination is understood. The *bodhisattva* realizes the sameness of all *'dharmas'* on account of their being baseless, signless, originless, unborn, detached, pure from the beginning, inexpressible, being similar to illusion, dream, or echo, and he gains insight into the non-duality of being and non-being. He sees that all the three worlds are mere thought-constructions *(citta-mātra)*. The perfection realized here is that of wisdom *(prajñā)*.

The meditations at this stage are directed towards man's ignorance, which, as we have seen, forms the beginning of the chain of 'dependent origination.' The ignorance lies in believing that the world has origin and destruction, and lodges souls. By not knowing the truth, people are moved by their merits and demerits, which produce the motives, the forces *(saṁskāra)*, which lead consciousness *(citta, vijñāna)* in its development. This consciousness again becomes contaminated by the contact with sensory material, leading to feeling, thirst, grasp-

52 Ibid., pp. 111-115.

ing, and utterly to rebirth. Knowing that in truth all things are non-originated, the *bodhisattva* pities those who under the influence of ignorance are caught in the circle of rebirth, which is the same as that of 'dependent origination.' It is a tree of suffering, that grows without any doer or feeler.

This stage culminates in the experience of a threefold release, that is characterized by experiencing things as being without substance *(śunya)*, seeing beings as non occasioned *(animitta)*, and being free from desire. The mind is turned towards knowledge free from attachment, which is the abode of perfect wisdom *(prajñāpāramitā-vihāra)*, and is free from thought, meditations, its objects, absorption, paranormal knowledge, and suffering.[53]

When reaching the seventh stage, the classical path *(mārga)* leading to liberation is already completed. For the *bodhisattva* this is not the end, because liberation for the Mahāyānist is not the cessation of all phenomena, but a state of sentient experience *sub specie aeternitatis*. What lies beyond this liberation fills the gap between arhatship and Buddhahood. The present stage is therefore called the far-reaching *(dūraṅgamā)*. It is an uncaused state, but with experience and activity. The *bodhisattva* now reaches perfection in method *(upāya)*, which implies:

- appearing as if with great merit and knowledge.
- comprehending the selflessness of the phenomena.
- standing firm in compassion, love, joy, and equanimity.
- being free from affliction, and freeing people from it.
- realizing the non-duality *(advaya)* of things.
- being merged in the Truth of all Buddhas.
- showing on the body the marks of a Buddha.
- experiencing past, present, and future as one moment.
- appearing in various aeons.

The bodily and vocal actions of the *bodhisattva* become pure, and he performs the worldly crafts spontaneously (after having mastered them at the fifth stage). He becomes a teacher of beings in the three thousand worlds. For their rescue he becomes like them, subjecting

53 Ibid., pp. 115-123.

himself even to death or the influence of heretical teachers, severing himself seemingly from the Truth by adopting worldly rites etc. But in all this he remains detached and does not become contaminated.[54]

The eighth stage is called the immovable *(acalā)*, and in it the perfection of resolution *(pranidhāna)* is realized. Established in truth, renunciation, tranquillity, and wisdom, the *bodhisattva* knows that all things are without origin, growth, change, and decay, and that they are by nature non-existent. In other words, he comprehends the 'thusness' (*tathatā)* of all things, which means that all things are like space. He has acquired peace *(śānti)*, and is above all activity and enjoyment. He reaps the fruit of his ways.

The *bodhisattva* is now ready to acquire the powers and infallibilities which characterize the Buddhas, for these are needed to bring all beings to the Truth. He becomes omniscient, i.e: he adequately understands all beings in their motives, and he becomes intuitively sure in all his doings. He needs these gifts to adapt himself to the beings which he must lead to salvation. He further develops control over the span of his life, his mind, action, aspiration, resolution, miracles, doctrine, and true knowledge. Now he has become a member of the Buddha-family.[55]

The ninth stage is that of good thought *(sādhumatī)*, and establishes the perfection of powers. The *bodhisattva* now knows of all phenomena whether they are good, bad, or indifferent, pure or impure, worldly or transcendental, conceivable or inconceivable, definite or indefinite, constituted or inconstituted. He knows all duties, and also the thought-habits of beings, their afflictions, actions, faculties, aspirations etc. He knows in what way a being is to be guided to the goal, and therefore adapts the teaching according to his judgement. He preaches the Dharma to all the worlds in a variety of ways.

The tenth stage is called cloud of Dharma *(Dharmamegha)*. It is that of the perfection of true knowledge, *jñāna*), and it completes the *theosis* of the *bodhisattva*, who becomes now submerged in the absorption of omniscience. He appears seated on a lotus of infinite splendour, and shines with a refulgent body. He is consecrated by the rays issuing from all the Buddhas. He has reached complete illumination. The *bodhisattva* now has become a Buddha himself, or in other words, a

54 Ibid., pp. 123-125.
55 Ibid. pp. 125-127.

'*tathāgata*.' He understands all the Truths of the Buddhas, and he can perform any miracle.[56]

Below the above is rendered in a schematic form.[57]

List of the stages of a bodhisattva

according to the 'Daśabhūmīśvara' and 'Bodhisattvabhūmi'

D. bh.	Bodhi-bh
	1. family-abode
prebodhisattva stages not named	2. aspiration-abode
1. joyous stage *(pramūdita-bhūmi)*	3. joyous abode
2. immaculate st. *(vimalā-bh).*	4. moral abode
3. shining st. *(prabhākarī-bh)*	5. meditation abode
4. radiant st. *(arciṣmatī-bh)*	6. wisdom abode
5. hard to conquer st. *(sudurjayā-bh.)*	7. noble truth abode
6. turned towards bodhi *(abhimukhī-bh.)*	8. dependent orig. abode
7. far-reaching st. *(dūraṅgamā-bh.)*	9. enjoyment abode
8. immovable st. *(acalā-bh.)*	10. unoccasioned abode
9. good thought st. *(sādhumatī-bh.)*	11. analysis abode
10. Dharma-cloud *(Dharmamegha-bh.)*	12. highest abode

T*HE 'BODIES' OF THE BUDDHA*. Characteristic of Mahāyāna is the idea of the different 'bodies' *(kāya)* of the Buddha. Already the Sthaviras had made a distinction between Buddha's body of form *(rūpakāya)* and his body of Dharma *(dharmakāya)*. The body of form was that of Śākyamuni, born in Kapilavastu, and having died in Kuśināgarī, a body prone to all human frailties. Through it, the Buddha was married, begot a son etc. It was the subject of the attack of his cousin Devadatta, it suffered from disease, and finally, when going into *nirvāṇa*, the Buddha was liberated from it. In this human body another body was found, it was the body of the liberating Teaching *(Dharma)*, handed over by the pupils, and finally written down in the Āgamas

56 Ibid., pp. 127-131.
57 Ibid., pp. 132-135

and Nikāyas. This latter body survived through the ages, while of the former only the relics could be honoured. Both bodies were devoid of any metaphysical dimension.

The Mahāsaṁghikas had a different conception of the 'bodies.' For them there did not exist individual Buddha's, such as the one born in Kapilavastu, but only one eternal and transcendental Buddha, manifesting himself in a variety of ways, through different births in many bodies. Accordingly, there are no Buddhas attaining enlightenment, but only one enlightened everlasting Buddha-existence, wherein are realized all the perfections and the whole teaching of all the Buddhas who have appeared in the worlds. This transcendental being was called the 'Buddha-body,' and it manifested itself in apparitional bodies. (called *nirmāṇakāya*) such as that of Śākyamuni and other individual Buddhas, who appear only for the sake of rescuing sentient beings from the circle of rebirth, but have no real being beyond the appearance.

Early Mahāyāna, such as found in the *Collection of the Eightthousand,* or in the work of Nāgārjuna seems to link up with the Sthaviras rather than with the Mahāsaṁghikas, for it also makes the distinction between the body of form and that of *dharma*. But the conceptions are more differentiated than in the earlier Sthavira-thought. In the first place the body of form no longer is restricted to the physical or visible aspect – there is also a body of subtle, i.e. imperceptible form, which is that out of which the visible body evolves –, in the second place, the body of Dharma is no longer formed only by the Teaching, but, besides, it consists of all those *dharmas* constituting a Buddha: virtues, meditations, wisdom, liberation, and insight into liberation. There also appears a third concept of the *dharma*body, that of a metaphysical principle *(tathatā)* underlying all appearance.

The Yogācārins or idealists drive the distinctions even further; they term the subtle body of form 'body of experience' *(saṁbhoga-kāya)*, and the gross they mention by the same name as the Mahāsaṁghikas *nirmāṇa-kāya*, and they admit thereby its apparitional character. The *dharma*body, again, was the body formed by the *dharmas* constituting a Buddha. Still later, four bodies became distinguished; as a metaphysical principle the *dharma*body was renamed, and called essence body *(svābhāvika-kāya),* and as a body purified by the Buddha-*dharmas*, it was named body of selfexperience *(svasaṁbhoga-kāya)*, while the older 'body of experience,' the subtle body of form, got the name of body of the experience by others *(parasaṁbhoga-kāya)*.

And in this way the Idealists restate the conception of the Mahāsaṁghikas, accepting the idea of the 'apparitional body,' and elaborating that of the Buddha-body. In doing so they base themselves on the *Descent on Lanka*, The *Collection of the 25,000*, and the *Lotus-sūtra*, from which comes the following passage, in which the transcendental Buddha speaks:[58]

> It is not to be considered, that Śākyamuni lately leaving his family life, and attaining illumination at Gaya said: 'I attained complete illumination countless ages ago, and since then I have been preaching the Dharma.' All that.I have said about the previous Tathāgatas, Dipaṅkara etc., and their *nirvāṇas* are my own apparitions. These were only my methods for expounding the Dharma ... Though I have not attained *nirvāṇa*, to rouse curiosity in the minds of the people and a desire to see Buddha, I say that the appearance of a Buddha is an exceedingly rare event.

The apparitional body.

The Idealists *(Yogācārins)* accept, with the Mahāsaṁghikas, the *Collection of 25,000*, the *Laṅkāvatāra* and the *Lotus sūtra*, the existence of an apparitional or worldly Buddha-body *(nirmāṇa-kāya)* as a kind of emanation from a transcendental personality, called *body of enjoyment*. It is a kind of copy of the eternal Buddha for use in the temporal world. The unlimited Buddha appears in it under the limitation of an earthly body with earthly faculties, and even with an earthly mind. Such bodies appear in all corners of the world for the sake of leading sentient beings onto the Buddhistic path. They are meant to appeal to common men, monks, and *bodhisattvas* who are not yet in one of the 'Ten Stages.' The highest Buddha, in addressing people, adapts himself to their level of understanding by adopting at will bodily forms, voices, and minds to suit the purpose of spreading the Doctrine. By his miraculous power, he can also make others appear in different forms,

58 pp. 311 ff, in Dutt, p. 152.

or he can speak through the mouths of others, e.g. through those of Śāriputra or Subhūti.

The apparitional body is in the ultimate sense unreal *(saṁvṛti)*, it does not exist apart from the true Buddha, on whom it remains dependent in all its manifestations, such as the practice of the six Perfections (the higher not being realized on the worldly level), persuading people to observe the moral code, and to comprehend the non-substantiality and non-duality of all things.[59]

The body of enjoyment.

The apparitional body is a form assumed by the transcendental Buddha for preaching to ordinary beings, who otherwise could not perceive his nature. In the early *Collection of the Eightthousand,* and in the work of Nāgārjuna, no mention is made of this apparitional body, but only of a 'body of form.' Of this form-body were distinguished a gross and a subtle type. The Yogācāra (Idealist School) gives to this subtle body of form an independent status, calling it the body of enjoyment *(saṁbhoga-kāya)*. The very name 'body of enjoyment' points to the fact that it is with this purified body, that the Buddhas experience and enjoy the *dharmas*.

Whereas the apparitional body is used by the everlasting Buddha to appear to, and preach to beings of crude and mediocre sensitivity, the body of enjoyment is used to preach the noble and metaphysical truths to the beings of higher sensitivity, the *bodhisattvas*, having entered one of the Ten Stages. Later still, an even more subtle body was conceived, perceptible not even to the *bodhisattvas*, but only to the Buddhas themselves. To distinguish this latter body from the former body of enjoyment, it was called 'the body of self-enjoyment' *(svasaṁbhoga-kāya)*, while the original 'body of enjoyment' was given the name 'body of enjoyment for others' *(parasaṁbhoga-kāya)*.

All three bodies are of aesthetic or phenomenal character; they appear with increasing splendour to beings of ever more refined sensitivity. By doing good works, one can develop the senses, become a *bodhisattva*, or ultimately a Buddha, and experience the pure and brilliant forms belonging to those planes of existence; by doing evil works one can degenerate the senses, making them only sensitive to

59 Dutt, pp. 152-156..

the most brute stimuli. For what we experience is an interpretation of the signs of the experience of others, and we can interpret these signs only insofar as we can mirror that experience in our own. When we have restricted ourselves by enslaving our experience by wrong practices, we can only recognize a wretch like ourselves. That's why ordinary beings cannot understand a Buddha in his own nature, and why a Buddha, for the sake of rescuing the spiritually crippled, must descent in apparitional bodies, using even brute stimuli to lure people away from the darkness into the light.

As the lower is contained in the higher, but not the other way around, the three bodies mentioned may be conceived as stages of emanation or effulgence. Looking from the standpoint of common people, the higher bodies seem like divine sources of life. Just as an apparitional Buddha sheds his light on all creatures living in an epoch, nurtures them as it were, and embodies the spirit of his time, in the same way the body of enjoyment is the embodiment of a world; it stands on a higher level of generality. It contains all excellences of such a world in principle; it is the possibility to assume all its forms. It is like a primeval matter, which is able to produce everything. Therefore in early texts it is called the state of which the nature is primeval matter *(prakṛtyātmabhāva)*.

The Buddhas, presiding over the differents worlds, have all their own body of enjoyment, perhaps because it was felt, that a world is nothing else but a unity of enjoyment, or divine experience. Such enjoyment pervades its whole world like the rays of the sun rewakening the dormant life. Some, the *bodhisattvas*, are touched directly by this light, others by its reflection in the apparitional body, like the nocturnal beings who catch the light of the sun only through its reflection in the moon.[60]

The body of Dharma.

Early Mahāyāna makes a distinction between the relative *(saṁvṛti)* and the Absolute *(paramārtha)*. Everything that can be object for the senses, the phenomenal, is by its nature relative. The two (or three) bodies of which we have spoken are – because they belong to different levels of the aesthetic – part of the realm of relative existence. This realm

60 Ibid., pp.. 157-162.

of the relative, phenomenal, or aesthetic is dependent on an absolute realm beyond all phenomena, and therefore beyond all distinctions, concepts, and description. It has neither form nor thought, is immutable, and unchangeable. It is the base and essence, not only of the Buddha, but of all living beings whatsoever. It is that in which only a *dharma* can be given. Being the substratum of everything, it is itself without substratum. It is unlimited and fills all space; it is the all-pervading eternal being or truth of all that appears under the limitation of an aesthetic perspective. Although it is different from the particular *dharmas* in not being particular and limited, and therefore objective, it is also non-different from them, because it is their very existence, their 'thingness' *(dharmatā)*. This base of every perspective is called 'suchness' or 'unique singularity' *(tathatā)*, 'voidness' (of meaning *[sunyatā])*,'body of dharma' *(dharmakāya)* or 'body of essence' *(svabhāvika-kāya)*. It can only be realized in one's own self.

The Buddhas as they are seen by the *bodhisattvas* and by themselves are beings of infinite power, splendour, and knowledge. Their nature is unfathomable for the common people. Now it appears, that this unfathomable Buddha-nature is not different from their own. The highest goal of everything, even of the Buddhas, is at the same time the universal base and essence of everything. The Buddhas in their apparitional bodies, and bodies of enjoyment, are different personalities, but in their essence, their body of *dharma*, they are the same. In other words, they all share the same body of *dharma*, and this they share with all sentient beings. The body of *dharma* comprises everything. What sets a Buddha apart from ordinary beings, is not his essence, but his knowledge. The common people and animals are blinded by ignorance, and because of that their essence is veiled to them. What the *bodhisattvas* aim at, and what the Buddhas realize, is the dispelling of this ignorance. Then the essence, the truth, is seen through true knowledge. This unveiled *dharma*body is also called 'the body of knowledge' *(jñānakāya)*. It is the knowledge- or truth-aspect of the body of (self)-enjoyment. In the clarity of this truth one recognizes the mirage-like nature of the *dharmas*, the phenomenal nature of the world, which is like illusion or dream.[61]

61 Ibid., pp. 162-170.

T*RUTH* In Mahāyāna philosophy one can distinguish – roughly speaking – two patterns of thought, that of the Madhyamaka (or Mādhyamika), the School of the Middle, following closely the earlier *Wisdom sūtras,* and that of the Yogācārins, the idealists, who take their departure from the *Descent* (revelation) *on Lanka.* Both schools accept a highest Truth. In the light of it, all things in the world are known to be non-dual *(advaya),* sharing the same nature, which is called 'suchness' *(tathatā).* It is the unique existence, everything else being mirage and illusion. To realize this Truth is to achieve liberation *(nirvāṇa).* This Truth is not something which comes to be at a certain point of time; it is eternal, inexpressible, unthinkable. It is, whether it is realized or not. Without it, nothing, not even the transmigrating existence would be. That's why it is said that there is no difference between liberation *(nirvāṇa)* and the circle of rebirth *(saṁsāra).* In these respects the two philosophical schools do not differ, the main difference being, that the Mādhyamikas do not want to go beyond a negative characterization of this Truth, which they denote as *Śūnya* (empty), while the Yogācārins show less hesitation, and equate their Truth with pure consciousness (i.e. consciousness not 'contaminated' by any ideas or impressions).[62]

Suchness.

At the basis of all Mahāyāna conceptions lies the insight in the fundamental unity of reality. All things can be denoted only by means of general classifications and generic characteristics. When I want to communicate my unique experiences, I must use words, which may be used for all kinds of similar experiences. When I see a cow eating grass, the words 'cow,' 'eating,' 'grass' etc. stand for all animals, herbs, and processes of a certain kind. By talking about grazing cows, I surely express some meaning, but it is impossible to convey the uniqueness and concreteness of the situation, which in all speech can only be presupposed. The basic insight of Mahāyāna now is, that the uniqueness, which distinguishes the individual situation from its general characteristics, is the very thing which sets reality apart from mere verbal exposition and mental image. Because language and imagination are by their very nature generalizing, the concrete, which is also individual and unique, falls principally out of their scope; we cannot reach it by

62 Summary of N. Dutt, *Mahāyāna Buddhism*, p. 152.

words or thought. Because of that we cannot make distinctions in it, for these we cannot make without thought, imagination, and words. Accordingly, we cannot speak about different kinds of uniqueness, and consequently we cannot speak about various unique things, since uniqueness by its very nature cannot be multiplied. The Mahāyānists, therefore, conclude that in their uniqueness all things are the same. There is only one unicity, individuality, in which all generalities are integrated. No longer it is the thing (the subject of our language and thought, i.e. the cow) which is the substance to be determined (by qualifying it). The word, the idea 'cow' is one predicate, explicating one aspect of the one unicity or singularity, the suchness *(tathatā)* of which there may be denotation but not connotation. Reality is one, unique, concrete, individual, irrepeatable, and everything which is not so, is not the reality, but is made up of mere ideas, words, imaginations.

The suchness, the unique reality, is also called 'emptiness' *(śūnyatā)*. This is not meant to deny reality, but it indicates, that things and phenomena in general have no existence as separate entities. Out of their place in the integral whole they are nought, but as the focus of the singular reality, they embody it completely. Accordingly, the reality, the ultimate truth, is not filled with substances, there is nothing beyond its own identity. In other words, in their ultimate uniqueness entities *are* the Unique Reality. This uniqueness is called by still other names, such as dharmahood *(dharmatā)*, sameness *(samatā)*, *dharma*body *(dharmakāya)*, dharma-container *(dharmadhātu)*. It is present in every being, but common people live in a merely general way; they consider themselves to be separate personalities, created by the carrying of a particular name, and the performing of a particular function, e.g. of being householder, workman, politician, Buddhistic monk. As long as people do not realize that they are not the general concept which they carry in their head, but the unique reality, this very reality remains dormant in them. As such it is called 'the embryonic Buddha' *(tathāgatagarbha)*.

The unique reality is not just a logical postulate. Our deeds and concepts must be validated in reality. If we act on the basis of wrong conceptions, reality will present us the bill. Only truth itself will not be refuted, on the contrary it is truth itself which tests all our efforts. In this way, truth, as the inexorable Law, directs the course of events.

We cannot escape it, whether we accept it or not. It calls us and corrects us.[63]

The veils of affliction and of thought.
Early Buddhism, especially that of the Sarvāstivāda type, concentrated itself on action. For it, liberation was the peace following upon the eradication of the roots of action. The thinkers of Mahāyāna consider this to be a one-sided conception of liberation. In this way, they say, one can become free from afflictions *(kleśa),* but without the accompanying insight into the true nature of the absolute, the 'suchness,' what one finds is not the true *nirvāṇa*, but a temporary, heavenly resting place.

There are two veils *(āvaraṇas)* hiding the truth:

1) that of the afflictions (*kleśāvaraṇa)*, which arise because people identify their personality with the body, the mind, and the other ultimate constituents of existence, as accepted by early Buddhism: feelings, perceptions, and inclinations.

2) that which prevents one to see the singularity of existence created by the ignorance, that through language and imagination presents us with a plurality of objects of knowledge *(jñeya)*, while in reality the whole of being is one and unique.

According to the Mahāyānists, the early Buddhists – which they call Hīnayānists (followers of the lesser career) – only succeeded in dispelling the veil of afflictions, because they knew, that the personality *(pudgala)* was not a real existent, but a bundle of phenomena of various kinds on which the idea of a personal unity was only projected. They did away with the idea of the ego; that made them free from attachment, and consequently from afflictions, but they did not question the reality of the plurality of the phenomena *(dharmas)*, which they accepted as ultimately real. They realized, say the Mahāyānists, the 'being without substance of the self' *(pudgalanairātmya)*, but not that the *dharmas* as a plurality of separate entities (events) are equally with-

63 Dutt, pp. 277-281.

out substance *(dharmanairātmya)*. Therefore they did not realize the ultimate singularity, which is the same as attaining 'illumination' *(bodhi)*. This realization was the privilege of Mahāyāna; it was a form of liberation in which not only rest was obtained, but also an insight that penetrates unhindered through the whole of existence, apprehending things in their uniqueness.[64]

Conventional and highest truth.

There are different ways of coping with reality. The common man just takes his personality and the world for granted. As long as he does not want to escape his earthly condition, this attitude to reality suffices in all normal practical affairs. For the Buddhist monk, who wants to escape from rebirth, to this normal world are added the realities of ethics and meditation, in short those of the noble eightfold path, the Buddhistic way of liberation. For the Mahāyānist all these practical approaches of reality are mere conventions. They make distinctions, which work, but ultimately do not correspond with truth. In fact, they are mere fancy *(parikalpanā)* or imagination. Our normal way of looking at things cannot penetrate into the truth, it remains entangled in the material of words, concepts, and mental images, and what we take as reality, in fact, is nothing else but a manipulating of this material, to create out of it our own illusions. These constitute the conventional truth *(saṁvṛti-satya)* of normal daily life. To find the real truth *(paramārtha-satya)* beyond our conventions we must drop our habitual perspectival standpoint, we must not look at the world from the angle of any particular existent, but merge our particularity in the singularity. Then, having occupied the one 'place' in the universe without location, we can know things in their unique nature, their 'suchness' *(tathatā)* or '*dharma*hood' *(dharmatā)*, without distorting this truth-knowledge by any perspectival point of view.

The Yogācārins (idealists) put the above in somewhat different words. What in the above was called practical or conventional truth, they call 'imagined' *(parikalpita)*, because since time immemorial, the idea of existence has been projected in our imaginations. This 'imagined' existence, which is, more correctly, an existence imputed on mere representations, constitutes at the same time the world as related

64 Ibid., pp. 174-177.

to consciousness, namely, when it is not interpreted as consisting of independent entities, but as the whole of objects immanent in, and part of one integral stream of consciousness. As such it can be considered as the phenomena existing in, and therefore being dependent *(paratantra)* on consciousness. This consciousness, itself not being dependent on something else, is the abode for everything to appear. It is the highest truth, and they call it the 'perfectly real' *(parinișpanna)*.[65]

T*HE UNITY OF NIRVĀṆA AND SAṀSĀRA*. The world of our ideas, representations, and conventions, is the world in which we are daily living. As this world consists of mere thought-constructions, designations, and symbols, there is nothing real in it; the world, which these mental tools create, is illusory, like a hallucination, or as images reflecting in the water. What does not really exist, also has no real origination and no real decay, it simply appears and disappears, it does not coalesce or disintegrate. As the whole world of the round of rebirth *(saṁsara)* is of this character, there is in it no real existence, no real origination, no real death; it is just the reflection of the one truth, appearing as many, because it is broken up by its different reflections: in the lake, in the pond, in the tank, in the bowl of water I hold in my hand. The reflection may be clear or troubled, as when e.g. the wind is rippling the water of the lake.

If worldly life is not real, it cannot be brought to an end by attaining liberation *(nirvāṇa)*. Being a reflection of the truth, it has no separate existence apart from it. The world does not come to an end at the attainment of liberation, only the mistaken conception of its substantiality disappears. The same world is not seen any more through the veil of misconceptions, but in the light of truth.

Saṁsāra and Nirvāṇa are really not apart. Nirvāṇa is nothing but the truth. As such it is present in, lies at the base of all appearance. Without the truth really nothing would be, and without something present, its truth cannot be captured. When one goes from *saṁsāra* to *nirvāṇa*, nothing changes, nothing vanishes, nothing comes to be. It is just a change of view, of condition, a clearing up of the sky, or like the lighting of a candle in a dark room. The truth of revolving life is

65 Ibid., pp. 254-264.

nirvāṇa, and the exposition of this truth in appearances is *saṁsāra*. Both cannot be torn apart, they are non-dual *(advaya)*, the same singularity.

The moment an individual realizes that he is this singular reality, that *saṁsāra* is identical with *nirvāṇa*, he becomes perfect, i.e. a Buddha. When a being attains a state of mind in which he cannot separate himself from any other thing of the world or from the absolute, he is said to have realized *nirvāṇa* in the Mahāyānic sense.[66]

66 Ibid., pp. 177-182.

Chapter 6
Madhyamaka

One of the most influential schools of Buddhism is the Madhyamaka (School of the Middle) founded by Nāgārjuna. We cannot actually tell wether the latter was an adherent of Mahāyāna. Although the Chinese ascribe to him some important commentaries on Mahāyāna works, in the works of which we may be sure that they are his, there is no reference to the Mahāyāna scriptures, not even to the *bodhisattva* ideal. All quotations in these works refer to the original *sūtras*, esp. of the *Saṁyukta-āgama*, and interest seems to be limited to the four noble truths and the doctrine of dependent origination. It is possible, that by focusing the attention on what in his opinion were the central issues of Buddhism, Nāgārjuna has been willing to cleanse Buddhism of its philosophical accretions for the sake of bringing it back to what he believed was the original lore of the Buddha. In conformity with the name of the school, we may conclude that he saw his teaching as the 'middle path' between extremes, fit to unite the different Buddhistic schools being on the verge of losing each other out of sight. Before all it may have been his intention to prevent the split between the ancient schools and rising Mahāyāna. For although Nāgārjuna may not have been a Mahāyānist himself, he does not criticize the new movement, while the non-Mahāyānist is generally very harsh in his criticism of the new creed. Whatever may have been Nāgārjuna's personal stand, his school developed on Mahāyāna lines. It obviously did not prove possible to bridge the gap between the old and the new. Already his immediate pupil, the Ceylonese prince Ārya-deva, professes his believe in the *bodhisattva* ideal.[67]

Criticism.

The essence of the mainstream of the Madhyamaka is the criticism of all metaphysical speculation. It does not propound a doctrine, but tries to free the way for Buddhist practice and experience by criticizing all viewpoints *(dṛṣṭi)*.

The object of the Buddhist path is the ultimate or absolute. About such an ultimate nothing definite can be said. All our affirmations and negations make sense only with reference to empirical reality. Here, when we affirm something, we take into account the place, the date, and the circumstances. For example: when I say 'the daughter of the barber is my mother,' this only makes sense if the barber is identified in the context of common experience. And when I deny something, it always implies, that the subject of my negation is empirically real. Even if I say: 'There is nothing here,' it implies that somewhere else there must be something, since otherwise such a negation could in no way be intelligible. Affirmation and negation, accordingly, can have no meaning beyond the bounderies of human experience. Any assertion or negation going beyond these limits, is meaningless. That's why you can say nothing definite about the ultimate (absolute) or other non-empirical notions, like 'the soul,' 'the world' (as a whole), 'substance,' etc. Every attempt to say anything definite on these subjects necessarily leads to contradiction. It is the sole task of the Mādhyamika philosopher to reveal these contradictions in every metaphysical doctrine, not to teach himself some opinion on abstruse matters. By disposing of all opinions, at the same time the road is prepared for religious experience. For true religion cannot grow on dogmatic soil.

From the above we must not conclude, that the Mādhyamika pleads for a kind of empiricist science. For him the empirical is the domain of the relative, and he believes, that it is the task of Buddhism to raise people from this domain into that of the absolute. This is the more important, and only here true freedom can be found. But this domain

67 Cf. D. J. Kalupahana, *Nāgārjuna, The Philosophy of the Middle Way* (N.Y. State University Press, SUNY. 19086, also A. K. Warder, *Indian Buddhism* (Motilal Delhi, 1970/80, p. 376.

is not open for description through language. The truth is unspeakable, only to be experienced inwardly. What can be spoken of is not the truth.

Life of Nāgārjuna.

Nāgārjuna was born, and died as a citizen of the Sātavāhana empire spreading from Saurāṣṭra to Andhra in Central India. His life is associated with the reign of king Gautamiputra or Pulumāyi II, around the beginning of the 2nd century AD. During the height of his career, he left his home to lecture at the monastery of Nālanda in the Ganges region. At the end of his life he again returned to the south, to the Andhra territory around Dhānyakaṭaka. There are many legends concerning his person. He is associated with the practice of alchemy, and he is said to have been familiar with the dragon-world, from which, they say, he brought to Nālanda. the collection of the 100,000 of the 'Wisdom *sūtras*.' The Sthavira schools, on the other hand, accuse him of having written it himself. But his association with the work is doubtful.

Works ascribed to Nāgārjuna.

There are some works, that can be ascribed with confidence to Nāgārjuna. Among these the Root Verses on the Madhyamaka should be mentioned in the first place. These are accompanied by his own commentary, and they form the basic text of the Mādhyamika tradition. Other theoretical works are the *Seventy Stanzas on Relativity (śūnyatā)*, the *Sixty Stanzas on Argument*, the *Exclusion of Opposition*. Further there are: the *Letter to a Friend* (the Sātavāhana king), the *Mendicant Bowl Sutra* and its 'Explanation,' *the Wave of Pearls*, and *Four Laudatory Hymns*. The Chinese, however, ascribe to Nāgārjuna also the *Great Treatise on the Wisdom Sūtras*, and the *Commentarial Treatise on the Ten Stages*. When they are right, Nāgārjuna must after all be considered as a Mahāyānist. A number of other works of less importance is ascribed to Nāgārjuna, among which tantric and medical ones.[68]

68 A. K. Warder, *Indian Buddhism*, pp. 375-376

Dates and works of Mādhyamika thinkers:

Works of Nāgārjuna (ca. 150 AD)

Root Verses on the Madhyamaka & Commentary (Mūlamadhyamakakārikā)
Letter to a Friend (Suhṛllekha)
Seventy Stanzas on Relativity (Śūnyatāsaptati)
Sixty Stanzas or Argument (Yuktiṣaṣtika)
Mendicant Bowl Sūtra (Vaidalyasūtra)
Exclusion of Opposition (Vigrahavyāvartaṇi)
Pearl Necklace (Ratnavalī)
Four Laudatory Hymns (Catuḥ-stava)
Great Treatise on the 'Wisdom Sūtras' (Mahāprajñāpāramitā-śāstra)?
Commentarial Treatise on the Ten Stages (Daśabhūmi-vibhāṣa-śāstra)?

Other thinkers

date AD	
200 ad., Āryadeva	*Work of 400 stanzas* (Catuḥśataka)
450 AD Buddhapālita	Mādhyamika-vṛtti
450 AD Bhāvaviveka	*Jewel in the Hand* (Karatalaratna) *The Torch of Reason* (Tarkajvāla) *Summary of Madhyamaka Things* (Madhyamakārtha-saṁgraha) *The Lamp of Wisdom* (Prajñāpradīpa) *Depending Origination according to Madhyamaka* (Madhyamakapratītyasamutpāda)
575-625 Candrakīrti	*The Clear Worded* (Prasannapadā) *Revelation of Madhyamaka* + comm. (Madhyamakāvatāra), Commentary on the *400 Stanzas* of Āryadeva
695-743 Śāntideva	Compendium of the Doctrine (Śikṣasamuccaya) Practice for Illumination (Bodhicaryāvatāra)

705-762 Śāntarakṣita	Ornament of the Madhyamaka ((Mādhyamakālaṅkāra)
713-763, Kamalaśīla	Lustre of the Madhyamaka (Madhyamakāloka)

SHORT HISTORY OF THE MADHYAMAKA. There can be distinguished four phases in the development of the Madhyamaka. In the first place there is the formulation of the Madhyamaka ideas by Nāgārjuna and Āryadeva. This phase runs from the middle of the 2nd century AD until the middle of the fifth century. Here the Madhyamaka is founded as a critical system. Its method is not to put forward its own standpoint, but to show that all standpoints whatsoever are untenable, because any one conceals implicit contradictions. The Mādhyamika brings these contradictions to light, contradictions which must be unacceptable to the one defending the standpoint. The method employed, accordingly, is that of the *reductio ad absurdum*.

We have already spoken of Nāgārjuna. His most important pupil was Āryadeva, who seems to have been a Ceylonese prince, living about 200 AD. Whereas Nāgārjuna directs his polemic mainly against the Ābhidharmika system (that of the Sarvāstivāda), Āryadeva directs it primarily against the rivalling non-Buddhist systems of the Sāṁkhya and the Vaiśeṣika. He does this in his chief work, called *The Work Consisting of 400 Stanzas*.

In the middle of the 5th century the school splits into two branches. One branch, led by Buddhapālita, remains loyal to the method of *reductio ad absurdum*, and is therefore called the *prāsaṅgika-school* (*prasaṅgika* being the Sanskrit term for *reductio ad absurdum*), the other, headed by Bhāvaviveka, holds, that in combatting opponents, on the occasion the Mādhyamika may adopt his own standpoint opposed to the one he wants to reject. His school is called the *svātantrika*-school, *svatantrika* meaning 'autonomous' or 'dependent on itself.' This name points to the fact, that the school can depend on standpoints of its own.

Bhāvaviveka seems to have been important in his time. He is characterized by his liberal-mindedness. For he recognized that all blessing did not come from the Mādhyamika position, and that the highest truth as explained by other systems also leads to salvation, even the truth of the non-Buddhist systems. He taught, that the realization of *śūnyata* (relativity) is not absolutely necessary to attain *nirvāṇa*. The Hīnayānists also reach final release. Nevertheless the Hīnayānist should be convinced of the universality of relativity *(śūnyatā)*. This does not imply the non-existence of things, but merely stands for the denial of the dogmatic assertion of existence. Relativity does not nullify things, but shows their real nature as devoid of essence. Bhāvaviveka also thought – in contrast to the adherents of the Prāsaṅgika School –, that relativity can be proved. He was an erudite, who wrote many books, such as: *The Jewel in the Hand*, the *Torch of Reason* (in which he displays a thorough knowledge of the Sāṁkhya, Vaiśeṣika, and Vedānta systems), the *Synopsis of the Subjects of the Madhyamaka*, the *Lamp of Wisdom* (being a commentary on the *Madhyamaka-kārikās*), and another commentary on the same, the 'Origination in Dependence according to the Madhyamaka.'

The third phase in the development of the Madhyamaka starts with Candrakīrti, who probably was active between 575 and 625 AD. His work is characterized by a severe criticism of the Svātantrika-school of Bhāvaviveka, and by a return to the method of *reductio ad absurdum*. He was born in the south, probably in Samanta, and was a pupil of Dharmapāla and/or Kamalabuddhi. Besides the Svātantrika school, Candrakīrti combats also Buddhist idealism and the Vedānta, which were in the ascendency in his time. He tries to make clear, that there can be no consciousness without an object, as the idealist holds; we cannot even apprehend it, much less remember it. To him such consciousness appears as the self *(ātman)* of the heretics in disguise. Idealism is also inconsistent with the truth of empirical reality, and with common sense. In practical matters, common sense should be defended against idealism. Important works of Candrakīrti are: *The Clear-Worded*, a commentary on the Madhyamaka Stanzas, *The Revelation of the Madhyamaka* with his own commentary, and a *Commentary on the '400 Stanzas' of Āryadeva*.

To the school of Candrakīrti we must also count Śāntideva (active between 695 and 743 AD). He is said to have been a prince of Saurāṣṭra, who came to Nālanda after an auspicious dream. His works are: *A Compendium of the Doctrine*, and *Revelation of the Practice unto Il-*

lumination. In Śāntideva's thinking there is a strong accent on devotion and spiritual discipline.

The fourth phase of the Madhyamaka is introduced by Śāntarakṣita and Kamalaśila. In these thinkers we find a mixing of the Madhyamaka tenets with those of Buddhist idealism. The Madhyamaka method is practised with regard to ultimate reality, but as concerns empirical reality, the idealist, and not the usual realist Madhyamaka position is defended.[69]

D*IALECTIC.* It is the conviction of Nāgārjuna, that the application of language to reality is inadequate. Language is by its nature general, and therefore it can never mirror the uniqueness of reality. Because of that no doctrine cast in the moulds of language and of thought – which is a correlate of language – can contain the truth. Thought and language constitute a way of coping with reality in an abstract way, but they do not convey its essence. This essence can only be touched in immediate experience, it cannot be rendered by any means.

The Mādhyamika tries to convince his opponents of the incompetence of language and thought by showing, that every doctrine when logically elaborated, leads to intrinsic contradictions. This is so especially when the bounderies of experience and common sense are transgressed, when, for example, one wants to say something about the general characteristics of the world as a whole (which never can become object of experience) or of the soul as an entity transcending the phenomena of inner experience. The Mādhyamika does not want to say anything definite on these subjects, but solely points to the incompetence of reason in the fields beyond daily experience. He also holds, that the categories which we use in describing the world in which we live do not reflect reality, but are structures imposed on it. In other words, categories, like 'substance' and 'causality' do not represent reality as it is in itself, but only the way in which we deal with it.

69 T. R.V. Murti, *The Central Philosophy of Buddhism* Allen & Unwin, London, 1955, '80, '87, pp. 87-103. The exposition in this chapter generally follows this work closely, although the reader will meet with some viewpoints not met in Murti's work.

The tetralemma.

The classical way of coping with the incompetence of reason in the field beyond experience is the *tetralemma.* Already the Buddha was confronted with such insolvable questions as: 'Is the world eternal or not?', 'Is the world infinite or not?', 'Is the soul mortal or not?', and 'Do the liberated live on after death or do they not?'. The questions were posed by the disciple Māluṅkyaputra and the wandering monk Vatsagotra. The Buddha refused to take the questions into consideration, since they were of no help to the solving of the only problem worthy of our concern, the problem of suffering and how it is to be overcome. For as there is no suffering beyond experience, it is obviously experience which we must analyse, instead of speculating about lofty realms. By trying to escape the confrontation with our own life, we obviously will not be able to put right what is wrong.

Unlike the Buddha, Nāgārjuna and other Mādhyamikas take the questions as posed by Māluṅkyaputra into consideration, not to answer them, but to show that they are unanswerable, and that every position defended with reference to them, necessarily leads to contradictions. This attitude of the Mādhyamika must be seen against the background of the rivalling liberation-schools. The Buddha refuses to enter upon the questions, because he is confronted with seekers for salvation, the Mādhyamika enters upon them, while he finds himself opposed to other movements of thought, claiming to offer a genuine path to salvation. He wants to expose the untrustworthiness of those claims, by showing that they are not based on sound thinking. How Nāgārjuna does this, we shall show through the example of causality. This was an important topic. For salvation is based on liberating practice, and the effectiveness of practice depends upon how action produces its result, and this is the core of the problem of causation. Now there were four important doctrines about the relation of cause and effect:

1) That there is identity between cause and effect,
2) That cause and effect are different,
3) That there is both identity and difference between them,
4) That there is neither identity nor difference between them.

These four theses at the same time represent the four possible logical alternatives, as conceived by Indian logic, for the relation between cause and effect (or between other items), the so-called 'tetralemma' *(catuṣkoti)*. The first two members of the tetralemma form the basic alternative offered by logic, but since in Indian logic the *tertium non datur* is not accepted, the two last members are added to cover the whole field of logical possibilities.

The first thesis, about the identity of cause and effect was defended by the important Brahminical school, called the Sāṁkhya. But what do you mean when you speak about the identity of cause and effect, the Mādhyamika asks. You obviously do not mean to say that cause and effect are identical in their manifest forms. For the Sāṁkhya the cause is the same thing as the effect, but in a non-manifest form, like the seed is the same thing as the tree, but with branches and leaves still unevolved. But if there is difference between cause and effect in that way, how can you maintain their identity? And how can a thing that is not manifest be a cause? For don't we observe, that things are only efficient insofar as they are manifest? What's the use of projecting an imperceptible tree into the seed as the cause of the visible tree? What do we gain by doubling the world in that way? The knowledge of causality that is practically useful, tells us that if this occurs that will happen. Knowing this you can anticipate events. But to say, that if this occurs, it must have existed earlier in an imperceptible manner, does add nothing to our practical understanding, and theoretically it is unwarranted.

The second thesis, held by the Ābhidharmika or Vaiśeṣika, that there is difference between cause and effect, also cannot be defended. For if things are different, i.e. if there is a radical fissure between them, there can be no connection between cause and effect, and the two cannot influence each other. Either nothing could be produced, or anything could spring from anything, which would result in the abandonment of causation. If there is no inner connection between cause and effect, this is tantamount to saying, that there is no causality at all. But the Ābhidharmika cannot accept this conclusion, since then there would be no longer a base for moral action, and for the liberation practice.

We now might be inclined to think, that the criticism of the first two alternatives would be an implicit vindication of the third, viz. that there is both identity and difference between cause and effect. This standpoint was defended by the school of Jainism.[70] But the Mādhyamika does not accept it. His argumentation, however, in this case seems not so strong. It rests on the idea that entities cannot have opposed aspects, and on the believe, that as far as cause and effect are identical, the arguments against identity may be put forward, and insofar as they are different, the ones against difference.·

The fourth alternative, according to the Mādhyamika, stands self-convicted, for to hold that there is neither identity nor difference between cause and effect, comes to the same as saying, that things are produced by sheer chance, and that would deprive all action of its meaning.

But how can all the four alternatives, covering the whole of the logically possible, be rejected? The answer: the logically possible does not cover reality. It is experience which prescribes its rules to logic, and not the other way around. Besides, the four alternatives are not concerned with what matters in causality. They reduce causality to the problem of identity and difference, and this is not the right entrance to the problem of efficacity and process.[71]

Relativity.

The meaning of the criticism of concepts as e.g. cause and effect, is that these do not represent things in themselves, but relations which are not inherent in reality, but only belong to the ways in which we deal with it.

The normal function of the mind *(buddhi)* is to contrive methods for the satisfaction of our needs and desires, and for the maintenance and regeneration of our life. As such the mind enters into relation with its objects. The relations are of manifold nature, and the active human mind can never separate itself from them. The relations are the different modes in which man approaches reality. We mistake these modes for reality itself, but really all distinctions we make in language and thought are not the reflections of distinctions in reality, but the

70 Jainism is a liberation school, contemporary with, and in origin akin to Buddhism, but it has a much more materialistic metaphysics. For more information one should consult e.g. the works of Von Glasenapp and Schubring.

71 T. R.V. Murti, *The Central Philosophy of Buddhism,* pp. 129-135.

projections of our intentions with it, of the relations in which we stand to it. These, again, are themselves expressions of our proclivities. It is, accordingly, relations which dominate practical life, not the individual entities entering into these relations. They express the way in which we want to use things. It is we who relate, and the relations thus projected are in reality nothing else but conceptual devices or imaginations *(vikalpa, prapañca)*. In normal life we can view nothing apart from our intentions and conceptions. They veil the truth from us. No phenomenon is given apart from its relatedness to us, that is, from the way in which we relate it to us. Nothing can be separated from this universal relativity. 'Things,' which we conceive as entities, are so conceived, not because of what they are in themselves, but because of the functional relations in which they are placed. But 'things' which are nothing but relational modes, are nothing in themselves. And this for the Mādhyamika is the same as saying that they are not real. It is relation that identifies and differentiates the world of apparent multiplicity.

From the multiple relations between mind and reality derive all our categories which all consist of pairs, which have no meaning apart from each other. The meaning of 'cause' cannot be conceived without that of 'effect.' It is the same with couples of concepts like 'substance' and 'attributes,' 'whole' and 'parts,' 'subject' and 'object,' 'agent' and 'activity,' 'self' and 'states' etc.

Man in his normal dealings cannot conceive the world as it is in itself, but only in the light of his own aims, as directed towards himself, converging in himself. Therefore he cannot touch the essence of things.[72]

The goal of dialectic

The dialectic or criticism exercized by the Mādhyamika finds its point of departure in the existence of a variety of philosophical systems opposed to each other, explaining everything from mutually conflicting points of view. This arouses suspicion concerning the claim of thought regarding its ability to acquaint us with reality. From this suspicion grows the spirit of criticism. The Mādhyamika becomes aware

72 Ibid., pp. 136-140.

of the subjectivity of thought. He starts his critical analysis of existing doctrines, showing that they do not reveal reality. They are based on human judgement, and this is nothing but human choice, human determination, whereas the real in itself must be independent of human choice. Doctrines are nothing but human ideas, human fancies, human decisions superimposed on reality.

Whereas the world in which we are actually living, acting, and thinking is of our own making, reality itself is not conditioned by human endeavour and activity. It is not stained by the activities of the mind, which differentiate practical life. The active mind, trying to satisfy its needs, sends its rays of attention, coloured by its present objectives, to elicit some object out of the unity of universal being, to incorporate it into the limited unity of the ego. The object is taken out of its rest into the subjectivity of a plan, a program; it loses its fullness, and becomes a mere utensil devoid of proper essence. The hammer I hold in my hand, is not a being to be treated with respect, but a tool for realizing my wishes. It is taken out of the realm of nature *(svabhāva)*, rest, and space into that of appearance, turbulance, and time. In this turbulance not only the object, but also the mind itself becomes divorced from the universal unity of nature, and becomes an individual creating its own fancied world. The spontaneity of the mind should be brought to rest, so that the succession of intentions or thought-forms may come to an end. The mind then is no more thinking, fancying, willing, grasping, but tranquil and perceiving. It does not place the present in the perspective of a goal in the future, but, on the contrary, is fully absorbed in what is there. It is reunited with the universal. This state is called 'wisdom' *(prajñā)*, and in it the mind is not any longer separated from reality, but it has become its subjective reflection. This is not anything besides reality, but to be in union with it. This unity of wisdom and reality is also called body of *dharma (dharmakāya)*.[73]

SUBSTANCE OR FLEETING EVENTS? The Mādhyamika criticizes the idea of the Ābhidharmist, that the self is nothing else but a stream of momentary events of different types in conjunction, viz. a

73 Ibid., pp. 121-143.

stream of intellective and conative events, with their objects, forms, and their perceptions and feelings. For if events are selfcontained and momentary it is not conceivable how they should influence one another. When there is no entity before and after, there is nothing which comes into being. Origination, duration, cessation are inexplicable like 'māya' or dream. Dependent origination means that things have no nature of their own, but that there is universal relativity. This means that the problem of change and permanence is approached in a way different than before. The question is no longer whether things are in themselves fleeting or permanent. This is an idle question. It is to point out, that change and permanence are interdependent notions. This says nothing about the nature of reality in itself, for this is never an object of thought, everything said is about reality as it is given to daily experience. In this context of experience, the changing and ephemeral has only meaning in relation to the permanent.

A special case of the idea of the permanent and the impermanent is formed by the concept of the self *(ātman)*. Here, the Abhidharma and the Brahminical view stand in contraposition. The Brahmins of Nāgārjuna's days accepted a permanent self as the subject of transmigration. For the Ābhidarmikas there was no such permanence, but the self was considered as a convenient name to indicate the series of psychic events belonging to one continuous stream of consciousness. In this stream there is no permanence at all; every phase of the stream perishes before another is born. If there is an illusion of permanence at all, this is only a name *(prajñaptisat)*.

For the Mādhyamika both conceptions are untenable. For if there is no self beyond the changing events or phenomena, then there would be as many selfs as there are events; obviously no unity of consciousness could be conceived of, and there would be no principle on the ground of which an event ought to be assigned to one stream *(saṁtāna)* instead of to another. In fact, there could not be a unity or continuity of psychic events. If the self, furthermore, is identified with a series of discontinuous events, this gives a problem with regard to moral responsibility. For there would be no permanent subject to reap the fruits of its deeds. Accordingly, the identification of the act with the agent does not account for experience. The self or substance integrates the acts. But the self also cannot be considered as totally different from the events. It is not even a true reality. It is merely thought to exist owing to thought-construction. And it has only empirical value. The self is neither identical nor non-identical with the events. The self is the egoity reflecting in the changing events, enjoying a semblance of independence, identity, and permanence. It is thus a construct *(vikalpa)* read into the manifold phenomena. If the self were a real entity, there should be agreement about it. On the contrary one's self is non-self for another and vice versa; and this should not be the case if it were an objective reality. The relation of self and events cannot be formulated in any conceivable manner.

But if the self is not a real entity, who then is the mover of the body? But how can an immaterial principle activate a material thing like the body, or the sense organs and mind etc.? Changeless and all-pervasive, the self is not active *(niṣkriya)*; and without action this self cannot be an agent *(kartṛ)*. It cannot even co-ordinate and synthesize the different events into a unity. On this condition too moral and spiritual life becomes impossible. An unchanging self cannot benefit by spiritual discipline. And in progress the self cannot be identical at any two stages of its development. Phenomenal life is product of the imagining function of the mind *(kalpanā)*. The real is beyond our conceptual patterns. The self has no meaning apart from the events and mental activity. The two are mutually dependent and hence unreal.

In spite of this, the combination-view of the Jains and Saṁmatīyas, viz. that the self is both permanent and impermanent, also is rejected. The individual is neither identical with, nor different from the states, says the Mādhyamika, thereby inconsequently taking up the fourth position of the tetralemma. It is admittedly difficult to formulate a conceivable relationship between the self and the changing events. It can only be said that there is mutual dependence, which means that there is no identity or difference.

After an examination of the several views *(dṛṣṭi)* with regard to the self, Nāgārjuna concludes: 'The self is not different from the events nor identical with them: (there) is no self without the events, nor is it to be considered non-existent.' There is neither self nor non-self, since these are subjective devices. The real as indeterminate *(śūnya)* is free from conceptual construction. It can be approached in numberless ways owing to the capacities of the aspirant for liberation. The divergent utterances of the Buddha are directed to people in different stages of development. For keeping them away from vice, existence of self may be accepted (moral responsibility). To get rid of attachment, selflessness is preached. For realizing complete freedom, the giving up of all views is insisted upon. Reality is transcendent to thought, and non-dual.[74]

T*HE HIGHEST WISDOM.* It was contended before, that the Madhyamaka is the criticism of all speculation and dogmatism. Its purpose is to free the mind from its presuppositions, which at the same time are the conditions of the normal way of life. The mind must be emptied from concepts and ideas. Only then the highest wisdom will arise, from which things can be seen in their own nature, and not in that which we have imposed on it by our own imagination. To see things as they really are, we do not need acquisition of information, but a purification of the intellect. It is a negative method to reach universality, the abolition of the restrictions which conceptual patterns impose.

The truth, reality, is covered by the veil of our conceptions, which in their tentative character must always be wrong in an ultimate sense. It is called the veil of knowables *(jñeyāvaraṇa)*. It is caused by the working of ignorance *(avidyā)*, which may be identified with the projective activity of the mind. Instead of being open to reality, the mind projects upon it its own fancies, and thus creates a 'shadow-world' of its own making, which hides the real truth from us. This shadow-world, this covering of the real, can be removed by disposing of the ideas which are at the base of it. Then the intellect *(buddhi)* becomes so pure *(amala)* and transparant *(bhāsvara)*, that no distinction can exist between the real and the intellect which apprehends it. Because of this lack of distinction between the truth and its apprehension, the absolute unity of them may be denoted by names indicating its objective or its subjective aspect, such as 'dharmahood' or 'highest wisdom' *(prajñāpāramitā)*, but really it is non-dual *(advaya)*.

The absolute as devoid of all determination is the inexpressible ground of all phenomena; it is devoid of the two extremes of 'is' and 'is not.' In the Madhyamaka the absolute is mostly denoted as 'highest

74 Ibid., pp.165-208.

wisdom'. This wisdom is the mind freed from conceptual restrictions, it is the mind-essence, the precondition of all conscious functioning. The discovery of this essence at the same time frees man from suffering, since it destroys ignorance, the basis of the afflictions *(kleśa)* of desire and aversion, which form the direct cause of suffering.

The highest wisdom is knowledge without the distinction of subject and object, it is truth as such, in which knowledge is not distinguished from its object, and essence not from existence. It is intuition without the differentiations of reason. It starts with the consciousness of illusion, and ends with the negation of this illusion. This illusion is the total and persistent conflict of reason, the interminable opposition of viewpoints:

> 'As the several philosophical views are views of reality, the Mādhyamika in being aware of the illusoriness of the views, is aware of the illusoriness of the world which is characterized by these views. For instance, in rejecting the different theories of causation, the Mādhyamaka has rejected causation as a constitutive factor of the real'[75]

Nature of wisdom.

The highest wisdom is a kind of intuition, but not a sensory one. It is not transitory, as it is the nature of all things. Though realized in its pristine form in the highest transic states, it is not a special faculty with a limited scope: it is the basis of all things *(prakṛtir dharmāṇām)*. It is the invariable form of knowledge of which other modes of apprehension are the species.

Dialectic removes the screen of thought-constructions, the obstruction and limitation obscuring intuition. In liberation there is thus only epistemic, but no ontological novelty. It is not gained by a special faculty, but by freeing the mind from its natural disposition to bifurcate and to conceptualize.

The highest wisdom is contentless intuition. There is nothing opposed to it. It is non-dual, not-bifurcated *(advaidhīkāra)*. The absolute, the entire reality is its content, and not any particular limited object. It is unfathomable *(gambhīra)*, immeasurable *(aprameya)*, infinite

75 Ibid., p. 216.

(asaṁkhyeya), inexpressible, too deep for words, too universal for distinctions to apply.

> 'The mind is freed from impediments *(āvaraṇas)*, is perfectly diaphanous, non-distinct from the real, and a description of the one is a description of the other. Intuition is the absolute.'[76]

In the intuition of the absolute is no consciousness of realization; it is self-forgotten,and not intent. This intuition precludes progress and surprise. It is knowledge of the entire reality once and for all, and does not depend on contingent factors, such as favourable circumstances and previous information. In it there is really no progress, although one can justifiably speak of a progressive falling away of the obstructions of this knowledge.

Wisdom is freedom

Freedom in Buddhism is in essence freedom from suffering. Suffering is impeded willing. This freedom from suffering is attained by the elimination of the root-causes, the afflictions *(kleśa)*: perplexity, desire, and aversion. Of these, the first is the direct expression of ignorance, which itself is the obscuring function of the projective activity of the mind. Therefore wisdom and freedom are not two parallel but independent processes. Freedom is the practical implication of wisdom. A person assailed by passions, and distracted by worldliness cannot perceive the truth. And only on perceiving the truth, one is completely freed from passions. Discipline can be divided into two stages: mind-control *(śamatha)* and contemplation *(vipaśyanā)*. And this discipline is directed towards the removal of the afflictions. In all Buddhistic thought this removal leads to liberation, but in the Madhyamaka much stress is laid on the fact, that these afflictions are themselves product of the projective function of the mind, i.e. of ignorance. This projection is subjective, and because subjective, one can be freed from it. Nāgārjuna says:

76 Ibid., p. 220.

> 'Of constructive imagination are born attachment, aversion, and perplexity, depending (respectively) on our good, evil, and stupid attitudes. Entities which depend on these are not anything by themselves. The affects are unreal'[77] … 'Freedom *(mokṣa)* is the cessation of *karma* and afflictions *(kleśa);* these arise from thought-construction *(vikalpa);* this ceases with the knowledge of their falsity *(śūnyatā).*'[78]

Openness is the antidote for all afflictions. When the real is not apprehended as an ens or a non-ens, there is cessation of imaginative projection *(kalpanā).* There can be no gain or loss, elation, or depression. The Dhammapada says:[79]

> 'Desire, know I thy root; from imagination *(saṁkalpa)* thou springest; no more shall I indulge in imagination; I will have no desire any more.'

The problem is essentially one of knowledge, insight into the nature of the real. The supremacy of the intellect, and its absolute power to control and eradicate the afflictions, is the rock on which the Mādhyamika spiritual discipline is built. Not the will, but the intellect is the supreme faculty to which others are subordinate. Truth is the highest value. Openness *(śūnyatā)*, as the dissolution of the conceptual function of the mind, is freedom.[80]

ABSOLUTE AND PHENOMENA. The Madhyamaka distinguishes between the absolute and the phenomenal. Corresponding with this distinction is the one between the highest truth and the empirical truth, the practical truth of daily life. The absolute is non-becoming and non-ceasing. We would call this 'eternal,' although this should not be conceived as the subsistence of an entity. The phenomenal is by its nature subject to birth and decay. Now there is really one reality, one truth, the absolute, the phenomenal is ultimately not a reality at all. Why then consider it? Because we are entangled in its illusion! Denying this would force us to take the illusion that we live in for the truth.

77 Madhyamaka-kārikā, 1.2, quoted by Murti.
78 Madhyamaka-kārikā, 5, quoted by Murti.
79 *Dhammapāda*, quoted in *Madhyamaka-kārikā*, quoted in Murti, pp. 350, 451.
80 Murti, pp. 238-242.

Why call our daily reality an illusion? Because it is composed of our own thoughts and imaginations. In reality we make distinctions between substance and quality, cause and effect, the one and the many. But these are the categories of our thought, and not reality as it is in itself. Likewise, we have all kinds of ideas about the world. These are so tenacious, that in looking at the world we really do not perceive anything else than the ideas we have projected upon it. We have closed ourselves up in a world of our own making. But this does not mean that all is illusion. Clearly we would not have been able to create our categories and ideas, if we had not been there, and we could not have projected them if there had been nothing to function as a coathook to hang it on. You can only project if there is something to project it upon. This substrate of all our thought, categories, and imaginations is the absolute. But this absolute is nothing but experience as such *(tattva)*, experience as cleansed from all its explicit and implicit judgments. This is the experience of the wise, who have abandoned themselves, who do not any longer interpret the world in the terms of their own needs and ideas. It is not the world as distorted by the petty ego, ready made for its own purposes, but the ego crushed by the overwhelming truth.

This truth is not something over and above the world, it simply is the world, but not the dissected world as it is given to our analytical distinctions, not some aspect, or part of it, but the world as an integral whole, as that by virtue of which, amidst all change there is still a point of reference. The world can be viewed as process or as being, and then we must take 'being' not in the sense of 'entity,' a 'something,' but as the ground on which only an entity can occur, as the canvas without which there can be no painting, and not as something depicted on it. Viewed as a process, the world consists of a plurality of things and events, each of which is subject to development, to origination, growth, subsistence, decay, and death. Nothing lasts, not the minutest thing endures. Of that what a thing is in this moment nothing remains in the next. We can grasp nothing substantial. In this the Mādhyamika goes further than the Ābhidharmika, for he even rejects atomic events, just because these would tend to become substances. But on the other hand, we cannot maintain that something originates and decays if we do not presuppose that it endures in the meantime. Without the duration of the changing, the very notion of origination and decay would lose its meaning, for if there does not originate something which endures, nothing originates, nothing changes, nothing dies. But this is exactly the point where the Mādhyamika wants to have us. Really nothing originates and nothing dies. But once you accept origination, change, decay, you implicitly accept duration, permanence. When you accept process and development, progress, decline, you also accept its causes and conditions. In the world of becoming, everything is a result that has a cause, and everything is a cause which will yield its consequence. Everything is caught up in a web of causal relations, nothing can stand by itself. At the same time every quality implies its opposite. Something can only be light because its environment is dark etc. But just because of this unbreakable causal interrelationship of things, we are able to view them in a different way. Because a thing is nothing in itself, but gains meaning because of the whole of the relations in which it stands, a thing can be taken as the whole of its implied references. Viewed like that, the thing is the whole of its implied causes and effects, the totality of its relations, and because nothing in the universe can be sundered, it is simply the whole of all relations given in a particular time and place. To view something in the perspective of the whole is to see its truth. Let's make this clear. A man is born and dies. In the meantime we may say that he exists. Before and after he does not. But although, the man is born and dies, the truth that he is born, and has died, does not perish with him. Although a man's existence is temporal, the truth of his existence in time is not temporal. And so it is with the truth of everything whatsoever. But then, do many truths exist coeternal? Can the truth of my existence be separated from that of yours? It seems not. A fully defined truth cannot be a limited statement, but implies the whole universe. Let's take the following example to make this clear. We can say that the English politician Churchill lived from 1874 until1965. We can take this for a truth, but it would be equally true to say, that he lived from 1849 until 1895. All truths that can be formulated are true within the context of a common universe of understanding. When I say 'Churchill,' most people will think of Winston Churchill, but more than a century ago, they would have thought of Randolph Churchill. When I speak of '1965,' I mean the year of the Christian era. All points on which we fix the truth are relative. To make these truths more stable we should specify them, specify Winston, specify the Christian era. But even such specification would not be understandable to any cognizer whatsoever, not to one living before the Christian era or after it having been fallen into oblivion, not to an extraterrestrial, if he exists. To describe the truth of the life of Churchill in a non relative way, clearly a description of the whole universe should be implied, in a language understandable to every possible intelligence. But we have no such language at our disposal, and we live too short to complete such a description. But still we intuitively clearly see that the truth of a fact does not die with it. We also can see that the truth of one fact cannot be isolated from any other one, in short, that every truth is anchored in the one truth, implying the truths concerning each particular. The Mādhyamika expresses all this, when he says, that truth is the concreteness of concrete things *(dharmānām dharmatā)*, the substrate of them *(prakṛtir dharmāṇām)*. No thing can stand by itself, they all depend upon each other, they have no nature of their own *(niḥsvabhāva)*, but there collective truth, their 'dharmahood' (essence) or substrate only stands alone *(akṛtima svabhāva)*. But are we to think that each perishable entity produces its part of the eternal truth? It is not that simple. Man is not simply a heap of living matter that comes into existence and subsequently fades away, but he is a cognizer, he even exists as such, and the object of knowledge as knowledge is truth, otherwise it would not be knowledge, but fantasy, idea, thought-construction *(vikalpa, kalpanā)*. Truth is not an object like a stone, to be touched, to be hewn, to be crushed. We cannot indicate the stuff out of which it is made. It is realized only by intelligence. One can have insight into it. We can say that truth is all things as they are, but this is not quite so, for we have seen that truth is transcendent to the existence of things. We then might say that truth is the knowledge according to reality, but this is also not quite so, for truth, by its nature is the object of knowledge. To avoid the impasse, we might say then, that truth is the culmination of both the subjective and the objective, the knowledge of the whole, but as it itself belongs to the whole, it cannot be itself outside the whole. The whole and its knowledge being co-finite, that's the truth. As knowledge it is wisdom, as the whole it is suchness (*tattva* or *tathatā*). This is what the Buddha experienced at the moment of his enlightenment. It is said that then he discovered the law of dependent origination; a lucid theory, thought Ānanda, his disciple. Not lucid, said the Buddha, deep and abstruse! For in enlightenment one does not discover an abstract law, but the causal interrelationship is experienced in its unique concreteness. If the Buddha saw, that from ignorance arise the inclinations, from inclinations consciousness, from consciousness form … until old age and death, it means that he saw that from this ignorance arose this inclination, from this inclination this consciousness etc. The realization of the universal interrelationship is not the general insight that things are interrelated – we may accept that as a platitude –, but the realization of the unique way in which they are interrelated. It is not just because of making the enlightenment more interesting, that it is said, that it is anticipated by the remembering of previous lives, by the insight into the lives and rebirth processes of others. All this points to the utter concreteness of the experience of truth.

As truth is without birth and decay, it is simply there, but it is not realized, because it is covered up by our thoughts, imaginations, categories, and ideas. This covering can be summarized under the headings of the 'mental faculty' *(buddhi)* and 'ignorance' *(avidyā)*. Normal life *(vyāvahāra)* is the truth, but covered up *(saṁvṛta)* by ignorance or mind. It is nothing apart from the truth, but the truth veiled, distorted, broken up, truth in the carnival mirror. To find the truth, you must remove the covering of ideas and fantasy, empty yourself of illusive meaning, and plunge into it. Thus freed from impediments *(kleśa)*, the truth bursts forth into the remotest corners of life. It's like the untying of a knot in a rope. The knot is not something different from the rope, but still it makes the rope less usable.

The absolute is known as the reality behind the phenomena, it is not itself phenomenal. It is the implicate of all things. It has no connotation but only denotation. The outward appearance shown by the phenomena obscures this true inner essence. By discovering, removing the superimposed character of phenomena, the true nature of the absolute is revealed. Technically this is called *'adhyāropāpavādanyāya,'* the method of the removal of the ascription. Phenomena are used as devices *(upāya)* to reach the unconditioned *(paramārtha)*, which is their end *(upeya)*. This is the only means of expressing the absolute. Although an ascribed characteristic may not constitute the real, yet it can indicate it as its ground. The absolute is the only real; it is not truly different from the phenomena. The difference is only epistemic, subjective, and not real. There is not the least difference between the absolute and the universe, says Nāgārjuna.

> 'The universe viewed as a whole is the absolute, viewed as a process it is the phenomenal – having regard to causes and conditions (constituting all phenomena, we call this world) phenomenal world. This same world, when causes and conditions are disregarded, (i.e. the world as a whole, *sub specie aeternitatis*) is called the Absolute.'[81]

Ignorance.

Ignorance *(avidyā)* is the non-apprehension of the real and its misapprehension as something else. It has two functions, one obscurative *(āvaraṇa)*, the other constructive *(asatkhyāpana)*. The two functions are interrelated: without the emergence of the unreal appearance, there could be no obscuration of the truth, and without misapprehension of the true nature of the truth, there could be no false notion about it. It is indulging in conceptual construction *(saṁkalpa)*. The truth is indeterminate *(śūnya)*; the viewing of it through thought-forms is ignorance, for instance, seeing it through categories like substance and quality *(dharma)*, one or many, existence or non-existence.

Ignorance has its origin in pointless attention or distraction *(ayoniśo manaskāra)*. The distracted mind does not confine itself to a point, to the thing at hand, but flits like a butterfly from the one to the other. It results in differentiating, identifying, synthesizing things. Wisdom, on the other hand, is intensity of concentration of mind *(nirvikalpa-jñāna)*, the thing is known then as it really is. Ignorance is beginningless but has an end. Together with the other afflictions *(kleśa)* it can be annulled. Ignorance itself is unreal *(māyā)*. If real, the products would be real and there would be no way of changing the world-process. If the afflictions belong to one's nature, how can they be abandoned? Afflictons (ignorance, desire, and aversion), works, and results are like fairy castles, mirages, dreams.[82]

81 *Madhyamaka-kārikā*, XXV, 9, tr. by T. Stcherbatsky in *The Conception of Buddhist Nirvāṇa.*, p. 48.

82 Murti, p. 238-242.

Two truths.

The Madhyamaka makes a distinction between the truth and the phenomena, between what is true in itself and what is true to the percipient. These two truths are called 'highest truth' *(paramārtha satya)* and 'covered' or 'conventional truth' *(saṁvṛtisatya)*. The first is knowledge of truth without distortion, the last reality as viewed through the veil of our ideas and categories of thought. The first only is truth in the ultimate sense, but the latter is not totally to be disregarded, since the practical life, that always forms the point of departure of the liberation path, is governed by these ideas and categories. Categories of thought and points of view distort the truth, which itself is nothing but the absence of thought, and the object of the innermost experience of the wise. It is so intimate and integral that we cannot be self-conscious of it. Conventional reality covers the truth, makes it appear otherwise. All things have two forms, according to the manner of apprehension: they can be apprehended as they are *(tattva)* or wrongly *(mithya)*. There is difference in quality but not in quantity between the absolute and the phenomena.[83]

FREEDOM. In the Madhyamaka, as in all Buddhism, freedom, identified with *nirvāṇa*, is not freedom of action, but freedom from pain and suffering. Since suffering is ultimately due to ignorance, it also consists in a being free from all illusion. This means for the Mādhyamika: being free from all perspectival viewpoints, doctrines, and categories of thought, being free from all ideas, imaginations, and thought-constructions *(vikalpa, kalpanā)*. It is thought and imagination (which forms the basis of all thought and language), that projects worlds in consonance with our desires, or worlds that threaten our comfort. It leaves us with the hopes and fears, desires and aversions, that blind us to the truth of the world that is really before our eyes, and within the reach of our touch. It makes that we really see our own projections, and reality only as subservient to these. The world, not willing to submit to our desires, causes that we suffer from them. If we do not accept the presence, but always want something else, live with

83 Ibid., pp. 228-255.

our thought in something else, life must always be unfulfilled, and this is painful. Do away with your imagined projections, then you will be freed from your desires. Freed from your desires you will be free from suffering. You live no longer with a frustrated will. Freedom is the total cessation of imagination *(sarva-kalpanā-kṣayo hi nirvāṇam)*. Ārya-deva says: 'Take away all.'[84] One should desist from vice, free oneself from the substance-view, and lastly give up all standpoints. These are the stages of progress. Freedom is a process of negation of ignorance and afflictions *(kleśa)*. The state of freedom, also called '*samatā*' (evenness) does not admit of degrees. It is Buddhahood itself. All beings carry it in themselves as a potential *(tathāgatagarbha)*, all living beings are endowed with the essence of the Buddha, but only by the path of the 'Ārya' it is realized. The immaculate, which is of spiritual nature, pervades all that exists. Beings are in various stages of purification, but one as Buddha. In the process of freeing oneself from ignorance and defilements, wisdom *(prajnā)*, which is one with the absolute, gradually becomes manifest.[85]

Freedom is spiritual.

The highest good is spiritual freedom. In the spiritual man there is no division between the surface motives and the deeper unconscious drives; he is not torn asunder by conflict and confusion, he is fully integrated and unified. This is done by wisdom *(prajnā)*. He has abandoned the defilements of ignorance, desire, and aversion. There is complete identity between the individual and the cosmic good. Egoity is absent. The pain of another being is one's own. All spirituality is the attainment of this universal interest and the elimination of private standpoints and values. The spiritual act is not a means to an end, it is the end itself. It therefore necessarily carries within itself the criterion of its efficacy and soundness *(pratyātma-vedanīya)*.[86]

84 *Catuḥśataka*, 3, VIII, 15, in Murti, p. 256.
85 Murti, pp. 256-58
86 Ibid., p. 260 [pp. 258-275].

Ajanta, mural, ca. 2nd century AD, Wiki Commons

Chapter 7
Idealism

Traditionally, Buddhism was divided into three 'disciplines': ethics *(vinaya)*, meditation *(dhyāna)*, and metaphysics *(abhidharma)*. In dealing with the Abhidharma and the Madhyamaka – although these two differ in intellectual outlook – we have been treating the lines of thought of those in Buddhism who had specialized themselves in the logic of the system. Now, in dealing with the system of idealism, also called 'Yogācāra,' we find the thought of those who had specialized themselves in the practice of yoga and meditation. The name 'Yogācāra' (practice of yoga) seems to make this perfectly clear. In origin, the Yogācāra, therefore, should not be considered as a separate school. Novices entering the community were selected according to their disposition. The more simple minded could become happy by applicating themselves to the Vinaya discipline, the intellectuals were fit to study the Abhidharma, and the mystical types could specialize in yoga. In the Madhyamaka we found, that language cannot reach the ultimate, which is transcendent in every respect. The mystic, however, holds that the ultimate, although not expressible in words, can be touched by experience. Whereas we find that the Mādhyamika dialectic robs the basis of any intellectual standpoint, so that no positive affirmation of the ultimate results, in the Yogācāra we meet with a shift from logic to experience, and in this field, not in the way of ratiocination, but in that of description of experience, of its structure and condition, something positive can be said.

The Yogācāra as a school of idealism, is said to have begun with Asaṅga, the brother of a Vasubandhu, in the 3d or 4th century, during the Kuṣāṇa reign. It originated later than the Madhyamaka of Nāgārjuna. The central theme of this idealistic Yogācāra is, that in the depth of meditation, when, the passions are conquered, and the world is abandoned, there still remains something to be affirmed, consciousness in its most pure and undifferentiated form. And this untainted consciousness, as the ultimate base and residue of all variety, is the matrix from which the world with its distinctions of time, extension, and relations springs. These are all painted on the canvas of pure consciousness, they cannot be without it. The purity of primeval consciousness is soiled by the distinctions of the world, created by the strokes of imagination. These distinctions do not represent real things – the only real thing being the canvas – but they are mere cognitions *(vijñaptimātra)*. They can, and should be cleansed away to return to original purity.

A second thought peculiar to this early form of idealism is that of the potential mind, the storehouse of consciousness *(ālaya-vijñāna)*. This thought was probably derived from the Vaibhāṣikas (Sarvāstivādins). As we have seen, these, distinguished between the actual appearance of a phenomenon *(dharma)*, which is momentary, and its eternal nature *(svabhāva)*. The store-consciousness of the early Yogācāras now can be considered as the sum-total and unity of *dharma*-essences, which are potentialities for life's appearance. The blank canvas of consciousness is not only a reality in itself, but also so many potential paintings. It contains, as it were, the seeds of possible occurrences, which always take the form of particular cognitions. Life lies dormant in this potentiality, which may be considered as a being, subconscious, awaiting the conditions on which it can manifest itself in one form or another. Time unfolds it. It also can be considered as the whole of dispositions *(vāsanā)* left over by the former acts of a stream of consciousness, which forms at the same time the potentiality for its future appearance. Later in the development of idealism, the term 'store-consciousness' was abandoned. We do not find it any more in Dignāga and Dharmakīrti, although these thinkers still hold to the idea of a body of subconscious dispositions, which, in fact, is the same thing.

For the Yogācāra, the absolute, as a universal consciousness cleansed of all distinctions, can be known by inner experience. It usually is called '*pariniṣpanna*,' and it is the realization. the apprehension of things as figments of the mind. As a rule, it is not possible to rise above the acceptance of the reality of the imagined *(parikalpita)* and dependent *(paratantra)* existence, the common world of daily experience, which functions as a practical truth. One does not see that it is really like a dream. These two, the absolute and the imagined existence, correspond to the 'highest' and 'covered truth' of the Madhyamaka.

How can imagination form its constructions, and how can it account for the orderliness of the apparent world? To answer this question, logic does not suffice, we should enter the field of the theory of knowledge (epistemology). In Indian terminology: we should investigate the laws of valid knowledge *(pramāṇa)*. In the West such a search for the basis of our knowledge and experience is also called transcendental logic, to contrast it with deductive logic, which goes from a set of axioms to a system of conclusions. Transcendental logic, on the other hand, reduces the complexity of our experience and knowledge to its basic elements, as e.g. sense data, apprehensions, concepts etc. It was Dignāga who made the means of valid knowledge *(pramāṇa)* the centre of his thinking. He wrote the *Pramāṇasamuccaya* (Compendium of valid means of knowledge). Dharmakīrti wrote on it a long commentary, the *Pramāṇavārttikam*. With these works we will deal in the following, but for the sake of completeness of exposition, we shall give a short survey of other authors and works in the tradition of idealism.

H*ISTORY*. The tradition of idealism seems to start with a certain Maitreyanātha, a vague figure, to whom are ascribed a few works, such as the *Basic verses of the Jewel-Casquet Section (Ratnagotravibhāga* or *Uttaratantra)* a work that as a whole rather should be attributed to a certain Sāramati (or Sthiramati I), living in the 4th century. It seems to have begun with the feeling that the interpretation of the *'Prajñāpāramitā'* as found in the Madhyamaka, with its strong accent on relativity *(śūnyatā)*, was in danger of losing the essential thing out of sight: liberation as something to be affirmed.

Besides the *Ratnagotravibhāga* and the *Ornament of Clear Insight* (*Abhisamayālaṅkara)*, possibly from the same writer, there are the works of Asaṅga, and his presumed younger brother Vasubandhu, who is sometimes distinguished from Vasubandhu the Sautrāntika, who, according to Frauwallner, lived a century later.[87] Asaṅga must be placed in the third or fourth century, and Vasubandhu, if he be his younger brother, accordingly, not much later. Works of Asaṅga are: the *Compendium of the Abhidharma, Section on Dharma and Dharmahood, Section on the Mean and the Extremes* (maybe of Maitreyanātha), *Ornament of the Mahāyāna-sūtras, Summa of Mahāyāna,* and *Treatise on the Stages of the Yogācāra.* Vasubandhu seems to have written a commentary on the *Sec-*

87 It was Prof. E. Frauwallner who put forward the hypothesis of two Vasubandhus in *On the Date [...] of [...] Vasubandhu* (Serie orientale, Roma, 1951). After initially having given credit to this hypothesis, I seriously have come to doubt it. A reason for this is that the development of logic in Buddhism, from Dignāga onwards, seems to be an elaboration of thought found in the works of Vasubandhu the 'Elder', the said brother of Asaṅga. Now, it is held by Frauwallner that Vasubandhu the 'Younger' wrote the *Abhidharmakośa*, and that the same was the teacher of Dignāga. It is a strange phenomenon then, that Dignāga for the development of his thought should have taken recourse to another Vasubandhu, stranger yet, that he as pupil should not have distinguished between his teacher and the old Master, not even seems to have been aware of this distinction. A like mistake is not plausible in the relationship master-pupil, Ascribing the logical works of Vasubandhu the Elder to Vasubandhu the Younger does not solve the problem. For why is there so much affinity between the thought of the logician Vasubandhu and the older Yogācārin?

It is said that the younger Vasubandhu was a Sautrāntika, the elder a Yogācārin. But this looks over the fact that the Vasubandhu of the *Kośa* speaks with due respect about the Yogācāra masters. Moreover, the tradition following Dignāga fuses Sautrānrika and Yogācāra ideas, and will later be named *Vijñānavāda* or *Yogācāra-Sautrānrika.* Will it then be absurd to suppose that the master on whom this tradition rests, Vasubandhu, was himself a *Yogācāra-Sautrāntika,* fusing Sautrāntika and Yogācāra thought? By the way; in *Die Philosophie des Buddhismus* Frauweallner makes clear, that he does not believe in his own hypothesis. On page 110 he introduces the *Pañcaskandhaka-prakaraṇa* as a work of Vasubandhu the younger and remarks that it is really a Mahāyāna treatise following the Yogācāra of Asaṅga. But this was a mark of Vasubandhu the elder. In treating the *Viṁśatikā* and the *Triṁśikā* under the heading of Vasubandhu the elder, on page 351 he says: 'Meiner Ansicht nach ist Vasubandhu der Jüngere ihr Verfasser, doch kann diese schwierige Frage hier nicht weiter erötert werden.' (According to my opinion V the younger is their author, but this complex question cannot be treated here). Stefan Anacker, in his Introduction to *Seven Works of Vasubandhu*, pp. 7-24, also defends the identity of the said two Vasubandhus. Compare also what I have said in note 15 of Ch. 2 of the present work. If the above hits the mark. some adaptation of the chronologies in this book will be needed. But, since I am not yet certain as to the most plausible chronology, I maintain the present provisional one.

tion on the Mean and the Extremes, and the so-called collections of the *Twenty Verses* and the *Thirty Verses*. He perhaps also wrote a work on logic, the *Exposition of Speech*, but those who accept two Vasubandhus often ascribe this work to Vasubandhu the Sautrāntika.

In that time, or a little earlier, there also appeared *'sūtras'* endorsing the idealistic standpoint. Of these we must mention the *Sūtra on the Freeing of the true Meaning*, the *Garland-Sūtra*, the *Revelation* (descent) *on Laṅka*, and the *Abhidharma-sūtra*. To this circle of early idealists and idealistic texts we must add a second Sthiramati who lived probably a little later than Vasubandhu, and who wrote a commentary on the 'Thirty Verses.' After this time, the tradition of idealism was continued in a modified form by Sautrāntikas with a strong logical and epistemological interest, who are also characterized by the fact, that they drop the separate concept of a storeconsciousness. The interest in logic was probably aroused by discussions with the Nyāya. Vasubandhu II (If he is to be distinguished from Vasubandhu I) possibly wrote the *Exposition of Speech* and through it brought his great pupil Dignāga to his epistemological researches, which inaugurated a second phase of Buddhist idealism. When we place Vasubandhu II in the 5th century, and take for a fact that Dignāga was a very young pupil when he met Vasubandhu (II) as a very old teacher, we can place 50 or 60 years between them, and place Dignāga at the beginning of the 6th century. He wrote the *Light on the Hidden Meaning Commentary*, a commentary on the *Exposition of Speech*, *Tail and Trunk-discourse*, *Critique of the Basis of Apperception*, *Drum of the Wheel of the Middle Term*, *Introduction to Logic*, and his chief work, the *Compendium of the Means of Valid Knowledge*. A pupil of his was Īśvarasena, but a generation later again appeared his true pupil, Dharmakīrti. He was for idealism what Candrakīrti was for the Madhyamaka. Both probably lived in the 7th century, and, perhaps, even shared one teacher, Dharmapāla. The great works of Dharmakīrti are, the *Commentary on the Means of Knowledge* with auto-commentary, the *Ascertainment of the Means of Knowledge*, and a small work the *Drop of Logic*. Again a century later we find Dharmottara writing commentaries on his works. Besides, the latter wrote independent works: the *Critique of the Means of Knowledge*, *Discourse on Exclusion*, *Proof of another World*, and *Proof of Momentariness*. We also should mention again Śāntarakṣita and Kamalaśīla, along

Dates and works of idealist thinkers

date AD	
250 ad, Maitreyanātha, Sāramati	*Jewel-casquet Section* (Ratnagotra-vibhāga)
250 ad	*Ornament of Clear Understanding* (Abhisamayālaṅkāra), *Freeing of the Proper Meaning* (Sandhinirmocanasūtra) *Revelation on Laṅka* (Laṅkāvatārasūtra) *Garlandsūtra* (Avataṁsaka) from which especially the *Double Order Abhidharmasūtra*
290-360 Asaṅga	*Compendium of the Abhidharma* (Abhidharmasamuccaya), *Section of 'Dharma' and 'dharma-hood'* (Dharmdharmatāvibhaṅga)
(Maitreyanātha)	*Section on the Mean and the Extremes* (Madhyānta-vibhāga) *Ornament of the Mahāyāna-sūtras* (Mahāyānasūtrālaṅkāra) *Summa of Mahāyāna* (Mahāyānasaṁgraha) *Treatise on the Stages of the Yogācāra* (Yogācārabhūmiśāstra)
400, Vasubandhu	*Work of Twenty Verses* (Viṁśatikā) *Work of Thirty Verses* (Triṁśikā) T*reasury of the Abhidharma* + commentary (Abhidharmakośabhāṣya) *Exposition of Speech* (Vādavidhi)
450, Sthiramati	*Commentary on* Triṁśikā
500-550, Dignāga	Light on the Hidden Meaning + Comm.(Marmapradīpavṛtti)

500-550, Dignaga	*Exposition of Speech Comm.* *Trunk and Tail Discourse* (Hastavālaprakaraṇa) *Introduction to Logic* (Nyāyamukha), *Critique Concerning the Basis of Apperception* (Ālambanaparīkṣa) *Drum of the Wheel of the Middle Term* (Hetucakraḍamaru), *Compendium of the Means of Valid Knowledge* (Pramāṇasamuccaya)
600 Īśvarasena	
650, Dharmakīrti	*Drop of Logic* (Nyāyabindu) *Ascertainment of the Means of Valid Knowledge* (Pramāṇaviniścaya) *Commentary on the Means of Valid Knowledge* (Pramāṇavārttikā (being a commentary on Dignāga's Pramāṇasamuccaya) *Proof of Other Streams of Consciousness* (Saṁtānāntarasiddhi),
725, Śāntarakṣita	Tattvasaṁgraha
735, Kamalaśīla	
800, Dharmottara	Commentaries on Dharmakīrti *Critique of the Means of Knowlwdge* (Pramāṇa-parīkṣa) *Discourse on abstraction* (Apohaprakaraṇa) *Proof of another World* (Paralokasiddhi) *Proof of Momentariness* (Kṣanabhaṅgasiddhi)
850, Haribhadra	
950, Prajñākaragupta	
950, Jñānaśrī	

with Haribhadra, who were mentioned earlier as Mādhyamikas, but who really represent a syncretism between the Madhyamaka and idealism. Last should be mentioned Prajñākaragupta and Jñānaśrī from the School of Bengal, but then we are already in the tenth century.[88]

DIGNĀGA. Dignāga was born in the Pallava country in the far south at a place called Siṁhavaktra near Kāñci. He became a monk and joined the Vātsiputrīya-school. But its doctrine of the 'person' seemed unintelligible to him. He therefore left the Vātsiputrīyas to study under the Sautrāntika master Vasubandhu, probably in Ayodhya. The greatest part of his life he lived in a rock-dwelling in Kaliṅga (Orissa), but he often visited the university of Nālandā. There he found his students and taught new doctrines on the theory of knowledge, and through it became the founder of a tradition. In the solitude of Kaliṅga he is said to have written his major work, the *Compendium of the Valid Means of Knowledge*. After its completion, he again travelled through India, but in old days he returned to his remote forest dwelling.

Dignāga developed the logical ideas of Vasubandhu into a critique of knowledge. You cannot make progress in the truth unless you have ascertained what the means of valid knowledge are. The theory of knowledge therefore replaces the old Abhidharma, and becomes the basis of all study and practice. Even the *sūtras* cannot be accepted without question.[89]

The reality of the external world.

In the *Critique concerning the Basis of Apperception*, Dignāga touches upon the problem of the reality of the external world. It is in this work, that he comes closest to the idealism *(yogācāra)* of Asaṅga. The work starts with an examination of the realism of the Vaiśeṣika which accepts indivisible atoms as the building bricks of the agglomerates that constitute the things of the visible world. Now Dignāga holds that an external thing must be either an atom, or an agglomerate of

88 Cf. A. K. Warder, Indian Buddhism, pp. 423-523.
89 Ibid., pp. 449-459.

atoms. If it can be proved that neither of these.can exist, it is proved that external things are not realities but ideas in the mind.

Firstly the idea of the atom as an infinitely small indivisible entity cannot be upheld. Although the reasoning seems not quite clear, the idea is like this: an entity, as far as it has extension must be divisible, since it must have an upper part and a lower part, a right part and a left part, and having this, there is a way between these extremes, ergo it must be divisible. On the other hand, if an atom has no extension, it also cannot have properties. Besides, having no extension, its multiplication cannot yield extension either. A mere point is just a nothing. The second idea of the Vaiśeṣika, that there are real agglomerates of atoms which function as independent entities, is also untenable. What is meant by such an agglomerate? That atoms in configuration form an image by themselves? But would that not be like denying the subjectivity of my seeing a crocodile in a cloud, and affirming that the cloud in itself is a crocodile? But admitted, that a configuration of atoms is the cause of my apprehending things in a certain manner, this does not say that it is the object *(viṣaya)* of my apprehension or apperception. For the object is the thing in the way it is apprehended, and not its presumed or real cause. The object, accordingly, in any way is an idea, an image given in consciousness. But since it was already proved that the atoms are fictions, a forteriori their configurations are fictions too. They cannot be the cause even of the apprehension of an object. What then is the cause? Here Dignāga defends the old Buddhist theory of *karma*. Every action leaves behind a trace *(vāsanā)* in the subconscious. Such a trace is like a seed, that in due time ripens in an actual experience, which is nothing else but the retribution of the original deed. The force of this ripening – Stcherbatsky calls it a *biotic force* – produces the actual apperceptions which constitute the apprehensions of the present sense data. In other words: one's dispositions shaped by one's former deeds, make one apprehend the in itself meaningless sense data, provided by the senses through conditioned spontaneity, in such or such a manner. The whole of these dispositions is the whole of the traces left in the subconscious, and constitutes what the earlier Yogācāras called the store-consciousness. It is the law of *Karma* which accounts for the regularity of the world, not natural law. The object of cognition (apperception or apprehension) is, accordingly, something experienced inwardly by consciousness, in introspection. It is nothing else but a figment of consciousness. Subject and object are both internal, they are distinctions within consciousness. There is no difference between the blue object and the sensation of blue. The same idea can be regarded as a cognized object and as the process of cognition.[90]

Theory of knowledge.

Dignāga has become famous not because of his metaphysical insights, but because of the way in which he developed his theory of knowledge on the basis of it. The thinking about knowledge *(jñāna)* traditionally constituted one of the concluding sections of the Abhidharma. For Dignāga it is the most important section of it, so important that he makes it the sole object of his investigations. Knowledge is the basis of all successful practice, also of the liberating practice. Therefore the theory of knowledge is preliminary to the Buddhistic way. The defence seems pragmatic – indeed it is – but this does not mean that knowledge in itself is defined pragmatically by Dignāga. Truth is not defined as success, but rather as knowledge in accordance with reality, or as the exclusion of what is not in accordance with it, viz. all conceptualization.

In contrast to the epistemology of the Nyāya[91], Dignāga accepts but two sources of valid knowledge: sensation *(pratyakṣa)* and inference *(anumāna)*. Religious authority *(śabda)* accepted by the Nayāyikas is not an independent source of knowledge, even the Buddha cannot be trusted on his words. As every other information, the words of the master should be tested in experience. 'Comparison,' also accepted by the Nayāyikas, is no independent source of knowledge either, since it can be reduced to inference. The two ways of gaining knowledge correspond to two basic functions of the mind: pure experience and imagining *(vikalpa)*. In fact, sensation is no means of knowledge at all, since it is identical with it *(jñāna avikalpa)*, which means, that sensation

90 Cf. T. Stcherbatsky, *Buddhist Logic* (vol 1), pp. 519-521.

91 The *Nyāya* is the brahminical counterpart of Buddhist logic. It is based on a much more realistic metaphysics. In addition to e.g. Dignāga, it takes as valid means of knowledge 'analogy' *(upamāna)* and scriptural authority *(śabda)*. Buddhism rejects scriptural authority. (certainly brahminical scriptural authority), and thinks 'analogy can be reduced to 'inference'.

as such cannot err. But sensation is seldom given as such. Most often it is blurred by the imaginations superimposed on it, which, again, are aroused by our desires. Pure sensation is really what remains when all imagining is removed *(pratyakṣa kalpanāpoḍha)*. It is what you see wih all implicit and explicit judgment suspended. It is experience beyond language, inexpressible because of its unique concreteness, since language, which is by its nature general, can only express the general. The object of experience is, accordingly, not a thing (*artha* [also 'meaning']). A thing is by its nature something classified, belonging to a genus *(jāti)*, having qualities, distinctions etc. Experience as such has none of all that. It is without imagination and concept. It is mere presence, with its sensory content, given without any interpretation. It seems that in this idea of sensation we find at the same time the concept of liberation. Inference, based on language, just guides our experience, veiled by imagination to pure, unveiled experience of truth. For in Dignāga's opinion, experience without implicit judgement is not just a chaos of impressions without order and meaning, as it would be thought of in the Kantian tradition, but on the contrary, reality in its most integrated form, not cut into pieces by intellectual distinctions. Apprehension does not constitute our reality, but obscures it. Non-apprehension is not nothingness but givenness.

Sensation.

Sensation reveals the proper marks of reality *(svalakṣaṇa)*. These constitute the uniqueness that cannot be rendered in words, since these by their very nature can only reveal the general characteristics *(samānyalakṣaṇa)*. When, for instance, looking at a lotus, we can just sit down and undergo the integral experience. This experience is in its infinite shades, in its vividness, in its being an integral whole, not to be rendered. It is just this experience, independent even of the fact whether I know that the flower before my eyes is a lotus or not. I can be overwhelmed by the scene without knowing where I am, what kind of waterflowers are before me, even forget about flowers at all and just see, smell, and hear; feel the wind or heat or whatever, experiencing suchness. I can approach the experience in language, especially of the poetic type, or by rendering it through any other art, but this remains a simulation, it cannot render the fullness, it is not the true thing, the thing in itself, i.e. in the way as it is given in its entirety in experience. For the thing in itself is here not something beyond experience but just the totality of the experience itself. Any remembering of this thing itself is just a faint image of the sensation, it is an echo, a picture. What is remembered is just the significant aspect of it. Really all our experiences – as long as they are not of the overwhelming type – do not present the fullness of experience but just significant selections from it. I shall give an example. I recently visited with my little daughter of three years old, and not able to read, an astronomical museum. There were at the spot several computers for the sake of testing the knowledge of whoever touches a button. A screen presents a question with three possible answers. You choose A, B, or C, and the computer answers with RIGHT or WRONG. After playing a while and asking my daughter to answer A, B, or C, another girl came asking for our place, and started again pushing buttons. My little daughter looking over her shoulder enthusiastically cried WRONG, WRONG! I was really a little perplexed; where had she learned to read? Well, the answer was simple, as she later explained to me: a RIGHT screen has another colour than a WRONG screen. But in selecting just the linguistic aspect of the experience, this totally had escaped my notice.

Sensation can be of different types. In the first place it can be the givenness of the data as presented by the five senses. For sensation is defined with reference to the sensory material and not with reference to its cause or object, for the latter is only an object of apprehension with its implied judgement, and not of sensation as such. In the second place there can be sensation of inner phenomena, such as feelings and mental acts as such (e.g. a phantasy conceived as phantasy and not as its objec). In that case the thing in itself and its object, its reference *(ālambana)*, coincide.

Inference.

We have seen, that there is the thing in itself, the unique concrete sensation as such, and its 'external' reference, that of which it is the sensation. This object of sensation, this reference, can never be given, it is always inferred, which means that at best it can be constructed out of abstracted sensory material. The inferred object therefore has no real existence. At best it is useful to guide experience in a good direction.

Imagination, conceptualization, language, and judgement are the pillars on which the process of inference rests. Inference in Indian thinking is a process which concludes from particular to particular: 'I see smoke over there, therefore there must be a fire.' But this process of inference is only possible through the mediation of the universal. When you do not know that smoke in general is always a sign *(liṅga)* of fire, you cannot infer a particular fire when you see a particular formation of smoke. But for the Buddhist there is no eternal idea 'smoke' which carries the implication of 'fire.' There is no real object corresponding to our words. With the exception of the Vaibhāṣikas, Buddhists-are nominalists. As for David Hume, for Dignāga concepts are labels attached to imaginations of a similar kind, and words again are representations of these labels. Words do not refer to real sensations, because the uniqueness of concrete experience is inexpressible. But still our everyday discourse is almost totally canalized by words and concepts, which characterize respectively wholes (in space), series (in time), and situations *(avastha)* [in space-time]. All these constitute abstractions from the fullness of concrete sensation and experience. If these abstractions have no real reference, but are based on mere imaginations, what then is their function? Well, they have the function of limitation. When I utter a sentence, this can by no means be a way to indicate a concrete empirical situation, but it certainly excludes a vast number of such possible situations. And in a limited situation such exclusion can go so far, that the contours *(ākara)* of a concrete sensation can be represented, just as the sketch of a building is the representation *(ābha)* of it. But such a sketch never includes the fullness of detail. It is always a combination of general characteristics *(sāmānyalakṣaṇa)*, which are nothing but figments of imagination. And imagination is illusory, because it is faint in comparison with real sensation; it is limited in the selection of its aspects, and besides arbitrary in the combination of these. It can never concretize in a full sensation, but sieves out the fullness of possibility. There is an indirect relation between words and reality. Words, which imply classifications, make dichotomies in the totality of knowledge. Though they do not relate directly to objects, it may be allowed, that they exclude a part of the totality, negate a part of it. The meaning of a word, the relation between words and objects, therefore, may be defined as 'the exclusion of what is other' *(anyāpoha)*. So by negation it is possible to bridge the gap between the universe of sensation and the unreal universe of imagining.[92]

Imagining is uniting something with a name, a class, a quality, an action, or a substance. It is the combined function of abstraction and representation. It represents abstracted aspects of fullness, and in doing so projects these on full experience itself. And so we create a future and a past consisting of non-existing things, we talk about things that are not present, see ourselves surrounded by existences to which we ascribe independence, while in reality there is no such independence. All the practical impulses of daily life are based on such illusory projections. The things of this world are conceived as logical subjects endowed with fixed amounts of qualities; they can be discretely explicated, while in reality it is the sensory field *(gocara)* that exists as filled with sense data, while the ascription of these to logical subjects rests on mental acts, projective fancies. These ascriptions can only take place on the screen of sensation, and are nothing apart from it.

Inference, based on the imaginative function of the mind, accordingly, does not yield truth in itself. A general conclusion never can be true, but it can close (wrong) roads of experience, and so guide to fuller experience, which is pure sensation.

D*HARMAKĪRTI* Dharmakīti was, just as many others of the important thinkers, born in the south. He was from Trimalaya (maybe Tirumalla). Born in a Brahmin family, he had received a corresponding education. But he was interested in Buddhism, and became a lay adherent. He wished to receive instruction from a direct pupil of Vasubandhu. There only was left the old Dharmapāla from whom he took the vows. He was much interested in logical problems, and therefore went to Dignaga's pupil Īśvarasena, because he was a direct pupil of the deceased master. He became the greatest interpreter of Dignāga's system. Even Īśvarasena conceded that Dharmakīrti understood Dignāga better than he himself did. This understanding became expressed in a great commentary on *Dignāga's Compendium of the Means of Knowledge*. Dharmakīrti's life passed as do the lives of Buddhist philosophers,

92 Cf. A. K. Warder, *Indian Buddhism,* pp. 456, generally on Dignāga: pp. 447-465.

'composing works, teaching, public discussion and active propaganda. He died in Kaliṅga in a monastary founded by him, surrounded by his pupils.'[93]

But Buddhism was already on the decline, Brahmanism and modern devotional Hinduism were in the ascendency. Dharmakīrti grieved about the absence of able pupils who would be able to continue his work. He was very pessimistic about the level of understanding his work would be able to find in the India of his days. He said: 'Mankind is mostly addicted to platitudes, they don't go in for finesse. Not enough that they do not care at all for deep sayings, they are filled with hatred and with the filth of envy. Therefore neither do I care to write for their benefit. However, my heart has found satisfaction in this (my work), because through it my love for profound and long meditation over (every) well spoken word has been gratified.'[94] And: 'My work will find no one in this world who would be adequate easily to grasp its deep sayings. It will be absorbed by, and perish in my own person, just as a river (which is absorbed and lost) in the ocean.'[94] He only found a worthy successor in his pupil's pupil Dharmottara. Afterwards his work was assimilated by Tibetan Mahāyānism, and to a lesser degree by Ceylonese and Burmese Theravāda.[95]

Two levels of truth.

Dharmakīrti's reasoning practically accepts two levels of truth. For developing his epistemology, he is content to accept the Sautrāntika ontology as a base. The exposition of this ontology and epistemology covers most of his work. But the Sautrāntika realism, accepting a reality built up out of evanescent atoms, or – in modern terms – 'quanta,' does not constitute the ultimate metaphysical truth. In fact, the Sautrāntika ontology hides contradictions, and to solve these, one must accept idealism, and explain the diversity of the given world not by external stimuli, but out of internal motivations. In the following, in the first place attention will be given to the prima facie ontology and epistemology, and only at the end, the final interpretation of the facts will follow.

93 T. Stcherbatsky, *Buddhist Logic* (vol i), p. 35-36.

94 Ibid., pp. 35-36.

95 Ibid., pp. 35-36.

Ontology.

Dharmakīrti is just like Dignāga in many respects a Sautrāntika rather than a Mahāyānist in the line of Asaṅga. He makes a distinction between the object as it is given immanently in consciousness and the external cause of this object. There seems to be a reality outside the person, which makes that in the mind a picture is formed. This picture, however, is not a copy of what is there outside. The mental picture presents a whole, while the cause consists of what could be called sense quanta or stimuli. These quanta or stimuli consist of the momentary flashes of e.g. colour quanta, having an impact on the sense of vision. One quantum cannot be noticed, but when a certain swell-value is reached the sense-organ is activated. There are perceived sense data of certain colours and shapes, and finally these are apprehended by consciousness. These apprehensions as particular wholes or things, extended in space and enduring in time, are nothing but constructions of consciousness; they are not the things as they are in themselves, but things constituted in and by consciousness itself. The real things are the flashing quanta that exist for one moment, but not without transmitting their activity to another quantum in the next moment, until by close vicinity this transmits its activity to a perceiving consciousness, which by the energy of these impulses creates its constructions: things, ideas, desires, great dreams, and illusions.

The minds themselves consist of series of apprehensions, being momentary flashings not unlike those of the quanta by which they are influenced. When not barred by external influences each one moment of apprehension transmits its activity to the next one, which therefore will be a consciousness-quantum very much similar to the one by which it was occasioned. This transmitting of impulse, produces the illusion of continuity and time. The senses and other organs are, as functions of the mind, rooted in it. They too exist as quanta to be influenced by other quanta, transmitting their impulses. They grow out of the stream of mind-quanta like branches and twigs from a tree.

Momentariness.

Concerning the momentariness of phenomena Dharmakīrti has the same thought as his Sautrāntika predecessor Vasubandhu. A quantum or event vanishes the moment after it appears, while things taken as substances do not exist at all. But, if nothing interferes, in the next moment a similar event is reproduced as was given in the previous. Destruction has no external cause, but is inherent in appearance. What is called 'destruction' is, that causes make that in the next moment not a similar, but a different event appears. And so it is with everything that can be considered as a 'being.' If quanta are momentary, then how long is a moment? It is just the time needed for one quantumleap.[96]

Causality.
Nothing perishes without transmitting its energy to the next instant. The appearance vanishes, but not the energy that caused it. The transmission of energy does not operate in a straight line. The power is dissipated to a certain extent. The effect is not a perfect reproduction of the cause, since there are subsidiary causes at work. The main cause itself is influenced by other causes, and under their influence produces side-effects in addition to its mere self-reproduction. The appearance in the next moment, therefore, always deviates somewhat from that in the previous, and there will be some other appearances besides. Nothing works in total isolation; everything stands in a network of causal influences. In every single appearance there are to be found echo's of the remoter parts of the universe.

There is a complex of causes *(hetusamāgri)*. A single event never emerges from another single event. It belongs to several complexes, which cause developments in different directions. But an event is never effective as part of a complex. By its own 'responsibility' it makes, together with other events, the complexes that are to occur. There is no real connexion between different events. That cannot be, since each event sets its own time. There is no time in the interval between events, which could measure their contemporaneousness. Time is a 'byproduct' of the transmission of actuality, and because of that cannot be a universal frame of reference to measure its own genesis. One event can only influence another by its own destruction. No two can exist at the same time. For if they did, they could not influence one

96 Cf. T. Vetter, *Erkenntnisprobleme bei Dharmakīrti*, pp. 14-18 (Wien 1964, Hermann Böhlaus) Taken Vetter's facts on Dharmakīrti for granted, his work is followed here, although by taking a different viewpoint, some of his information will appear here in a somewhat different light.

another, i.e. they would not appear, be no event at all, but timeless potentialities, virtualities, in other words: mere ideas.

The accumulation *(sañcita)* of events is the object of perception. The number of what in Whiteheadian terminology could be called 'throbbing actualities,' represents the 'swell value' that stimulates the sensorty system, which in turn is he condition for the apprehemsion of an object, i.e. of its mental presentation. It reveals in an image the attack of amassed events on the sensory system. When the image arises, the sensory stimuli have already vanished; when the stimuli arise, the bombing of events has already passed. The mental image presents what is no more there.

The main effect of a cause is not its perfect copy, but something similar but nevertheless different. There is a series of events, that is selected as such from 'eventual chaos,' just because it presents a succession of sameness of appearance with only slight modification. Any previous event of such a series is called immediate antecedent *(sāmānantara-pratyaya)*. A series of such events is called born out of the same *(sajātiya)*, and as a whole is termed 'stream' *(saṁtāna, saṁtati)*. Dharmakīrti even calls the immediate antecedent with the Sāṁkhya term *upādāna* (what is assimilated, incorporated, apprehended, i.e. the material cause).[97]

Mind.

Just as sensory events, the mind forms a series of events. It is the ultimate medium of actuality. Its true nature is counteracted by ignorance, acts of volition, and desire. It is the purpose of Buddhism to free its true nature, its virtues, such as faith, compassion, friendliness, and wisdom. This can only be done by mental training in which the root of all vice, ignorance, is attacked. This ignorance is the misplaced acceptance of an 'I' the futileness of which must be realized in the concept of I-lessness *(nairātmyadṛṣṭi)*. Then, together with ignorance, thirst is removed, and the veil consisting of all vices taken away from the mind, leaving it in its pristine purity with all its emanating virtues, such as compassion and wisdom. In principle the roots of rebirth are then destroyed. But motivated, not by desire, but by duty, by the vow to save all beings, the mind can remain qualified by pure volition, and

97 Ibid., pp. 18-25.

enter rebirth again, not because of unfree passion, but by free choice. This is the way of rebirth proper to the *bodhisattva*. In this respect Dharmakīrti is a Mahāyānist, although in many other respects a Sautrāntika.[98]

The means of knowledge.

The aim of knowledge is to regulate meaningful action. And successful action is itself the test case for valid knowledge. Knowledge enables purposeful action, and purposeful action validates knowledge.

There are two means *(pramāṇa)* for establishing knowledge, one primary and one secondary. Primary is sense-awareness *(parokṣa)*, or sensory perception. Here we become acquainted with all that is new in reality, and it is that on which all intuition is based. The secondary means is constituted by inference *(anumāna)*. There is yet a third means of knowledge, which really is not a separate means at all, since it is based on the first two. One might call it authority, but it is certainly not unquestionable. The testimony of a man who has proved his trustworthiness by his way of life, can be accepted. This testimony itself is based on experience and inference, and again, even when accepted, the knowledge should again be validated in practice by whoever accepts it.

All knowledge, based on these means, derives its primary ascertainment from intuition. A logical or causal connection can be intuited in only one act of perception. Repeated verification does not yield a higher amount of certainty, since necessity cannot be derived at all from the contingency of time. The value of sensation and experience lies in the fact that they present the object of intuition not that they constitute it. Although truth is eternal, it must be given in temporal succession. Therefore intuition can err. Error can only be ruled out by living according to your intuitions. When they lead you astray into misery and bondage, they must be set aside; when they guide you to freedom, they must be accepted.[99]

98 Ibid., pp. 25-27.
99 Ibid., pp. 27-41

Perception.
Perception is presentation free from imagination and without error. It yields the proper, unique, and individual nature of things *(viśeṣa)* without the interference of the conception of general characteristics *(samānya).* General characteristics are not something real. They are nothing else but the similarities given in the representations of memory and expectation. They are the vague ideas that form the objects of our words and not the distinct givenness of actual perception; they are not immediate presentations, the individuality of which can never be rendered in words.

But although true perception is distinct, not all that is distinct is true. Ordinary perception functions as an instrument of action. It may deceive us, as e.g. in the case of the rope mistaken for a snake. It is the practical test that must verify perception. What guarantees truth? Firstly, a real thing is always object of more than one sense, and besides it can serve an objective aim, and it can be the point of departure of the realization of further aims.

Error not based on imagination mingled with perception, can be based on defects of the sense organs.

There are four kinds of perception: sensory, mental (paragnostic), the appearance of mental phenomena [feelings, acts of will, and so on (in which case the object is given in its entirety)], and yogic perception (in which things are seen which are not present before the sensory perception). The last kind of perception creates its own object. In that sense it is akin to imagination, but it is distinct from imagination because it is not vague.[100]

Inference.
There are three elements contained in every inference: the reason (or cause) *[hetu]*, the predicate, and the (logical) subject. In all cases the predicate is the implication *(vyāpti)* of the reason, and the cause the implication of the effect: if the reason is true, then also the predicate is true; if the effect is there, than also the cause is to be found.

There are three types of inference: (1) those inferring essence or implied quality, called 'reasons of essence' *(svabhāvahetu)*; (2) those inferring a cause, called 'causes of effect' *(kāryahetu)*; and (3) those in-

100 Ibid., pp.37-41.

ferring the non-existence of something (the logical subject) from the absence of something (an effect or property), called 'not having experienced' *(anupalabdhi)*. A little confusing is, that the word '*hetu*' is used here in two different senses, that of 'reason' and that of 'cause.' When used as 'reason' in the first type of inference, it stands for that which contains an implication; when used as 'cause' in the second type of inference, it stands for the implication, i.e. the necessary presupposition or antecedent.

To make the three types of inference clear, we give an example from each of them. Here (s) stands for 'logical subject,' (p) for 'predicate,' (r) for 'reason,' (c) for 'cause,' and (e) for 'effect.'

1) inferring essence	This (s) is a tree (p), because it is an oak (r)
2) inferring a cause	There (s) is smoke (e), [r], therefore there must be fire (c) [p]
3) inferring absence	There (s) is no water (r) therefore there is no river (p)

The first kind of inference is used for 'proving' the Buddhistic verities: 'Something is perishable because it is (given in perception)'; 'It is painful, because it is perishable'; 'It is not-I, because it is painful.'

Unlike the first kind of inference, which is based on language, the second kind of inference may be based only on images or mental representations. In the first place this kind of inference is used to conclude to a series when confronted with a sign of it. If I see the posture, I conclude to the man, and, when I am mistaken, when I see the rope, I conclude to the snake. But I can also reason from the effect to a subsidiary cause, as I do when concluding from smoke to fire. [101]

101 Ibid., pp. 28-31.

Buddha.

As a further means of knowledge the word of the Buddha is introduced. It is not an unquestionable authority. No one can be trusted just on his word, not even the Buddha. Firstly his way of life must make it probable that he does not lie, and secondly it must be asserted that he has something to say that is not evident to everyone. Only a man like that can be expected to reveal the highest goal of action, for only to such a one it is accessible. Once the highest goal is attained, action may come to an end, unless another aim is set, not that of the liberation of the self but of the whole of suffering mankind. And that was the aim of the Buddha's actions. Through these the world is instructed concerning the means of liberation, since, having reached the goal himself, the Buddha knows how to achieve it, and he can teach others about the way leading to it.

As all knowledge, also that accepted from the Buddha should always be validated in practice. Its instruction should be precisely followed, and, only when it is seen that this leads to the goal of liberation, its truth is to be affirmed. The knowledge concerned is about what to do and what to avoid. This knowledge is born from the Buddha's great compassion *(mahākaruṇā)*, and this compassion is at the same time the guarantee, that his teaching is not born from selfish interest. This compassion was acquired by long training through innumerable births. Because of all this the Buddha is considered as a means of knowledge.[102]

Goal and practice.

Intuition, perception *(pratyakṣa)*, is the goal of all action. The ultimate perception is the immediate vision of what until then was merely understood, the four noble truths. Then the ignorance causing dependent origination is overcome, and there is realization of the 'not-I.' In the work of Dharmakīrti this notion of ego-lessness generally takes the place of the noble truths as the ultimate realization of insight. This ego-lessness is also called 'emptiness' *(śūnyatā)*. The vision of emptiness only then makes an end to rebirth when it is practised until the wiping out of the last trace of an 'I,' which comes to the same as the eradication of ignorance.

102 Ibid., pp. 31-34

But not only the error of the acceptance of an 'I' is abandoned. All things are now cognized according to truth. Ignorance takes things, as we imagine them, for existent, but they are not the way we present them. Although not absolutely non-existing, we misrepresent them. That wrong idea of things disappears in intuition, which is knowledge without mental construction *(nirvikalpa jñāna)*. What is thus intuited transcends language, for language is bound to conceptual understanding, which, again, is bound to thought-construction or imagination. Reality in final intuition is contemplated in its own nature and uniqueness. It is here given as the thing in itself *(vastumātra)*. If this is realized, one rises above selfish desire, and acts only for the sake of others *(parārthakriya)*.

But already in daily life we participate in reality. It is not *mere* imagination. Every true experience possesses a moment of fulfilment and emanates something of truth. The realization of an aim in daily life is different from its expectation. And the real appearance of a thing in perceptive experience must be distinguished from its vague representation. But the daily 'fulfilment' of experience, from moment to moment, is not the final end, because it can yield the opposite from what is desired, and also, because one here is still busy to realize the freedom from which only it becomes possible to help others.

For final realization the denial of the 'I' is required, but to live for the sake of others requires something in addition, an insight into universal truth. That insight grows from a thinking of perception, which, by way of so being thought, transforms into what is called contemplation. That is at the same time the highest praxis, because it dissolves the duality of ordinary perception. All duality of 'I' and 'world' is overcome.

Perception in daily life has not yet reached that integral state. It is on the one hand means to the knowledge of an object, on the other hand end. Compared with fancy, which only expects the goal, it presents some shade of the truth. But it is the virtue of imagination that, in this situation of partial fulfilment, it projects the final goal. It seeks to procure desired perception and avoids the opposite. In the process of inference it is a means of knowledge, i.e. when used in a regular and not in a random way. Therefore, perception and inference (using language and imagination) are useful as long as the final end of intuited integrity has not been reached. These useful means stand apart from the sheer deception that never leads to verification, and does not still the passions.[103]

Understanding

There is a cleft between intuitive perception, the goal of all activity, and rational thought. Intuition presents reality, thought copes with mere ideas, fancies, representations. These are the things on which both language and thought are based. Thought, therefore, is not directly in touch with reality, with truth. Intuition is forceful, representation is faint, the first is unique, individual, the second general. One should say, the two have nothing in common. But then, inference was accepted as a valid means of knowledge, which means that it can learn us something about reality. If there is, however, an unbridgeable gap between between reality and thought, how can the latter learn us something about the former?

The way to solve the problem, is to range thought under action. Therewith, admittedly, it lies outside the realm of intuitive truth, but still it has a pragmatic value. Thought yields conclusions. These cannot be taken as truth without any further inquiry, they must stand the practical test. They must lead us to our aims or else be rejected. However, used with precaution, inference indicates the right direction of practice.[104]

Apoha

Things as given in perception are unique and individual. As such they cannot be classified, but according to their function, they can. For although things do appear differently in every perception, and not even one thing does appear twice in the same manner – let alone that different things could be given as identical – they do perform the same functions, serve the same aims. On the ground of sameness of function classes or categories of things can be sundered from other classes. A 'category' is not something in itself; like all concepts it performs a function, which is selecting a group of particulars fit for a certain

103 Ibid., pp. 34-37.
104 Ibid., pp. 41-63.

purpose. This process is called *apoha* (sundering or selection). And so, although things are unbridgeably separated in their individual uniqueness, they are grouped in conformity with the function and destiny, that constitute their meaning. And so things are separated from other things on the ground of human expectation. Now there are methods to build justified expectations and to avoid haphazard ones. These methods are based on the processes of inference of which we have made mention before.[105]

Logical implication

One way of avoiding error in our expectations is the making explicit of the logical implications of a concept. We are endowed with vague and intuitive notions of the meaning of things. But by inferring its implications we can articulate it. If something is an oak, we know it is a tree, that its wood is of such and such a quality, and although no fruit is visible, we can be sure that in due time it will yield acorns. When we clarify what is implied in the concept, we cannot deceive ourselves in our expectations. Once we have recognized something as a shell, we cannot mistake the silvery lustre for silver, but know that it only can be mother of pearl. One concept implies many categories and qualities; all these contain their own implications. And some of these may conflict with the (mistaken) idea and expectation we have of the general concept in which these many qualities are integrated. Therefore making explicit what is in the nature of the class, curbs our projected hopes which constitute the will o' the wisp that leads us astray. Perception, provided that it is not defective, in itself never deceives us, because it does not imply concepts, and therefore has no implied qualities. What on the practical field of our expectations settles the right and the wrong, is the conflict of concepts with experience. Our hopes are directed to a goal, which, as something lying in the future, is never factually present but always represented by imagination. The force of this imagination may cover the present perception, and make that it is taken for what it is not. Inference aids us in establishing the conflict of the implications of the concept, projected by our hope, with actual perception, so that we see that the idea cannot match the

105 Ibid., pp. 47-63.

perceptive content, and acknowledge that it is a projection. The first way of avoiding error, accordingly, is a clarifying of thought.[106]

Representations

Action is aim-directed. Aims as not yet realized are represented in images. Such images differ from the concrete impressions of perception in not being detailed but schematic. They leave out the uniqueness, and in doing so, they are able to represent some species. They form moulds which can contain different specimens of the same type. This fact makes, that representations (schemata) can be associated with words. The representations are a special sort of mental phenomena. They constitute the ever changing forms of the mind. They are the mind-matter, evolving without beginning, but their forms and schemata are stamped by ever new impressions: Impressions leave a schema (idea: *vāsanā*) in the mind, which after vanishing from the present becomes latent, and is thus preserved (i.e. renewed) until it is re-enacted, be it in a conscious memory or in the recognition of a new impression of something similar. In the last case, the schema may be adapted. In this way, the representation is the mediator between the general concept and the concrete impression. Being always a representation of a goal, the schema aims at realization in a corresponding impression. It is like a seed *(bīja)* which ripens into the actual fulfilment of the desired sensation. The fulfilment is not possible if principally the idea has no corresponding impression. Ideas can match an impression, as the idea of water and the concrete sensation of it, or they may not, as e.g. in seeing water in a mirage. But there are ideas which are completely baseless, such as the figments of metaphysical speculation, as e.g. the idea of primeval matter *(pradhāna)*. The water of the mirage cannot stand the practical test: it cannot quench thirst, and besides, it cannot be given to more than one sense; but for the speculative fancies there is not even a test.

Ideas based on impressions and stimuli yield practical understanding – although they cannot copy real experience in its uniqueness – for they can serve to distinguish one thing from another. Every real experienced thing serves an aim. E.g. a cow gives milk. The individuality of each particular cow is irrelevant to this function. 'The idea itself

106 Ibid., pp. 47-49.

does not fulfil the aim ... but the aim is connected to the image, and it can be fulfilled if the image sprouts from an impression, and fits in with the schema of an already existing idea.'[107] Such a representation covers a field of reality and is therefore called 'real as covering' *(saṁvṛtisat)*. It guides action to the proper place. The real thing fulfils the goal, the water fulfils the goal of satisfying thirst, being recognized by the idea which in itself cannot quench thirst. Although the real thing is thus different from the idea, the latter still is useful, for the idea does not fit in with non-watery things. Although it does not satisfy me, it guides me to my satisfaction. The idea eliminates undesired impressions of reality. Mistakes are still possible if the lead-idea is not sufficiently articulated. Then the mirage can be taken for water etc. 'The mould must fit ever more tightly around the particular and the expectation of an aim, corrected by experience, must be coupled to ever more precise representations.'[107]

Meaning and judgement

Individual reality is beyond representation and language. Still our ideas with their implicit meaning, i.e. judgement, have practical value. How is this possible? The answer is, that the idea as such is not completely congruent with reality. It is schematic, whereas reality is detailed. But because of that, one idea can cover a range of concrete phenomena, phenomena that perform a similar function, but it excludes the (individual) phenomena which do not perform that function. And, since in practical matters, it is the realization of some function that counts, the individual difference of phenomena, although constituting the ultimate theoretical truth, is of no practical value, just as little as is the individual difference between the individual acts that satisfy my objectives. If I want to quench my thirst, it does not matter whether I go to the the well or to the cistern. What matters is, that I am saved from exhaustion.

In thought the individual things are thus represented by images of a general and schematic character. Under the influence of actual experience, this vague inner image becomes the subject of semantic refinements. The water I drink appears with a certain colour and a certain taste. New ideas, accordingly, are seen to specify the general idea of

107 Ibid., pp. 49-59.

water, and the range of phenomena covered by the now specified idea of water, becomes smaller. For only the overlap of say the idea of 'water,' 'blue,' and 'salty' presently covers the subject of experience. But even these qualities that actually come to experience in a cognition, do not render the uniqueness and individuality of the reality before me. For this reality is not a combination of different general ideas, of which each can be sundered apart, but a singularity of which there is no second. Besides the three qualities mentioned, it has infinite distinctions that escape any particular cognitive act. But although escaping judgement and the projection of meanings, it is this which constitutes the perceptive element in every cognition. Judgement, by projecting a schematic idea, sunders the perceptive content according to its criteria. According to human aims, the same stone can be classified as a hammer or as a grinder. The same piece of wire can be used either to conduct electric current or as a rope. This process of sundering or sorting things according to our practical categories is called '*apoha*'. It takes the form: 'This *(idam)* is "P".' Here 'this' is the mental representant of the thing categorized, and 'P' is the category predicated. Such a judgement (i.e. a projection of meaning) contains a truth and a falsity; a truth insofar as it sets apart the thing from other things that cannot fulfil my aims (in this sense the nature of the thing provides the reason for my judgement), a falsity insofar as the thing in its uniqueness and individuality is more than a mere expedient, viz. a fullness that cannot be exhausted in any finite process of imagination and nomenclature.[108]

Word and sentence

Words represent meanings and judgements in language. They are only meaningful in the arrangement of a sentence. The purpose of spoken or written language is to rouse the corresponding representations in the mind of someone else. And these lead the person adressed to the thing intended; it makes him do or understand something. Language does not represent a system of self-contained meanings (connotations), but is merely denotative. Its main function is to select possibilities. This negative process of sundering out, excluding, what is not desired, creates the illusion of a positive meaning, but in reality it is

108 Ibid., pp. 54-59.

only a selection-criterium, since the meanings stand for the selecting schemata that guide the mind by limiting its scope and direction. Limitation and exclusion are coterminous with language. There are no words or images pertaining to everything. The fact that language and meaning always direct one towards something, implies that pure theoretical knowledge is impossible. Even philosophical works aim at something; they intend to have some effect on others, to serve them, to guide them to somewhere. Even if one doubts whether anyone can understand, the purpose of convincing is still there.[109]

The idealist solution of the problem of knowledge

Dharmakīrti made a distinction between the representation , the schema, selecting a group of particulars according to functionality, and the perception, i.e. cognition free from representations and error. What is the mark of this distinction? Whereas e.g. a visual perception and a visual representation have in common that both present a visual image, they differ insofar as the one (the representation) presents the image of a fixed type, which selects from the unbounded field of vision finite forms of a certain shape, while the other presents the whole field in its complex fullness and diversity. While the representation yields us one finite scheme, the perception provides us with a complex variety, which is the very field of application of the different finite schemes. Therefore the very presence of multiplicity in perception proves that it is free from representation.

But now, there is the Sautrāntika teaching, that a multiplicity of momentary atomary events causes a cognition in the mind. When the cognition appears, the cause has already vanished. Besides, the matter-events are separate, while the cognition imposes upon it a unity of form, in which the separate units do not appear. If this is so, the true objects, the atomary events, are not perceived. What is actually perceived, is what Dharmakīrti counts as a representation, a schema imposed upon a plurality, covering it. On the Sautrāntika presupposition the multiple object of cognition could not be given in perception, but, in fact, the multiplicity, variety, diversity is given in it. Therefore, the theory of disparate momentary atoms causing cognition must be

109 Ibid., pp. 59-63

abandoned. There is no object transcending the immanent content of perception. At the same time the idea of truth as the correspondence of idea and reality must be given up. And no longer can subject and object be considered as two.

Knowledge now springs from the inner conditioning and spontaneity of the mind itself. But if such is the case, the theory of causality requires a reinterpretation. Up to now, schemata, representing aims, were explained out of the latent imprints of past impressions. These imprints are to be considered as the sunken worlds of countless lives, lying outside the rays of present attention. Actual representation then is the re-enactment of these imprints in a schematic form. With one stamp can be made many prints, which all differ somehow in individual character. The working of experience is exactly opposite: out of many imprints, i.e. latent impressions of experience, is made one schematic representation. These representations, selecting aims according to function, guide our action in the world. Perceptive experience, itself cause of the imprints, and the retribution of deeds, were explained in the Sautrāntika view – which is Dharmakīrti's own prima facie view – by the causality between entities in the real world outside, and by its impact on the particular stream of mind. As now this external world has dissolved in immanence, actual (perceptive) experience, and retribution of deeds, must be explained within mind itself. This means that, besides representations, also experience and retribution are conditioned by imprints instead of being conditioned by external factors.[110]

three aspects of consciousness

The act of knowledge has three facets: there is not only the distinction between knowledge and the known, the object, in which knowledge is conscious of a certain shape attributed to something; there also is the fact that the act is selfconscious. Neither the selfconsciousness nor the object are something apart from the knowing act. Already early Buddhism renounced the idea of a knower beside the act of knowing. However, the Sarvāstivāda and Sautrāntika had introduced the external object in the form of ephemeral atoms into Buddhistic epistemology. This object, moreover, is at best cause of the form cognized

110 Ibid., pp. 63-71.

in consciousness. The appearing form does not mirror it and must be attributed to the projective faculty of the mind. But why then accept these atoms, this external object at all? As no object is conceivable apart from its being known, it is a strange thing that there should exist entities that in not being able to appear in their own shape, can never be objects of any cognizing act. It is better to conceive subject and object as being inherent in the knowing act itself.

The coercion which is implied in perception need not be explained by some working from outside, but is also understandable from the working of the previous moment in the stream of consciousness *(samanāntara-pratyaya)*, which may be taken as the sole condition of the present. The subconscious dispositions in this stream *(sūkṣma-manovijñāna)* carry with them the ripening retributable deeds (acts of volition) of the past. Perception is, accordingly, merely the retribution of deeds immanent in the development of consciousness. This consciousness is now conceived as a stream that has swallowed the other four elementary phenomena of early Buddhism as aspects of its own essence.

Just like the object, also the subjective side of the cognition is immanent in the act of knowledge itself. The cognition is self-conscious, which means that the realization 'I perceive' may accompany all my perceptions. Of every perception it can be said afterwards 'I have perceived.' Every act of knowledge is evident in itself. Knowledge projects an object, but by that very act it candles the light in which it sees itself. And this lightening of self-consciousness, in fact, is the true purpose of all cognitive acts. Knowing is revealing: the light of the sun reveals the world, but it needs no lamp to reveal itself. If knowledge should not be visible in itself, the whole world would be in darkness.

But even the immanence of the object in consciousness does not constitute ultimate truth. Like it was shown, that the logical distinction between concepts does not fit the uniqueness presented by perception, so also the difference between knowledge, subject, and object is merely based on an artificial distinction. For the wise, experience is a wholeness that cannot be torn apart. Only the ignorant here see difference.[111]

111 Ibid., pp. 71-77.

The pure light of true knowledge

When there is no real world outside the mind, the whole process of liberation becomes an interplay between truth, or true knowledge (that pervades everything) and ignorance. Ignorance hides and covers the true nature of the mind, which in reality itself is truth. Mind is bound by inner confusion and mental blockings, unaware of its own nature, but freed by the practising of the Buddhistic path, it displays its innate happiness and truth through the whole of space, be it, that by sheer compassion a free mind, a *bodhisattva*, can choose to take on new bodies for the sake of guiding the world to the ultimate goal, i.e. freeing all minds from the illusion of oppressive objectivity and externality.[112]

The problem of intersubjectivity

Dharmakīrti wrote a work on the repudiation of solipsism *(saṁtānāntara-siddhi)*. He was therefore aware of the problem which the interpretation of intersubjectivity yields in the context of idealism. He solves the problem by stating that the representations of our own body, feelings, thoughts etc. differ from those of the mental life of others. The first have the form 'I speak', 'I go' etc, the second the form 'he speaks,' 'he goes' etc. Just as the form of the first points to my own experience, from the form of the second we must conclude to the experience of other streams of mind. The establishment of others, accordingly, is similar as in realism, only making a shortcut. The reasoning of the realist concludes from another body to another mind, the idealist concludes from a different form of representation to a different will. These different wills all have their own workings and the collectivity of these workings constitutes the intersubjectivity of our world. That different minds can share their illusions is like people suffering from the same eye-disease, who share each other's optical distortions of vision.

But what sets one stream of mind apart from another? We saw it was will. But if will, and its workings, as the principle of individuation is set aside, then mind is no longer characterized, it seems, by different individual appearances. Therefore in the final knowledge, when there is no more ego, no more desire, the idea of plurality must vanish from the mind. As long as there is a world constituted by collective aims and

112 Ibid., pp. 83-88.

works, there must be assumed other minds, but if there is no longer a diversity of willing, and no more limitation of knowledge, idealism cannot any longer establish plurality. It also does not want to do so.[113]

113 Cf. T. Stcherbatsky, *Buddhist Logic* (vol. 1), pp. 521-524..

Borobudur, Java, 4e, 5e century, Wiki Commons

Part II

Buddhism In China

Buddhism entered China as early as the first century, but in the period of disunity, after the collapse of the Han-dynasty, between 221 and 589 AD, it became a considerable force. From the beginning it was of an early Mahāyānist form. We find ideas akin to the Indian Madhyamaka. And also early Māhāyana *sūtras*, such as from the '*Ratnakūṭa*' collection or from the *'Instruction of Vimalakīrti' (Vimalakīrti-nirdeśa-sūtra)* were held in high esteem. These thoughts were brought to China by the Dharmaguptakas, an offshoot of the Sarvāstivādins, but apparently with Mahāyānistic leanings.

Buddhism in China spread from the east. Important was the Indian enclave Chotan in the Tarim Basin. From here came the Indian prince Kumārajīva, who as a Chinese captive translated many Buddhist texts in the second half of the 4th century and in the beginning of the fifth. But already a few hundred years before his appearance in China, there were established some rivalling schools. Most of these schools tried to make Buddhism understandable to the Chinese mind by pointing to its analogies with Daoism. The relativity or 'voidness' of all phenomena *(śūnyatā)* was compared with the ideas about 'non-being' of Lǎozi and Zhuāngzi. Probably it was this affinity of the Mahāyāna ideas with Daoism, that especially favoured the spread of this type of Buddhism. But Mahāyānism, it must be stressed. does not reject the classical *Three baskets.* It took them over from the Sarvāstivādins and the Dharmaguptakas, and the resulting Chinese *Tripiṭaka*, called in Japanese the

Taishō-tripiṭaka, is more voluminous than any other. It even contains many classical *Theravāda* works. Until the rise of the Sòng dynasty (about 1000 AD) Buddhism became the major intellectual force.[1]

1 Cf. Fung Yu-lan, *A History of Chinese Philosophy*, Princeton 1953/1983. Here part II, pp. 239-240. My exposition of Chinese philosophy is much indebted to this work of Fung, especially to Ch. VII of part II of this great work (using the translation of Derk Bodde). I felt the need of including something of Chinese Buddhism also in this work. Here thorough work already been done, I made ample use of it and spared my energies for the scrutiny of those parts of Buddhist history less well systematized. In the following, text between square brackets are my additional remarks.

Chapter 8

The Assimilation of Daoism

In this same period of the rise of Buddhism, there was also a revival of Daoism. The syncretistic spirit of the time failed to see the principal difference between the two streams of thought. One felt that only different names were used for the same realities. The 'non-being' (wú) of the Daoists was just another name for the 'emptiness' (*śūnyatā*) of the Buddhists. Sages of Buddhist and Daoist origin were compared by Sūn Chuò (4th century). Also Daoist terminology was used to explain Buddhist ideas. This was called the *method of analogy*. So was, e.g. the method of resignation as practised in yoga equated with the principle of non-activity *(wúwéi)* of Daoism.

T*HE SIX HOUSES.* The earliest Buddhism in China was known to be divided in six '*houses*' and seven *schools.* There are no actual texts left from this period, only some scattered quotations in the *Zhōngguān-lùn sū* (Commentary on the Mādhyamika Śāstra), and the sub-commentary on the same work, the *Zhōnglùn sūjì*, written by the Japanese monk Anchō between 801 and 806 AD. The difference between *houses* and *schools* solely consists in that the first *house* contains two closely akin but variant schools. The other *houses* coincide with the *schools.* The schools (houses) are:

1) School of original non-being *(Běnwú)*
2) Variant school of original non-being *(Běnwú yì)*

3) School of matter as such *(Jísè)*
4) School of non-being of mind *(Xīnwú)*
5) School of impressions *(Shíhán)*
6) School of phenomenal illusion *(Huànhuà)*
7) School of causal combination *(Yuánhuì)*

The school of *original non-being* was founded by Dào'ān (312-385). He wrote a work called *Xìngkòng lūn* (Treatise on the emptiness of the nature of things), now lost. What we know about the work is, that it defended the idea, that the five groups of elementary phenomena: consciousness, conation, sense data, feeling, and apprehension (the so-called *skandhas*) have no true reality. Their nature is empty (*śūnya*, *kōng*). It therefore taught the early Mahāyāna doctrine of the non-substantiality of phenomena *(dharma)*, also called in Sanskrit *dharma-nairātmya*. The second (variant) school was headed by Fǎshēn (286-374). He said that all things have evolved from original non-being. It seems that here the idea of the voidness of the elementary phenomena is dressed in a more Daoist terminology.

The third school is that of *matter as such*. It teaches that sensory things are *empty*, i.e. that they lack a permanent nature of their own. It does not accept that the atomary basis of this matter is empty too. The idea seems to be, that sensory forms are necessarily related to consciousness. The mind imposes the perceptible form on the cause of perception, the invisible atoms which activate the senses. What is perceived therefore is not real, but its causes, the atoms, are. The idea expressed here, accordingly, seems to be akin to that of the Indian Sautrāntika.

Also reckoned to this school, is Zhīdūn or Dàolín (313-366), but his teaching is really different. It is again Mahāyānistic. Mind and matter are 'empty' in the sense that they only exist in dependence on something else. They exist only as a result of causation and not in themselves. But as such, as caused and dependent existence, there is no place where they do not exist. But the cause of matter is not an atomary matter in itself, but probably antecedent matter which·itself is again dependent on its antecedents.

The fourth school is that of *non-being of mind*. It was developed by the teacher Zhú Fǎwēn. It does not want to deny the reality of things as such. But when there is no clinging to things, the mind is empty of their apprehension, i.e. the mind does not conceptualize the world. Other schools considered this doctrine to be a heresy.

The school of *stored impressions* is the fifth. In the Sòng period (420-478) appeared Yú Fǎkāi. He said:[2]

> 'The threefold world is the abode of the night (of mundane existence), and the mind and consciousness are the source of the great dream (taking place during that night). All the (phenomena of) existence which we now perceive are the apparitions of that dream. When we awaken from it and the long night gives way to day, the consciousness which gives rise to illusion becomes extinguished and the threefold world is all (seen to be) empty. At this time it (the mind) no longer has anything from which to be produced, yet there is nothing it cannot produce.'

The commentator Anchō remarks, that this school distinguishes a highest and a lower truth. The lower truth is the world seen through illusion, while the highest truth represents the emptiness of all things. Taking into consideration also the name of the school, we may safely conclude, that here we find a Chinese version of the Yogācāra.

The sixth school is that of *phenomenal illusion*. It is associated with the teacher Dàoyī (early 5th century). He says that the *dharmas* of ordinary truth are illusion.[3]

> 'All *dharmas* are equally illusory, and constitute what pertains to ordinary truth. But the spirit *(shén)* is genuine and not empty, and as such pertains to the highest truth. For if this spirit were likewise empty, to whom could the Buddhist doctrine be taught, and who would there be to cultivate its path, renounce the world, and become a sage?'

The seventh school is that of *causal combination,* headed by Yú Dàosuì, who says, that being as worldly truth results from the combining of causes. With the abandonment of causes non-being results. And this is the highest truth.[4]

2 Fung Yu-lan, *History*, part ii, p. 256.

3 Ibid, p. 257.

4 Ibid. pp. 239-58

SĒNGZHÀO. In Buddhism there is a fundamental contrast between *nirvāṇa* and *saṁsāra*. It is the contrast between the absolute *(bhūtatathatā, zhēnrú)* on the one hand and time on the other. Thinkers of the period of disunity equated this contrast with the Daoist one between *non-being (wú)* and *being (yǒu)*, *quiescence (jìng)* and *movement (dǒng)*, between *non-activity (wúwéi)* and *activity (yǒuwéi)*. In this period we find more than a mere stressing of analogies, we find original thinkers, of which Sēngzhào (384-414) is one of the most important.

He was a poor monk from Jīngzhào. He lived as a copyist and from this he derived his learning. He was attracted by mysticism. Hence came his admiration for Lǎozi and Zhuāngzi. But he lacked something in them, which he found in the *Vimalakīrtinirdeśa sūtra*. After reading it, he said: Now I know where I belong. He thereupon became a Buddhist monk, well versed in the *Tripiṭaka*, but with a special fondness for Mahāyāna, esp. of the Madhyamaka type.

Zhào was a contemporary of Kumārajīva and worked together with him at the translation of the *Pañcaviṁśati-sāhasrika-prajñāpāramitā*. Kumārajīva praised him for his understanding and his style. His works are gathered in the *Book of Zhào*.

Movement.

We shall say something on Sēngzhào's affinities with the Madhyamaka and on his concept of wisdom.

As regards the first, we find, that, similar to Nāgārjuna, Sēngzhào analyses the notions of *movement* and *rest,* and of *existence* and *non-existence,* choosing for a middle way between the extremes of interpretation.

Zhào's idea of movement is that of the movement of time. Reflecting on it, he contends that no thing from the past comes into the present and that the present never changes into the past. Things past are immutable. The truth of their being such and such, their particular situation at their specific moment, is there for ever. Likewise, the actuality that is the present is there for ever as actuality, as spirit *(shén)*. Truth and spirit are beyond change. Only seemingly the present transforms into the past. Therefore, change, movement, is only illusory appearance. But that illusion is the world of time to which our notions refer.

The fact is, that there is no permanent identity. The thing now is different from the thing a moment ago. New existence is added to the past, which thereby in itself remains unaffected. Each individual moment remains in place at its relative position in time or history. It can never fail to be conditioned by the preceding moment and to condition by itself the next moment. The present moment cannot fail to be conditioned by the previous. Therefore, in the present is contained and preserved the amassed working, the total efficacity of everything that has passed. For *karma* can never perish. 'A mound borrows its completion from the first basket full of earth;' 'The finishing of a long journey depends on the first step taken.'[5]

Because phenomena have no permanent identity, they neither change (or move) nor remain the same (be in rest). But since still there appears phenomenal change in the sense that different moments have different contents, it may also be said that phenomena *(dharma)* change in appearance while being quiescent.

Existence.

Sēngzhào writes: 'All things are really in one way non-existent and in another way not non-existent. Because of the former fact, though (seemingly) existent, they are not existent. Because of the latter fact, though (seemingly) non-existent, they are not non-existent.'[6]

This is, because things are subject to causation; their being is dependent on other (former) being, and not self-contained. For if things would be self-contained, they would be eternal. In the same way, the non-being of things is also relative, non-eternal, and dependent on conditions. Both, the existence and non-existence of things are dependent, conditioned, relative. That's why existence and non-existence are themselves relative towards each other in the same way as the coming to be (appearance) and vanishing (disappearance) of things. The being of things is not absolute, and their non-being is still manifested in forms, and is, therefore, not absolute either.

The popular view of being as 'being there,' and of non-being as 'being absent' is accepted by Zhào. But what is there is not (ultimately)

5 Fung Yu-lan, *History*, part ii , p. 262.
6 Ibid., p. 264.

real. Things exist in one sense, but not in another. If 'being' does not mean that things are real, and 'non-being' does not mean that they are obliterated without trace, the being and non-being, though different terms, express the same basic meaning.[7] Being and non-being are not antithetic but complementary. Things neither exist nor do they not exist, or, they are both, existent and non-existent.

Wisdom.

Zhào interpretes wisdom *(prajñā)* as sage-wisdom. If this sage-wisdom may be ranged under knowledge at all, it is a very special kind of it. For in ordinary knowledge, there is a distinction between the knower and the known and such distinction is absent in sage-knowledge, which culminates in the highest truth *(paramārtha-satya, zhēndì)*, and this can never be objectified as some particular entity to be known. In *On Prajñā not being Knowledge* Zhào writes: 'Because wisdom is assumed to know what is to be known, and to apprehend the qualities (of things), it is said to be knowledge. But since absolute truth inherendy lacks any phenomenal qualities, how is it to be known?'[8]

Knowledge and the *known* are relative terms, and what is relative is also conditioned. Relative and conditioned existence cannot be absolute, and therefore ordinary knowledge cannot entail the truth. Something becomes 'known,' and therefore objective, because of the objectivating activity of the mind, and, inversely, the knowing act arises because of the *something* being given to it. Both, the knowing and the known, cause each other mutually.

But truth is something uncaused, and this it is, that wisdom is concerned with. It is not a something which can be apprehended in a concept. 'Hence real knowledge, when it regards absolute truth, never apprehends what is known (as does ordinary knowledge). Since it does not do this, how can such wisdom know?'[9] Therefore 'wisdom' could be better called the absence of knowledge. 'The sage, by means of the Prajñā, which has no knowledge, illumines the absolute truth which has no phenomenal qualities.'[9] 'Void and unmoving, it *(prajñā)* has no

7 Ibid., p. 265.
8 Ibid,. p. 266
9 Ibid., p. 267.

knowledge, yet knows everything.'[9] In wisdom the mind is not fixed on any particularity, but in it everything becomes transparant. It is the actuality of life and the world, that which Sēngzhào calls the 'real quality *(shí xiāng)* of all things.' It is that actuality apart from which no event occurs. The things appearing in it are as illusory as the worlds created by an illusionist, but although the things given are illusory, the experience of them is real. As things, taken from their experiential context, they are non-existent, but seen as the actuality of experience, they constitute wisdom. Zhào writes in a letter to Liú Chéngzhī: 'The development of knowledge reaches its apex within (the sphere of) qualities. But since the *dharmas* fundamentally do not (really) possess such qualities, how can sage-wisdom be knowledge?'[9] Sage-wisdom is 'knowledge of what is quality-less.'[9] It is the power to reveal the real quality of things. And this power is revealed by emptying the mind from particularities.

> 'Wisdom knows not, yet it illumines the deepest profundity. Spirit *(shén)* calculates not, yet it responds to the necessities of the given moment *(yīng huì)*. Because it calculates not, spirit shines in lonely glory in what is beyond the world. Because it knows not, wisdom illumines the mystery *(xuán)* beyond mundane affairs. Yet, though wisdom lies outside affairs, it never lacks them. Though spirit lies beyond the world, it stays ever within. Hence the sage is like an empty hollow. He cherishes no knowledge. He dwells in the world of change and utility, yet holds himself to the realm of non-activity *(wúwéi)*. He rests within the walls of the nameable, yet lives in the open country of what transcends speech. He is silent and alone, void and open. *(On Prajñā not being Knowledge)*.[10] Therefore Ratnakūṭa says: 'Without mentation, he yet acts.' And the Fàngguāng says: He (the Buddha) in his state of motionless enlightenment, establishes all the *dharmas* in their places. That is why the footprints of the sage, though a thousandfold, all lead to the same end...'[11]

10 Ibid., p.268: from *On Prajñā not being knowledge* (Zhàolùn, pp. 71-72, p. 109 of translation Liebenthal).

11 Ibid., pp. 268-69 (*Zhāolùn*, Liebenthal p. 73.)

By not knowing the sage has insight into everything, and by not acting intentionally, he accomplishes everything, guides events to their proper solution.[12]

DÀOSHĒNG. A contemporary of Sēngzhào was Dàoshēng (360-434), like the former a pupil of Kumārajīva. He was a quick-witted man from Jūlú. On coming in contact with a Buddhist monk, he himself became converted to the monastic life, and travelled to Cháng' ān, where he met Kumārajīva.

His understanding is said to have penetrated beyond words. Words, as symbols, according to him, have the purpose to lead to an understanding of ideas, but once these are understood, words are no longer of any avail. By approaching texts too philologically, you often become blocked in your understanding of their meaning. You should forget about the fish-trap and catch the fish.

Shēng's cherished doctrines were, that good deeds do not entail retribution, that Buddha-hood is achieved by instantaneous enlightenment, and that the nature of enlightenment is hidden in every being, and can be realized even by unbelievers.

Retribution.

There is only indirect evidence of Shēng's ideas on retribution. We are told, that Shēng held, that good deeds do not entail retribution. The idea behind this must be the old Buddhist thesis, that the one proper way to behave is by disinterested action. Action that is not motivated by desire does not result in karmic retribution, just as water does not stick to a lotus leaf. It is the action of the enlightened one, of the one who has come to awakening.

Besides this general insight in Shēng's ideas on the matter, which is suggested by Indian Buddhist tradition, the only thing that may elucidate more particularities of Shēng's lore is a treatise by Huìyuǎn (334-

12 Cf. Fung Yu-lan, *History*, pp. 358-270.

416): On the Explanation of Retribution, which possibly is inspired by Shēng. We will quote here a part of this work, given by Fung:[13]

> 'If we investigate the natures of the four major elements, so as to understand the basis from which our physical forms are received, (we see that) they (each) depend on something else, and it is thus that they constitute one common whole. Physical life is no more than some thrown-away dust, and its rise and annihilation belong to a single span of transformation. This is (the truth) to which the insight of wisdom and sword of knowledge lead us. Through it we may ride the natural cycle of coming and departure, so that despite the coalescence and dispersion (of physical bodies), it is no longer we (who undergo these changes). Inhabiting innumerable bodies during our Great Dream, though we actually dwell in the midst of being, yet we identify ourselves with non-being. How, when this is so, can there be divisions in what comes to us, or can we have any ties of greedy love?
>
> Suppose this truth is acquired by our minds before others become conscious of it. Then, regretting the failure of our solitary goodness to achieve merit (for others), and being conscious of our duties as beings possessed of prior understanding, we straightway expound the great Way *(Dào)* in order to illustrate its teachings: herein consist the virtues of love *(rén)* and altruism. It is as if the I and the not-I are mutually joined, so that there is no antithesis in the mind between the two. Should we then encounter sword-play, we lose ourselves in mystic contemplation. Should we join in battle, we meet the situation as if encountering good friends. Should we wound somebody, not only can no harm to our spirit result, but there will not be even the killing of physical life. It was thus that Mañjuśrī, holding his sword, was rebellious in manner, yet conformed with the Way. Had he continued brandishing his lance and raising his sword to the end of time, it would still have been to no purpose. Such a person as this may transform the whole world either by civil or military means. No reward will be received for such great merits, but what punishment, on the other hand, will be entailed?'

13 Fung Yu-lan, *History*, pp 272ff., following the *Collected Essays on Buddhism*, compiled by Sèng-yòu (*Hóngmíng jí*, in Taishō no. 2102, vol. 52, pp. 1-96.

By considering the opposite of this and examining its operation (in life), we can understand retribution. By pushing into affairs and seeking their underlying meaning, we can talk about punishment. Let me try to describe these. The effects of causation and products of change follow a definite course. Ignorance is the course of the net of delusion. Greedy love *(rāga, tān'ài)* is the storehouse for the various (mortal) ties *(lěi)*. The following of these two principles obscures the functioning of the spirit, and it is because of them that good and bad fortune, blame and calamity, operate. Because ignorance beclouds the understanding, feeling and thought become clamped to external objects. Because greedy love saturates the nature, the four elements cohere to form the body. By their cohering in the body a boundery comes to be fixed between the I and the not-I. By the clamping of feeling an agent of good and evil arises. If there be a boundery between the I and the not-I, the body is then regarded as belonging to the I, and thus cannot be forgotten. If there be an agent of good and evil, a greedy love for life results, so that life can no longer be sundered. In this way one becomes willing to sleep in the great dream and be blinded by delusion. Doubt is hugging to the breast during that long night and there is nothing but attachment. The result is that failure and success push after one another, and blessing and calamity follow on each other's heels. With the accumulation of evil, divine retribution comes to itself. With the committing of sin, hell meets out its punishment. This is the unavoidable fate without a shadow of a doubt…
Thus the retribution of punishment or blessing depends upon what are stimulated by one's own (mental) activities. They are what they are according to these stimuli, for which reason I say that they are automatic. By automatic I mean that they result from our own influence. How then can they be the work of some Mysterious Ruler?'

Instantaneous enlightenment

For Shēng's idea, that Buddhahood is attained by instantaneous enlightenment *(dŭn wú)*, we again, have no direct information. We know about it through a work of a contemporary, the *Discussion of Essentials (Biàn zōng lùn)* by Xiè Língyùn (385-433).

The basic idea is, that there are two concepts of enlightenment, the one – instructed (according to these thinkers) by the Buddha himself – teaches it is achieved gradually through learning, the other – brought forward by Shēng and, Xiè Língyùn – says that, as truth is one, whole, and eternal, it can be grasped only as a whole, and at once, and not gradually and partially. The second thought is also alleged to have the support of Confucius.

The idea of gradual enlightenment implies, that with the gradual eradication of *ignorance* through learning, also the bonds with worldly existence are gradually overcome. Such process can take countless rebirths. The other thought is suggested by the concept of 'emptiness.' For as long as there is something left, there is no emptiness, and, accordingly, the '*mysterious way of the sage*' has not been reached; the 'mirror' of the mind has not yet been fully cleansed, and therefore cannot represent the 'abstruse and mysterious.' This truth is something that is not 'known' as something objective, but is subjectively realized. Learning can only gradually increase 'knowledge,' but in 'knowledge' the truth remains external; it is merely an increase in believe *about* the truth, but not truth itself as experienced. In 'knowledge' this truth is only *represented as an object of hope* Because of this directedness of learning and 'knowledge' at truth, it may lead to it, although there cannot be a gradual mastering of it. For the realization of truth is not a conquest of being, but the leap into the void of non-being *(wú)*. It is therefore realized in a flash of insight, when all the ties of being have ended Only then the permanent is attained. For 'What is temporary is false; what is genuine, permanent. The temporary has no permanence; permanent knowledge has no falseness. How, with the impermanence of false knowledge, can one invade the genuineness of permanent knowledge?'[14]

There is an objection against the idea of sudden enlightenment, brough forward by a certain military officer, Wáng Hóng (379-432). He says: 'If the faith derived from instruction gives not even partial entry into illumination it is then merely a blind faith in the sages. In such a case, truth will not be the concern of one's mind – a fact which

14 Fung, p. 279: from *Discussion of Essentials (Biàn zōnglūn by Xiè Língyùn).*

may be truly called the height of blasphemy. How then, can (such faith as this) act for daily advancement?'[15]

Xiè Língyùn quotes Shēng as having replied to this objection in favour himself and Xiè. This is the only thing that we have of him on the subject verbatim, provided Xiè quotes him correctly:

> 'Examining what Xiè Yǒngjiǎ (Língyùn) says, I find myself in complete agreement. It seems to be wonderfully good, and I cannot but quote it with joy. The problem raised by you is vitally important and I hope you will understand (Xiè's meaning) after thinking the matter over carefully. Now I myself should like to try to outline the ideas I have derived from his statements, in order thus to express my joyful feelings. He maintains that there cannot be.faith without knowledge; in fact, the faith derived from instruction is itself knowledge. The truth obtained through this knowledge, however, remains external to the self. Even so, by utilizing (such knowledge), it (truth) may be approached by the self. Hence, why should not the (knowledge in question) help to induce daily advancement? On the other hand, since such knowledge is not an integral part of ourselves, how can there through it be any partial entry into illumination? Since truth is seen (even) in something external, this means that there is no complete darkness. But since the knowledge does not lie within us, this also means that it cannot yet produce illumination.'[16]

THE IMMORTALITY OF THE MIND. There have been preserved some collections of polemical debates concerning Buddhism: the *Collected Essays on Buddhism (Hóngmíng jí)* compiled by Sēngyu (445-518), and the *Further Collection of Essays on Buddhism (Guǎng hóngmíng jí)*, collected by Dàoxuān (596-667). These debates are for a large part concerned with the clash between the traditional Indian and Chinese ideas about the nature of the soul, spirit, or mind. Indian thought in general, and also Buddhism, embraces the idea of the transmigration of the soul, or, what may be slightly different, of rebirth. For the Chi-

15 Ibid., p. 281 (from *Biàn Zōnglùn*).

16 Fung, pp. 280-81 (from *Biàn Zōnglùn*; entire chapter of Fung on Shēng, *History*, part II, pp. 270-284.

nese mind this life on earth is more decisive. Not denying completely the existence of an afterlife, the idea of a return of the personality on earth for penance or further perfection is generally absent. This life is a one-time occurrence, not to be repeated over and over again. The idea of sudden illumination on the one hand, and that of gradual emancipation, through a course of many lives, are naturally coupled to these two differing points of view. If life occurs but once, there is no time for a gradual preparation – in which you are born first in the Buddha-family, subsequendy become a lay-adherent, then a stream-enterer, and finally an *ārya* (noble) and an *arhat* (saint), to be, henceforward, 'no more for this world.' If liberation is to happen at all, it must be here, as an illumination in this life.

The opponents of Buddhism say, that the spirit *(shēn)* is inseparable from the body, and, when the body perishes, the spirit does likewise. The commonness of this thought in the Jìn period is illustrated by a fragment of Huìyuǎn in the *Hóngmíng jí* in which he tries to repudiate this thought.

> 'A questioner may say: ... The endowment of the vital force *(qí)* is confined to a single life. With the termination of that life it melts away again so that there is nothing left but non-being. Thus soul *(shēn)* [spirit, mind], though a mysterious thing, is a product of the evolutions of the *yīn* and the *yáng*; evolving, they produce life, and again evolving, they produce death. With their coalescence there is a beginning, and with their dispersion an end. By extending this principle, we may know that soul [mind] and body evolve together, so that from their origin onward they do not constitute separate sequences. What is fine and coarse both belong to the one vital force, and from beginning to end share the same dwelling. As long as the dwelling is intact, the vital force remains coalesced so that there is a spirit. Upon the disintegration of that dwelling, the vital force dissipates so that the intelligence is extinguished. With that dissipation, what has been received returns to the great origin. With that extinction, there is a reversion to nothingness. This return and reversion to the final end is a natural process. Who is there to make it thus?
>
> But suppose that they (body and soul [mind]) are originally different from one another. Then it is simply a case of different vital forces com-

bining with one another, and having combined, of evolving together. In this way too, the soul [mind] finds a place in the body, as fire does in wood. During life it can be sustained, but with the final desintegration it must perish. According to this principle, with the departure of the body the soul dissipates, no longer having a place in which to live, just as with the disintegration of the wood the fire becomes quiescent, no longer having anything on which to support itself.

Even supposing that it is obscure and difficult to decide whether (body and soul [mind] are (originally) the same or separate from one another, (irrespective of which theory is correct), the doctrine of being and non-being can be sustained only on that of coalescence and dispersion. 'Coalescence and dispersion' is the inclusive term applied to the evolutions of the vital force and to its myriad fluctuations between birth and extinction. Therefore Zhuāngzi says: 'The life of man results from the coalescence of the vital force. Its coalescence is life; its dispersion, death. If then life and death are but consecutive states, what have I to grieve about?' The ancients who were skilled in talking about the course (of nature) have surely been able to arrive at the truth. If it is really as (I have described it), the highest principle is that of concentration (of the vital force) within a single life. With the conclusion of this life there is no further evolution. This theory is possible to investigate.[17] In reply I say: What is the soul [mind]? It is a spiritual something of the finest essence. Being of the finest essence, it cannot be portrayed by the lines of the hexagrams (of the *Book of Changes*). That is why the sages speak of it as a marvelous something, whose aspect cannot be determined, nor its deep meaning plumbed, even by persons of superior wisdom. Yet those who (now) talk about it use ordinary knowledge to create doubts, causing everyone to become equally self-confused. The making of such false statements has already gone far…

Zhuāngzi has uttered a profound statement on the Great Origin when he said: 'The Great Lump (the universe) toils me through my life and rests me in death.' Again he says that life is man's halter, and death is a return to the real. From these statements we may know that life is a great calamity, and its absence is a return to the origin. Wénzi has quoted the Yellow Emperor as saying: 'The body suffers destruction but the soul undergoes no change. With its unchangingness it rides

17 Fung, pp. 286-7 (Huìyuǎn in *Hóngmíng jí*).

upon change and thus passes through endless transformation.' While Zhuāngzi says further: 'To have attained to the human form is a source of joy. But in the infinite evolution, there are thousands of other forms that are equally good.' From these statements we may know that life is not something coming to an end with a single transformation and having no return as it pursues creatures (in various forms of existence. Although these two philosophers do not fully reach the truth in what they say, they have heard something of its partial meaning. In your discussion, without investigating the doctrine about the alternation of life and death, you have suspected that coalescence and dispersion are (restricted to) only the single evolution (of a single lifetime). Without thinking that the course of the soul is that of something marvelous and spiritual, you say that what is fine and what is course come to an end together. Is this not deplorable?

As for your comparison of the fire and the wood, it originates from the writings of the sages. However, you have lost its correct outline and so have brought it forward unclearly without proper investigation ... Let me explain and study it from the point of view of fact. The transmission of fire by fuel is like the transmission of the soul by the body, the fire being transmitted to another bundle of fuel just as the soul is transmitted to another body. The earlier bundle of fuel is not the same as the later bundle; from this we may understand the mystery of the manner in which 'the fingers come to an end.' Nor is the earlier body the same as the later body; from this we may understand the profound way in which our spiritual faculties operate.

Doubters, seeing that the body decays after a single lifetime, suppose that the soul perishes with it. This is like seeing how the fire comes to an end on one piece of wood, and then saying that it is completely extinguished for all time. Such is an distortion of what is said in 'The cultivation of life' (ch. of the Zhuāngzi), and fails to probe deeply into its real character.'[18]

An attack on Buddhism is found in the work of Fàn Zhèn: *Essay on the Extinction of the Soul* (also contained in the *Hóng Míng Jí*).

18 Ibid., pp. 288-9.

> 'The body is the substance of the soul; the soul is the functioning of the body ... The relationship of the soul to its substance is like that of sharpness to the knife, while the relationship of the body to its functioning is like that of a knife to sharpness. What is called sharpness is not the same as the knife, and what is called the knife is not the same as sharpness. Nevertheless, there can be no knife if the sharpness is discarded, nor sharpness if the knife is discarded. I have never heard of sharpness surviving if the knife is destroyed, so how can it be admitted that the soul can remain if the body is annihilated?'[19]

Fàn Zhèn further says, there is no distinction between body and soul; man is but one substance, not to be dissected into independent parts.

World-denial and the state

The reasons for this criticism of the Buddhist conception of the mind were not only theoretical. The other-worldliness of Buddhism induced people to depreciate civil-life, the state. It might easily lead to a neglect of civil-duties, of which the discarding of family life was seen as a prominent example; and this might do harm to the state. Buddhism from the outset was critical against worldly rule and might be a potential menace to established authority.[20]

19 Ibid., p. 290 (Fàn Zhèn, *Shén Miè lùn* in *Hóng míng jí*).
20 Cf. Fung Yu-lan, *History*, part II, pp. 291-2 on Fān Zhèn's motivation.

Chapter 9

Later Buddhist Developments

With the national unity under the Suí (590-717) and Táng (618-906) dynasties, the influence of Buddhism increased. An important figure, inaugurating this time, was Jízàng (549-623).

JÍZÀNG. Jízàng is said to be of Turkestan ancestry, but was actually born in Nanjing. When he grew up there, he came into contact with Buddhism, and became a monk. He wrote many works, among which commentaries on the *Mādhyamika Śāstra*, the *Śata-śāstra*, and the *Dvādaśa-nikāya-śāstra.* He belonged to the Mādhyamika school of Buddhism, called in Chinese *Sānlùn* school (Three Treatises school). His ideas were rather scholastic and little original. One of the main features of his thought was the *theory of double truth (èrdì)* as was expounded in his *Essay on the Double Truth (Èrdì Zhāng)*

He bases himself in that work on the *Prajñā-pāramitā-upadeśa Śāstra* (doubtfully ascribed to Nāgārjuna) and the other Mādhyamika works already mentioned. The essence of all these works is, according to Jízàng, to develop the theory of the Double Truth, and to clarify the way that avoids the two extremes, viz. that of being and non-being, *saṁsāra* and *nirvāṇa* and so forth.[21]

The Double Truth exists on three levels. 'The first explains that to speak of being *(yǒu)* is mundane *(shí)* thruth, but of non-being is Absolute *(zhēn)* Truth.

21 Fung, pp. 293-299.

The second explains that to speak either of being or non-being is to fall into the two (extremes), and so is mundane truth. To speak of neither being nor non-being is to avoid the two (extremes), and so is Absolute Truth…'[22] About the third level the following is remarked.[23] 'At this point, to say that there either are or are not two (extremes) is mundane truth; to say that there neither are nor are not two (extremes) is Absolute Truth.'

The three levels of double truth have in common that they aim at renouncing ordinary believes. Ordinary people take the *dharmas* for existing, but these have no cause of existence and are empty. In renouncing ordinary believes, people are led from the mundane into the real, so that one may become a sage.

On the first level the ordinary idea of existence is renounced, on the second the idea, that the denial of 'being' is 'non being' is renounced, and it is pointed out, that truth never can reside in the extremes. Permanency and impermanency, *saṁsāra* and *nirvāṇa*, are all extremes to be transcended. Here accepting one of the extremes is embracing mundane truth. The rejection of both extremes is the *middle path* leading to the highest truth.

Speaking about the third level Jízàng continues:[24]

> Yet in this assertion [viz. the rejection of the extremes on the second level] there still lie two extremes. Why? (It has been said that) the two (extremes) are both one-sided, and that what belongs to neither of them, is the *middle path.* (In actual fact, however) one-sidedness is one extreme, but centrality is another. Thus one-sidedness and centrality still result in two extremes, and *this* being so, (in the third stage, the belief in either of them) is called mundane truth. But the denial of both, one-sidedness and centrality, constitutes the middle path which is the highest truth. All the teachings made by the Buddhas to cure the ills of sentient beings, never go beyond these concepts. Therefore they expound the Double Truth according to these categories.

22 Fung, *History*, part ii, pp. 294-5: from Jízàngs *Essay on the Double Truth.*
23 Ibid., p. 295.
24 Ibid., p. 296.

When the idea of the double truth is pushed to the extreme, even emptiness and *nirvāṇa* cannot stand, for also these appear as extremes that have relative existence only.

> 'Emptiness, and being of this sort both alike pertain to sentient beings, and therefore must both be discarded ... For what reason? Because everything perceived by the senses is void and illusory, and so is to be discarded. However, it is not merely illusion that is to be discarded, for 'reality' too does not (actually) exist. The reason is, that reality exists only because originally there is illusion (i.e. only as the antithesis of illusion). No illusion, and therefore no reality: herein is manifested the pure and correct path. It is variously called the *'Dharmakāya,'* the 'Correct Path' *(zhèngdào)* or the 'Real State' *(shíxiāng).*' ... 'Hitherto [in Hīnayāna] it was said that one must discard the practice of clinging to the passions as realities ... and that by discarding these six modes of existence, the *nirvāṇa* of the Tathāgata would be gained. But now it is made clear that, whereas, when there is life and death *(saṁsāra)*, there may be *nirvāṇa*, as soon as there is no life and death, then there is also no *nirvāṇa* ... Life and death and *nirvāṇa* are equally illusory, whereas the denial of both, life and death and *nirvāṇa* is called the Real State.'[25]

But at the same time the way is opened for the acceptance of everything: Since unreal phenomena are the same as the real state, they coincide with it.

XU*ÁNZÀNG*. Xuánzàng (596-664) has become famous for the account of his pilgrimage to India. He crossed the Himalayas in 633 and spent ten years in the native continent of Buddhism. From India, he returned to the Chinese capital Cháng'ān in 645, carrying with him 657 Buddhist texts. The rest of his life he filled with completing 75 translations.

Xuánzàng was especially interested in the work of Vasubandhu and his commentators. This interest gives his work – in contrast to that of many other Chinese Buddhists – a very Indian character. He is especially known for the translation of an idealistic work of Vasubandhu,

25 Ibid., 297-8.

the *Triṁśikā*' (*Wéishí sānshí lùn, Treatise in Thirty Stanzas on Mere Ideation)*, and its commentary by Dharmapāla, the *Vijñaptimātratā-siddhi (Chéng wéishí lùn, Establishing of the Doctrine of Mere Ideation)*. Xuánzàng's work was not confined to mere translation, for his translations also imply elaboration with the help of commentaries.

All is relative to the mind.

According to Vasubandhu and Xuánzàng, there are two fundamental errors, the believe in an independent ego *(ātman, wǒ)*, and that in the independence of existence *(dharmas, fǎ)*. The *School of Mere Ideation (Wéishí)* wants to destroy these errors by pointing out, that both are baseless or hollow *(śūnya)*. Ego and world have no existence apart from the mind. Their appearances are all mental representations dependent upon the evolutions of consciousness, which can be equated with mind, conscious as well as subconscious.[26] Ego and *dharmas* are all products of consciousness.

Consciousness comprises eight kinds of activity, falling under three categories: 'maturing consciousness' (*vipāka-vijñāna, yìshúshí*, intellection *(manyanā, sīliang)*, and 'representation' *(vijñapti, liǎobié)*. Here the maturing consciousness is the eight kind of mind-activity, intellection the seventh and representation includes the other six: the five types of sensory perception, and their mental coordination as the sixth.

Seeing that ego and *dharmas* are dependent on consciousness, and that they are without nature *(svabhāva)* of their own, one understands the unsubstantiality of the soul and its objects *(pudgala-nairātmya & dharma-nairātmya)*. But, because the consciousness on which they depend is real, they cannot be said to be altogether unreal or 'hollow' *(śūnya)*.

With this doctrine, two current ideas in Buddhism should be set aside, one – maintained by e.g. the *Sarvāstivādins* – holding that the external world is real, and the other – put forward by the *Mādhyamikas* – saying that the mind itself is as baseless as anything else, declaring everything to be 'hollow' *(śūnya)*. By asserting the substantiality of things, one transgresses their actual givenness in consciousness, and by denying consciousness, one denies the very actuality of experience.

26 Fung., p. 300.

By avoiding these two errors, one breaks away from rebirth.[27]

The *Chéng wéi shí lùn* here follows a middle path for which even the middle way of the *Mādhyamika* is an extreme.

Four levels of consciousness.

'Impure' consciousness, i.e. consciousness under the influence of desire and the passions, manifests itself under the double aspect of subject and object. What is objectively perceived is called 'perceived division' *(lakṣaṇa-bhāga, xiāngfēn)* what is actually perceiving as subject, is called perceiving division *(darśaṇa-bhāga, jiànfēn)*. Both these divisions are not separate entities but they are dependent on something else, of which they are just aspects, viz. the underlying consciousness. In the form of self-consciousness – which is itself a third division of consciousness *(sva-saṁvitti-bhāga, zìzhèng)* – the separate acts of object-consciousness are related to the unity of experience of one single stream of consciousness, of which these acts are just differentiations. Because of this relatedness to a stream of experience there can be memory, recognition, and knowledge, and without these neither objects nor subjects could be apprehended. But with this relating of straight perception to self-consciousness, the divisions of consciousness are not exhausted, for the very distinction between object- and self-consciousness points to the fact, that there also must be a reflective awareness *(svasaṁvitti-saṁvitti, zhèngzìzhèngfēn)* that is conscious of both, the object-perception *and* its relation to a unity of conscious experience. This makes four divisions or levels of consciousness, all taken together.

All these are evolutions or differentiations of one basic consciousness. 'Evolution (*biàn*, Skr. *pariṇāma*?) seems to consist of two parts (subject and object) … It is in dependence upon these two divisions that the ego *(ātman)* and things *(dharmas)* are established.[28]

But the existence of what is thus manifested, is illusory. Ego and things are not separate existences, but hypostazations of the subject-object-division within consciousness. They correspond to a polarity

27 Ibid., p.301

28 Ibid., p. 303: from Xuánzàng's *Completion of the Doctrine of Mere Ideation* (Chéng wéishí lùn) / Vijñaptimātratā-siddhi [being a translation of the work of Dharmapāla, which is itself an elaboration of Vasubandhu.

within consciousness and are not entities existing outside – and independent from – consciousness. Only the inner consciousness, which causes the appearances with their inherent polarity, is real in the true sense.

Store-consciousness.

According to the *Chéng wéishí lùn*, the substratum of all actual manifestations of consciousness, is the store-consciousness *(ālaya-vijñāna, zàngshí)*. This store-consciousness is the same as the maturing consciousness *(vipāka-vijñāna)* mentioned before. This and the defilements of existence condition one another.

Here, under the 'defilements of existence' we must understand the sensory impressions with their corresponding feelings and cognitions – pertaining to the normal life of desire – which can be beneficial or non-beneficial. Such impressions, with their mental digestions, do not pass without a trace when they vanish from the present, but are retained in an all-encompassing – and partly non-actual-consciousness, called 'store-consciousness,' which may be translated by 'memory' in a very broad sense – i.e., it is more than actual remembering, a kind of reservoir from which actual rememberings are re-enacted. It might also be termed 'subconscious,' or – to use a term of Anagarika Govinda – 'subliminal consciousness,' but it *also includes* actuality. Xuánzàng's idea is, that it is a kind of spiritual matter, which becomes *impregnated* by the impressions, feelings, and cognitions (phenomena, *dharmas*) of actual experience. When the store-consciousness is called the eighth consciousness,' then it is impregnated by the other seven consciousnesses, viz. 'mind-consciousness' (on which later), and the sensory cognitions.

The *impregnations (vāsanā)*, the retentions of actual experience, characterize their particular streams of consciousness, and provide them with dispositions of their own. These dispositions are like seeds, which develop under the influence of new impregnations, until they bear fruit in the actual facts of a particular life. Bad dispositions result in misery, and good ones in a happier life. Therefore the store-consciousness is also called 'maturing consciousness.' Because it is conditioned, impregnated, by various impressions, it also develops in a variety of ways, in accordance with the quality of the 'seeds' it is carrying. This development is a process of continuous causation: every impregnation by an impression is cause of a development issuing in an effect, which again has the nature of an impression, and this, again, causes the substrate-consciousness to be impregnated, engendering a new development, and so on, into infinity. Cause and effect form a closed cycle, which, in truth, is nothing else but the circle of *saṁsāra*. They constitute the endless transformations of the particular store-consciousness, which, because of its incessant change can be said to be neither perishable, nor permanent. For change itself goes on forever.

As regards the seeds contained in the substrate-consciousness, Xuànzáng refers to three theories, one – perhaps of some *Sarvāstivādins* – says, that the seeds are innate ideas of consciousness; a stream of consciousness contains all possible seeds, but these ripen according to the impregnations provided by the impressions of particular experience. These cause one seed to ripen and another to remain barren. Another theory – of the *Sautrāntikas* – holds that the seeds themselves are constituted by the impregnations, and therefore are not innate; they are sowed. A third theory holds that both kinds of seeds do occur. Xuànzáng himself seems to hold to the third opinion.

Seeds can, furthermore, be divided into 'pure' and 'impure' ones. The impure ones keep the stream of consciousness entangled in the world of desire, the pure ones cause the stream to transform into higher, transcendental worlds, such as the various paradises and heavens, or the formless world.

Also those things which we consider to be external, are evolved by seeds resting in the store-consciousness. Mountains and rivers are not simply given. We have learned to apprehend them. And these apprehensions are the fruits of particular impregnations, acquired in the antecedent learning-process of a consciousness-stream in *saṁsāra*.

But, as mountains and rivers are the outcome of an individual learning process, how can they constitute our common world; how can there be intersubjectivity?

Men are born in intersubjectivity, because of a similarity in their karmic merits. To be born as a man on earth, requires seeds and impregnations of a certain type. E.g. most men are disposed to desire women, and therefore they have been born in a world that may gratify this desire. The seeds of mountains and rivers are in all of us, for, if not, we would not have been born in this world, but in one in which there are no mountains or rivers. The more similar the *karma*, the more closely will physical conditions after birth resemble, and this resemblance constitutes the commonness of our world. The people whom we frequently meet, are those placed closest to our own condition, and therefore with them we can most easily communicate. But note, that it is comparatively easy to come to a global understanding of each other's environment but difficult when you want to get into the *particular* details.[29]

The seven active forms of consciousness.

The store-consciousness is what is impregnated by – and stores the impressions of – the other consciousnesses. It seems like a female principle that produces according to the seeds by which it is inseminated. It is the living matter that gives birth to all the variety of existence. It is the dim background of daily consciousness, carrying in itself the hidden motives and dispositions issuing in a particular form of practical life.

It is active, intentional experience which conditions the growing forces of unconscious life. This active consciousness is of seven types, falling apart into two main groups, on the one hand, understanding, intuition, or reason, on the other, sensory discrimination. Sensory discrimination provided by the sensory functions is called 'gross,' while understanding and the store-consciousness are called 'subtle.' The gross functions operate inconstantly, conditioned as they are by various factors, but the subtle forms of consciousness are always present, since their conditions are generally fulfilled.

It is understanding *(manas)* which effectuates self-identification. It considers the store-consciousness (falsely) as an identity and holds it for an ego *(ātman)*. As such, it clings to it. In this clinging we see the understanding under the influence of four afflictions *(kleśa's)*: ego-ignorance, ego-belief, self-conceit, and self-love.

> 'Ego-ignorance means lack of understanding. It is to be ignorant of the (true) nature of the ego, and deluded as to the principle that there

29 Fung, part II, pp. 304-312.

> is no ego. Ego-belief means the clinging to (the principle of) ego. It wrongly imagines certain things to be an ego when they are not so. … Self-conceit means pride. Basing itself on the belief in an ego, it causes the mind to assume a high and mighty air. … Self-love means a greedy desire for the self. Because of its belief in the ego, it develops deep attachments for it.[30]
>
> These four, by their constant rise, disturb and pollute the innermost mind (the *ālaya-consciousness*), and cause the outer (i.e., the remaining seven) operating consciousnesses perpetually to produce defiling elements. It is because of these (four) that sentient beings are bound to the cycle of transmigration [rebirth] without being able to escape.'[31]

Not only the understanding, but sensory and mental discrimination also contribute to the identification of an ego. The function of discrimination consists of the five senses and thought *(mano-vijñāna)* as the sixth, which co-ordinates the various sensory data into a coherent scheme. Making a distinction between the outside world and its own psycho-physical frame, it identifies the latter as its ego, forms a definite image of it and clings to that image, considering it to be the ego. This second identification is not present without interruption. When through some sensory defect or in sleep the presentation of sensory forms is interrupted, also this identification is interrupted. But this is not so in the case of the identification of the understanding – which is nothing but the synthetic function of identification – with the store-consciousness, which endures also in the absence of conscious mental activity.

The active forms of consciousness, understanding and sensory discrimination, do not exist separated from the store-consciousness, in fact, they are just its fruits or products. Therefore also the various identifications, made by means of various faculties, must be considered as forms of the underlying consciousness itself. What is generally called 'ego' and '*dharmas*' are both evolved out of the store-consciousness. They have no separate existence. The mistaken belief in such separate existence causes the clinging to such imagined existences, which can

30 Ibid., part ii, pp. 312-3: from *Chéng wéishi lùn.*

31 Ibid., p. 313.

take the form of ego-clinging or *dharma*-clinging. The *Chéng weíshí lùn* says:[32]

> 'The ego-clingings are, generally speaking, of two kinds: (1) that which is innate, (2) that which results from mental discriminations. The ego-clinging which is innate, is perpetually present in the individual, owing to the internal causal influence of its false perfuming [impregnations] which has been going on since beginningless time. Thus, without depending on (external) erroneous teachings or discriminations, it spontaneously operates. That is why it is called innate.'

But the innate clinging again is of two kinds: (1) the identification of the understanding with the store-consciousness, and (2) the identification of thought and understanding with the psycho-physical frame, both of which have been mentioned already above. The clinging due to mental discrimination, on the other hand, depends on external factors and is due to wrong instruction.

Also the external world has no existence independent from the store-consciousness. But the belief in such an existence also here causes a clinging to it. Also this clinging is partly innate and partly taught. And this clinging is differentiated in a similar way as the clinging to the ego.

In all this the understanding takes the individualized mental images arising from the store-consciousness and considers them to be true ego and true *dharmas*. In the same way, thought makes that the psycho-physical complex also can be held for the ego and external phenomena for an objective world.

All consists of the mind's immanent differentiation.

Understanding, and sensory perception, although in reality not different from the one basic consciousness, are called 'evolving,' because they both display a subjective and an objective aspect, the so-called perceived part *(lakṣaṇa-bhāga)*, and the perceiving part *(darśana-bhāga)*. When we examine perception, then the perceiving part is called 'thought' or 'discrimination' *(vikalpa)*, and its object is that 'what is

32 Fung, part II, p. 316

thought' *(vikalpita)*. Both, the thinking and what is thought, are no real and separate entities, but are aspects of the one act of consciousness. In other words, the subject and the object are both immanent in consciousness, their transcendence of the consciousness-sphere is only seemingly. 'According to the correct principle, there are definitely no 'real' ego or *dharmas* aside from what is thus evolved from consciousness' ... there are no real things apart from these two aspects. Therefore everything phenomenal (*yǒuweí* [noema]) and noumenal (*wúweí* [noesis]). everything seemingly real and false alike, is all inseparable from consciousness. There are no real things apart from consciousness. But this is not meant to deny that mental functions, *dharmas*, etc., as inseparable from consciousness, do exist.[33]

> 'Therefore everything is 'Mere Ideation.' But, as for false discrimination itself, it may definitely be accepted as an established fact. For 'mere' does not deny the *dharmas* etc., as long as they are inseparable from consciousness, and in this sense 'open space' *(ākāśa)* and so forth, do exist. In this way we avoid the two extremes of either adding (something to consciousness) or reducing (consciousness to nothing). The meaning of 'Mere Ideation' is established, and so we are able to keep to the middle path.'[34]

But as everything is mere ideation, does this not result in solipsism? To say that there is nothing apart from consciousness, does not mean that there are no other streams of consciousness *(saṁtāna)*. What use, then, would the Buddha's preaching of the Dharma have had? Although it is true, that the mind of others cannot be perceived directly, it is perceived indirectly by means of one's own objectivations of it.

The three natures of reality and their true essence.

All existence may be regarded as having three natures *(svabhāva, xìng)*:

1) the nature of dependence *(paratantra-svabhāva, yītāqǐxìng)*,
2) the nature of imagination *(parikalpita-svabhāva, biànjìsuǒzhíxìng)*,

33 Ibijd., p. 318.
34 Ibid. p. 318-9

3) the nature of ultimate reality *(pariniṣpanna svabhāva, yuánchéng-shíxìng)*.

The first nature presents reality as it is given in naïve experience. The facts of life are given in a conditioned way, but are not reflected upon. They just keep the minds of people conjured up by their incantation. They suggest an existence that is not really there. But although existence is suggested, it is not randomly given, it is conditioned by all the factors that constitute one of mind's moments. Here, everything that is given, is so, because it is conditioned *(paratantra)* by other phenomena. It is not something in itself, it is only what it is, because of its relation to other things and moments. But this spell of existence develops into an opinion, stating that the phenomena of life are not there because of their dependence on other phenomena, but that they are the expression of the confrontation between a real existing ego and things existing in themselves. This opinion, accordingly, projects imperceptible entities, substances or essences, behind the perceived facts of experience. Such opinion consists of mere mental constructs, and is therefore called 'imagined' or 'mentally constructed' *(parikalpita)*. This nature of things is that of a mistaken reflection. To come to the insight, however, that such independent essences, entities, or substances are not required to uphold phenomena, and do not even exist, constitutes the right knowledge concerning reality. It recognizes, that in truth there is no independent subject behind, and apart from, the processes of seeing, thinking etc., and no independent objects behind, and apart from, the being seen in the process of seeing. One knows now, that ego and substantial things are but 'hollow' concepts, mere words without a real reference. This double 'hollowness' of reality, the hollowness of the ego *(pudgala)* and hollowness of phenomena *(dharma)*, constitutes the highest truth *(pariniṣpanna)*. Reality – subjective and objective – is seen then as relative to, and as evolved from the mind.

Up to now, the three natures were related to the subject-object character of experience, that suggested real entities and a real ego, although these notions have practical reality only insofar as they are conditioned by causation. They are false insofar as they are considered to be substantial (i.e. unconditioned), true, however, only if seen to be *devoid* of substantiality. The subjective and objective aspects of experience were considered to be the mere presentations of the mind. As such, mind, at least, seemed to be truly existent. But mind itself is nothing apart from the succession of its phenomena, and so it too must be dependent on causes, and is not an in itself existing entity, a self-identity. Just as with objective phenomena and the ego, this fact of dependent existence can give way to a merely imagined hypostazation of the mind – the wrong view –, but also to the true insight, that the genuine existence of the mind is not phenomenal or even thing-like, but that in appearance merely it is phenomenal (truly a tautology), and in its essence it is void or indeterminate.[35]

This void and indeterminate essence is the true nature of the mind, and – since mind is the true nature of all things – also of all things. It is known as genuine thusness *(bhūtatathatā, zhēnrú)*. In the light of this essence, reality is not false, for this nature is constantly there, immovable. It is also called container of the *dharma (dharmadhātu)* and realm of reality *(bhūtakoṭi)*. The *Chéng wéishí lùn* says about it:

> 'For the *Bhūtatathatā*, which is revealed by the 'emptiness' of the non-ego, there is neither 'being' nor 'non-being.' It is sundered both from the 'road of mind' and 'road of words.' It is neither identical with, nor different from, all the *dharmas*. As it is the genuine principle of all the *dharmas*, it is called the Dharma-nature *(fǎxíng)*... In order to refute the idea that it does not exist, it is said to exist. In order ro refute the idea that it exists [as a thing], it is said to be empty. Because one cannot say of it, that it is baseless or illusory, it is said to be real. Because its principle is neither false nor perverted, it is called *bhūtatathatā*.'[36]

The road to wisdom.

To come to an understanding of things in the light of truth is not easy. One can admit that the world exists only relative to the mind, but this in itself does not change experience. And, after all, to free experience from its fetters is the aim of Buddhism. The transformation of experience requires more than an intellectual assent, it implies that we

35 Fung., p. 328-332.
36 Ibid., p. 332.

abandon our wrong habits and inclinations, and purify our feelings and desires. Only in this way, mere knowledge can become wisdom, i.e. truth as practised.

The transformation-process needs discipline and *cultivation,* and these proceed in five steps or stages:

1) The first step is *making preparations (saṁbhāra).* According to Xuánzàng, the keeping of the eightfold path is preliminary even to the intellectual understanding of the phenomenality of the world and the self;
2) The second step is that of *intensified effort.* It means, cultivating oneself to the point, that one is able to decide and to select;
3) The next step is that of *unimpeded understanding.* As a result of effort, practical life becomes transparant to the intuition. It is the insight into the truth held by the *bodhisattvas*;
4) The fourth step is called *exercising cultivation.* It is the practical application of the insight won at the preceding stage.
5) The last step is that of *final attainment.* 'It is abiding in the unsurpassed perfect wisdom *(bodhi)*'[37]

The road to wisdom requires so much effort, because of the 'impregnation' of the store-consciousness. In other words, one's physical and mental deeds have endowed one's personality with a habituality of acting that cannot easily be altered. Our habits – especially our bad ones – stick to us, and cannot simply be cleansed away. Such vices are called *kleśa*, and they are a barrier *(kleśāvaraṇa)* to the true way of life. In the same way our habitual way of looking at things forms a barrier to true understanding, the so-called *jñeyāvaraṇa* (veil of knowables). The two barriers correspond to the ideas of 'ego' and 'world.' Believe in the ego means, being ruled by its desires, and its corresponding pernicious habits. Belief in an independent, objective world, means belief in the food for these desires. Belief in an ego and in the world, are, therefore, not merely intellectual positions, rather they are the implications of normal, daily, social life, which rule all human relationships; they are even its condition. To break away from it, is nothing less than a complete conversion. It needs the intensified effort of the second stage,

37 Fung. p. 333.

which in practice means the Buddhist course of studies, a philosophical investigation into the 'names' and 'essences of things.' In this way a man discovers, that the things he takes for granted, are merely his own suppositions, and also it comes to his mind, that, since 'what is taken' [the objects] does not exist …, and since no real objects exist apart from the consciousness which takes them, how can real consciousness itself exist apart from the objects which are taken by it? For what is taken and what takes are in mutual dependence one on the other.[38] Here begins the arising of the first worldly truth, which is the insight into the emptiness or relativity of the subjective and the objective.

But, although the relativity of subject and object is understood at the second stage, the relativity of 'being' and 'non-being' (emptiness, indeterminateness) still escapes the mind. To obtain this insight in the third stage, one realizes the insight into the *essential thusness of things (bhūtatathatā),* which in the fourth stage results in the great conversion or 'metanoia,' that radically changes one's life, disposing of the *veils of vices* and *of wrong knowledge.* By removing the vices, *nirvāṇa* is gained, by removing wrong knowledge, enlightenment *(bodhi)* is experienced. And so, the fifth stage of *final attainment* is reached. All pollution is swept away, and the untainted harvest of religious life is gained. It is pure, perfect, and clear, and it is called *storehouse realm.* The eight consciousnesses by now all have been transformed into true knowledge or wisdom *(jñāna).*

These taintless, purified consciousnesses, having withdrawn from the world motivated by desire, again return to the world, but now to one motivated by compassion. It is the motivation of the *Bodhisattvas,* who, coming from a motivational complex that is entirely different from that which generally rules our world, form a heaven in the midst of the banalities of daily drudgery – until all are saved.[39]

38 Fung., p. 335
39 Cf. Fung, *History*, part II, pp. 299-338 (On Xuánzàng).

Chapter 10
Three Schools

Later Chinese Buddhism came to be centred in three main schools, the *Huàyán* or Garland-school, following the *Avataṁsaka sūtra*, the *Tiāntái* school, named after a mountain, following the *Saddharma puṇḍarīka* or Lotus-sūtra, and the *Chán* school, the school of meditation *(dhyāna)*, better known by its Japanese name *Zen*.

FÀZÀNG AND THE HUÀYÁN SCHOOL. Xuánzàng's extreme idealism met with resistence. Fàzàng (643-712) was one of Xuánzàng's co-operators in translating, but he came to disagree with the latter's ideas, and left the translation-hall. He was of Sogdian ancestry. His grandfather came – like the kinsmen of Jízàng-from present day Turkmenistan.

After breaking with Xuánzàng, he independently started to develop the ideas of the monks Dǔshùn (557-640) and Zhìyán (602-668). This means that he developed the thought of the *Avataṁsaka-sūtra* (Garland-sūtra), and so contributed to the growth of the Chinese Huàyán (Garland) school.

He explained the *Garland-sūtra* to the usurper-empress Wū, or Zé-tiān, but the mere theoretical teaching proved to hard for her understanding. Fàzàng directed her attention to a gold lion in the palace-hall, and succeeded in explaining to her – using the lion as an example – the intricacies of the relation between matter and form. In this way it was said – was born his *Essay on the Gold Lion*. In it, he explains ten principles:

1) Origination through causation,
2) The emptiness of 'matter,'
3) The three natures,
4) The revelation of what is without quality,
5) Non-generation,
6) The five teachings,
7) The mastering of the ten mysteries,
8) The embracing of the six qualities,
9) The achievement of 'bodhi,'
10) The entry into nirvāṇa

1. Origination through causation.

Fàzàng makes a distinction between the gold, from which the lion is made, and its form. The gold is compared to the true being of the world, the imperishable nature, the unborn 'realm of principle.' (The lion-form, on the contrary, which is compared to the phenomenal world, is entirely dependent on causes (here the work of the artist), and is nothing in itself. The gold is the '*dharma*'-nature, which lies within the *womb of the Buddha (Tathāgata-garbha)*. It is in its own nature complete, self-sufficient, clear, pure, perfect, and brilliant. It is for ever unstained, beyond the processes of pollution and purification: aloof, but at the same time omnipresent. It is the one truth behind the variety of appearances; it is the substantial cause of all that exists, but its forms of appearance need secondary causes, just as the gold needs the artisan to form the lion. This truth is also to be compared to the one nature of ocean-water, and the phenomena to its surface-waves, not differing from the water in substance, but only in aspect and concept.[40]

2. The emptiness of 'matter.'

The idea of the 'emptiness of matter' does not refer to 'matter' in the Western sense of the word. Meant is the Indian word *rūpa*, which points to anything phenomenal or aesthetic. Its 'emptiness' means, that the outer aspect of the lion is void, while only the gold of which

40 Cf. Fung, *History*, part II, pp. 339-42.

it is made, is real. 'Matter' here, accordingly, refers to the form, and not to the gold that *we* would designate as 'matter.'

The phenomena of the world are all manifestations of illusion *(māyā, huàn)*. Lacking an inherent nature, they are empty, but inasmuch as they present seeming qualities, they are existent. 'The best thing (to say) is that illusory matter (form, *rūpa*), inasmuch as it lacks any inherent substance of its own, cannot be differentiated from emptiness; and that genuine emptiness, being all-perfect, penetrates to what lies beyond existence. By viewing matter as empty we achieve great wisdom *(mahāmati)*, so that we do not abide in the circle of life and death *(saṁsāra)*. By viewing emptiness as matter (form) we achieve great pity *(mahākaruṇā)*, so that we do not abide in *nirvāṇa*.'[41]

Emptiness is not complete annihilation, since it does not exist apart from form, just as form does not exist apart from emptiness. Emptiness is not itself thing-like, it is merely the relativity of phenomenal existence. The emptiness is as the gold, which, although genuinely existent, necessarily must assume some phenomenal appearance, while this appearance in itself has no substantiality whatsoever. 'For emptiness separated from matter (form) becomes complete annihilation, while matter (form) separated from emptiness becomes something real.'[42]

3. *The three natures.*

The *Essay on the Gold Lion says*: 'The fact that, from (the point of view of) the senses, the lion exists, is called its (character [nature] of sole imagination. The fact that (from a higher point of view) the lion only seemingly exists, is called its (character [nature] of) dependency on others. And the fact, that the gold (of which the lion is made) is immutable in its nature, is called (the character [nature] of) ultimate reality.'[43] The distinction made here, is basically the same as that made by Xuánzàng. The hypostazation, the ascribing of independent exis-

41 Fung, *History*, part II, pp. 342-43: from *Xiù Huàyán aòzhǐ wàngjìn huányuán guān* (Cultivation of the contemplation of the mysterious meaning of the *Avataṁsaka*, for the extinguising of false thought and returning to the origin).

42 Ibid., 342-43.

43 Ibid., *Essay on the Gold Lion (Jīn shīzi zhāng)*.

tence to the lion, is the nature of sole imagination, the acceptance of its practical and relative existence is called its nature of dependency on others, and the immutability of the gold stands for the underlying nature of the mind, which constitutes *ultimate reality,* and to which the lion in ultimate analysis should be reduced. But for Xuánzàng even the mind proved at the end only to have relative existence; Fàzàng's ultimate mind, on the other hand, proves to be genuinely ultimate, not to be dissolved again by further analysis.[44]

4. Revelation of what is without quality.

Concerning this principle Fàzàng continues: This means that the gold completely includes the lion, for apart from the gold, the lion itself has no qualities *(lakṣaṇa)* that may be seized. This fact is therefore called that of the qualityless.[45] And also he says: To contemplate the qualityless is (to complete) the fact that the qualities of the tiniest particle of matter *(guṇa)* arise out of the evolutions of the mind. Their position is false and has no reality, so that when seizing them one does not get them. From this we may know that the qualities of matter are void and non-existent, being products of the mind and completely lacking any inherent nature of their own. This fact is called the qualityless.[46] Because things have no substance, they also cannot bear qualities; these too are projected by the mind.

5. Non-generation.

The Gold Lion says, concerning this principle: 'This means, that when we see this lion as something that has been generated *(shēng),* it is only the gold that has generated it. External to the gold, there is nothing else. Thus, whereas the lion undergoes generation and destruction, the gold itself incurs neither increase nor decrease. This fact is therefore called that of non-generation.'[47] In another work, the *Hundred*

44 Ibid., pp. 342-3.

45 Ibid., p.344 *(Jīn shīzi zhāng).*

46 Ibid., pp. 344-345: from *Hundred Theories in the Sea of Ideas of the Acataṁsaka sūtra (Huàyán jìhài bǎimén).*

47 Ibid. p. 345 *(Jīn shīzi zhāng).*

Theories in the Sea of Ideas of the Avataṁsaka-sūtra, (Huàyán jīng jìhǎi bǎimén), Fàzàng makes himself more clear. He says, that mind is the cause of qualities *(guṇa)*, which are its mere projection. But this elementary projection, again, influences the mind, which consequently evolves its apprehensions, ideas etc., which it cannot do without the stimulus of some – seemingly – external object. But, as this all is a merely illusory process, nothing real, i.e. nothing substantial, nothing having existence in itself is generated.[48]

6. *The five teachings.*

Fàzàng distinguishes five levels of Buddhist teaching:[49]

1) *That of the adherents of the Lesser Vehicle (Hīnayāna).* The characteristic of their teaching is, that they reject the permanency of outward appearances, which, in their opinion, come to be and perish every moment.

2) *The elementary teaching of the Greater Vehicle (Mahāyāna).* At this level, one sees, that things do not undergo origination and destruction by themselves, but are – even in their atomary existence – dependent on the projective function of the mind.

3) *The final teaching of Greater Vehicle.* Herein one realizes, that, although things are dependent on the mind, not existing in themselves, they still should be accepted in the way in which they are presented. In spite of their transcendental illusoriness, their practical value remains unaltered.

4) *The instantaneous teaching of the Greater Vehicle.* Here one discards the concepts of being and emptiness, to remain in a state of conceptless non-attachment. This is the experience of instantaneous enlightenment.

5) *The perfect teaching of the One Vehicle (ekayāna).* In the previous

48 Ibid, p. 345.
49 Ibid., pp. 346–47

stage, the *individual* mind has abandoned the question as to its own existence and non-existence. But one must know, that, after all, it is mind – now not individual but absolute mind – which, as an all-pervading light, manifests all things.

7. *The mastering of the ten mysteries.*

This seventh principle constitutes one of the most abstruse aspects of Fàzàng's teaching. In it, he enumerates ten theories or *mysteries,* all elucidating a side of the Avataṁsaka lore. In general, these ten mysteries try to inculcate universal relativity, but two types of relation are central: that between the *subjective* mind and its *objects*, the phenomena – which relate as the container and the contained – and that between whole and parts. These relations are elaborated in the first six 'mysteries.' The last four mysteries cope with the problems of (7) infinite regression, (8) the revelation of truth by means of the phenomenal, (9) the continuity of time, and (10) absolute mind.

Here follow the 'mysteries' under their original names:[50]

1) *Simultaneous completeness.* Here Fàzàng treats the relativity of the lion's gold and its form. The gold is the subjective intelligence, the form the phenomena of which it is aware. Both should not be considered as different parts of the absolute mind, but each of them presents this absolute in its completeness. The subjective covers the whole of existence, and, at the same time, the objective covers the same whole.

2) *Pure and mixed attributes of various store-houses.* The whole of the absolute mind is differentiated in various individual streams of consciousness (store-houses). Each of these individual streams implicates the whole of existence (absolute mind). While thus comprising the infinite, it still remains a finite and limited existence. While *having* in itself the pristine, pure, unstained, and undifferentiated mind, it still is an individual limited by its impurities and characteristic dispositions.

50 Ibid., pp.349-355.

3) *Mutual compatibility between the dissimilarities of the one and the many.* Mind and phenomena both cover the whole field of being (1), yet they do not mingle or interfere with one another. They represent the same whole from different sides.

4) *Mutual freedom among things.* The parts – the individuals constituting the whole of absolute mind, do not mutually exclude one another, nor do they bar the other's influence; they all mutually pervade one another.

5) *Hidden and displayed co-relation.* Between the subjective mind and its objects exists a relation of complementarity. You cannot determine both at the same time by your attention. When you fix the one, the other becomes indefinite. And when you globalize your attention in order to catch both sides, both are given in a mixture of vagueness and articulation.

6) *Peaceful compatibility of the minute and the abstruse.* Here the same is asserted as under (5), but now applied to the relation between whole and parts. Although (the) all is present in everything, only one thing at a time can lead attention.

7) *Indra's net.* If, according to (2), each part implicates the whole, then the lion – which here stands for the whole – is multiplied in all its parts; each part carries a 'copy' of the whole. But since every 'copy' of the whole, once more, contains all its parts, and these parts, again, bear yet another copy of this whole, the whole of absolute mind is infinitely reflected in itself. In fact the very process of self-reflection constitutes by its endless repetition the impression of a seeming multiplicity. It is like the net of Indra, which is sticked by jewels of which each one reflects all the others, each of which is itself reflecting all the others, so constituting an infinite regression.

8) *Relying on phenomenal things in order to elucidate truth.* By recognizing that it is ignorance which projects phenomenal reality, in this *démasqué* of phenomena, truth is revealed.

9) *Variable formation of the ten aspects of time in sections.* Everything phenomenal is momentary. Its existence lasts but a moment. Each individual moment has a past, present, and a future. Again, each of these have their own past, present and future, so that these nine aspects of time together with their unity in the moment, constitute ten aspects of time. The nine divisions of the moment form a single sequence. They are not separable parts of time, but relative distinctions, which mutually permeate each other.

10) *Excellent achievement according to the evolutions of the mind only.* Neither the subjective intelligence, nor the objective phenomena have any nature of their own. They are both, in their relativity, evolutions of the absolute mind which is beyond the distinctions of whole and part, and of subject and object.

8. *Embracing the six qualities.*

Again, here something is said about the relation between *whole* and *parts.* The lion, as a whole, is said to have the quality of *generalness,* the five sense organs, as parts of the whole, that of *particularity.* But, because whole and parts arise from the same cause, they have something similar in common, the quality of *similarity.* On the other hand, the fact that they do not overlap in function is their quality of *diversity.* The combining of the several organs into a whole, is their quality of *integration,* but their occupying distinct positions, is their quality of *differentiation.*[51]

What is said about the lion and its organs, can be said about any relation between whole and parts, and with respect to any phenomenal thing whatsoever.

9. *The achievement of bodhi*

Fàzàng equates *bodhi* with the 'Way' *(Dào)* and enlightenment *(jué).* It means that all things, even before being composed, have been in a state of 'calm extinction.' 'By avoiding both attachment and renun-

51 Fung, p. 355

ciation, we gain the road to bring us to the sea of Omniscience.' … Comprehension of the fact that from time without beginning all the illusions have fundamentally no reality, is called 'enlightenment'. The final embodying of all wisdom is called the achievement of *bodhi*.[52] It is like the awakening from a dream, in which there is nothing real, no solid reality. Phenomenal reality is like a rope mistaken for a snake, and later – in enlightenment – it is recognized as what it really is. But delusion and enlightenment stand in a mutual relationship to one another. They are not separate or successive realities. The pure mind consists in the comprehension of the sameness of illusion and non-illusion. Once enlightenment is obtained, the illusory itself becomes real, so that it is no *other* reality in which the enlightened enter. But, having changed states, the former existence is understood as ignorance.[53]

10. Entry into nirvāṇa.

In *nirvāṇa*, the qualities of phenomena and of the subjective mind have both disappeared; the sticking vices are no longer produced. 'Beauty and ugliness are both merely so many manifestations, and the mind is tranquil like the sea. Deluding thoughts are all extinguished, and there remain no compulsions. We cast off our bonds, emerge from our barriers, and eternally abandon the source of suffering. This is called *entry into nirvāṇa*.'[54] There is no longer a *distinction between the knower and the known, between subject and object*. 'The experience of the Buddha-realm means the emptiness of matter [stimuli] *(guṇa)*, absence of personal ego *(ātman)*, and the absence of phenomenal quality ([aesthetic form] *lakṣaṇa*)… However, having experienced entry into the realm, one may not dwell forever in calm extinction, for this would be contrary to the teaching of the Buddhas. One should teach what is beneficial and joyous, and (for this purpose) should study the expedients and wisdom of the Buddhas.'[55] Because of their wisdom, the Buddhas do not abide in *saṁsāra*, but because of their compassion they cannot stay in *nirvāṇa*.

52 Ibid., p. 356 *(Jīn shī zhāng)*.
53 Ibid., pp. 355-6.
54 Ibid., p. 356 *(Jīn shī zhāng)*.
55 Ibid., *Huàyán yīhāi bǎimén*

Epilogue.

One of the fundamental insights of Fàzàng is, that the subjective and objective both cover the whole field of existence, without barring each other's spheres or conflicting with one another. This is only possible, when both, the subjective and the objective, are not separate entities, but different *modes* of apprehending the same underlying being. This thought became standardized in the formulation of Chéngguān, the fourth patriarch of the Huàyán school (ca. 700), who said that the *Avataṁsaka-sūtra* speaks of four kinds of dharma-containers *(dharmadhātu, fǎjiè)*, those of *phenomenon,* of *noumenon,* of *unimpededness between noumenon and phenomenon,* and of *unimpededness between phenomenon and noumenon.*

A second important aspect of Fàzàng's thought is, that he, unlike Xuánzàng and most earlier Buddhist schools, adopts the idea of an absolute mind as contrasted to the individual mind. Fung[56] interpretes this as an adaptation to the Chinese mind, but this change to an objective idealism can better be interpreted as Vedantic influence upon the Buddhism of the *Avataṁsaka-sūtra*, which was already there before it came to China. It is striking that, as contrasted to the work of Xuánzàng, we here find – in the context of the interpretation of the *Avataṁsaka* – introduced many Vedāntic terms and similes.

THE FÀHUÀ, OR LOTUS SCHOOL FROM THE TIĀNTÀI MOUNTAINS. Whereas the Huàyán school follows the *Avataṁsaka-sūtra*, the Tiāntài school highly estimates the Lotus-sūtra *(Saddharma-puṇḍarīka, Lotus of the Good Law).* Its third patriarch was Zhíkǎi (538-597), who lived in the mountains which gave the school its name, and who followed Huìwén (550-577) and Huìsī (515-577) as leader. Zhíkǎi himself wrote many works on meditation techniques. The philosophical tenets of the school are laid down in the *Mahāyāna Method of Cessation and Contemplation (Dàchèng Zhìguān Fǎmén),* ascribed to Zhíkǎi's predecessor Huìsī. But actually it must be a work from after the 8th century. The following exposition is based on it.[57]

56 Ibid., p. 359.

57 CF. Fung, *History*, part ii, pp. 361-62: from *Mahāyāna Method of Cerssation and Contemplation (Dàchèng Zhìguān Fǎmén),*

Absolute mind.

The school of *Tiāntài* adopts – even with more emphasis than the Huàyán school – the idea of an absolute mind, which is known under two names, which differ in connotation: *bhutatathatā* (*zhēnrú,* genuine thusness) and *tathāgata-garbha* (*Rúlái zàng*, womb of the Thus-become). *Bhūtatathata* stands for the absolute mind in its undifferentiated, eternal, and all-pervading aspect; *tathagata-garbha* has a double meaning, firstly, it can denote *bhūtatathatā* as yet explained, but it also stands for the absolute mind in its world-including aspect, as the container of the whole of apparent diversity.

The whole world has the absolute mind as its substance, it is nothing apart from it. All things depend on it to have their being. Considered as substances they are only illusory appearances, which seemingly come into existence, and, again, seemingly go to destruction. In reality they consist of one single mind only. The *Awakening of Faith,* ascribed to Aśvaghoṣa, and quoted in the *Mahāyāna Method*, says about this: 'That in all things, which for all time has been independent of speech, terms, and mental causation, and which in the final analysis is everywhere the same, undergoes no change, and cannot be broken or destroyed: such is the one mind, which is therefore named the *bhūtatathatā*.[58] The absolute as 'Buddha-womb,' on the other hand, is also the absolute as related to the world of appearances; it is the container of this whole illusory world. But this fullness of all possible and actual reality is at the same time the inner essence of every individual existence. This means, that in essence every individual being encompasses the whole world of actual and possible appearances. All activity and appearance is a function of the one silent essence or absolute mind, which comprises the good as well as the bad: the pure and impure actualities and the pure and impure potentialities. This accent on the presence of good *and* evil is typical of the *Tiāntài* sect, and probably derives from Daoism. Accordingly, the womb of the Thus-become is everywhere undifferentiated (or empty) and adamantine in substance and reality, but in its functions *(yòng)* it is diverse and implicates the

58 Fung. *History*, part II, pp. 361-62: from *Mahāyāna Method of Cessation and Contemplation (Dàchèng Zhìguān Fǎmén).*

natures and manifestations of the variety of things. So there lies difference in what is without difference.[59]

The *Method* says with regard to this:

> 'How can I say this? What I mean is that it is not like a lump of clay, made up of a large number of particles of earth. How so? Because this lump of clay (regarded as an entity), is false; it is only its particles of earth that are real. Therefore, whereas each such particle has its own distinct substance, it is only through their combination that the lump of clay becomes formed, and thereby comes to contain all the distinctions of these many particles.
> Such, however, is not the case with the *Tathāgata-garbha*. How so? Because the *Tathāgata-garbha* is something genuine and real, a perfectly harmoniously undivided whole. Hence the *Tathāgata-garbha* is, in its totality, the nature of a single hair-pore that belongs to a single sentient being; (at the same time) it is, in its totality, the nature of all the hair-pores of that sentient being. And as in the case of the nature of the hair-pore, so in that of the natures of each and every other thing that there is in the world. As in the case of the nature of a single sentient being, so in that of the natures of all sentient beings of this world, and likewise of all the Buddhas who transcend this world. They are (each and all of them) the *Tathāgata-garbha* in its totality.'[60]

Three natures.

Practical life is explained by the theory of *karma*. The store-consciousness becomes impregnated by impure deeds, and this creates a condition of ignorance. In this ignorance, the seeds of the impure deeds bear fruit. This whole process evolves within the single mind, which is its only substance. This substance is the highest nature, comparable with the highest nature of Xuánzàng. Likewise the two other natures, already found in Xuánzàng and Fàzàng – designating various degrees of reality – are accepted: the *dependent nature (paratantra)* and the *nature of discrimination (*corresponding to that of *sole imagination* of Xuánzàng).

The highest nature, called 'nature of reality,' transcends all limita-

59 Fung, pp. 361-364.
60 Ibid., p. 364

tions, but, being bound by the impurities of life – i.e. conditioned by time – it is called 'store·consciousness' *(ālayavijñāna)*. This is the nature of dependency *(paratantra)*. The world as apprehended by the six senses and the thinking mind are called 'nature of sole discrimination.' These three natures stand to each other in a relationship comparable to that of water, stream, and waves. *Water* is the universal nature, *stream* is the nature possessed with a tendency, and the *waves* are the outward manifestations of this tendency. The *stream* or store-consciousness is the whole of seeds awaiting fruition. Considered as immutable substance, it is called 'pure mind,' but with a view to its evolving manifestations, it is called 'store-consciousness.' Therefore it comprises truth and diversity. The highest nature also has a double aspect, according to whether it is apprehended in its immutable aspect or with reference to its relation to appearance, or, in other words, according to whether it is the nature of sentient beings or of the Buddhas. The single mind unaware of itself is active, but self-conscious it is tranquil; tranquil it is pure, active impure. In the same way, the store-consciousnes – which is mind in relation to forms – has a pure and an impure aspect: directed to liberation it is pure, given to vices it is impure. Likewise also the nature of sole discrimination has a pure and an impure aspect.

Sole discrimination poses things as real. Clinging to things thus apprehended, the mind is deformed by its illusions, and develops particular tendencies. It exists in correlation with the dependent nature *(ālaya-vijñāna)*. For by accepting things as real, the mind develops tendencies and becomes store-consciousness, and this, again, manifests itself by positing things as real. Realizing this mutual dependency, the absolute is understood, and the store-consciousness becomes pure.[61]

The universal and the individual mind.

If all beings have the single mind as their substance, why then do they experience sometimes things in common, and at other times not? There is a universal substance common to every individual being, which is responsible for the common elements in experience, but at the same time, beings differ among each other, because their respective streams of consciousness are characterized by the 'impregnations'

61 Ibid., pp. 365-69.

caused by their particular deeds. The kind of deeds common to the history of all people, constitutes the common world of mountains, rivers etc. in which we live. But those deeds which are characteristic of particular beings and mark their individual history, ripen into the particular characteristics of the different lives of particular beings. The line between common and individual *karma* is also that which forms the barrier between the world outside and that inside, between the experience of the so-called objective world and that of one's own body, feelings, and mental phenomena. The first is there for all, the latter can be experienced only by one's own inner sense. Each type of conduct makes a hidden nature, resting in the absolute, reveal itself to common or individual experience.[62]

The integration of all things.

All things are connected in a relation of mutual compatibility. The absolute comprises the eternal essences of all things, but hidden from manifestation. As these are all integrated in the one essence of the Buddha-nature, their evolution in time and space, in the realm of sensory experience, also cannot cause contradictions regarding particular manifestations. Each nature within the Buddha-nature would be nought if this Buddha-nature would therein not be present in its entirety. Likewise in each manifestation of such a nature the universal nature is present as a whole. There can be no phenomenon in which the single mind is not given uniformly and integrally. The differences presented by these diverse phenomena have relative existence only. They are in the way as they are given in a single mental act. Phenomena belonging to different acts, cannot be brought into a direct relationship with one another. We can talk about 'large' or 'small,' 'long' or 'short,' but these have only subjective and relative existence. We may experience a mountain as big, and a mustardseed as small, but both can in the experience of a single man be made to look small or big. Only in their relative existence in the single act, the one is big and the other is small. And in that act, the 'small' and the 'big' are abstractions from the full mind that is present entirely. It lies in the nature of the mind that it can only represent the compatible, that it can only act by

62 Fung, pp. 365-69.

unifying. Therefore it harmonizes all things. 'Each and every particle of matter is a manifestation of all the Buddha realms of the ten directions.' 'The three ages and, in fact, the totality of time, become, when understood, a single instant.'[63] All things can be integrated, because as manifestations they have no reality in themselves but are dependent upon mind to be shown. All things are merely the functioning of the mind, conditioned by its previous functioning.[64]

Cessation and contemplation.

Man is trapped in the circle of *saṁsāra*, because he sticks to the ideas, concepts, and attachments that form his world. To escape from it, one must follow the path of spiritual cultivation. Then finally, the original, pure mind will become manifested, such as is the case in 'cessation' *(nirodha, zhǐ)* and contemplation *(guān)*.

'Cessation' is the same as the experiencing of *nirvāṇa*. It is described as the experiencing of the unsubstantiality of the *dharmas*. At the same time it is the stopping of the stream of illusory thoughts. The mind's activity becomes calmed like an ocean of which the waves are stilled, the same water, the same world, but without its usual turbulent agitation. In this state there is no active life. One sits down, merged in absorption. If this state would not be interrupted, it would mean – after some time – the end of life itself. But since for Buddhas and *bodhisattvas* there still remains the task of saving the world from suffering, after having been merged in it, they again rise from this state with a mind in, what is called by Fung, a state of 'contemplation' *(guān)*. What is this 'contemplation'? Through it we know, that although things are illusory, they still have a relative existence in the sense that they are caused, and thus follow the laws of causation, i.e. that of *dependent origination*. The manifestations which we consider as our world are not given at random, but in the frame of an ordered whole. It is contemplation or introspection that enables philosophical reflection, and this establishes for example the theory of the *Three Natures*. It makes it possible to expound the Teaching, coming back from the state of

63 Ibid., p. 374 *(Dāchéng zhíguān)*.
64 Ibid., pp. 370-375.

absorption, like the voyager, who, having come back from a marvelous country, describes to others the way that he once went himself.[65]

In cessation one loses all sense of plurality. One becomes the one mind and assumes all sentient beings as a perfect body. There is the 'calm limpid purity' of inner silence. 'It functions without appearing to function, and acts without appearing to act. All things are originally everywhere the same, and so too is the nature of the mind. This then is the profound nature in its essential substance.'[66]

> 'The achievement reached by contemplation is that of manifesting the essential nature of the mind so that it functions without interference with the world of physical things, and spontaneously emanates the potentialities of all things, both pure and impure... because of the achievement of cessation, one is not polluted by the world. Yet because of the achievement of contemplation, one is not restricted to silent inactivity. Or, finally, because of the achievement of cessation, one functions yet remains ever still. But because of the achievement of contemplation, one stays still yet remains ever functioning.'[67]

In this concept of liberation, the world as such is not set aside: 'Only eliminate the ills, but not the things. The ills consist in the sensory clingings, but not in the great functioning self.' ... Although we know that the existence of things, is not (real) existence, we also know that this does not prevent their non-existence from existing.[68] When the mind is purified from its attachments, it can enter the world without being soiled by it.

Pure and impure natures.

The universal mind contains in itself all natures as potentialities for manifestation, the pure as well as the impure. Now, the substance of all beings, ordinary living men and animals, as well as Buddhas and bodhisattvas, is nothing but this universal mind, and therefore all be-

65 Fung, pp.375-378
66 Ibid., p.374 *(Dāchéng zhíguān)*
67 Ibid.
68 Ibid.

ings contain in themselves both natures, the pure and the impure. One cannot make or destroy the innate natures, neither the pure nor the impure, but one can make them manifest by either performing good or bad deeds. By doing wrong, the mind's bad nature is impregnated by bad *karma*, and the being thus impregnated stays in a bad condition, having bad experiences, while the being performing good deeds, impregnates the mind's pure nature with good *karma*, and thereby causes the pure nature to appear, which eventually may result in becoming a saint, *bodhisattva*, or Buddha, beings who realize the highest experiences. But these different kinds of actions, and the habitualities resulting from them, do change nothing in the hidden nature of all things, which is beyond creation and destruction, they only pertain to the phenomenal, the illusory sphere of appearance. In reality there is nowhere a difference in nature.[69]

Ignorance and enlightenment.

If both the pure and the impure natures are inherent in the universal mind, which functions in every being, why then is the one better than the other? It is said that the impure, although springing from the mind, is opposed to it, and that the pure is following it. This comes to the same as saying, that pure deeds issue in a self-knowledge of the mind, and bad deeds result in ever graver forms of ignorance. Although both the Buddhas and the ignorant partake of the impurities of the world, only the latter are lost in them, whereas the Buddhas are aware of their illusory nature. The ignorant lack enlightenment *(bodhi* or *jñāna)*. Because of this enlightenment, a Buddha, although he enters the cycle of rebirth, and performs impure acts, he can do this as a being from another order, like an actor entering a stage-setting. But unlike a normal actor, he is aware of the fact that his co-actors take the play for reality and act according to that, being subject to real hopes and fears. He must convince them of the fact that it is all just a play and thereby free them from their agonies. He teaches living beings that all the world is but the product of the mind.

This kind of enlightened action in the world, as being caused and conditioned – like all other mundane acts – is called 'nature of de-

69 Ibid., pp. 378-380.

pendency' in its pure aspect. Because it is – like actions motivated by desire – purposive, it is called 'nature of intentional thought' in its pure aspect. In this way a Buddha partakes of all the three natures, also the lower ones, but in acting in the world, he is motivated in a way diametrically opposed to the motivation of ordinary beings; while the latter try to satisfy their desires, the Buddha only acts to save others. He does not aim at his own well-being, since all his wishes are already stilled and fulfilled. He knows, and in this knowledge lies the ultimate satisfaction. Being in the world, he never abandons enlightenment. He possesses the wisdom by which he is always aware of the pureness of the inner mind, and this awareness, again, is nothing else but the pure mind being aware of itself. So it is in the Buddhas, that the universal mind comes to know itself.[70]

The intellectual position of the Tiāntài school

The teaching of theTiāntài school is influenced by the thinking of Xuánzàng and the Huàyán. In all these forms of thinking the mind constitutes the ultimate principle. But from Xuánzàng onwards, there is a progressive shift from subjective to absolute idealism. For Xuánzàng the seeds of things were contained in the store-consciousness. But of these there were many streams, corresponding to the multitude of living beings. The seeds in the different streams were the outcome of different types of *'karma,'* and the *'karma'* was conditioned by different seeds. Here we find a philosophy of process. The actuality of our world is not something pre-established, but is nothing but the horizon formed by the similar perspectives held by consciousness-streams conditioned by similar deeds. The world is more or less an accidental outcome of the merit of our deeds.The world does not have a hard kernel; it is nothing beyond the floating phenomena of life. In the Huàyán we find a universal mind as the functioning principle in every particular mind. Every mind has individual being by virtue of this transcendental mind, which is waiting to be discovered by religious searchers. Here something divine enters the Buddhist scene. The accent on this universal mind is even stronger in the Tiāntài school. Here the universal mind is called the womb of the Buddha *(tathāgata-*

70 Fung, pp. 380-83.

garbha). It does not carry merely particular potentialities, but, as an absolute mind, it carries the entire realm of possibility. All is contained in its all-embracing nature, which, at the same time, is hidden in each and every being. Good and evil are pre-established in it, and are the unavoidable characters in the script of the cosmic drama. Even the Buddhas cannot change this, they only distinguish themselves from other beings by not being deceived by the utter realism of the scene – which suggests that it is reality and not a play –, and by curing others from such deception. In this concept of the universal mind comprising the whole of the phenomenal process in detail, the Tiāntài goes further in its 'Platonic' realism than the Huàyán. For by absorbing all phenomena in the universal nature, and letting become manifest only that which already is, the phenomena of the world become less illusory than in earlier forms of Buddhism; they are no longer opposed to the absolute, but share in it, by being contained in it.

The utter consequence of this thought was brought forward by Zhànrán (711-782). He says, that the universal mind is not only present in living beings, but also in the constituting particles of inanimate matter. The Buddha-nature is in every particle of dust. Thus, mind is no longer merely a principle of life, but also of existence. The nature of all, of the whole, is present in the minutest of its parts. For the better performance of their role, the script of the entire drama is copied for the distribution among even the least conspicuous figurants. Whether the water is clear or muddy, it does not lose its nature of wetness. Whether mind is self-conscious (limpid) or unaware of its own nature, it does not lose its nature of perceptivity, of noting.[71]

T*HE CHÁN SCHOOL* The *Chán* school, better known as Zen, is probably the most uniquely Chinese of all Buddhist schools. It is said that it was brought to China from India by Bodhidharma, who allegedly worked in China during the reign of emperor Wū (502-549). Between him and the Buddha – one says – there was a continuous line of patriarchs, transmitting their esoteric teaching without words from mind to mind. There is no evidence for such a tradition – but how could there be for a tradition without spoken or written expres-

71 Ibid., pp. 383-86.

sion? Leaving the historicity of Bodhidharma for what it is, we do better to seek the real roots of Chán in the Chinese tradition itself. We have seen, that Chinese Buddhism had an early and a later start. In its early phase it was brought into connection with Daoism. This phase culminated in thinkers like Sēngzhào and Dàoshēng, of whom the first made much of equating the Buddhist principle of relativity or emptiness *(śūnyatā)* with the Daoist 'non-being' *(wú)*, and the second stressed another principle, also of Daoist origin, viz. that of instantaneous enlightenment *(dǔn wú)*. Both these principles play an important role in Zen.

The later start of Chinese Buddhism inaugurated with Xuánzàng, who was a faithful representative of the Indian Mere-ideation school of Vasubandhu. Here there is much less Daoist influence. While the Huàyán and Tiāntài schools are more or less free interpretations and elaborations of the idealist principle, the Chán school takes up the line of the earlier tradition of Chinese Buddhism, influenced on the one hand by the Madhyamaka tenet of relativity, interpreted as 'emptiness,' and on the other by the Daoist idea of the sudden break-through of wisdom.

A line of patriarchs is said to have handed down the meditative practices of Chán (which is the Chinese rendering of Indian *dhyāna* or 'meditation'). The first is the Bodhidharma already mentioned, the second Huìkě (487-593), followed by Sēngcàn (?-606), Dàoxīn (580-636), and Hóngrěn (602-675). After that the school split into a northern and a southern branch, the former headed by Shénxiù (ca. 600-706), and the latter by Huìnéng (638-713). Especially in the southern school much emphasis was laid on the doctrine of instantaneous enlightenment. This southern school continued the Zen-tradition, while the northern school fell into oblivion.[72]

Wisdom

As with Sēngzhào, wisdom *(prajñā)* is a kind of knowledge that is not knowledge; it is the intuitive certainty in following the right path, and – being identified with the real thing – a knowing of the real quality of things. It is the same as emptiness, *nirvāṇa*, and enlightenment.

72 Fung, pp. 386-88

There are no gradations in this enlightenment or wisdom, once gained it is gained completely. It is complete identification with truth.

What is this truth? There are two interpretations: one says that it is nothing at all, something completely without quality and undefinable; the other interpretation says that it is the mind from which all things arise, without which nothing can be, because it makes everything appear. As such it is also called 'original nature' or 'Buddha-nature.' Comprehending the real quality of things is the same as comprehending this mind and perceiving its nature in oneself. The first interpretation seems to base itself on Sēngzhào, the second on Dàoshēng.

All Chán adherents, however, subscribe to the following five points:[73]

1) *The highest truth or first principle is inexpressible.*
2) *Wisdom cannot be cultivated.*
3) *In the last resort nothing is gained.*
4) *There is nothing much in the Buddhist teaching.*
5) *In carrying water and chopping wood: therein lies the wonderful Dào.*

1. The highest truth is inexpressible.

In the line of the *Prajñā-pāramitā* tradition, in Chán the highest truth is not something that can be objectified; therefore it also cannot be put in a verbal statement. Truth is something to be lived rather than something to be said. Therefore, like the Buddha himself, Chán is averse to metaphysical speculation. It is not really a philosophy, but a quest for the truthful way of life. This is achieved by 'not being linked with all things.' 'What is this?' asked the lay Buddhist Páng Yùn. To him master Dàoyī replied: Wait until at one gulp you can drink up the water in the West river, and I will tell you.[74] Dàoyī could not answer and should not answer, and this really was the answer.

73 Ibid., pp. 388-90
74 Fung, pp. 390-93; op. cit., p. 393.

2. Wisdom cannot be cultivated.

There is a poem by Huìnéng that runs as follows:[75]

Originally there was no 'Bodhi-tree,'
Nor was there any mirror.
Since originally there was nothing, Whereon can the dust fall?

The poem must be read in the light of the following story:

'Mǎzǔ (Dàoyī) lived in the Chuánfǎ monastery on the Southern Peak. There he occupied a solitary hut in which all alone he practised meditation *(chán)*, paying no attention to those who came to visit him.

One day Huáiràng kept grinding a brick in front of the hut, but Mǎzǔ still paid no attention. This having continued for a long time, Mǎzǔ finally asked: 'What are you doing?' The teacher (Huáiràng) replied that he was grinding to make a mirror. 'How can a mirror be made by grinding bricks?' asked Mǎzǔ. Replied the teacher: 'If a mirror cannot be made by grinding bricks, how can a Buddha be made by practising meditation?''[76]

The gist of all this is, that since the state of freedom is radically and totally different from the state of bondage by works, it is impossible to gain this state by means of works, that is, by conscious effort. For conscious effort is a form of attachment, albeit an attachment to the highest good, and freedom is only to be gained by an abandonment of all attachment, a letting loose of all fetters. Freedom is the absence of any object (body, Bodhi-tree) and of any self (mind, mirror). In that case there is nothing to be purified by conscious effort. Liberation is always there for the one who is prepared to see it, it is not something to be made or to be accomplished by 'angry preparations.' Because there is in liberation not something that comes to be, there also is no gradual emancipation. One cannot be partly in bondage and partly in freedom. Freedom is realized all at once. This is what is meant by 'sudden enlightenment.'

75 Ibid., p. 391: from *Sūtra spoken by the sixth Patriarch, Teacher of the Buddhist Truth (Liùzǔ dàshū fǎbǎo tánjīng).*

76 Ibid., pp. 391-92: from *Recorded Sayings of Ancient Worthies (Gǔzūnxu yǔlù)*

What is this state of freedom? Is it a state of real nothingness, as may be suggested by the fact that in it there is an absence of objects? No, this is not meant. In freedom one still goes on living, for how could there be freedom in the absence of someone to be free? The absence of objects merely points to the absence of the subject-object relation. The mind of the liberated is not intent on any object, neither in a cognitive nor in a practical sense. In the same way it is not conscious of itself, for what reason this mind also can be termed a *no-mind*. The fact is, that the mind cannot any longer be distinguished from its content. Because the mind is not filled with the virtual reality of something it *would like* to know or *would like* to have, but is really filled with the true reality of what is before us, the fragrance as smelled, the savour as tasted, the colour as seen, it does never transcend actuality. It is not attracted by the pleasant, nor repulsed by the loathsome. It is simply experience as such enjoyed in a neutral and placid mood. Apart from it there is no world-shocking enlightenment or freedom. It is just taking the ordinary facts of life without hurry or worry·[77] Xiyùn said:

> 'If you understand this, what need to be driven hither and thither? The only thing to be done is to rid yourself of your old *karma*, as opportunity offers, and not create more from which will flow new calamities.'[78]

This, however, does not mean to do nothing at all, but simply to act without a deliberate mind. Dàoyī says:

> 'The intrinsic nature (of man) is already enough. Not to be clamped either to good or evil is all that a man engaged in spiritual cultivation needs to do. To cleave to the good and eschew the evil, to contemplate emptiness, and to enter the state of concentration: all these are deliberate activities…'[79]

Again, Huáihài says: 'To have a polluting love for either the sagely or the mortal spheres is to have emotions, and thereby to lack the Buddha-na-

77 Ibid., pp.393-399.
78 Ibid., p.393 *(Gŭzūnxu yŭlù)*
79 Fung, p.394.

ture. But if, vis-à-vis these sagely and mortal spheres, including all things existent and non-existent, you have no mind that selects or rejects; if, in fact, you do not even have the idea of selection or rejection – this is to lack emotions and thereby to possess the Buddha-nature. It is called lacking them simply because one is not tied to them. This is not the same as the absence of the feeling of a tree, a stone, the empty air, a yellow flower, or the blue-green bamboo.'[80]

The wise stays in the midst of the world but is not stained by it, because he is not in the state of affliction *(kleśa)*, but in that of *bodhi*. He does good deeds, but not with an eye on the good result. Not that for him causality does not operate, but in his state there is nothing that can contribute to his well-being. Therefore, although things appear to him, there is nothing he *acquires;* he is already one with all.

3. *In the last resort nothing is gained.*

Achieving enlightenment is not gaining something. What one was deluded about before is the same as what one is now enlightened about. Before entering the Path, mountains were mountains and rivers rivers, and after enlightenment, again, mountains are mountains and rivers rivers. And just as the common man 'wears his clothes, eats his food, relieves his bowels, and passes water,' so does the sage.[81] Searching enlightenment is like riding an ass in search for the donkey. Qīngyuǎn said: 'There are only two diseases: one is riding an ass to search for the ass; the other is riding an ass and be unwilling to dismount. One should not search for the ass at all. Thus the deluded state of mind ceases to exist. But if, having found the ass, one is unwilling to dismount[82], this disease is most difficult to cure. I tell you, do not ride the ass at all. You yourself are the ass. Mountains, rivers, and plains are all the ass. Why do you ride on it? If you ride, you cannot cure your disease. But if you do not ride, the universe in all directions becomes one wide expanse. With these two diseases expelled, nothing remains

80 Ibid., p. 394
81 Ibid., p. 401.
82 Ibid., p. 400.

to affect your mind. This is spiritual cultivation. You need do nothing more.'

'Before enlightenment there is no spiritual cultivation that can be deliberately practised. After it, there is no Buddhahood to be achieved.'[83] Dàoyī says: 'We speak of enlightenment in contrast to delusion. But since there is originally no delusion, enlightenment also cannot stand.' This is what is known as 'obtaining that is not obtaining,' and this it is what is meant when it is said that 'in the last resort nothing is gained.'[84]

4. *There is nothing much in the Buddhist teaching.*

The practice of Chán is sometimes described as the *gold and ordure method*. Like the master of Qīngyǔan said: Before it is comprehended it is all like gold; after it is comprehended, it is all like ordure. Chán entails nothing great, nothing fantastic, nothing secret or abstruse. It is sometimes said, that the Buddha had a secret doctrine, but that his pupil Mahākāśyapa did not keep the secret. According to Dàoyīng (9th century) this means that: As long as you do not understand, it remains a secret of the World-Honoured One (the Buddha); but once you do understand, it becomes the unkept secret of Mahākāśyapa.[85] If there is a secret, it is an open secret.

The cosmological and psychological theories of early Buddhism are regarded in Chán as superfluous furniture. They are useless, and should be done away with. What is really important does not transcend the simple facts of daily life. Doing the things that everyone does, but with an equanimous mind, that is all that's needed. Yìxuán (Lǐnjí) asked his teacher Huángbò (Xīyùn) three times about the main tenets of Buddhism, and three times received a beating. Later, under another teacher, he attained enlightenment. He recognized: 'At bottom there is nothing very much in Huángbò's Buddhism.[86] As the *Transmission of the Lamp* makes clear, this must be said not only of the Buddhism of Huángbò, but of all Buddhism.

83 Ibid., p. 400
84 Ibid., 400-1
85 Ibid., p. 402: from Transmission of the Lamp (*Chuándēng lù*)
86 Fung, p. 402: from Transmission of the Lamp *(Chuándēng lù)*

In carrying water and chopping wood: therein lies the wonderful Dào.

The mind of the sage is not different from that of ordinary men. For the 'ordinary mind is the Dào.'[87] Enlightenment is nothing else but a re-entering ordinary humanity. It is even a transcending of sagehood. After coming to understand the other side, you come back and live on this side, tell the *Sayings of the Ancient Worthies*.[88]

The sage does not act in another way than the ordinary man, but since he left ordinary life to go to the other side, and returned again from there, to him his acts have a different significance. What before enlightenment was lust and anger, after that is called Buddha-wisdom. The enlightened do not *act* different, they *are* different. To have unpolluted wisdom one must simply empty one's mind. Huáihài says: Daily go out, stay at home, or sleep, but in every word you say, do not attach yourself to the things of purposeful activity. Then, whatever you say or wherever you look, all will be unpolluted.[89] In the work of Páng Yùn we read: 'Spirit-like understanding and divine functioning lie in carrying water and chopping wood.'[89]

Although doing the same acts as ordinary men, the wise do not evoke retribution. This is because their acts are done without selfish interest. Of acts in themselves it cannot be said whether they are sinful or not.

> 'Whether there is sin or not, depends on the man. If he be greedy for all things, both 'existent' and 'non-existent'; if his mind be set on selecting and rejecting; and if he be unable to pass beyond the three phrases [i.e. 'being,' 'non-being,' and 'neither being nor non-being'] – then it may be positively stated that this man has sin. But if he go beyond the three phrases, if his mind be like a void emptiness, and if he not even think about this void emptiness, then it may be positively stated that this man is without sin.'[90]
>
> 'To eat all day yet not swallow a grain of rice, to walk all day yet not tread an inch of ground, to have no distinction during that time be-

87 Ibid., p.403
88 Ibid., p.405.
89 Ibid., *(Gŭzūnxu yŭlù)*
90 Ibid., p. 404 *(Chuándēng lù)*

> tween object and subject, and to be inseparable from things the livelong day, yet not deluded by them: this is to be the man who is at ease with himself.'[91]

He is amid the phenomenal, yet devoid of the phenomenal. For the one on the Buddhist path this state, if ever, is very difficult, and only with strenuous effort to achieve, but after enlightenment having come, it goes effortless, spontaneous. In all his acts, he does not assert his being. That's why it is said, that he is identified with non-being. He has abandoned his opposition to his nature. Neither the man as such, nor his environment are given up, only the attitude towards oneself and towards the environment has changed. He is no more disabled and dissatisfied. It is his response to reality that constitutes the Dào. In his spontaneity activity is the same as non-activity. Not being involved, he yet functions.

Thus Chán brought Buddhism back to the world.

91 Ibid., p. 404

Pagoda, Wiki Commons

Part III
Buddhism in Japan

As far as philosophical and religious thinking is concerned, Japan is much indebted to China. This is so in spite of the fact that the Japanese temper is very different from the Chinese, and that it has a very specific aesthetic sense of its own. Although Japan has a religion of its own soil, Shinto, this never became philosophically articulated, close as it is to nature religion.

Among the philosophies imported from China, Buddhism occupies the first place, but also Confucianism had a considerable influence on the Japanese mind. From the beginning there was a development of Buddhism in which strong Confucianist elements were assimilated. It was only in the Tokugawa period (16th-19th century) that Confucianism became the predominant stream of thought, and, to a certain extent, was opposed to Buddhism. Daoism never was able to seize as much importance in Japan as it did in China. It seems that Shinto has taken over that role. Often it is said that this Shinto religion is indigenous, but in fact also this Shintoism has grown out of indigenous shamanism, which underwent strong Buddhist and Confucianist influences.

The types of Buddhism that can be found in Japan are the same as that are found in China. We find here the philosophies of Tiāntái and Huàyán, which bear in Japan the respective names of *Tendai* and *Kegon*. Chán is known under the name *Zen*. Important for Japan are also the Pure Land *Jōdo*) sect and the Mantra sect introduced by Kūkai. Also these sects were already known earlier in China, and even in India, although we have not mentioned them. But in the Japanese situation they have become of particular importance.

Although Zen is not the only form of Buddhism known in Japan, and one of the latest to be introduced, the Zen way of life had so much impact on Japanese affairs, influencing the aesthetics of poetry, tea-ceremony, flower-arrangement, garden-architecture etc., that we will here mainly pay attention to Zen Buddhism, and especially to a Zen master who gave to Chinese Chán a specific Japanese flavour. This master is Dōgen, whose *Shōbōgenzō* (The Eye and Trasury of the True Law) is a work of considerable influence. In 1227 he introduced in Japan one of the two Zen schools that are still important there today, viz, the Sōtō school, which is based on the teaching of Xìngsī (677-744). The other branch of Zen is the Rinzai school, which follows the teaching of Huáiràng (?-775) and Yìxuán, who is also called Lĭnjí (Rinzai in Japanese).

As an example of this school we will say something about Hakuin (1685-1769).

Common in both these schools is the quest for enlightenment or the natural and unfettered way of life. This is called *satori* in Japanese. The difference between these two schools is as Alan Watts[1] remarks, that the Rinzai school seems to strive after *satori*, and it seems that this means that the intensity of it is proportionate to the feeling of doubt and seeking that precedes it. But this characteristic renders the Rinzai school vulnarable to the reproach of the Sōtō school, that such a *satori* which is relative to a doubt cannot be ultimate and must retain some dualistic character. The Sōtō school, on the other hand, seems to emphasize mere motiveless action. This is based on the knowledge that the Buddha nature is not something to be searched for, but is an ever present reality which only should be recongnized. We might say that this latter conviction is the more philosophical in character, and it can be no accident that the most philosophical of all Japanese Zen masters, Dōgen, introduced it.

1 Alan Watts, The Way of Zen, Penguin 1962, p. 130

Chapter 11

The Character of Japanese Buddhism

Typical characteristics of Japanese Buddhism – and of Japanese thinking in general – are an inclination to the concrete and – as Nakamura[2] calls it – an orientation towards the·limited human nexus; i.e. thinking tends not to be universal but is centred around the particular conditions of the Japanese situation and society. The love for the concrete and phenomenal expresses itself e.g. in the lack of abstract concepts and in the tendency to translate the abstract into the concrete picturing of natural scenery in poetry or painting. A striking example of the 'translation' of a Chinese philosophical poem by Kūkai is given by Nakamura.[3] The Chinese version reads:

Whatever is phenomenal is impermanent
Its essential characteristic is appearance and disappearance
When these appearances and disappearances come to repose,
tranquillity is comfort.

The version of Kūkai reads:

Although fragrant in hue
(blosoms} are scattered
For everyone life is impermanent
This morning I crossed the uttermost limit
A shallow dream I will not dream, nor will I become intoxicated.

2 Hajime Nakamura, *Ways of Thinking of Eastern People,* Honolulu, 1964, 1985, ch. 35, passim

3 Ibid., p. 499.

The connection of Buddhism with the Japanese social nexus is exemplified in the way in which it was introduced in Japan. The original Buddhism was far from a state religion. Kings were placed in the same category as robbers. And people were advised to avoid them as much as possible, and, if they cannot escape them, be on their guard. But in Japan Buddhism was introduced as a present from the Korean king to the Japanese emperor and it was at first the religion of the nobility. Around the middle of the 6th century, the king of Paekche (in Korea), Syöng Myöng, sent a mission to Kimmei (the emperor of Japan) with presents, among which an image of the Buddha and several *sūtras*. He praised these highly, saying that even Confucius did not reach the knowledge contained in it. Especially the sculpture of the Buddha was highly admired by the emperor and his court. Traditional Japanese religion did not know works of art of this type. It contributed to the acceptance of Buddhism in Japan. At the end of the 6th century Japan lost much of her domains on the Korean peninsula, also the allied kingdom of Paekche. Many Korean refugees fled to Japan and took with them their Buddhistic culture.

It was prince Shōtoku (574-622), who saw in Buddhism the moral base on which to build the Japanese state. By the time he undertook the service of the imperial throne in AD 593, Buddhism in Japan only spread among immigrants, tradesmen and members of the royal family. The royal family thought that the idea of one truth might contribute to the consolidation of their sovereign power. Instead of taking refuge in the 'Dharma', Japanese Buddhism paid homage to the eternal Buddha. This Buddha was brought into connection with ancestor and emperor worship. This Japanese stress on the Buddha as the eternal aspect of sovereignty, made Buddhism much more nationalistic in character than in India or China, where much more stress was laid on 'dharma' (law) and the community (*saṁgha*). So it was said by Shinran (founder of the Shin sect of Jōdo Buddhism) that Shōtoku 'found in Buddhism a universal basis for the relationship between the ruler and the ruled. His inspiration helped in achieving national unity and in subduing the clannish spirit under it.'[4] For this aim of achieving national unity, Shō-

4 Shōson Miyamoto, *The Relation of Philosophical Theory to Practical Affairs in Japan:* in *The Japanese Mind*, ed. Ch. A. Moore, Honolulu, 1967, p. 6.

toku also used Confucianist ideas. He accepted the Doctrine of the Mean and also the *yīn-yáng* dichotomy of later times. The idea of the mandate of heaven was used to establish the central authority of the court. He omitted, however, the doctrine found in the Mencius, that heaven can withdraw its mandate when the sovereign fails in justice, and bestow it upon someone else, thus making the blood-succession of the emperor into something absolute. The motivation for all this need not be sought for in a power-hunger from the side of the imperial family, but rather in the necessity of establishing national peace in a land apt to be tormented by clan feuds. This is why Shōtoku is often considered as the father of the Japanese nation.

Chapter 12

Buddhist Sects

Shōtoku had been far from a sectarian. But already soon two types of Buddhism became predominant in circles of the court and the nobility, viz. the Tendai and the Shingon sects. In the Nara-period (710-784) also the Kegon (Huàyán) sect became quite influential. The Kegon philosophy, however, will not be dwellt upon here, since no substantially new development is seen in Japan beyond the Chinese original.

It seems to have been the esoteric character of the Shingon sect, and its willingness to accept the traditional gods of Japan, including the sun-goddess Amaterasu – from which the emperor is said to be a descendant –, that made it the court religion par excellence. And although the Tendai sect theoretically is less apt to compromise, it too did not show an exclusive attitude towards traditional thinking. So it was said: *'Kyūchū Shingon Koge Tendai'* (Esoteric Shingon for the imperial court rites and esoteric Tendai for aristocratic ritualism).

Saichō, or Dengyō Daishi (767-822), introduced in Japan the Tendai (Tiāntái) form of Buddhism. This school bases itself mainly on the *Saddharma-puṇḍarīka sūtra* (Lotus of the True Dharma Sūtra), in Japanese called the 'Hokke'-sūtra. The basic features of this sect are the same as already discussed when the Chinese Tiāntái was spoken of. It is stated that only a Buddha can realize the true state of all *'dharmas'* (here 'objects' or 'things') as they are, i.e. their 'thusness' or 'suchness.' In experience, this thusness is manifested in various modes. But these modes belong to the realm of relativity. They can be changed and expressed in words. But the thusness (the *'to tí,'* the essence) escapes verbal determination and change. Now, it seems, that only an indirect knowledge of this essence is possible, viz. by completion of the knowledge of its relative expressions. In fact this completion actually is the essence of things. And so essence as such is ultimately not something in itself.

This is the highest truth. All things have in themselves this reference to an ultimate end, although they are in various modes of actuality. In their limited actuality they are, so to say, pregnant with truth, and only because they incorporate truth they can be passing into and from actuality.

The world of living beings is divided into several realms, from the lowest inmates of hell to the Buddhas (the enlightened ones). But what has been stated above about the completion that constitutes the essence of things, indicates that these realms are not separate. In each thing the natures of all others are present, although in varying degrees of actuality. The all is the one and the one the all. Because of this, all beings have the potentiality to become complete, to become Buddha(s) (although this may require many incarnations). This Buddhahood can be contained in one thought (or flash of consciousness), which, spreading through the universe, awakens all things, so that they may enter existence.[5] The distinctive feature of Japanese Tendai now seems to be its concern for the protection of the Japanese state. According to Nakamura there exists in Japanese thinking in general a tendency of substituting the real for the ideal. The Japanese state, with its emperor, seemed suited to take the place of the absolute. So it was already Saichō, who coined the term *'Dai Nippon'* (Great Japan). But it was Nichiren (1222-1282), the founder of the new 'Hokke' sect, who further elaborated the Tendai doctrine into a more national way of thinking. The Buddhist thinking was simply transformed in a way of worship and salvation. This was one aspect of the process of making Buddhism spread among the people in the Kamakura period, the time of the decline of the power of the nobility and of the rise of the warrior and lower classes. The more populist version of the Tendai doctrine now told that it was enough to recite the title of the *Hokke-sūtra*, in Japanese 'Namumyō Horengekyō,' and to worship the guardians

5 Shinshō Hanayama, *Buddhism of the Great Vehicle*, in *The Japanese Mind*, pp. 36-37.

of the four quarters, with among them, besides the founders of the Tendai sect, also the sun-goddess and ancestor of the imperial house, Amaterasu Ōmikami.

The Shingon sect was introduced in Japan by Kūkai, also named 'Kōbō Daishi.' It is also called the Mantra School, or, in Chinese, the School of *Zhēnyán*. It has a strong mystical character. Kūkai was born in 774 as a member of an aristocratic family. He was destined to enter governmental service. But against the wishes of his family he decided to study Buddhism. It is said that in his youth, after he left the university of Nagaoka, he used to meditate in the mountains. Here he developed a close feeling with nature and he learned to look at natural phenomena as divinities in the traditional Japanese way (as also in the Shinto religion) under the influence of diverse religious sects. So he believed that the gods (*kami*) permeated nature, and that they were the offspring of Izana-gi and Izana-mi, the creators, the parents of Amaterasu, who are the origin of the entire universe. Amaterasu is the sun-goddess, pervading with her rays the entire universe, and she stands in a direct blood-relationship to the imperial house. This point is of importance, because it provides the clue to the fact, that Kūkai's later Buddhism was brought into connection with the imperial house and the Japanese state. It is said that in a dream Kūkai was summoned to study the *Mahāvairocana sūtra*, popularly known in Japan as the *Dainichikyō*. Both the Sanskrit and Japanese refer in the title of the *sūtra* to the radiance of the sun. It suggests the idea of a Buddha-nature that as a sunlike light shines in and through all things.

Thus the affinity between Buddhahood and Amaterasu, with her connection to the imperial house, is here clearly felt. The Buddha is seen as the *Dainichi Nyorai*, 'the Great Radiant Tathāgata' (name for the Buddha as one who has thus become), and this again is the same as the 'body of Dharma.'

For gaining better understanding, Kūkai went to China to study under a Tantric master. This was Huíguǒ, who welcomed him as his successor. Under him he studied Sanskrit and the arts for thirty months and then went back to Japan loaded with *mantras*, *maṇḍalas*, *sūtras*, and the attributes needed for esoteric practice, as the 8th patriarch of Shingon Buddhism.

Kūkai's thinking has developed a reputation for being inaccessible, esoteric. This is true, however, only in a certain respect. The *mantras* and *maṇḍalas* used for meditation in Shingon are only transmitted from master to pupil and are not made public in print or any other form. In this respect one may speak of a secret doctrine. But this secrecy does not mean that Shingon in its essence is irrational or follows blind authority, and that its mysteries cannot be corroborated by experience. On the contrary, experiential 'verification' is extremely important. The difference between the so-called exoteric teaching and the esoteric teaching of Shingon is the following. The exoteric teaching proceeds from the incarnate historical Buddha, and is addressed to an audience with physical ears, but the esoteric teaching proceeds from the *'Dainichi Nyorai'* (or *Mahāvairocana Buddha*), which is a spiritual entity permeating the whole universe as a kind of light. Its teaching goes without words or speech, without any material interference. It speaks, so to say, directly to the heart, though this heart should first be opened by the meditation on *mantras* and *maṇḍalas*. Another difference between the esoteric and the exoteric way is that in the latter emancipation is a gradual process, sometimes only fulfillable in many incarnations, whereas in the former all beings are able to realize enlightenment immediately.

The *'Dainichi Nyorai'* preaches and teaches the *dharma*. This means that by his all-pervadingness he reveals the truth in every experience. In everything he is immediately present. This revelation of truth also can be considered as the grace (*kaji*) of the 'Dainichi Nyorai.' By his meditation the monk can partake of this grace and truth, which offers itself in the symbols of deeds, words, and representations, more specifically: handpostures (or *mūdras*), *mantras* and *maṇḍalas* (or regular patterns). The 'Nyorai' in truth penetrates the transparant universe. But to one, who has not yet realized this transparancy, it communicates in symbols. Thus the Buddha enters in me, and I enter the Buddha. Then Buddhahood is obtained in this very body and the mind has become its clear mirror.

The obtainment of Buddhahood is in last analysis no obtainment at all. Since in truth the 'Nyorai' pervades all, also man's nature, and that of all sentient beings, is in truth already enlightened. All things 'abide in the great enlightened mind. All sentient beings are innate *bodhisat-*

tvas.' They only have been bound by greed, hatred, and delusion.[6] More than an acquisition, enlightenment is rather a recognition. It is the meditating on Shingon symbols that can lead to this recognition and free men from the attachments mentioned.[7]

In the Kamakura period (1185-1333) the influence of the lower classes as a political and cultural factor became stronger. A large part of the power fell in the hands of the warrior class, which in Japan should be distinguished from the nobility and is closer to the peasant population. Also tradesmen got a more prominent place. It was time for a religion that could appeal more to the masses. This religion was the so-called 'Jōdo'-Buddhism, basing itself on the *Sukhavati-vyūha-sūtra* (Sūtra on the arrangement of Paradise). It is also often referred to as the Pure Land sect. This version of Buddhism too was not a Japanese creation; it existed already in India. But in Japan it became particularly important. We may compare it to the Bhakti movement in India. Here liberation is not gained by an intellectual enlightenment, as it is in so many other forms of Buddhism, but by the devotional invocation of the name of Amitābha Buddha *(Amida-butsu)*. Only the faith in the Buddha of eternal light and life makes that one will be reborn in his paradise or Pure Land. The faith was already introduced in Japan in earlier days, but it spread widely through the activities of Hōnen (1133-1212), leader of the Jōdo sect and his disciple Shinran (1173-1262), founder of the 'Jōdo-shin' sect.

'Jōdo' has always been a lay-religion. It was preached by Hōnen that the present time was one of decay, and that the severeness of the monks and Buddhas of old could not be practised anymore in this time. Man cannot attain enlightenment (*satori*) anymore by discipline. So meticulous rules and the cultivation of virtues and meditation were disposed of. It was a tenet of Hōnen, that one should in regard of all this 'renounce, shut, ignore, and throw away.'[8] And it was stressed that any man or woman, be he a monk, a noble, hunter, prostitute, or a robber, could be reborn in Pure Land solely by faith in Amitābha and by the invocation of his name. Shinran went even further than

6 Y.S. Hakeda, *Kūkai, Major Works*, p. 86, quoted in D.E. Shaner, *The BodyMInd Experience in Japanese Buddhism*, New York, 1985, p .78.

7 D. E. Shaner, *The BodyMInd Experience in Japanese Buddhism, a phenomenological study of Kūkai and Dōgen*, New York 1985 (SUNY), pp. 68-77.

8 H. Nakamura, *Ways of Thinking of Eastern People,* p. 566

his master, who still made it a rule to invocate the name of 'Amida' 70,000 times a day. If you believe in the 'Amida-Buddha' you need repeat his name only one time, and you will at once be reborn in the Pure Land, and not at the moment of death, as Hōnen and his Chinese predecessors would have it. The presupposition of this view of Shinran is, that paradise is already present in this world of impurity and delusion. It is – to use a biblical phrase – in this world, although not of this world. A further difference between the old form of Pure Land Buddhism and the new form is, that the older form recognized a distinction between being born in Pure Land and entering '*nirvāṇa*,' but for Shinran both are one and the same thing. And so by the grace of 'Amida,' he maintains, amidst the impurity of this world, 'without being delivered from afflictions, one attains *nirvāṇa*.'[9] One becomes absorbed in the boundless compassion of Amitābha.

Man was considered to be of evil nature, in the sense of not being able by himself to do the right thing. Only by grace he can be saved. Although it was already accepted that even sinners could be saved, Shinran even stated, that as even the good man could enter the Pure Land, how much more the sinner. For this reason the sect was even persecuted, being considered as anti-social for going sofar as almost praising wrong-doing.

Sofar we have spoken mainly about the religious side of the Pure Land movement, but the more philosophical side is not absent. Shinran considered himself as the transmitter of an outstanding philosophical tradition. He had a high esteem for Nāgārjuna, Vasubandhu, Tánluán, and Shàndào. And in Jōdo in general the doctrines of the relativity of all existence, of the nexus of cause and effect, and of ultimate reality *(dharmatā-yukti)* were fully developed.

The inability of man to save his own soul, places him in a position of dependency and humility. But this is made into a structure of being. Existence in this world is being completely dependent upon others, i.e. all things are mutually determined in a causal nexus. There are two kinds of causes, the direct, or material causes, such as the seed is in relation to the plant, and adventitious causes (amongst others the effective causes) such as the water and sunshine that help the plant grow. All these causes are themselves determined by yet other

9 Ibid., p. 501.

causes in an infinite succession. So a plant like rice is determined by a chain of causes filling the whole universe, and that is why the whole universe can be said to be contained in one grain of rice or in one particle of dust. Man, again, is dependent on rice, and so the whole universe supports us as the 'natural grace' of Amitābha. That's why man should be grateful. But once you know that you are in this state of dependency, you can also see how much others are in need of you. And you should feel repentance for your sins and work for the welfare of all beings. Thus being born in the Pure Land by conversion is not the end of activity. In Shinran's vision the one reborn stays on earth. He discovers the unborn state in the midst of the born and dying. It is a state beyond duality in which, as a channel of grace, one is united with what is unborn but begetting. This is ultimate and natural being. Shinran wrote a short essay on it. The work is known as *Jinen hōnishō* (Essay on Naturalness). Therein he makes a synthesis of the idealist thought of Vasubandhu and the Madhyamaka of Tánluán (Donran). It is not by conscious design, but by the vow of the Buddha that one attains to the ultimate realm. By virtue of this absolute, which is formless, and known as something existing by itself, all things come into being. It is the means by which we know what reality is by itself, a realm of meaningless meaning.[10]

10 Shōsan Miyamoto, *The Relation of Philosophical Theory to Practical Affairs in Japan*: in *The Japanese Mind*, pp. 13-14.

Great Buddha, Nara Japan, Wiki Commons

Chapter 13
Zen Buddhism

Zen-philosophy may be considered as an inner contradiction. There is no more severe critic of theoretical constructions than Zen. Its aim is rather to sublate thinking to open up a silent world, which is a space for life and practice. Nevertheless one can try to describe the structure of the Zen world and Zen experience.

The starting point of Buddhism was the human condition. In the history of Buddhism this humanistic beginning was sometimes almost lost out of sight, because of an elaborately developed metaphysics. Much stress was laid on concepts such as the Mind, considered as a universal principle, Nature, wisdom, or 'the real' *(dharma),* and vacuity or nothingness as the basis of empirical existence. Zen interprets this historical heritage again as something not standing apart from man. It tries to redirect human life back to a way of experience that precedes the separate subsistence of things and men, and to restore the original unity of the actual occurring. This is often done in a most practical and non-theoretical way, viz. by means of meditation. In fact, the word 'Zen' is a Japanization of the Indian word for meditation: *dhyāna.* The Zen concept of '*zazen*' stands for nothing else but sitting in meditation. By this sitting in meditation one is supposed to realize a state of enlightenment, i.e. the aforementioned life preceding separate subsistence. This is done by revealing man in his absolute selfhood in meditation, prior to any objectivation. Thus in Zen one tries to transcend the subject-object dichotomy. To that end, the field of the intellect must be abandoned and one must simply be or 'become' oneself. Then at the same time all particular limitations of the original ego are transcended.

Zen posits the correlation between subject and object (or ego and world). A change on the subject side always corresponds with one on the object side, and vice versa. But in this correlation the subject is always the determining factor. A particular existential mode of the subject actualizes the world in a particular mode corresponding to it. The structure of the subject determines the structure of the world of objective things. When, accordingly, man feels that the world of his experience is not the true reality, then some change on the subject side is required to re-establish this truth. We first must get awake to see the things as they really are.

What is this awakening? It consists – as was already alluded to – in the giving up of the notion of the self-subsistence of things and of myself as something subsisting among those things. Thus the origin of this life, and of this world of things, the actuality itself, is discovered. This actuality is like an act of perception, the subject and the object of which are not separated from it. These are, as it were, withdrawn in original experience. In this experience no conscious identifications take place. This experience is often called 'wisdom' *(prajñā)*. It is contrasted with normal cognition or *vikalpa* which is characterized by acts of identification, combination, and differentiation.

To see a thing as this particular thing, is from the outset seeing it under the limitation of a particular essence, e.g. its 'appleness.' But since, as in all Buddhistic thinking, a thing in Zen is seen as determined by its relations to the myriad of other things, all the essences of all other things are involved in the this-ness of this apple. Taking an apple is taking the whole world in the form of an apple. An apple is not merely an apple. It is now seen as an apple because consciousness posits it thus. To see the apple in its original indetermination, one must inhibit the positing function of consciousness. This is also described as looking at it with no-mind (*wú xīn* Ch.). Then, after the sublating of all essences, the reality *(Dharma)* lights on. This kind of consciousness Zen wants to have as the normal state. It is also called the 'non-abiding mind' *(aprașțhita citta)*. It is not a state of unconsciousness, it is a fluid and unscattered consciousness in a state of vigilance.[11]

11 Cf. T. Izutsu, *Toward a Philosophy of Zen-Buddhism*, Boulder 1982, pp. 1-17.

The universal and individual aspects of consciousness.

We have seen, that in Zen the empirical subject or ego is not considered as a selfsubsisting entity. The ego is not an autonomous and substantial entity which is in itself the subject of its activities. On the contrary; from the standpoint of the individual the actus should rather be ascribed to a universal entity inhabiting all the performances of the individual. This entity is often called the *tathāgata-garbha* (literally: the germ or foetus of 'what [or who] has thus become,' i.e. the matrix of Buddhahood). It is also, and especially in Zen and other forms of Chinese Buddhism, designated as 'Mind.' This is not some private or divine mind, but the whole field of reality. Reality only reveals itself in actual experience. Every individual experience now must be considered as one actualization of the whole field, it is one conscious moment here and now in the sea of other similar acts. From the standpoint of this experience here and now, however, these other actualities are revealed. Thus they appear as the latent source from which actualities become manifest. As such the Mind (also 'no-mind') works in all concrete activities. It is the universal in the particular to which all actual being should be ascribed. The empirical ego can be called selfhood, because all its movements are actualizations of what is its real selfhood, i.e. pure perceptive consciousness. In the same way all objective correlations of subjectivity are actualizations of the Mind. This ultimate governing principle is something which runs through the subject-object relationship and which makes this very correlation become actualized. It should not be regarded as a supra-sensible substance. There is nothing beyond pure experience and its potentiality. This whole of experience in the various beings is, as we have said, called 'Mind.' It cannot be known as something objective. To know it in its living experience, 'body and mind must drop off.' To achieve this, these first must be recognized as objectified entities. By doing so, one retreats in the sphere of creative actuality. The world, i.e. the Mind, now becomes devoid of subsistent identities. This state of voidness of substance is also called the state of emptiness *(śūnyata)*. In this state also the subject, insofar as it is considered as a substantial entity among other entities, is sublated. Thus beyond the substantiality of the empirical self a pure non-subsistent self as pure actuality is discovered. Here all limitation of essence is lost sight of. Life is not anymore looked upon through the veil of essences or conceptual determination *(māyā)*, it rather takes it own course as such, unhampered by wilful thinking or practice. Life like this is called wisdom *(prajñā)*. It is an ever lucid awareness of a fluid unbroken reality in pristine purity. It is a light that illuminates all. This sea of actuality is in Zen, as already said before, often described as Mind *(xīn)*. This is not an idealist view which reduces everything to thought or ideas. This Mind is the world of experience before it is broken up into the so-called mind and thing, prior to subject and object. And this, again, is synonymous with *wú xīn* or 'no mind'. This mind is also called *xīn fǎ* (Ch.) (mind reality). Mind in the ordinary sense is but an abstraction. So all things are but one mind. Out of this reality emerge subject and object. The Self sees its own self reflected on all things as two mirrors facing each other without being between them even a shadow of a thing.[12] One's own subjectivity is actualized in the objective world and the objective world is actualized in the subjectivity. The whole correlation of the subjective and the objective is one single perceptive act. And this is considered as the self-manifestation of the cosmic Mind. But there is no manifestation, no factual concreteness, outside individuals.

Lǐnjí (J. Rinzai), the founder of the Zen school named after him, says:[13]

> 'What do you think is reality? Reality is nothing other than the Mind-reality. The Mind-reality has no definite form. It permeates and runs through the whole universe. It is, at this very moment, in this very place so vividly present. But the minds of the ordinary people are not mature enough to see this. Thus they establish everywhere names and concepts, and vainly search after reality in these names and letters.'

The Mind-reality actualizes itself in the individual minds of the persons. 'In the eye it acts as sight; in the ear it acts as hearing; in the nose it acts as the sense of smell; in the mouth it speaks; in the hand it grasps; in the foot it walks. All these activities are originally nothing but one single spiritual illumination, which diversifies itself into

12 Isutzu, pp. 34-35
13 Ibid., p. 39.

harmonious correspondences. It is because the mind in this way has no definite form, that it can act in every form'.[14]

Typical of Lǐnjí is now, that he likes to present this Mind-reality as the universal Man which he also calls: the Man without ranks. When wisdom arises this Man manifests himself.

> 'O venerable friends, you should directly grasp the Man who is pulling the wires of these shadowy phenomena behind the scenes. If you but realize that the Man is the ultimate source of all Buddhas, any place in which you actually are at the present moment is the ultimate and the absolute place for you, Brethren!'[15]

By becoming the direct actualization of the reality, Man becomes the master of the place in every situation. He lives in the concrete persons. Whatever the individual does is done by the universal. The universal acts through the limbs of the individual. But the two persons are in fact one.

Two Schools.

Two important ramifications of Zen must be mentioned here: the 'Zazen-only school' *(Sōtō-shu)* and the 'Kōan' school *(Rinzai-shu)*. Zen was introduced in Japan in the Kamakura period (12th and 13th centuries) through the channel of these two rival sects. The Sōtō (Cāodǒng) School, which was brought to Japan by Dōgen (1200-1253), goes back to Xīngsī (677-744), Dǒngshàn Liángjiē (807-69), and his disciple Cāoshàn Běnjí (840-901). It is also known as the School of silent Illumination. This is because in it the importance of sitting in meditation is endorsed above all else. Enlightenment cannot be a sudden happening; it must be a process of gradual maturing. Only after long periods of training in meditation can the real nature of the self, i.e. of being, be realized. So the Sōtō School is also mentioned as the school of gradual enlightenment, in contrast to the Rinzai School, which is called the school of sudden enlightenment.

14 Ibid.,p. 59
15 Ibid, p. 40.

The Rinzai School goes back to Yìxuán (or Lǐnjí, J. Rinzai) died 867). But the present form of Rinzai in Japan rather goes back to Dāhuì, J. Daie) who collected *'kōans'* so that they might be used for training the monks. In this particular form it was introduced in Japan by Eisai (1141-1215). The Rinzai School advocates sudden enlightenment and is very dynamic in contrast to the static attitude of the Sōtō School. The school rejects sitting in meditation as an exclusive way of gaining enlightenment. This is a falling into the devil's pit. Even meditation here is considered as dynamic. It is a turbulent activity of the mind. A 'kōan' (riddle) is given to the student, which problem he should grapple with body and mind, while sitting in meditation. In this way the meditation becomes a kind of spiritual battlefield. The *'kōan'* becomes an 'iron ball of doubt' and exhausts the mental resources of the disciple. Suddenly the 'ball' breaks up into pieces and the self-nature is realized. This enlightenment is a sudden event.[16]

The practice of Sōtō consists in serene, quietistic contemplation. A (merely) practical distinction is made between a surface level and a depth level of consciousness. On the surface we find images and concepts. It is the realm of logical and object-centred thinking, as one experiences when one is in the normal waking state. But at the same time the depth level remains undisturbed. The situation is comparable to the relation between the turbulent waves and the calm depth of the ocean. Psychic energy must attain a state of intense concentrated unity, so that the mind might witness its own depth level which is invisible in normal consciousness. So sit unmovingly as a rock in half or full lotus-sit with rythmically regulated breath. Thus one must submerge in inner concentration, but this has nothing definite on which to focus. It is not fixed on a riddle or a *maṇḍala*. Only the mind sinks beyond ideas and concepts. Dōgen saw in this practice the actualization of Buddhahood itself, i.e. the oneness of being. For him enlightenment and the practice of sitting meditation is one and the same thing. In it one is aware of the utter fullness of existence. One becomes a crystallization of universal life.

The Rinzai School regards this practice as quietistic and says that it runs counter to the spirit of Zen. Nányuè, a disciple of Huìnéng, already warned that Zen does not consist in sitting or lying down. Do-

16 Isutzu, p. 162-3

ing only this, one never reaches the 'mind.' And also Dāhuì said that you never should regard sitting as something supreme and referred to the Sōtō masters as false Zen masters. It is true that meditation is also practised by Rinzai, but here it is not an emptying of all thought, but a being fixed on the *'kōan'*.[17]

As representative examples of the two schools, in the following we pay attention to the thinking of Dōgen (1200-1253), founder of the Sōtō sect in Japan, and to Hakuin (1685-1769), a reformer, mainly inspired by the Rinzai sect. As we have done with the philosophies of India and China, we will omit the modern developments. The closer one comes to one's own time, the more difficult it becomes to make representative selections. However, we here at least must mention the name of the Kyōto school – of which Nishida and Nishitani are the most important representatives – as a school of thought relating the tradition of Dōgen to modern Western thinking, especially to the phenomenological tradition. Furthermore we must mention D.T. Suzuki as the one who did much to make the Rinzai type of Zen more accessible to the Western public.

D*ŌGEN*. Dōgen was born in 1200 as son of an important politician. At the age of two he lost his father, possibly as a result of a political murder. At the age of seven, also his mother became ill, and died. Probably because of these tragic happenings, we find that his work is imbued with a sense of the fleeting character.of life. Already at a young age he requested his family to allow him to become a monk, which permission was given only reluctantly.

He was initiated at mount Hiei, the centre of Tendai Buddhism. He there studied the various forms of Buddhism under abbot Kōen. But already soon he was troubled by a burning question: if it is true that – as the *sūtras* say – all living beings are endowed with Buddha-nature, why then should one strive for it? On mount Hiei he could not find a satisfying answer. He visited some other monasteries to find the answer to his question. And finally he met with Eisai, the introducer of Rinzai Zen. Eisai is said to have answered Dōgen on his question: 'All the Buddhas in the three stages of time are unaware that they are

17 Isutzu, ibid..

endowed with Buddha-nature, but cats and oxen are well aware of it indeed.'[18] This answer made some impression on the young monk. He decided to study Rinzai Zen under Eisai's guidance. But the latter died the following year. So he had to continue his study under his disciple and successor Myōzen. But although Myōzen was an honest man, he could not teach Dōgen what he did not embody himself. So in 1223 Myōzen and Dōgen together undertook a journey to China for the deepening of their knowledge of the Zen way of life. After entering the harbour of Mingzhou, Myōzen right away started his monastery tour, Dōgen, on the other hand, stayed some time aboard of the ship, probably to adapt himself to the new environment or to recover from his seasickness. On board he met with a simple older monk who came to buy some Japanese mushrooms. He was much impressed by the plain and simple life of this man. Despite his old age, the man still worked hard as a cook. And again Dōgen wondered why all this toil was needed. So he posed a version of his old question to the cook.

> 'On hearing my remarks, he broke into laughter and said, 'Good foreigner! You seem to be ignorant of the true training and meaning of Buddhism.' In a moment, ashamed and surprised at his remark, I said to him, 'What are they?' 'If you understand the true meaning of your question, you will have already realized the true meaning of Buddhism,' he answered. At that time, however, I was unable to understand what he meant.'[19]

Coming from the ship he went to Tiāntōng monastery. Here he was again disappointed. Not only he did not find the answer to his question, but also he was treated with discrimination, because of his being a foreigner. He was put in lower rank than was in accordance with his Buddhist age (the years passed after entering a monastery for the first time). He visited some other monasteries without much benefit. Then he returned to Tiāntōng, hearing that the old abbot had died and was replaced by the then famous Rújīng (1163-1228). In this man he finally found the master he was looking for. Rújīng laid great stress on zazen.

18 Y. Yokoi, *Zen Master Dōgen, an introduction with selected writings*, New York, Tōkyō, 1976, 1981 (Weatherhill), p. 28.

19 Ibid., p. 29.

One day he found one of the monks in the medition-hall dozing away. Rebuking him he said: 'The practice of zazen is the casting away of body and mind, so why are you dozing?' Upon hearing this Dōgen experienced something that is often called 'enlightenment.' He went to Rújīng, prostrated, and said:'I casted away body and mind.' Dōgen here discovered what was to be the guiding insight of his whole further life, viz. that there is no enlightenment without practice or activity and that in fact practice and enlightenment are one and the same thing.

So he went on practising at Tiāntōng for a few other years. In 1227 he went back to Japan with copies of the Cāodǒng (Sōtō) Zen texts. In Japan he found Buddhism, even Rinzai, more badly in decline as when he left. He moved to Kōshō-ji temple, where he had a meditation hall built. There he started his lessons in zazen (sitting meditation). He also advocated a sober attitude. Soon he had so many pupils that he had to build a new hall. In this time also he was already busy writing his main work, the *Shōbōgenzō*. Gaining more influence, he met with more and more adversery from the side of the established Buddhist orders. This compelled him to flee from the site of Kyōto to a region at the east-coast; known as Echizen province (present day Fukui prefecture). Here he founded Eihei-ji (Temple of eternal peace), which is there unto the present day and is the biggest monastery of Japan. Dōgen remained there working for the rest of his life until in 1252 he became fatally ill. Fruitlessly searching for a medical cure, he died the next year in Kyōto.[20]

Against syncretism.

Dōgen is a very straightforward thinker with the character of a reformer. He very sharply rejects the syncretism of the Chinese Buddhism of his days. Confucianism and Daoism are very inferior to Buddhism. They cannot even be compared with it. Let alone that they could form a triposd of truth together with Buddhism as was often held. Daoism and Confucianism are merely human lores. They merely teach the service of the emperor and filial piety, the latter seen as a method of regulating the household, besides, the teaching of Daoism

20 Ibid., pp. 30-38

is unethical. And its idea of spontaneity is diametrically opposed to the Buddhist lore of universal causality. The works of the Chinese thinkers are even inferior to those of Brahmanism. For while they seem to agree with Brahmin thought in equating the Self with the absolute, they do not accept, like the Brahmins do, the law of *karma*, which implies the retribution of work even beyond physical death. In general Dōgen has very little respect for Chinese thinkers, not even for Zen Buddhist thinkers. The only one he really respects is his master Rújīng. In his vision India is the centre of the world, Japan is but a barbarous nation, and, what is really unfair, he even dares to call China a 'small' country. It appears that Nāgārjuna is the patriarch he most often quotes with due respect.[21]

Enlightenment

In the thinking of Dōgen it is impossible to make a distinction between cosmological and psychological thinking on the one hand, and thinking concerning release or enlightenment on the other. Even less than in many forms of Indian Buddhism, it is here the intention to outline a metaphysical structure. All attention is directed to what might be called 'true experience'. Such experience is simply what it is. It is not a positing of ideas; it recognizes no distinctions. There is no 'me' experiencing some 'other'. It is just the flowing stream of life meeting with no opposition whatsoever. One might call his thought a 'monism of experience.' There is – and this is very typical of Dōgen – no opposition at all between mind and matter. The mind and the world are the same entity. There is no spiritual substance that never dies contrasted to a perishable body, i.e., there is no soul dwelling in a corporeal frame. In a passage in the fascicle *Bendōwa* (Story of Buddhist Practice) Dōgen explains himself in clear terms:

> 'From the beginning Buddhism has taught that body and mind are one, and substance and form are not two different things. Be certain that this was taught in both India and China. Furthermore, in Buddhism, both imperishability and perishability are not to be separated as

21 Dōgen Zenji, *Shōbōgenzō*, 4 vls., tr. Kōsen Nishiyama and John Stevens, Tōkyō 1975, 1984 (Nakayama Shōbō) part III, pp. 21, 85ff., 96-101.

> body and mind, or as substance and form. Where does the body perish and the mind abide? In Buddhism there is no *nirvāṇa* apart from the cycle of life and death. Moreover, if you mistakenly think the mind is eternal and consider it to be the true Buddhist wisdom that is beyond life and death, you should recognize that the very mind you are using is bound to the cycle of life and death – this is very futile.'
>
> 'In Buddhism mind and body are one; then how can it be that the mind abides and the body perishes? … Furthermore do not think that the cycle of life and death should be eradicated – that is an enormous mistake. It must be clear that Mind is the original gate to the true teachings of Buddhism and includes the entire essence of phenomena, which cannot by any means be divided into different aspects such as body and mind, life or death, enlightenment or *nirvāṇa*. All phenomena, all the myriad forms of existence are only this one Mind; nothing is excluded.'[22]

There is no distinction at all between the world and the experience of it. Accordingly, there is no world that could perish after the spirit has withdrawn from it. All phenomena are transient and abiding at the same time. That is why life and death exist together in each moment. Both are, as it were, the same thing seen from a different angle. To know this is enlightenment and freedom. The unity of being (or what is here the same, non being) simply is all there is. It is also enlightenment and freedom itself. This should only be recognized and understood.

The essence of Dōgen's teaching about enlightenment is, that it is not something apart from the experience of the phenomenal. The universe is proclaiming the actual body of the Buddha. Mountains and rivers proclaim the law when they are not taken as mere sense data but as the focus of the fullness of meaning that is the entire universe. In this sense everything is the universe. I am, the mountain is, and the most trifling thing is. Only when all phenomenal things have become the Buddha, there is enlightenment. Then one also perceives oneself as all things. The Mind has become everything. And one forgets oneself as a particular existence. All things as they are experienced constitute the Mind. Things as experienced have no permanence. Every-

22 Ibid, part i, p.56.

thing is utterly transient. It is devoid of fixed essences. Every moment of fleeting existence is just what it is. It does not transform from one state into the next. That would presuppose an underlying and persisting substance. There is only the new phase of experience replacing the old. Every moment of experience is a new·creation. Things are taken as they are seen from the eternal present. They are viewed *sub specie aeternitatis*. When life is experienced like this, all human practice has become actualization of enlightenment. It means that one penetrates and masters each thing. This does not mean that one can comprehend all things intellectually. Even for the enlightened one the world is too complex for that. It means that the things of this world are not beclouded any more by the projection of our ideas about them. So nothing escapes the mere 'receptive' perception, there is no more distorting perception. In this sense this experience can also be called 'emptiness,' since no content beyond the actually given is projected in what we experience. The concept forming function of the mind is subdued, and thus it is said that one experiences with 'no-mind.' This attitude of the enlightened is also called 'wisdom.' In this wisdom-experience, the seer and the seen are joined in one actuality. One is in this experience not conscious of an 'ego,' nor is one conscious of separate objects as independent substances. Here life is a unity: 'body and mind have fallen off.' And because the stream of experience is in all of its phases as it is, pointing to nothing beyond itself, it also can be said to be of absolute character. Dōgen calls this way of experience also *hotsubodaishin* (true experience of the mind). The experience of this kind does not mean that one lives in a meaningless stream of mere sense perception. Such a sense perception is itself a mere abstraction from experience as lived. It is more like daily experience, in which things simply can be called by their name. But it is a 'daily life' that does not cling to the past nor grasps to the future. It is absorbed in the present. And by this very absorption in every moment the whole universe is given, including even the past and the future.[23] In this way every location and time includes all the elements of existence. This experience must be harmonized with bodily action. Not only is life experienced as a unity, but one's actions should also tend towards a unity and a completeness of life. One should spread the true life

23 Sh. part I, p.13.

among all living beings. Receptivity and activity should melt together. This harmonizing of the spiritual and the physical is called by Dōgen *shinjitsunintai* (the real body of man).[24]

Everyone possesses the Buddha-mind by nature, but without practice and training it remains dormant or it becomes obscured by the tendency of the mind to fixate concepts and entities. And thus the flux of wisdom is broken up. But when the Buddha-mind is manifested, then it is seen that all things constitute the Buddha-mind and the Buddha-mind encompasses all things. At all times this universe is the Buddha-mind. 'The sky can collapse and the earth disintegrate but Mind will remain.'[25]

Time and Being.

Time is an important concept in Dōgen's thinking. For him 'existence' is time itself and time is existence. All the elements that make up our existence, our skin, flesh, bones, and marrow, are related with, and emerge through time and causality. But this nexus of time and causality is a complete existence, encompassing the whole of time and pervading the infinity of space. We ourselves are that nexus. All things exist within us as given in time, because we ourselves only exist as time. Time is not different from the structure of experience, or, – what is the same – it is not different from the mind. Time is complete in each instance, i.e. each instant covers the entire past and future and the infinity of space. Each instant is an eternal present. As long as the present is, it covers all, but as soon as it is no more – as it were –, it still is as one of an infinity of moments contained in the now actual present. This means that time has two aspects, a fleeting aspect and an abiding. The fleeting aspect never escapes the grasp of constancy. When time is passing, it is still retained in time-as-all-encompassing-eternity. Time never can escape from itself. It is the all-pervading Mind in which everything is connected with everything in a web of mutual implications. The tree is implicated in my time, but I am implicated in the tree's time. And both times are but abstractions from abiding time, the time that does not move, because there is

24 Ibid., p. 13
25 Ibid., p.19

nothing outside itself in which it might move. 'When body and mind thus emerge, the elements are unified, and time and existence function together.'[26] This means that things, and we ourselves, reach existence when their duality, their being conceived as separate existences, is given up, and between the one and the other no opposition is seen anymore. Then the universe is one body and mind, mind as body, and body as mind, since, as we saw earlier, also subject and object are abandoned as abstractions.[27]

Causality.

One of the features of Dōgen's thinking is his concept of universal causality. Causality is the endless process of transmigration determined by acquired merit. So it is not the deterministic type of causation that until recently was generally accepted in the West. It presupposes a freedom to do the good as well as – of course – a freedom to do the wrong. This concept of transmigration must not be considered as a soul flying from one body to another. Such a concept of an independent soul, disguising itself in different bodies, and finally abandoning them all, is not accepted by Dōgen. It is rather the phenomenal realm itself that migrates from one time to another time. The phenomenal man transmigrates from this life to the next, again into this world, or into a heavenly world, or into hell. The whole world migrates from one world cycle or *kalpa* to another. But also every change within this life is a process of transmigration. Life is not continuous but jumps from one moment or *kṣaṇa* to the next. There are 65 *kṣaṇas* in the time needed to snap your fingers and about six and a half billion in a day. Every action in this way produces its inevitable result when its merit has ripened, be it in this life, the next, or in one or more of the subsequent lives. No one, not even an enlightened one, can escape this causality. Enlightenment follows Buddhist practice as its result. There is no opposition between a real world of enlightenment and an unreal phenomenal realm. The causal nexus of the phenomenal world is utterly real, and there is no enlightenment existing in separation from it. Good and evil also are clearly distinguished, and there is no place

26 Sh. p. i, p. 42.
27 Ibid. pp. 68-72

where one can go beyond it. Every good action produces its beneficial results and all evil leads to misfortune or even to hell. The causal nexus is inescapable and unending. There is no great ocean of enlightenment that one may attain after death. After death always awaits a new existence in accordance with the *karma* (work) accumulated in this and previous lives. It means that no one can escape from suffering unless by working unceasingly in conformity with the Buddhist precepts. There is no easy way out. Any escape from causality would mean its denial. And the denial of universal causality is according to Dōgen the denial of the essence of Buddhism. This essence can be summarized as the Law of the preservation of *karma*. This is the answer to Dōgen's question posed as a young monk: why men must work unceasingly in spite of the fact that every being is said to be endowed with Buddha-nature. There is no innate nature apart from work.[28]

Zazen.

Dōgen's school is well known for laying much stress on *zazen* (sitting in meditation) as the means to obtain enlightenment or to arrive at the unity of existence. 'The goal is to have a full lotus posture of your body and a full lotus posture in your mind; and you must have a full lotus posture in the state where body and mind have fallen off.'[29] *Zazen* must be identified with the Buddhist Law. In the lotus posture one realizes *samādhi* in body and mind. *Zazen* – says Dōgen – is the practice of all Buddhas and patriarchs. In it one experiences self-fulfilment, i.e. being immersed beyond duality. This is called *jijuyu samādhi*. It is that in which everything exists, but only in *zazen* it is realized.

> 'Even if you sit for only a moment in jijuyu samādhi the Buddha-mind seal is imprinted in your body, mind, and words; simultaneously, the entire phenomenal world is also imprinted with the Buddha-mind seal – all space is enlightenment … The variety of phenomenal objects themselves are Buddha's enlightenment … They all expound the most profound form of *prajñā* (wisdom).[30]

28 Ibid. part iii, pp. 96-101.
29 Ibid. part i, p. 125.
30 Ibid. p. 149.

This all is achieved by finding absolute quiescence through sitting in *zazen*. It is not that now the whole world in its infinite detail is brought to consciousness. This is impossible. It is just by abandoning consciousness of the particular that one can reach this state in which one becomes all things without consciously knowing them.

HAKUIN. Hakuin was born the 25th of december 1685. He grew up in a simple family which belonged to the Nichiren sect. As a child he displayed a remarkable gift of memory, learning hundreds of village songs by heart, and remembering almost every word of a sermon on the Lotus-sūtra. After being severely shocked by a sermon about hell, he became a truth-seeker. He requested his parents to permit him to enter the life of a monk. Finding no satisfaction for his spiritual needs, he wandered from temple to temple until he finally met Etan, an old priest who in a rough manner instructed him in the wisdom of Zen. As answer to his questions being only beaten and thrown from walls, finally he experienced a sort of enlightenment.

> 'One day, in the morning, I wandered round the town of Iiyama on my customary alms-begging route. I was walking alone when a wonderful idea about the Way came into my mind, of which I could not rid myself. I became so obsessed with this idea that I did not notice where my feet carried me. Suddenly I found myself, without knowing how I had come there, at the door of someone's house where I was begging alms. For a long time I was standing there, so absorbed in the new idea that the master of the house who had ordered me to go away over and over again finally in exasperation took up a writing brush and hurled it at me.'[31]

Hakuin was wounded, but remained in the state he was, until he suddenly clapped his hands and laughed. After relating the story to Etan, the latter told him to take the vows and deepen his new insight.

Hakuin took his vows seriously, and eventually became ill, because of a too harsh practising of meditation, symptoms of which are being

31 Hakuin Zenji, *The Embossed Tea Kettle* (O ra te gama), *and other works*, tr. R.D. M. Shaw, London 1963 (Allen & Unwin), p. 17 (Introd.).

mentally distressed and suffering from physical fatigue. He found the cure in a kind of Daostic yoga, which he considered to be the elixer of life. It was so effective that even in old age he boasted still to have his teeth. But what had started as a health cure, also helped him to improve his thinking and to facilitate mystical introspection.

All the time Hakuin was wandering around. On receiving a message that his father was dying he returned home. After the latter's death he took residence in Shoinji-temple, a desolate place. Here he lived in poverty as a village priest. Daily he practised his introspection yoga, and – also because of the quiet and simple surroundings – he became healthier every day. He also had a strong social feeling, and lived in close contact with the poor peasantry, suffering under the hardships of the Tokugawa Shogunate. His loath against its rule is expressed in his popular sermons in dialect, in which he revives the shocking hell-experience of his youth, now populated with magnates and purple-robed abbots.

Gradually he acquired fame as a preacher and as an author, and a flock of disciples gathered around him. He describes them in poetical language:

> 'They live scattered about to the east and the west, within ten or twelve miles. They live under conditions of great suffering, in old decaying houses, temples, and broken down tombs, which they rent as hermitages. Distressed in the mornings, pained with bitter evenings, starved in the daytime, frozen at night, nothing passes through their mouths but vegetables and barley flour ... The very gods must surely shed tears for them, the demons must surely put the palms of their hands together and pray for them.
>
> 'When these men first came here, they looked like Sogyoku and Kan, so attractive were their looks, and their skin shone like fine oil. But before long they were like Toho and Kato, their bodies dried up, their faces haggerd. If one met them on the shores of the lagoon they were like bent up wizened things. If they were not in truth very bodhisattvas of men ... what pleasure could there possibly have been for them in crowding together here for such a long time?'[32]

32 Ibid, p. 28-29

In Shoinji Hakuin remained for the rest of his life, only leaving when invited to preach somewhere. He died January 1769. Posthumously he was given an honorary title.

Unlike Dōgen, who introduced Sōtō Zen, Hakuin is influenced by Rinzai Zen. Whereas Dōgen sees himself as a restorer of original Indian Mahāyāna Buddhism, and as a criticizer of syncretism, Hakuin's position is much less rigid. He does not make a secret of the fact that he had much benefited by Daoist practice. He respected the Zen Master Shoju as his teacher for meditation. But he was well aware of the dangers of a too harsh meditation, that only results in an emaciating of life. Be it that you find discerning stillness, if after it you die of exhaustion, who will benefit from it? So you have to take care of your life by protecting the life-spirit. The preserving of the life-spirit is accomplished by the method of 'introspection.' This method he learned from the master of the second half of his life, Haku-yu, an old hermit, living, according to the description of Hakuin in a cave on a mountain. Haku-yu's only possessions were three books: the *Doctrine of the Mean* (ascribed to Confucius), the *Laozi*, and the *Vajracchedika* (Diamond cutter) *sūtra.* This clearly suggests the tripod of Confucianism, Daoism, and Buddhism, which Dōgen abhorred so much. The most salient features of Haku-yu's lore are a health therapy consisting of a breathing technique and an inner brewing of the life-elixer, by concentrating the energies of the body in its lower part and especially in the abdomen. These techniques are unmistakably of Daoistic origin. Although they cannot be found in classical Daoism, such techniques were developed in a later and more popular Daoism, the most important aim of which was the acquiring of physical immortality. As a Buddhist, Hakuin advocated the active life of Zen, teaching: no work, no food. He severely criticized the quietistic attitude of just passively sitting in meditation in a spot far from the world. Meditation is only genuine when it takes place in the middle of the full life, in the very performance of one's abilities. But this active life was backed by a Daoistic health lore. Since without good health one cannot even reach intelligence and wisdom, let alone accomplish some work of importance.

The realm of the absolute.

The fundamental tenet of Hakuin's thinking is the unity of reality. All things, life and death, all different spirits – also the *dharmas* or the elements of existence – and the Buddha-nature, are in essence but one. Reality is but of one nature only. 'All aspects of the universe – the relative and the absolute – are but one in reality.'[33] All things are – or are contained in – one Mind. There is nothing outside the Mind. Objectively, the visible universe is, as it were, objective Mind, and on the subjective side there is – taken apart from its objective content – pure awareness, which is also Mind. This Mind can be considered as an all-encompassing entity. In this way it is viewed as an expanse, but at the same time it is considered as the essence of all there is. As an essence, it can also be called the Buddha nature, and as an expanse it can be called the Buddha- or Dharma-body. Between the essence and its incorporation, there exists an unbreakable correlation. The one cannot be without the other. The truth is for Hakuin that the universe and its absolute essence, the Buddha-nature, are identical. Without sentient beings there is no Buddha, and without the Buddha there are no sentient beings. Throughout the universe there is no place where the absolute is not, and there is no sentient being which does not possess its wondrous nature.[34] The ultimate essence of all things can also be termed the eternal present. Its extension is infinite. Everything, coarse and fine, the outer and the inner, come out of, and merge into, this infinite. But the human condition is that this is not realized. Man identifies himself with his own limited shape and his own limited abilities. In this way he has acquired a limited essence, constituted by fixed notions. In doing so he creates an illusory world of his own that keeps him entangled in the world of transmigration. He does not escape anymore from the creations of his own individual and limited mind (as contrasted to the universal Mind). To reunite himself with the universal, with the Buddha, man should transcend his own created limitations by abandoning intentionality, such as desires and lusts, likes and dislikes – which are the cause of his limited notions –, and work for the good of all creatures. Then one will rediscover the eternal calm

33 *Tea Kettle,* p. 111
34 Ibid. p. 122

of the omnipresent Mind. One is merged again in the infinite. This is, according to Hakuin, 'the casting away of body and mind' of which Dōgen spoke.[35]

Hakuin makes a fundamental distinction between the Buddha-nature and the non-Buddha nature. The Buddha-nature is the essence of the unlimited Mind as we have described above. It is the realm of non-birth. The non-Buddha nature consists of the *dharmas* or elements of existence as far as they are represented in the limited, individual mind. From this emerges the notion of a limited self. When we know, that this self with all its objects of sense is but an offspring of our own heart, we at once transcend the limited existence and see the eternal in which and by which it is.

The individual mind creates itself a limited path (as far as environment is concerned) through time, of which the future is determined by its own impulse and direction. This individual mind – because it is without shape – persists even after the disintegration of the physical body, which is characterized by shape. After that it creates a new body in conformity with its choices and actions in life. This can be a new earthly body of human or other type, but also a hellish or heavenly one. Only when the attachments that constitute this mind are dissolved, can liberation of the cycle of rebirth occur. This is the attainment of *nirvāṇa*. In this case the mind is said to have given birth to a Buddha. So your mind can lead you to hell or to liberation. This liberation is also the self becoming the 'non-self.' And this is nothing else but the stopping of the painful and narrow thinking.

The Buddha nature thus attained, is nothing else but the primary essence of all sentient beings. It is called 'the true heart,' *bodhi*, or *nirvāṇa*.' It is also the utter tranquillity that is the essence of the universal Mind, perpetual light, seeing nothing and doing nothing. It is the 'knowledge of the Buddha-heart.' It illumines the whole universe, 'it sends forth the bright light of the great mirror of absolute wisdom, so that all the chief duties of the law are exhaustively fulfilled during the ages of illusion'[36] It is immediate presence of undifferentiated nature without anything inside or outside. There is not something apart from it. It is unhindered *samādhi*. All good works come to an end in

35 *Tea Kettle*, pp. 110-128
36 Ibid., p.116.

it. Then the very body becomes, as it were, transformed in it. Typical of Hakuin is also that, just like Lĭnjí, he likes to speak here about the 'True Man' or the 'True constant Man.' This 'true man' is the man in which the Buddha-nature is displayed without hindrance. It is man as one with the universal. He also speaks about man's original dignity or 'true personal dignity.' This gives Hakuin's Zen the humanistic character so typical of the Rinzai sect.[37]

Karma and liberation.

Hakuin says that 'work' or *karma* has no outward shape. It is something persisting beyond physical dissolution. The law of *karma* dictates that every action and every intention leads to its proper result. What we sow, that we shall reap. What we sow in this life comes to fruition, sometimes in this very life, sometimes in the next. And, again, the life which we lead now is a result from our work in former existences. Our works lead us onwards. No one can escape from the evil he has created by his own activities. 'The seeds sown are seeds sown in the mind, and these seeds come up in unexpected places, here one, there ten thousand, and each must reap the pains and grieves of eternity.'[38] 'Good works lead us to a good place, bad works lead us to a bad place. The stage screen changes. We put on different stage dressings... This is the law of life and death.'[39]

But when one abandons attachment to this transient world, this entanglement in the web of *karma* is dissolved. No more is there any hell of one's own creation. One realizes the purity and calm of the universal Mind, and one is absorbed in the thought of 'non-thought.' This is what is also called 'enlightenment.'[40]

The analogy of man and society.

Often it is seen that an analogy is stressed between individual man and the cosmos as a whole. It is the theme of micro- and macrocosmos. Hakuin sees a similar analogy, but it is peculiar to him that he sees this

37 Ibid., p.111.
38 Ibid., p.162.
39 Ibid., p.158.
40 Ibid., p.158, 163-164.

analogy not between the individual and the cosmos, but between man and society. Like there is in a state a controller or Lord who unifies the country, so there is in man the mind that gives unity to all conceptual and spiritual activity. With the officials and retainers of the ruler correspond the mental vigours. As the basis of society there are the common people. With these correspond the vital energies responsible for physical well-being. Now just as a state can only be sound when the ruler and his retainers care for the well-being of the people, so meditation cannot be successful when life is neglected. When the mind and the will consume all energy, the physical frame will collapse and nothing can be achieved. This is just like a nobility living in luxury, which will eventually bring ruim to the state as a whole.[41]

Bibliography

This bibliography is far from complete. Since this work is meant primarily for the philosophically interested public, and not for the philologist, this list mainly offers translations of original texts, and includes only a few text editions. That's the reason why some of the works mentioned in the text are not included in the bibliography, for although they have been very influential, they have until now not been translated into Western languages. But even many translations will have escaped my attention. Again, the list of secundary literature is very selective.

Translations of basic texts can be searched for under the name of the author or under the name of the translator. Since sometimes the authorship is uncertain, these works also can be searched for under title. Generally this procedure is only to be followed when more then one work is ascribed to one author, otherwise only the name of the author is included in the list. Secundary literature is only included under the name of the author.

Abhidhammatthasaṅgaha – See under Zan Aung and Narada Thera.

Abhidharmakośabhāṣya of Vasubandhu – See under Vallée Poussin and Pruden.

Abhidharma-samuccaya of Asaṅga – See under Rahula.

Abhisamayālaṅkara – See under Conze and Obermiller.

Amṛtakara – See under Tucci.

Anacker, Stefan – *Seven works of Vasubandhu, the Buddhist Psy-*

chological Doctor, Delhi 1984, 1986, Motilal. Contains: *Vādhavidhi, (A Method for Argumentation), Pañcaskandhaka-prakaraṇa (A Discussion of the five Aggregates), Karmasiddhi-prakaraṇa (A Discussion for the Demonstration of Action), Viṁśatikā-kārikā (The twenty Verses and their Commentary), Triṁśikā-karikā (The thirty Verses), Madhyanta-vibhāga-bhāṣya (Commentary on the Separation of the Middle from the Extremes)* [work of Asaṅga], *Tri-svabhāva-nirdeśa (The Teaching of the three Natures).*

Aṅguttara-nikāya – See under Woodward .

Āryadeva – *Catuḥ-śataka*, See under Lang.

Asaṅga - *Abhidharmasamuccaya*, See under Rahula, *Mahāyāna-saṁgraha,* See under Lamotte, *Bodhisattva-bhūmi*, look under Willis, *Commentary on Vajracchedika*, See under Tucci.

Atthasālini of Buddhaghosa [commentary on the *Dhamma-saṅgani]*, See under Maung Tin.

Avadāna-śataka, See under Feer.

Avataṁsaka-sūtra – *The Great Means Expansive Buddha Flower Adornment Sūtra*, by T'ang Dynasty national master Ch'ing Liang. Translated from the Chinese Hua Yen Ching by the Buddhist Text Translation Society of the Sino-American Buddhist Association, San Francisco, 1979-1982. See also under Cleary.

Banerjee, N.V. (tr.)- *Dhammapada*, [includes text in Devanagari and Roman characters], Delhi, 1989.

Barnett, Lionel D. (tr.) – *The Path of Light (Bodhicaryāvatāra* of Śāntideva), London 1909, John Murray.

Barua, Benimadhab & Sailendranath Mitra (tr.) – Prakrit *Dhammapada* [based upon M. Senart's Kharoshti manuscript], Calcutta, 1921, 1988.

Bays, Gwendolyn (tr.) – *The Lalitavistara-sutra; The Voice of the Buddha, the beauty of compassion,* 2 vols. [translation of the French version of Foucaux], Berkeley,1983.

Bechert, H. – *Die Lebenszeit des Buddha*, Göttingen, 1986.

— *Bruchstücke Buddhistischer Versammlungen, I, Die Anavataptagātha und die Sthaviragātha*, Berlin, 1961.

Bendall, C. & W.H.D. Rouse (tr.) – *Śikṣa-samuccaya of Śāntideva, A compendium of Buddhist Doctrine,* London, 1922, 1990.

Bijlert, Viktor. A. v. – *Epistemology and Spiritual Authority; the development of epistemology and logic in the old Nyāya and Buddhist school of epistemology,* with an annotated translation of Dharmakīrti's *Pramāṇa-vārttika* II *(Pramāṇasiddhi),* Vienna, 1989.

Blofeld, John (tr.) – *The Zen Teaching of Huang Po on the Transmission of Mind,* London, Rider, 1958.

Bodhicaryāvatāra of Śāntideva, See under Barnett, Sharma, Steinkellner.

Bodhisattvabhūmi of Asaṅga, look under Willis.

Boin, look under Webb-Boin.

Borsig, Margareta von – *Sūtra von der Lotosblume des wunderbaren Gesetzes* [Saddharma-puṇḍarīka], translated in German from the Chinese text of Kumārajīva, Darmstadt, 1993, Wissenschaftliche Buchgesellschaft.

Brüll, Lydia – *Die Japanische Philosophie; eine Einführung,* Darmstadt, Wissenschaftliche Buchgesellschaft, 1989.

Buddhaghosa – *Atthasālinī,* See under Maung Tin, Sammohavinodaṇi, See under Ñanamoli, Visuddhi-magga, See under Ñyanatiloka (German tr.), Ñanamoli, and Maung Tin (Eng. tr.).

Burnouf , M.E. (tr.) – *Saddharmapuṇḍarīka, Le lotus de la bonne loi,* traduit du sanskrit, accompagnie d'un commentaire et vingt et un memoires relatifs au Bouddhisme, Paris, 1852, 1989.

Candrakīrti – parts from *Prasannapadā,* See under Stcherbatsky (Eng. tr. in Tbe Conception of Buddhist Nirvāṇa), May (Fr. tr), Schayer (Germ. tr.), Lamotte (Fr. tr.), and De Jong (Fr. tr.). Madhyamakāvatara, See under Fenner.

Carter, J.R. & M. Palihawadana (tr.) – *The Dhammapāda; A new English translation with the Pali text and the first English translation of the commentary's explanation of the verses,* Oxford, 1987.

Chalmers, Lord R. (tr.) – *Majjhima-nikāya, Further Dialogues of the Buddha,* 2 vols, London, 1927, reprint Delhi, 1988.

Chan, Wing-tsit – *A Source Book in Chinese Philosophy,* Princeton, University Press, 1969, 1972.

— (tr.) *The Platform Scripture, Tbe Basic Classic of Zen Buddhism,*

New York, 1963, St. John's University Press.
Chatterjee, K.N. (tr.) – *Tattvasaṁgraha, Sthirabhāvaparīkṣa of Śāntarakṣita,* Calcutta 1988.
Chaudury, Sukomal – *Analytical Study of the Abhidharmakośa,* Calcutta, 1983, KLM.
Cleary, Thomas (tr.) – *The Flower Ornament Scripture,* [a translation of the Avataṁsaka-sūtra], vol. I, Boulder, 1984, vol. II, Boston, 1986, vol. III, Boston, 1987
Cone, M. & R.F. Gombrich (tr.) – *[Vessantara Jātaka], The Perfect Generosity of Prince Vessantara: a Buddhist Epic,* Oxford, 1977.
Conze, Edward (tr.) – *The Large Sūtra on Perfect Wisdom, with the Divisions of the Abhisamayālaṅkāra,* London, Luzac, 1961.
— (ed. & tr.) – *Vajracchedika Prajñāpāramitā,* Rome, 1957, Serie Orientale Roma XIII, Istituto Italiano per il Medio ed Estremo Oriente.
— *Buddhist Thought in India, three phases of Buddhist philosophy, London,* 1962. Reprinted with corrections, 1983.
— (tr.) *Buddhist Wisdom Books, containing the Diamond Sūtra and the Heart Sūtr*a, London, 1988.
Cowell, E.B. (tr.) – *Jātaka Stories of the Buddha's Former Births,* bound in 3 vols., Cambridge 1895-1913, reprint 1981.
— with F. M. Miiller & J. Takakusu (tr.) – *Buddhist Mahāyāna Texts,* Oxford 1894. Reprint 1985, Sacred Books of the East, 49. Contains: *Buddhacarita of Aśvaghoṣa, the larger and the smaller Sukhavati-vyūha-, Vajracchedika-, larger and smaller Prajñā-pāramitā-hṛdaya-, and Amitāyur-dhyāna-sūtra.*
Dhammapāda – See under Müller, Carter, Banerjee, Barua.
Dhammasaṅgaṇi – See under Rhys Davids.
Dharmakīrti - *Pramāṇa-vārttika,* See under Bijlert, *Pramāṇa-viniścaya,* See under Vetter & Steinkellner, *Vādanyāya*, See under Much.
Dhātukathā – See under U Narada .
Dīghanikāya – See under Rhys Davids, Walshe (Eng. tr.), and Franke (Germ. tr.).
Dignāga (Diṅnāga) – *Pramāṇa-samuccaya,* See under Hattori.
Dōgen Zenji – *Shōbōgenzō,* See under Nishiyama.

Dutt, Nalinaksha – *Mahāyāna Buddhism*, Delhi, 1978, Motilal.
Emmerich, R.E. (tr.) – *Suvarṇabhāṣottamasūtra, The sūtra of Golden Light,* 1990 (2nd revised edition), Sacred Books of the Buddhists.
Ensink, Jacob – *The Question of Rāṣṭrapāla* [Rāṣṭrapāla-paripṛccha], Zwolle 1952
Fausbøll, V. (tr.) – *Sutta-nipāta*, See under Müller.
Feer, L. – *Cent legendes bouddhiques; la centaine d'Avadanas, commançant par Porna* (Pornamukha-avadāna-śataka), Paris, 1891, 1979, Annales du Musee Guimet, 18.
Fenner, Peter G. – *The Ontology of the Middle Way,* Dordrecht, Kluwer, 1990, Studies of Classical India. Includes a translation of the Madhyamakāvatāra of Candrakīrti.
Forke, Alfred – *Geschichte der alten chinesischen Philosophie,* 2nd edition, Hamburg, 1964, Universität Hamburg, Abhandlungen aus dem Gebiet der Auslandkunde, 25.
— *Geschichte der mittelalterlichen chinesischen Philosophie,* 2nd edition, Hamburg, 1964, Universität Hamburg, Abhandlungen aus dem Gebiet der Auslandkunde, 41.
— *Geschichte der neueren chinesischen Philosophie*, 2nd edition, Hamburg, 1964, Universität Hamburg, Abhandlungen aus dem Gebiet der Auslandkunde, 46.
Foucaux, P. E. de (tr.) – *Le Lalitavistara, l'histoire traditionelle de la vie du Bouddha Śākyamuni*, Paris, 1884, 1988.
Franke, R.O. (tr.) – *Dīghanikāya, Das Buch der Iangen Texte des buddhistischen Kanons in Auswahl ubersetzt*, Göttingen & Leipzig, 1913.
Frauwallner, Erich – *Geschichte der indischen Philosophie*, 2 vols., Salzburg, 1953-56, Otto Müller Verlag.
— *On the Date of the Buddhist Master of Law Vasubandhu,* Serie Orientale Roma, Rome, 1951.
— *Die Philosophie des Buddhismus,* Berlin, 1958, Akademie Verlag.
Friedmann, D. L. (tr.) – *Madhyanta-vibhāga-ṭika* [of Sthiramati], *Analysis of the Middle Path and the Extremes, being a commentary on the 'Madhyanta-vibhāga'* of Asaṅga. The translation is restricted to the first part of the commentary. Utrecht,

1937. Reprint, 1984.

Fung Yu-lan – *A History of Chinese Philosophy* (tr. Derk Bodde), 2 vols., Princeton, 1953, 1983, Princeton University Press.

Govinda, Anagarika – *The Psychological Attitude of Early Buddhist Philosophy*, London, 1961.

Hakeda, Yoshito S. (tr.) – *Kūkai, Major Works*, New York, 1972, Colombia University Press.

Hakuin Zenji – See under Shaw.

Hanayama, S. – *Buddhism of the One Great Vehicle*, in The Japanese Mind , ed. Ch. A. Moore, Honolulu, 1967.

Hattori, M. (tr.) – *Dignāga, On Perception: being the Pratyakṣa-pariccheda of Dignāga's Pramāṇasamuccaya, from the Sanskrit fragments and the Tibetan versions,* Cambridge, Massachusetts, 1968, Harvard University Press.

Hoogcarspel, Erik – *Nāgārjuna, The Central Philosophy, Basic Verses.* Amsterdam, 2005, Olive Press

Horner, L B. (tr.) – *Majjhima-nikāya, The Collection of the Middle-lenght Sayings*, 3 vols. London, 1954-59, reprint, 1987-1990.

— & P.S. Jaini (tr.)- *Pannasa Jātaka, Apocryphal Birth Stories,* vol. *I, Jatakas* 1-25, London, 1981, Sacred Books of the Buddhists, 38. Vol. II, See under Jaini.

— (tr.) – *Vinaya-piṭaka, 'Tbe Book of Discipline,* 6 vols., London, 1938-1966. Reprint: 1982-1988, Sacred Books of the Buddhists, 10, 11, 13, 14, 20, 25.

Huángbò, See under Blofeld .

Huìnéng – *Liùzu dùshī fǎbǎo tánjīng* (Liu-tsu Ta-shih Fa-pao T'an-cìhing.), See under Rouselle, Wong Mou-lam, Chan, and Lu K'uan-yu.

Hurvitz, L. (tr.) -[Saddharma-puṇḍarīka], *Scripture of the Lotus Blossom of the Fine Dharma.* Translated from the Chinese of Kumārajīva, reprint New York, 1982.

Izutsu, T. – *Toward a Philosophy of Zen-Buddhism*, Boulder, 1982.

Jaini, P. S. (tr.) – *Pannasa-Jātaka, Apocryphal Birth-Stories*, vol. II, London, 1983, Sacred Books of the Buddhists, 39.

Jātaka – See under Cowell , Cone, Horner, and Jaini.

Jha, Ganghanatha (tr.) – *Tattvasaṁgraha* [by Śāntarakṣita], with the commentary of Kamalaśīla, 2 vols., Baroda 1937-1939, reprint, 1986, Gaekwad's Oriental Series.

Johnston, E.H. & A. Kunst (tr.) – *Vigrahavyāvartani* (of Nāgārjuna), *The Dialectical Method of Nāgārjuna.* With Introduction and notes by K. Bhattacarya, Delhi, 1986.

Jones, J.J. – *Mahāvastu*, translated from the Sanskrit, 3 vols., London 1949-195.6. Reprint, 1976-1987, Sacred Books of the Buddhists, 16, 18, 19.

Jong, J.W. de (tr.) – *Cinq chapitres de Ia Prasannapadā* [Candrakīrti], Paris, 1949, Guethner.

Kalupahana, David J. (tr.) – *Nāgārjuna, The Philosophy of the Middle Way (*Mūlamadhyamaka-kārikā), Albany, 1986, State University of New York Press, SUNY series.

Kamalaśīla – See under Tucci and Jha.

Kambalapāda – See under Tucci.

Karma-siddhi-prakaraṇa of Vasubandhu – See under Anacker.

Kathavatthu – See under Zan Aung.

Kern, Hendrik (tr.) – *Saddharmapuṇḍarīka or The Lotus of the True Law,* Oxford, 1884, reprint Delhi, 1980.

Kūkai – See under Hakeda.

Lalitavistara - see under Poppe, Foucaux, and Bays.

Lamotte, Étienne (tr.) – *La somme du grand véhicule d'Asanga* (Mahāyānasaṁgraha), lnstitut Orientaliste, Louvain-la-neuve, 1973.·

— *L'Histoire du bouddhisme indien, des origines a l'ère Śaka,* lnstitut orientaliste de Louvain, 1958. (English translation, look under Webb-Boin)

— (tr.) Mahāprajñāpāramitā-Śāstra, *La traité de Ia grande vertu de sagesse,* lnstitut Orientaliste de Louvain, 1944-1949.

— (tr.) – (ch. 17) of the *Prasannapadā* of Candrakīrti, in Melanges Chinois et ·Bouddhiques, vol. 4, 1936, published by 'L'lnstitut Belge des Hautes Etudes Chinoises,' Brussels.

— (tr.) – *Vimalakīrti-nirdeśa, L'Enseignement de Vimalakirti,* Louvain-la-Neuve, 1987, Bibliotheque du Museon, 51, Publication de L'lnstitut Orientaliste de Louvain, 35.

Lang, K. (tr.) – *Āryadeva's Catuḥ-Śataka*, Copenhagen 1986,

Indiske Studier,7.
Laṅkāvatāra-sūtra – See under Suzuki.
Liebenthal, Walter (tr.) – *The Book of Chao* (being a complete translation of the work of Seng Zhao), Peiping, 1948, The Catholic University of Beijing.
Lozang Jamspal, Ngawang Samten Chopel & Peter Della Santina (tr.) – *Nāgārjuna's Letter to King Gautamiputra* (Suhṛllekha), with explanatory notes and preface by his Holiness Sakya Trizin, Delhi, 1978, Motilal.
Lu K'uan-yu (tr.) – *The Altar Sutra of the Sixth Patriarch* [Huìnéng], in Lu's *Ch'an and Zen Teaching*, London, third series, 1962, Ryder & Co.
Madhyanta-vibhāga-bhāṣya of Vasubandhu [commentary on the work of Asaṅga or Maitreyanātha], See under Anacker.
Mahāprajñāpāramitā-śāstra – ascribed to Nāgārjuna, See under Lamotte.
Mahāvastu - See under Jones.
Mahāyāna-saṁgraha of Asaṅga, See under Lamotte.
Majjhima-nikāya – See under Chatterjee, Chalmers, and Horner.
Masson, Jeffrey Moussaieff – *The Oceanic Feeling: the origins of religious sentiment in ancient India*, Dordrecht, 1980, D. Reidel, Kluwer.
Maung Tin, Pe (tr.) – *The Expositor (Atthasālinī) of Buddhaghosa,* edited and revised by C.A.F. Rhys Davids, London, 1920/21. Reprint 1976, Pāli Text Society.
— (tr.) *Visuddhimagga, The Path of Purity of Buddhaghosa,* London, 1923-31, reprint 1975, Pāli Text Society.
May, Jacques (tr.) – *Candrakīrti: Prasannapadā Madhyamakavṛtti, Douze chapitres traduits du sanscrit et du tibetain,* Paris, 1959, Adrien-Maissonneuve.
Miyamoto, Shōsan – *The Relation of Philosophical Theory to Practical Affairs in Japan*, in The Japanese Mind, ed. Ch. A. Moore, Honolulu, 1967.
Mohamad Shah, Jildi (tr.) – *De Basisverzen van de Ratnagotravibhāga*, Leiden, 1988, University paper.
Mookerjee, Satkari – *The Buddhist Philosophy of Eternal Flux,*

Calcutta, 1935, Delhi,1975, 1980, Motilal.

Much, M.T. – *Dharmakīrti's Vādanyāya,* Sanskrit Text Übersetzung und Anmerkungen, 2 parts, Vienna, 1991, Kommission für Sprachen und Kulturen Siidasiens, 25.

Moore, Charles A. (ed.) – *The Japanese Mind,* Honolulu, 1967.

Mūlamadhyamaka-kārikā of Nāgārjuna, See under Kalupahana and Hoogcarspel.

Miiller, F. Max (tr.) – *Dhammapāda, A Collection of Verses. With Suttanipāta, A Collection of Discourses,* translated by V. Fausbøll, London 1881, reprint, 1988, Sacred Books of the East.

Murti, T.R.V. – *The Central Philosophy of Buddhism*: a study of the Mādhyamika system, London, 1955, Reprint 1987.

Nagao, Gadjin M. – *Mādhyamika and Yogācāra, a study of Mahāyāna philosophies,* Albany, 1991, State University of New York Press, SUNY series.

Nāgārjuna – *Mūlamadhyamaka-kārikā,* See under Kalupahana, Hoogcarspel, *Suhṛllekha,* See under Lozang Jamspal, *Vigraha-vyāvartani,* See under Johnston,

Mahāprajñā-pāramitā-śāstra, See under Lamotte.

Nakamura, Hajime – *Indian Buddhism: a survey with bibliographical notes,* Japan, 1980, Delhi, 1987, 1989 (Motilal).

— *History of the Development of Japanese Thought,* 2 vols., Tokyo, 1969, Kokusai Bunka Shinkokai (Japan Cultural Society).

— *Ways of Thinking of Eastern Peoples,* India, China, Tibet, Japan (ed. Philip P. Wiener), Honolulu, 1964, 1985, University of Hawaii Press.

Ñānamoli, Bhikku (tr.) – *The Path of Purification* (Visuddhimagga) by Bhadantacariya Buddhaghosa, Colombo 1956, paperback reprint in 2 vols., Berkeley, London, 1976, (Shambala).

— (tr.) – Sammoha vinodaṇi [of Buddhaghosa], *The Dispeller of Delusion,* London, 1987, Sacred Books of the Buddhists

— (tr.) – *Peṭakopadesa, The Piṭaka Disclosure, according to Kaccana Thera,* London, 1964. Reprint, 1979, Pali Text Society, Translation series, 35.

Ñānamolo, Bhikku (tr.) – *Paṭisambhidhamagga, The Path of Discrimination,* introduction by A.K. Warder, London, 1982,

Pali Text Society Translation Series,86-87.
Narada Thera (tr. & ed.) – *A Manual of Abhidhamma (Abhidhammatha-saṁgaha)*, 2 vols., Colombo, Vājirārāma, 1956, 1957.
Nishiyama, Kosen & John Stevens (tr.) – *Shōbōgenzō, The Eye and Treasury of the True Law,* 4 vols., Tokyo, 1975-1983, Nakayama Shōbō.
Norman, K.R. (tr.) – *Sutta-Nipāta, The Group of Discourses, with alternative translations* by I.B. Horner and W. Rahula, vol. I, London, 1984, Pali Text Society Translation Series, 44.
— (tr.) – *Theragātha, The Elders' Verses I,* London, 1969. Reprint, 1990, Pali Text Society Translation Series, 38.
Ñyānatiloka, Mahathera (tr.) – *Der Weg zur Reinheit (Visuddhimagga) of Buddhaghosa*, Konstanz 1989, Verlag Christiani.
Obermiller, E. (tr.) – *Abhisamayālaṅkāra (*by Maitreya) [German translation], Acta Orientalia, XI, Leiden, agency E.J. Brill, 1932.
Oetke, Claus – *'Ich' und das Ich: Analytische Untersuchungen zur buddhistischen brahmanischen Atmankontroverse,* Wiesbaden, 1988, Steiner Verlag.
Oldenberg, H. – *Buddha, sein Leben, seine Lehre, seine Gemeinde,* Stuttgart & Berlin, 1881, 1923.
Pañcaskandhaka-prakaraṇa of Vasubandhu, See under Anacker.
Paṭisambhidamagga – See under Ñānamolo.
Paṭṭhāna – See under U Nārada .
Peṭakopadesa – See under Ñānamoli.
Piatigorsky, Alexander – *The Buddhist Philosophy of Thought: Essays in interpretation,* London, Dublin, 1984, Curzon Press.
Poppe, N (tr.) – *Lalita-Vistara; The twelve deeds of the Buddha.* A Mongolian version of the Lalitavistara, Wiesbaden, 1967.
Prajñāpāramitā-hṛdaya-sūtra – See under Conze and Cowell.
Prajñāpāramitā (large) – See under Conze.
Pramāṇa-samuccaya of Dignāga – See under Hattori.
Pramāṇa-vārttika of Dharmakīrti – See under Bijlert.
Pramāṇa-viniscaya of Dharmakīrti – See under Vetter & Steinkellner.

Pruden, L.M. (tr.) – *Abhidharmakośabhāṣyam* (of Vasubandhu) [from the French version by L. de Ia Vallée Poussin], Berkeley, 1988.

Rahula, Walpola (tr.) – *Le compendium de la superdoctrine* [being the, Abhidharma-samuccaya of Asaṅga], Paris, 1980, Publication de l'Ecole Française d'Extreme-Orient (78).

Rāṣṭrtrapāla-paripṛccha – See under Ensink .

Ratnagotravibhāga-kārikā – See under Mohamad Shah.

Rhys Davids, C.A.F. (tr.) – *Buddhist Psychological Ethics* [Dhammasaṅgaṇi], London, 1900, 1974, Pāli Text Society Translation Series, 41.

— & H. Oldenberg (tr.) – *Vinaya Texts*, 3 vols. London, 1881-1885. Reprint 1974-1975, Sacred Books of the East, 13, 17, 20.

— & T.W. Rhys Davids – *Dīgha-nikāya, Dialogues of the Buddha* , 3 vols., London, 1899-1921. Reprint, 1977-1989, Sacred Books of the Buddhists, 2-4.

— & F.L. Woodward (tr.) – *Saṁyutta-nikāya, The Book of kindred Sayings or Grouped Suttas,* 5 vols., London 1917-1930, Reprint, 1982-1990, Pali Text Society Translation Series, 7, 10, 13, 14, 16.

— (tr.) [Therigātha and Theragātha], *Psalms of the Early Buddhists,* London, 1909-1913. Reprint 1980, Pāli Text Society Translation Series, 1,4.

Rouselle, Erwin – *Das sutra des sechsten Patriarchen*, Frankfurt, 1930, 1931, 1936, Sinica, vol5., 177-191, vol. 6, 26-34, vol. 11, 131-137,202-210.

Saddharmapuṇḍarīka – See under Burnouf, Kern, Hurvitz, and Borsig.

Sammohavinodaṇi of Buddhaghosa – See under Ñānamoli.

Saṁyutta-nikāya – See under Rhys Davids & Woodward.

Śāntarakṣita – *Tattvasaṁgraha*, See under Jha and Chatterjee.

Śāntideva – *Bodhicaryāvatāra*, See under Barnett, Sharma, and Steinkellner.

Sarvāstivāda Abhidharma – no translations (except in Japanese).

Schayer, Stanislaw – *Ausgewählte Kapitel aus der Prasannapadā,* Cracow, 1931.

Schumann, Hans Wolfgang – *Der Historische Buddha: Leben und Lehre des Gotama,* München, 1990, Diederichs Gelbe Reihe.

Sengzhao – See under Liebenthal.

Shaner, David Edward – *The BodyMind Experience in Japanese Buddhism: a phenomenological study of Kūkai and Dōgen,* Albany, 1985, State University of New York Press, SUNY series.

Sharma, Parmānanda (tr.) – [Bodhicaryāvatāra], *Śāntideva's Bodhicaryāvatāra* (Sanskrit with translation, based on Prajñākaramati's Pañjika), 2 vols., Delhi, 1990.

Shaw, R.D.M. – *Hakuin Zenji, the Embossed Tea Kettle* (o Ra Te Gama), and other Works, London 1963, Allan & Unwin.

Śikṣasamuccaya of Śāntideva – See under Bendall

Stcherbatsky, T. – *The Central Conception of Buddhism, and the meaning of the word 'dharma,'* London, 1923, Calcutta, 1956, 1961, Susil Gupta.

— *The Conception of Buddhist Nirvāṇa,* Leningrad, 1927, Delhi 1968, 1977, Motilal.

— *Buddhist Logic,* 2 vols., Leningrad, 1930, New York, 1962, Dover. The latest reprint, is as far as I know, by Motilal in Delhi, date unknown to me.

Steinkellner, E. (tr.) – [Bodhicaryāvatāra of Śāntideva], *Der Eintritt in das Leben zur Erleuchtung*: Lehrgedicht des Mahāyāna, München, 1989.

— Translation of ch. II. of Dharmakīrti's *Pramāṇa-viniścaya* – See under Vetter.

Sthavira-gātha – See under Bechert.

Sthiramati – look under Friedmann.

Suhṛllekha of Nāgārjuna – See under Lozang Jamspal

Sukhavativyūha – See under Cowell.

Sutta-nipāta – See under Müller, Fausbøll, and Norman.

Suvarṇaprabhāṣa – See under Emmerich

Suzuki, Daisetz Teitaro (tr.) – *Laṅkāvatāra Sūtra,* London, 1932, Routledge & Kegan Paul.

Thera & Therigātha – see under Rhys Davids and Norman.

Thera-Abhidhamma – *Dhammasaṅgaṇi*, See under Rhys Davids, *Vibhaṅga*, See under U Thittila, *Dhātukathā*, See under U Narada, *Paṭṭhāna*, See under U Narada, *Kathāvatthu*, See under Zan Aung.

Thomas, E. J. – *A History of Buddhist Thought,* London 1963.

Triṁśikā-kārikā of Vasubandhu – See under Anacker.

Tri-svabhāva-nirdeśa of Vasubandhu – See under Anacker.

Tucci, G. (tr.) – *Minor Buddhist Texts*, Rome, 1956-1958. Reprint, 1986. Contains: (first part) Asaṅga's commentary on the *Vajracchedika*, Analysis of commentary on it by Vasubandhu, *Navaśloki* of Kambalapāda, *Catuḥstavasamārtha* of Amṛtakara *Hetutattvopadeśa* of Jitari, *Tarkasapana* of Vidyākarasanti, with an appendix containing the Gilgit manuscript of the *Vajracchedika,* edited by N.P. Chakravarti; (second part), First *Bhāvaṇakrāma* of Kamalaśīla: Sanskrit and Tibetan text with introduction and English summary.

U Narada (tr.) -*Discourse on the Elements* [Dhātukathā], London, 1977, Pali Text Society Translation Series, 34.

— (tr.) – *Conditional Relations* (Paṭṭhāna, 2 vols., vol. I, London, 1969, Luzac & Co.) Vol. II, London 1981, Routledge & Kegan Paul, both volumes published by the Pāli Text Society, Translation Series, 37, 42. Translation from the Chaṭṭasaṅgāyana Text of the Seventh Book of the Abhidhamma Piṭaka

U Thittila - *The Book of Analysis* (Vibhaṅga): the second book of th.e Abhidhamma, Piṭaka, translated from the Burmese Chaṭṭhasaṅgīti Edition, Oxford, 1988, Pāli. Society Translation Series, 39.

Ui, Hakuju – Article about the Buddha's date, according to Nakamura in Indo Tetsugaku Kenkyii, vol. 2, pp. 1-112, Tokyo Koshisha, 1926.

Vādhavidhi of Vasubandhu, – look under Anacker.

Vajracchedika-sūtra – look under Conze, Cowell, and Tucci.

Vallée Poussin, Louis de Ia – *L'Abhidharmakośa de Vasubandhu* [being a translation of the Chinese version of Xuánzàng], Paris, Paul Guethner; Louvain, J.B. Istas, 1923-1931 (6 vols.). For the English translation, See under Pruden.

— (tr.) – Vijñaptimātratāsiddhi, *La Siddhi de Hiuan-Tsang,* 2 vols., Paris, Paul Guethner, 1928-29.

Vasubandhu – *Abhidharma-kośa*, See under Vallée Poussin, *Vādhavidhi, Viṁśatikā, Triṁśikā, Tri-svabhāva-nirdeśa, Karmasiddhi-prakaraṇa, Pañcaskandhaka prakaraṇa,* and *Madhyānta-vibhāga-bhāṣya, Triṁśikā* also in Frauwallner, 'Die Philosophie des Buddhismus.'
Venkata Ramanan, K.– *Nāgārjuna's Philosophy, as presented in the Mahāprajñāpāramitā-śāstra,* Vermont & Tokyo, 1966, Reprint Delhi, 1975, 1977, 1987, Motilal.
Vetter, Tilmann – *Erkenntnisprobleme bei Dharmakīrti*, Vienna, 1964, Hermann Bohlaus.
— *The Ideas and Meditative Practices of Early Buddhism*, Leiden, 1988, Brill.
— *Der Buddha und seine Lehre in Dharmakīrti's Pramāṇa-vārttikam: Der Abschnitt über den Buddha und die vier edlen Wahrheiten im Pramāṇasiddhi* 1990, Wiener Studien zur Tibetologie und Buddhismuskunde, 12.
Vetter, T. & E. Steinkellner – Pramāṇa-viniścaya of Dharmakīrti, 3 vols., vol. I. ch. I. Pratyakṣam, ed. & tr. by T. Vetter, Vienna 1966, Svārthānumānam, ed. by E. Steinkellner, Vienna, 1973, vol. III, ch. II, Svārthānumānam, tr. by E. Steinkellner, Vienna, 1979, Osterreichische Akademie der Wissenschaften, Phil. -hist. Klasse, Sitzungsberichte, I: 250, 3, II: 267, 4, III: 358.
Vibhaṅga – See under U Thittila.
Vidyākarasanti – See under Tucci.
Vigrahavyāvartani of Nāgārjuna – See under Johnston.
Vimalakīrti-nirdeśa-sūtra – See under Lamotte and Boin.
Vimśatikā-kārikā of Vasubandhu – See under Anacker.
Vinaya Piṭaka – See under Rhys Davids and Horner.
Visudddhi-magga of Buddhaghosa – See under Maung Tin and Nyānatiloka.
Walshe, M. (tr.) – *Dīgha Nikāya, Thus have I heard: the long discourses of the Buddha*, London, 1987.
Warder, A.K. – *Indian Buddhism*, Delhi, 1970, 1980, Motilal.
Warren, Henry Clarke – *Buddhism in Translations,* New York, 1979, Atheneum.
Watts, Alan – *The Way of Zen*, New York, 1957, Harmond-

sworth, 1962-1975, Penguin, Pelican
Webb-Boin, S. (tr.) – *History of Indian Buddhism: from the origim to the Śaka era* by E. Lamotte, Louvain, 1988.
— (tr.) – *Vimalakīrti-nirdeśa, The Teaching of Vimalakīrti,* rendered into English from the French translation by Lamotte, with introduction and notes, London, 1976, Sacred Books of the Buddhists, 32.
Willis, J.D. (tr.) – *Tattvārtha chapter of Asaṅga's Bodhisattvabhūmi. On Knowing Reality*, Delhi, 1989.
Wong Mou-lam (tr.) – *The Sūtra of Wei Lang* (or Hui Neng). New ed. by Christmas Humphreys, London, Luzac & Co., 1947.
Woodward, F.L. & E.M. Hare (tr.) – Aṅguttra-nikāya, *The Book of Gradual Sayings, or more numbered Suttas*, (5 vols.), London, 1932-36, Pāli Text Society.
Xuánzàng – *Chéng wéishi lùn – Vijñapti-mātratā-siddhi, being an elaboration and translation into Chinese of the work of Dharmapāla, being itself a commentary on the Thirty Verses of Vasubandhu.* See under Vallée Poussin.
Yokoi, Y. – *Zen Master Dōgen: An Introduction with Selected Writings*, New York, Tokyo, 1976, 1981, Weatherhill.
Zan Aung, Shwe (tr.) & C.A.F. Rhys Davids (ed.) – *Compendium of Philosophy* tr. of Abhidhammattha-saṅgaha, London, 1910, Pali Text Society Translation Series.
— (tr.) & C.A.F. Rhys Davids – *Kāthavatthu, Points of Controversy or Subjects of Discourse.* London, 1915. Reprint, 1979, Pali Text Society Translation Series, 5.

Index and Glossary

A

Abhidhamma – Pāli for Abhidharma: 8, 76, 78, 81, 82, 96, 99, 346, 348, 349
Abhidharma – Corpus of canonical scriptures, with a content of theoretical psychology, date a few hundred years later than sermons and order rules: 8, 29, 70, 71, 75, 76, 77, 78, 79, 81, 91, 97, 101, 102, 123, 133, 145, 181, 197, 200, 201, 202, 204, 206, 337, 347, 350
Abhidharmakośa – *Treasury of the Abhidharma*, major work of Vasubandhu, 5th or 6th century: 70, 79, 102, 119, 123, 129, 200, 340, 349
Abhidharmakośabhāṣya – like *Kośa* + autocommentary: 202, 337
Abhidharmasamuccaya – *Compendium of Abhidharma*, work of Asaṅga: 202, 338
Abhidharmasūtra – Yogācāra Mahāyānasūtra: 202
Ābhidharmika – referring to Abhidharma: 173, 177, 187
abhijñā – paranormal gifts: 153
abhimukhī – sixth stage of the bodhisattva path: 154, 157
Abhisamayālaṅkāra – *Ornament of Clear Understanding*, Idealist Mahāyānasūtra: 202, 340, 346
absolute 8, 13, 16, 23, 25, 29, 48, 55, 61, 109, 110, 117, 118, 120, 127, 128, 129, 135, 138, 143, 146, 162, 165, 168, 170, 183, 184, 185, 186, 187, 190, 191, 192, 193, 198, 199, 238, 239, 240, 241, 272, 273, 274, 276, 277, 279, 280, 284, 285, 301, 304, 309, 313, 317, 322, 324, 328, 331, 332
abstraction 203, 210, 316, 324
acalā – 8th bodhisattva stage: 156, 157
accumulation 23, 214, 244
actuality 96, 103, 126, 213, 214, 238, 241, 255, 256, 284, 289, 304, 314, 315, 316, 324
adhicitta – training of the will: 153
adhimokkha – Pāli for *adhimokṣa*: 92
adhimokṣa – resolve: 111
adhimukti – true aspiration for becoming a Buddha: 151
adhiśīla – good conduct: 152
adhyāropāpavādanyāya – method for removal of mental prtojection: 190
adhyātma-āyatana – internal base of perception, the sense organs with the mind: 118
adosa – P. for adveṣa: 94, 96
advaidhīkāra – non bifurcated: 184
Advaita Vedānta –Upanishadic school affirming there is only

absolute consciousness: 148
advaya – non-dual: 155, 163, 168, 183
adveṣa – freedom from aversion: 116
āgama – any one of five groups of canonical sermons: 157, 169
āhāra – food: 99
ahetuka-cittāni – mental states, not causing retribution: 97
ahiṁsā – non violence: 116
ahirika – shamelessness: 94
ahrīkya – ibid. irreverence: 115
aim 24, 27, 54, 57, 58, 83, 95, 120, 162, 215, 216, 218, 219, 222, 223, 225, 252, 263, 284, 300, 313, 330
ākāśa – space: 102
ākara – shape: 209
ākāsa – P. ākāśa: 99
akusala – unwholesome: 90, 97, 111
akusala cittāni – unwholesome mental states: 97
ālambana – external object as cause of perception: 208
Ālambanaparīkṣa – *Examination of the Cause of Perception*, work of Asaṅga: 203
ālaya-vijñāna – storeconsciousness: 198, 256, 279
almightiness 136
alobha – being without greed: 94, 96, 116
altruism 243
amala – ubstained: 183
Amarāvati – ancient town in ancient India
Amaterasu Ōmikami – Japanese Sun Goddess: 305
Ameshapenta – saints of Zoroastrianism: 135
Amida-butsu – Jap. for Amithabhā 307
Amitabhā – unmeasured splendour, name of the Buddha of Western paradise: 135, 307, 308, 309
Ānanda – disciple of Buddha: 75, 190
anapatrapya – lack of scruples:115
Anchō – Japanese monk, commentator: 235, 237
Andhra – central-east part of India: 142, 146, 171
Aṅguttara-nikāya – Ascending Collection of canonical sermons: 77, 338
aniccattā – P. impermanence: 99
animitta – uncaused: 155
anottapa – P. anapatrapya: 94
anumāna – inference: 206, 215
anupalabdhi – not perceived, inferring absence: 217
anyāpoha – exclusion of the other: 210
Apara-śaila – early Mahāsaṁgha sect: 72
apatrapya – aversion of things objectionable 116
āpo – waters: 99
Apoha – epoche, abstraction: 11, 220
Apohaprakaraṇa – *Discourse on Abstraction,* work of Dharmottara

203
appearance 20, 21, 83, 90, 103, 117, 119, 121, 125, 137, 158, 159, 167, 180, 190, 191, 198, 213, 214, 216, 219, 233, 239, 263, 268, 269, 277, 279, 283, 299
apperception 8, 16, 85, 86, 87, 88, 89, 91, 92, 93, 99, 101, 102, 108, 109, 111, 201, 203, 204, 205
apprehension 16, 49, 53, 55, 83, 87, 91, 103, 111, 137, 183, 184, 191, 192, 198, 205, 207, 208, 212, 236, 237
apramada – care, tending the good: 116
aprameya – unmeasurable: 184
aprāpti – immunity: non-acquisition: 104, 105
apratisaṁkhyanirodha – cessation without insight, kataleptic state recognized by Sarvāstivādins: 121
aprasṭhita citta – non-abiding mind: 314
arcismatī – 4th stage of bodhisattva path: 154
arhat – saint of Theravāda: 36, 58, 66, 247
artha – meaning, thing: 207
Āryadeva – pupil and successor of Nāgārjuna in Madhyamaka School: 170, 172, 173, 174, 193, 338, 343
Asaṅga – Founder of Yogācāra School: 197, 199, 200, 202, 204, 212, 337, 338, 339, 341, 344, 347, 349, 351
asaṁkhyeya – innumerable: 185
asatkhyāpana – constructive: 191
āśaya – resting place: 153
Aśoka – 65, 66, 67, 68, 70, 72, 148
aśraddhā – lack of faith: 114
āsravas – the influences: 35
ātman – self: 174, 181, 254, 255, 258, 275
atom 117, 118, 204, 205
attachment 42, 43, 114, 120, 153, 155, 165, 183, 186, 244, 271, 288, 333
attha-paññatti-vīthi – graspimg of the meaning: 89
Atthasālinī – *The Interpreter*, work of Buddhaghosa: 78, 339, 344
auddhatya – restlessness: 114
autonomy 24, 105, 107
āvaccana – sphere: 97
āvajjana – being alerted: 87
Avanti – town in Mahārāṣtra: 30, 76, 144, 146
āvaraṇa – veil: 191
avastha – situation: 119, 209
Avataṁsaka-sūtra –Garland-sūtra, idealist Mahāyāna text: 141, 202, 267, 269, 270, 272, 276, 338, 340
avidyā – ignorance: 35, 41, 94, 183, 190, 191
avijjā – P. avidyā: 94
avijñapti – seed of subtle matter that causes retribution: 104, 107, 124, 125
avyakata – P. for avyākṛta: 90

avyākṛta –neutral, unevolved: 111
Ayodhya – town in North-India: 204
ayoniśo manaskāra – distraction: 191

B

background consciousness 87, 89, 90, 97, 100, 101
Bahuśrutīya – Mahāsaṁgha sect: 72
bāhya-āyatana – outward senses: 118
Bāṇa – poet from the time of Harṣa: 148
Benares 33, 36, 39, 40, 41
Bendōwa – part of *Shōbōgenzō*: 322
Běnwú – School of Original Non-Being: 235
Běnwú yī – Variant School of Original Bon-Being: 235
Bhadrāyanīyas – subsect of Vātsiputrīyas: 72
Bhagavad Gītā – Song of the Lord: 138
Bhāgavata – Vaiṣṇava sect: 143
Bhakti movement – movement of (theistic) devotion: 307
Bhāskaravarman – king of Assam: 147, 148
bhāsvara –transparent: 183
bhava – becoming: 40, 42, 154
bhavāṅga – Thera name for store-consciousness: 87, 109
bhavatṛṣṇā – desire for becoming: 101
Bhāvaviveka – Madhyamaka philosopher: 172, 173, 174
bhūmi – stage: 152, 157, 338
biān – evolution: 255
biānjīsuǒzhíxìng – nature of imagination: 262
Biān zōng lūn – *Discussion of Essentials*, work of Xie Ling-yun: 244
bodhi – enlightenment: 12, 134, 154, 157, 166, 264, 265, 268, 274, 275, 283, 290, 332
Bodhicaryāvatāra – *The Revelation of the Practice unto Illumination*, work of Śāntideva: 172, 338, 339, 347, 348
bodhicitta – mindset of a bodhisattva: 151
Bodhidharma – Zen saint: 285, 286
bodhisattvas – Mahāyāna saints: 131, 133, 134, 135, 136, 141, 142, 146, 151, 152, 153, 154, 155, 156, 157, 159, 160, 161, 162, 169, 170, 215, 228, 264, 282, 306, 329
bondage 8, 27, 35, 40, 41, 46, 51, 82, 215, 288
Book of Changes 248
Book of Zhào 238
Brahmanism 136, 143, 145, 150, 211, 322
Brahmins 33, 181, 322
Buddha-body 158, 159
Buddha-family 156, 247
Buddhaghosa – Buddhist Hīnayāna philosopher: 45, 76, 78, 338, 339, 344, 345, 346, 347, 350
Buddhapālita – Madhyamaka phi-

losopher: 172, 173
buddhi – function of feeling, judgment: 178, 183, 190

C

Caitika – sect of Mahāsaṁgha: 146
caittā – mental factors, Sarvāstivāda: 102
caitya –temple: 146
calana – vibration of background consciousness: 87
calm 24, 25, 133, 134, 136, 274, 275, 282, 318, 331, 333
Candragupta I – first ruler of Gupta dynasty: 146
Candrakīrti – prominent member of Prasaṅgika school of Madhyamaka: 142, 148, 151, 172, 174, 201, 339, 341, 343, 344
Cāodŏng – Ch. Sōtō Zen: 317
Cāoshàn Bĕnjí – one of the founders of the Sōtō School of Zen: 317
Cashmere 9, 67, 71, 143, 144, 148, 149
Catuḥśataka – *Work of 400 stanzas*, by Āryadeva: 172, 193
Catuḥ-stava – *Four Hymns*, by Nāgārjuna: 172
catuṣkoti – tetralemma: 177
catya – cheating: 115
causality 175, 176, 177, 178, 226, 290, 322, 325, 326, 327
causation 8, 12, 36, 41, 44, 56, 57, 176, 177, 184, 236, 239, 244, 257, 262, 268, 277, 281, 326
Cedi – royal house of Ganges region, 2nd century BC: 9, 145
cessation 155, 181, 186, 193, 281, 282
cetanā – volition: 91, 103
cetāsika – P. mental factors: 86, 90
Chán – Ch. Zen: 12, 267, 285, 286, 287, 291, 293, 297, 298
chanda – conscious volition: 92, 93, 111
Cháng'ān – Chinese capital 1st millennium: 253
change 24, 46, 48, 89, 109, 119, 120, 121, 125, 129, 133, 136, 148, 156, 167, 181, 187, 188, 238, 239, 241, 244, 248, 249, 257, 263, 276, 277, 283, 285, 304, 314, 326
Chéngguān – 4th patriarch of Hua-yan School: 276
Chéng wéishí lūn – *Vijñaptimātratā Siddhi, commentary on Vasubandhu's Triṁśika by Xuanzang:* 254, 255, 263
Chotan – Indian enclave in Tarim Basin: 233
citta – mind: 52, 82, 84, 86, 91, 102, 110, 111, 154, 314
cittaguññatā – proficiency of mind: 96
cittakammaññatā – adaptability of mind: 96
cittalahutā – agility of mind: 96
citta-mahābhūmika dharma – ten neutral mental faculties in Sarvāsrivāda: 111
citta-mātra – mind only: 154

cittamudutā – flexibility of mind: 96
cittāni – mental states: 86, 97
cittapassaddhi – tranquillity of mind: 96
citta-vīthi – mental process: 84
cittujjukatā –rectitude of mind: 96
cognition 15, 16, 44, 45, 46, 48, 49, 55, 87, 91, 92, 103, 110, 111, 205, 206, 224, 225, 227, 314
compassion 95, 96, 133, 152, 153, 155, 214, 218, 228, 265, 275, 308, 338
conation 48, 236
concentration 34, 37, 38, 61, 91, 92, 102, 111, 191, 248, 289, 318
conditioning 41, 53, 81, 83, 85, 108, 124, 128, 129, 153, 226
Confucianism 297, 321, 330
Confucius 245, 300, 330
continuity 39, 84, 85, 87, 181, 212, 272
conventional truth 166, 192
criticism 41, 120, 142, 169, 170, 174, 177, 178, 179, 183, 250
cuti – P. moment of death: 86

D

Dāchéng zhíguān 281, 282
Dāchèng Zhīguān Fǎmén – Mahayana Method of Cessation and Contemplation, by Huisī: 276, 277, 281, 282
Dainichikyō – Mahavairocana Sutra 305
Dainichi Nyorai – The Great Radiant Tathagata: 305, 306
Dai Nippon – Geat Japan: 304
dāna – alms giving: 152
Dāo – The Way: 13, 236, 243, 274, 287, 292, 293
Dào'ān – founder of School of Original Non-Being: 236
Daoism – Taoism: 233, 235, 277, 286, 297, 321, 330
Dāolín – early Chinese Buddhist: 236
Dàoshēng – Chinese Buddhist philosopher: 11, 242
Dāoxīn – 4th patriarch of Zen: 286
Dāoxuān – *compiler of Guang Hongming ji, Essays on Buddhism:* 246
Dāoyī – teacher of School of Phenomenal Illusion: 237, 287, 288, 289, 291
Dāoyīng – Zen Master, 9th century: 291
Daradas – Mongolian tribe, perhaps Tatars: 148
darśana-bhāga – subjective aspect of consciousness: 260
Daśabhūmīśvara –Mahayana work on the bodhisattva: 152, 157
Daśabhūmi-vibhāṣa-śāstra – commentary on the above, doubtfully ascribed to Nagarjuna: 172
Dengyō Daishi – Saichō, founder of Japanese Tendai: 303
dependent origination 7, 21, 36, 41, 42, 43, 44, 47, 48, 61, 62,

68, 154, 155, 169, 190, 218
desire 35, 37, 38, 39, 40, 44, 46, 48, 49, 50, 53, 54, 58, 59, 61, 92, 93, 97, 101, 111, 112, 113, 114, 115, 116, 120, 135, 153, 155, 159, 184, 185, 186, 191, 193, 214, 219, 228, 242, 255, 256, 257, 258, 259, 265, 284
Devaśarman – author of Dhātukāya: 79
dhamma – P. dharma: 82, 85
dhammachanda – noble desire: 94
Dhammapāda – Work of early Buddhism: 81, 186, 339, 340, 345
Dhammasaṅgaṇī – *Enumeration of the dharmas*, work of P. abhidhamma: 77, 81
Dhānyakaṭaka – town in Andhra, birthplace of Nāgārjuna: 145, 151, 171
dharma – Buddhist law, or category of mind: 75, 80, 81, 82, 84, 85, 99, 103, 104, 105, 107, 108, 111, 119, 123, 125, 126, 128, 129, 137, 138, 158, 162, 164, 180, 191, 198, 236, 239, 254, 260, 262, 263, 268, 276, 300, 306, 313, 348
dharmabody – Ther corpus of Buddhist teaching: 138, 158, 162, 164
dharmadhātu – absolute: 164, 263, 276
Dharmagupta – founder of early Buddhist School: 77
Dharmaguptakas – early Buddhist School: 8, 72, 76, 77, 233
dharmahood 138, 164, 166, 183, 189, 202
dharmakāya – corpus of Teaching: 126, 129, 138, 139, 157, 162, 164, 180
Dharmakīrti – idealist philosopher, epistemologist: 11, 15, 70, 148, 149, 151, 198, 199, 201, 203, 210, 211, 212, 213, 214, 215, 218, 225, 226, 228, 339, 340, 345, 346, 348, 350
Dharmamegha – Cloud of Dharma:, 156, 157
dharmanairātmya – voidness of being: 166
Dharmapāla – philosopher: 70, 174, 201, 210, 254, 255, 351
dharmas – categories of being: 9, 77, 78, 81, 82, 84, 85, 98, 99, 102, 103, 109, 127, 137, 138, 139, 142, 153, 154, 158, 160, 162, 165, 237, 241, 252, 254, 255, 256, 259, 260, 261, 263, 281, 303, 331, 332
Dharmaskandha – *Groups of dharmas*, work of Sarvastivada abhidharma: 78
dharmatā – dhrmahood: 138, 162, 164, 166, 189, 308
dharmatā-yukti – ultimate reality: 308
Dharmayaśas – apostle of China: 77
Dharmadharmatāvibhaṅga – *Analysis of dharma and dharmahood*, work of Asaṅga: 202

Dharmottara – idealist thinker: 149, 201, 203, 211
Dharmottarīyas, – early school: 72
dhâtu – element: 97, 98
Dhātukathā – book of Abhidharma of Theras: 77, 340, 348, 349
Dhātukāya – Corpus of Elements, work of Sarbastivada abhidharma: 78
dhyāna – meditation: 6, 54, 154, 197, 267, 286, 313, 340
dialectic 10, 175, 179, 184, 197
Dignāga – epistemologist and logician: 10, 70, 147, 198, 199, 200, 201, 202, 203, 204, 205, 206, 207, 209, 210, 212, 340, 342, 346
diṭṭhi – viewpoints: 94
disposition 83, 86, 87, 89, 91, 113, 184, 197
Doctrine of the Mean 301
Dōgen – Japanese Zen philosopher: 13, 17, 298, 307, 317, 318, 319, 320, 321, 322, 323, 324, 325, 326, 327, 330, 332, 340, 348, 351
dǒng – movement: 238
Dǒngshàn Liángjiē – a founder of Soto School: 317
Donran – Tanluan, Ch. Mādhyamika 309
dosa – P. aversion: 94
duḥkha – suffering: 37, 92
dǔn wú – sudden enlightenmet: 244, 286
dūraṅgamā – 7th bodhisattva stage: 155, 157
duration 99, 181, 187, 188
Dǔshūn – Monk of Huayan School: 267
Dvādasa-nikāya-śāstra – *Treatise on the Twelve Groups*, doubtfully ascribed to Nāgārjuna: 251
dveṣa – aversion: 94, 112

E

ego 22, 39, 40, 42, 49, 52, 152, 165, 180, 187, 218, 228, 254, 255, 258, 259, 260, 261, 262, 263, 264, 275, 314, 315, 324
ego-lessness 218
Eihei-ji – Soto temple in Japan: 321
Eisai – Rinzai monk: 318, 319, 320
ekaggatā – concentration: 91, 111
ekayāna – school of Buddhism: 271
emanation 139, 159, 161
enlightenment 11, 12, 36, 54, 158, 189, 190, 241, 242, 244, 245, 265, 271, 275, 283, 284, 286, 287, 288, 289, 290, 291, 292, 293, 298, 306, 307, 313, 317, 318, 321, 322, 323, 324, 326, 327, 328, 333
epistemology 15, 27, 151, 199, 206, 211, 226, 339
èrdī – double truth: 251
Èrdī Zhāng – *Essay on the Double Truth,* Jizang 251
Essay on the Gold Lion 267, 269
event 84, 85, 86, 99, 100, 103, 125, 159, 181, 212, 213, 214,

241, 318

F

fǎ – dharma: 254, 316
fǎjiè – dharmadhātu: 276
Fān Zhèn – author of *Essay on the Extinction of the Soul*: 250
fǎxíng – dharmahood: 263
Fǎzāng – Founder of Huayan School: 267, 268, 270, 271, 272, 274, 276, 278
feeling 20, 22, 43, 48, 49, 53, 54, 55, 85, 91, 92, 98, 103, 111, 135, 136, 137, 148, 154, 199, 236, 244, 290, 298, 305, 329
feudal 143, 146, 147
filial piety 321
force 20, 67, 89, 103, 104, 106, 107, 109, 125, 135, 137, 139, 186, 205, 221, 233, 234, 247, 248
freedom 10, 19, 24, 25, 40, 50, 56, 62, 70, 82, 83, 89, 93, 100, 101, 102, 108, 109, 170, 183, 185, 186, 192, 193, 215, 219, 273, 288, 289, 323, 326
fruition 8, 44, 54, 104, 106, 125, 128, 279, 333
Fung Yu-lan – author *History of Chinese Philosophy*: 234, 237, 239, 242, 243, 250, 342

G

Gandhāra – region in northern India: 143, 144, 148, 149
Gandharva – alf: 108
Garland-Sūtra 201
Gautamiputra Śatakarṇi – a king: 145
Gaṇḍavyūha – part of Avataṁsaka 141, 142
genus 207
gocara – field: 210
Greek 143, 144, 148
Greeks 144
groups 7, 20, 31, 37, 39, 40, 41, 42, 45, 48, 51, 52, 59, 78, 94, 95, 106, 118, 236, 258
guān – contemplation, vipassana: 269, 281
Guǎng hóngmíng jí – *Further Collection of Essays on Buddhism*: 246
Gujarāt 144
guṇa – quality: 270, 271, 275
Guptas – royal house: 9, 146, 147

H

hadayavatthu – heart: 99
Hakuin – Jap. Zen Master: 13, 17, 298, 319, 328, 329, 330, 331, 332, 333, 342, 348
Han-dynasty – Ch. dynasty: 233
Harṣa – king: 147, 148, 149
Hastavālaprakaraṇa – *Trunk and Tail Discourse*, by Dignaga: 203
hell 35, 44, 56, 57, 58, 59, 60, 61, 152, 244, 304, 326, 327, 328, 329, 332, 333
hetu – cause, reason: 216, 217
Hetucakraḍamaru – *Drum of the Wheel of the Middle Term*, by Dignaga: 203
hetusamāgri – combination of

causes: 213
Hiei – mountain in Japan, with monastery: 319
highest good 193, 288
highest truth 10, 12, 163, 166, 167, 173, 186, 192, 237, 240, 252, 262, 287, 304
hiri – shama: 96
Hokke-sūtra – Lotus sutra: 303, 304
Hōnen – founder of Jap Pure Land sect: 307, 308
Hóngmíng ji – *Collected Essays on Buddhism*: 243, 246, 247, 248
Hóngrĕn – 5th Zen patriarch: 286
hotsubodaishin – true experience of mind (Dogen): 324
hrī – shame: 116
Huáirāng – Zen Master: 288
huān – maya, illusion: 269
Huángbō – Zen Master Xiyun: 291
Huànhuà – Zen Master: 236
Huāyán – Garland School: 267, 269, 270, 275, 276, 277, 284, 285, 286
Huāyán jīng jìhăi băimén – *Hundred Theories in the Sea of Ideas of the Avataṁsaka Sutra*, by Fazang: 270
Huíguŏ – Mater of Mantra School: 305
Huīkĕ – 2nd patriarch of Zen: 286
Huīnéng – 6th patriarch of Zen: 286, 288
Huīsī – 1st patriarch of Tiantai: 276
Huīwén – 2nd patriarch of Tiantai: 276
Huīyuăn – author of *On the Explanation of Retribution*: 248
humanistic 313, 333
Hume 209
Husserl 80
Huṇas – Huns: 147

I

I 7, 15, 16, 17, 19, 20, 21, 22, 23, 24, 36, 44, 45, 50, 51, 52, 53, 54, 59, 60, 70, 79, 84, 85, 92, 159, 163, 167, 170, 180, 186, 188, 199, 200, 207, 208, 209, 211, 214, 217, 218, 219, 223, 227, 228, 234, 238, 243, 244, 246, 248, 250, 278, 287, 299, 306, 320, 321, 323, 325, 328, 346, 348, 350
idealism 126, 127, 128, 149, 151, 174, 175, 197, 198, 199, 201, 204, 211, 228, 229, 267, 276, 284
ignorance 7, 22, 35, 36, 39, 40, 41, 42, 43, 44, 45, 46, 49, 50, 52, 53, 58, 59, 66, 94, 114, 153, 154, 155, 162, 165, 183, 184, 185, 190, 191, 192, 193, 214, 218, 228, 244, 245, 258, 259, 273, 275, 278, 283
illumination 134, 154, 156, 159, 166, 245, 246, 247, 316
illusion 39, 46, 48, 49, 138, 139, 154, 162, 163, 181, 184, 186, 187, 192, 212, 224, 228, 236, 237, 239, 253, 269, 275, 332
imagination 46, 49, 90, 138, 163,

165, 166, 183, 186, 192, 193, 198, 199, 207, 209, 216, 219, 221, 224, 262, 269, 278
implication 11, 15, 185, 209, 216, 217, 221
impregnation 257, 264
impressions 43, 45, 48, 49, 52, 53, 57, 91, 92, 106, 163, 207, 222, 223, 226, 236, 237, 256, 257, 258, 273, 320
inclination 46, 107, 151, 190, 299
indriya – sense organ: 99
Inference 11, 207, 208, 209, 210, 216, 221
influence 7, 35, 36, 39, 40, 41, 42, 49, 50, 58, 59, 66, 90, 135, 137, 138, 140, 142, 143, 146, 147, 148, 153, 155, 156, 177, 181, 213, 223, 244, 251, 255, 256, 258, 260, 273, 276, 286, 297, 298, 305, 307, 321
information 29, 36, 70, 83, 84, 87, 89, 100, 103, 107, 151, 178, 183, 185, 206, 213, 244
insight 7, 16, 25, 35, 40, 58, 94, 95, 109, 112, 113, 120, 128, 133, 134, 151, 152, 154, 158, 163, 165, 166, 186, 189, 190, 218, 219, 242, 243, 245, 262, 263, 264, 265, 321, 328
instantaneous enlightenment 242, 244, 271, 286
intention 27, 46, 53, 59, 67, 106, 111, 113, 135, 169, 322, 333
intersubjectivity 11, 228, 257
intuition 184, 185, 215, 219, 258, 264
īrṣyā – jealousy: 115
issā – P. jealousy: 94
itthi-purisa-indriya – genitals, male and female: 99
Izana-gi, Izana-mi – ancestors of sun goddess: 305

J

Jain 143
Jainism 145, 149, 178
Jambu tree 54
Japanese state 300, 304, 305
jātakas – birth stories: 31
jāti – birth: 42
javana – full apprehension: 87, 93
Jayapīḍa – king of Cashmere, 8th century: 149
Jayasiṁha – king of Cashmere, 12th century: 149
Jayendravihāra – Buddhist monastery in Cashmere: 149
jiānfēn – subjective side of consciousness: 255
jijuyu samādhi – special form of samadhi attained in zazen: 327
Jinen hōnishō – *Essay on Naturalness*, by Shinran: 309
Jīng – quiescent: 238
Jìn period – period of Ch. history, 265-419: 247
Jísè – School of Matter as Such: 236
jīvitindriya – life principle: 91
Jízāng – Chinese Mādhamika: 251, 252, 267
jñāna – insight: 101, 156, 191, 206, 219, 265, 283

jñānakāya – body of knowledge: 162
Jñānaprasthāna – *Method of Knowledge,* work of Sarvastivada Abhidharma: 78
Jñānaśrī – idealist thinker: 203, 204
jñeyāvaraṇa – veil of ideas: 183, 264
Jōdo – Pure Land sect: 297, 300, 307, 308
judgement 11, 89, 100, 108, 109, 156, 180, 207, 208, 209, 223, 224
jué – bodhi, enlightenment: 274

K

kaji – grace: 306
Kaliṅga – Orissa: 30, 145, 204, 211
kalpa – world cycle: 326
kalpanā – imagination: 182, 189, 192, 193
kāma – erotic love: 35, 154
kāmachanda –desire for pleasures: 93
Kamakura period – period in Jap. history: 304, 307, 317
Kamalabuddhi – Mādhyamika thinker:174
Kamalaśīla – hybrid idealist: 173, 201, 203, 343, 349
Kāmarūpa – Assam: 147
kāmatṛṣṇā – desire for pleasures: 101
kami – Jap. gods: 305
Kāñci – town in south India: 204
Kaṇiṣka – king of the Kushans: 79
Kāṇva – early royal house: 143
Kānyakubja – capital of Harṣa: 147
Karatalaratna – T*he Jewel in the Hand,* work of Bhavaviveka: 172
karma 35, 42, 58, 59, 60, 61, 62, 90, 97, 103, 108, 114, 135, 186, 205, 239, 258, 278, 280, 283, 284, 289, 322, 327, 333
kartṛ – agent: 182
karuṇā – compassion: 95, 96
kāryahetu – 'causes of effect', i.e. reasons which infer a cause: 216
Kathāvatthu – book of Thera-abhidharma: 77, 79, 349
Kāthiawār 144
Kātyāyana – disciple of the Budha 76
Kātyāyanīputra – author of *Method of Knowledge:* 79
kaukṛtya – worry: 112
Kāśyapa – disciple of Buddha: 75
Kāśyapīyas – early sect: 76
kausīdya – depressiveness: 114
kāyaguññatā – proficiency of body: 96
kāyakammaññatā – adaptability of body: 96
kāyalahutā – agility of body: 96
kāyamudutā – flexibility of body: 96
kāyapassaddhi – restfullness of body: 96
kāyujjukatā – rectitude of body: 96
Kegon – Jap. Huayan: 297, 303
Khāravela – King of Orissa: 145
Kimmei – early emperor of Japan 300

kleśa – affliction: 114, 165, 184, 185, 186, 190, 191, 193, 258, 264, 290
kleśāvaraṇa – veul of afflictions: 165, 264
kōan – Rinzai riddle: 317, 318, 319
'Kōan' school – Riddle School, of Zen:317
Kōbō Daishi – Kukai, founder of Jap. Mantra School: 305
Kōen – Zen abbot, teacher of Dogen: 319
kōng – empty: 236
krodha – anger: 115
kṣaṇa – moment: 326
Kṣanabhaṅgasiddhi – *Proof of the Division of Moments*, work of Dharmottra: 203
kṣānti – patience: 153
Kṣemagupta – Brahmin king of Cashmere, ca. 950: 149
kuśala – wholesome: 90, 111
Kūkai – founder of Mantra School in Japan: 297, 299, 305, 306, 307, 342, 343, 348
kukkuccha – worry: 95
Kumārajīva – apostle of Buddhism is China: 77, 233, 238, 242, 339, 342
kusala – wholesome: 90, 111
Kuṣāṇas – Mongolian tribe: 9, 144, 145, 146, 148
Kyōto 319, 321
Kyōto school 319

L

lakṣaṇa – visible appearance: 119, 255, 260, 270, 275
lakṣaṇa-bhāga – objective side of consciousness: 255, 260
Lalitavistara – *Detailed account of Buddha's Charm,* Mahayana scripture: 54, 141, 142, 338, 341, 343, 346
Lamotte, E., 30, 68, 70, 75, 76, 79, 99, 105, 125, 129, 135, 142, 338, 339, 343, 344, 345, 350, 351
Laṅkāvatāra-sūtra – *Descent on Lanka,* Idealist Mahayana Sutra: 141, 344
Lǎozi – founder of Daoism: 233, 238
law 8, 56, 59, 60, 80, 81, 109, 190, 205, 300, 322, 323, 332, 333
lěi – mortal ties: 244
Leibniz 21
liǎobié – mental representation, vijñapti: 254
liberation 13, 33, 34, 35, 36, 37, 38, 40, 41, 50, 51, 54, 56, 57, 58, 59, 81, 82, 86, 90, 94, 95, 97, 100, 102, 110, 112, 113, 114, 120, 121, 134, 135, 136, 137, 155, 158, 163, 165, 166, 167, 176, 177, 178, 182, 184, 185, 192, 199, 207, 218, 228, 247, 279, 282, 288, 307, 332, 333
life-elixer 330
Lǐnjí – reformer of southern Zen

School, Rinzai: 291, 298, 316, 317, 318, 333
lobha – greed: 94
logic 20, 21, 22, 177, 178, 197, 199, 200, 201, 206, 339
Lotus-sūtra 159, 267, 276, 328

M

macchariya – egoism: 94, 95
mada – complacency: 115
Madhyamaka – School of the Middle Way of Nagarjuna: 10, 163, 169, 170, 171, 172, 173, 174, 175, 183, 185, 186, 191, 192, 197, 198, 199, 201, 204, 233, 238, 286, 309
Mādhyamakālaṅkāra – *The Ornament of the Madhyamaka*, by Śāntarakṣita: 173
Madhyamakāloka – *The Lustre of the Madhhyamaka*, work of Kamalaśīla: 173
Madhyamakapratītyasamutpāda – *The Origination in Dependence According to the Madhyamaka*, ascribed to Nagarjuna: 172
Madhyamakārtha-saṁgraha – *Summary of the Meaning of the Madhyamaka*, by Bhavaviveka: 172
Madhyamakāvatāra – *Revelation of the Madhyamaka*, by Candrakirti: 172, 341
Mādhyamika – referring to the Madhyamaka: 142, 148, 151, 163, 170, 172, 175, 176, 177, 178, 179, 180, 181, 182, 184, 186, 187, 188, 189, 192, 197, 235, 251, 255, 345
Mādhyamika-vṛtti – *Commentary on the Madhyamaka* by Buddhapalita: 172
Madhyānta-vibhāga – *Exposition of the Middle and the Extreme* by Maitreyanatha: 202, 350
Magadha – Bihar: 9, 30, 33, 144, 146, 150, 151
mahābhūtāni – the five elements: 116
Mahādeva – founder of Mahāsaṁgha: 66, 67, 68, 72
Mahākāśyapa – Kaśyapa, disciple of Buddha: 65, 291
mahāmati – great iunderstanding: 269
Mahāprajñāpāramitā-śāstra – *Large Treatise on the Wisdom Sutras*, ascribed to Nagarjuna, but doubtful: 172, 344, 350
Mahārāṣṭra 145, 146
Mahāsaṁgha – Lay branch of early Buddhism: 70, 72, 76
Mahāsaṁghikas – referring to the Mahāsaṁgha: 8, 65, 68, 71, 72, 76, 123, 141, 142, 158, 159
Mahāyāna 9, 123, 126, 129, 133, 134, 135, 136, 139, 140, 141, 142, 145, 147, 149, 150, 151, 152, 157, 158, 161, 163, 165, 166, 169, 200, 202, 233, 236, 238, 271, 276, 277, 330, 338, 340, 341, 344, 345, 348
Mahāyānasaṁgraha – *Summary of Mahāyāna,* by Asaṅga: 202, 343
Mahāyānasūtrālaṅkāra – *Ornament of the Mahāyānasūtras*, by

Asaṅga: 202
Maitreya – Future Buddha: 134, 146, 346
Maitreyanātha – Early Mhayana author 199, 200, 202, 344
Māluṅkyaputra – Pupil of Buddha posing the wrong quesdtions: 50, 51, 176
māna – self conceit: 94, 112
manas –mind: 38, 52, 80, 102, 258
manasikāra – spontaneous attention: 91
manaskāra – attention: 91, 111, 191
mandate of heaven 301
mano – in composita for manas: 82, 89, 259
mano-vijñāna – mind consciousness: 259
mantra – short sentence for meditative repetition: 305, 306
Man without ranks 176, 317
manyanā – intellection:: 254
mārga – way: 155
markṣa – hypocrisy: 115
Marmapradīpavṛtti – *Light on the Hidden Meaning Commentary*, by Dignaga: 202
mātṛka – cathechesis: 75, 78
matsarya – envy: 115
matter 12, 17, 20, 22, 29, 36, 49, 50, 87, 98, 104, 106, 107, 110, 117, 118, 161, 189, 222, 223, 225, 236, 242, 246, 256, 258, 267, 268, 269, 270, 275, 281, 285, 322
Maurya – Early Buddhist dynasty: 30
māyā – illusion: 115, 139, 191, 269, 316
maṇḍala – regular pattern for meditation: 318
means of knowledge 11, 199, 206, 215, 218, 219, 220
median path 61
meditation 25, 33, 34, 38, 40, 54, 58, 66, 97, 112, 114, 136, 153, 154, 157, 166, 197, 198, 211, 267, 276, 286, 288, 306, 307, 313, 317, 318, 319, 321, 327, 328, 330, 334
Meghavāhana –king of Cashmere: 149
Mencius 301
middha – absebt mindedness: 94, 95, 112
middle path 169, 252, 255, 261
middle way 8, 61, 238, 255
Mihirakula – king of the Huns: 147, 148
mithya – deceptive: 192
Moggaliputta Tissa – said author of *the Controversial Issues* (Kathavatthu) 77, 78, 79
moha – mental blindness: 94, 114
mokṣa – liberation: 186
momentariness 110, 119, 212
motivation 108, 212, 250, 265, 284, 301
movement 23, 49, 80, 87, 94, 99, 109, 117, 134, 169, 238, 307, 308
muditā – joy: 95, 96
Mūlamadhyamakakārikā – *Root*

Verses of Madhyamaka, Major work of Nāgārjuna 172
Myōzen – Companion of Dogen: 320

N

Nāgārjuna 10, 145, 158, 160, 169, 170, 171, 172, 173, 175, 176, 181, 182, 185, 191, 198, 238, 251, 308, 322, 342, 343, 344, 345, 348, 350
Nāgārjunikoṇḍa – town in Andhra: 146
nairātmyadṛṣṭi – There is no self apart from its appearance: 214
Nakamura – Modern Japanese philosopher 31, 76, 142, 299, 304, 307, 345, 349
Nālandā – place in Bihar, where the great monastery was: 204
nāma-paññatti-vīthi – grasping of the name: 89
nāma-rūpa – name and form: 42
name and form 42, 43, 44, 45, 52
Namumyō Horengekyō – mantra of the Hokke sect: 304
ñāna – insight: 97, 101
Nányuè – disciple of Huineng: 318
Nara-period 303
Narasiṁha – Gupta king: 147
Nārāyaṇa – name of Viṣṇu: 135
natural forces 103, 104, 107
necessity 71, 215, 301
nikāyas – canoinical scriptures (P): 30
nirmāṇa-kāya – body of appearance 158, 159
nirodha – cessation: 281
nirvāṇa – 12, 36, 82, 83, 101, 110, 121, 163, 167, 238, 251, 252, 253, 265, 268, 269, 275, 281, 286, 332
nirvikalpa-jñāna – knowledge without admixture of imagination: 191
Nishida – Japanese philosopher: 319
Nishitani – pupil of Nishida: 319
niḥsvabhāva – being without essence: 189
niṣkriya – inactive: 182
noble truths 7, 36, 37, 154, 169, 218
noema 261
noesis 261
no-mind 289, 314, 315, 324
Nyāya – logic: 201, 206, 339
Nyāyabindu – *Drop of Logic*, by Dharmakirti: 203
Nyāyamukha – *Introduction to Logic,* by Dignaga: 203

O

occasion 79, 84, 97, 101, 109, 173
omnipotence 133, 135
omniscience 133, 136, 152, 156
Orissa 30, 204
ottapa – scrupulousness: 96

P

Paekche – kingdom in Korea: 300
Pāli: 30, 31, 61, 71, 75, 76, 78, 79, 81, 344, 347, 349, 351

pañca-dvāra-vīthi – the five doors of the senses: 89
pañcaviṁśatisāhasrika – 141
Pañcaviṁśati-sāhasrika-prajñāpāramitā – Widom Scripture of 25.000 verses: 238
paññā – P. wisdom: 95, 102
paññindriya – P. faculty of understanding: 95, 96
paradise 50, 55, 140, 307, 308
Paralokasiddhi – *Proof of Another World*, by Dharmottara: 203
paramārtha-satya – highest truth: 166, 240
parārthakriya – acting for the sake of others: 219
parasaṁbhoga-kāya – subtle Buddha-body, to be seen by bodhisattvas: 159, 160
paratantra – dependent on others: 167, 199, 261, 262, 278, 279
parikalpanā – imagination 166
parikalpita – imagined: 166, 199, 262
pariniṣpanna – the absolute: 167, 198, 262
pariṇāma – evolution: 129, 255
parokṣa – sense perception: 215
Pāṭaliputra – capital of Magadha: 65
paṭhavi – P. earth: 99
paṭisandhi – rebirth consciousness: 87
Paṭṭhāna – *Conditional Relations*, work of Thera Abhidhamma: 77, 81, 346, 349
Peṭakopadesa – inependent work on abhidharma, preserved in Pāli 29, 49, 51, 52, 53, 54, 76, 85, 102, 133, 151, 153, 171, 185, 204, 211, 212, 224, 243, 345, 346
perception 15, 16, 42, 49, 87, 90, 100, 118, 119, 127, 137, 214, 215, 216, 217, 218, 219, 220, 221, 222, 225, 226, 227, 236, 254, 255, 260, 314, 324
person 29, 49, 51, 52, 53, 54, 85, 102, 133, 151, 153, 171, 185, 204, 211, 212, 224, 243
phassa – contact: 91
phenomenology 16, 80
phenomenon 80, 81, 82, 83, 106, 110, 118, 119, 124, 128, 179, 198, 200, 276, 280
Philosophy 4, 17, 81, 89, 170, 175, 178, 234, 314, 339, 342, 343, 344, 345, 346, 350, 351
pīti – zest, joy: 92
potentiality 126, 198, 304, 315
prabhākarī – the shining, 3rd stage of the bodhisattva: 153, 157
pradāsa – approving of objectionable thimngs: 115
pradhāna – primeval matter of Samkhya: 139, 222
prajñā – wisdom: 240, 241, 251, 287, 340
Prajñākaragupta – late idealist thinker: 203, 204
Prajñāpāramitā-sūtras – *Wisdom Sutras*: 141
Prajñā-pāramitā-upadeśa Śāstra

– *Teaching of the Wisdom Sutras*, ascribed to Nagarjuna, doubtful: 251
Prajñāpradīpa – *The Candle of Wisdom*, by Bhavaviveka: 172
Prajñaptiśāstra – *Treatise on Conventional Denotation*, work of Sarvastivada Abhidharma: 78, 79
prajñaptisat – being as an immanenty object of consciousness: 181
Prakaraṇapāda – *Discussion Section*, work of Sarvastivada Abhidharma 78
prakṛti – primeval matter of Samkhya: 139
prakṛtyātmabhāva – thr state that has prineval matter as nature: 161
pramāṇa – valid means of knowledge: 199, 215
Pramāṇa-parīkṣa – Investigation of the Valid means of Knowledge: work of Dharmottara: 203
Pramāṇasamuccaya – *Compendium of the Valid Meansd od Knowledge*, by Dignaga: 199, 203, 342
Pramāṇavārttikā – *Long Commentary on the Valid Means of Knowledge*, by Dharmakirti: 203
Pramāṇaviniścaya – *Ascertainment of the Valid Merans of Knowledge*, by Dharmakirti: 203
pramuditā – The Joyful, 5th stage of the bodhisattva: 152
pranidhāna – resolve, resolution: 156
prapañca – expanse, the universe: 179
prāpti – immunity: 104, 105, 106, 124
praśrabdhi – mental dexterity: 116
prāsaṅgika-school – Madhyamaka School, using the method of reductio ad absurdum: 173
Prasannapadā – *In Clear Words*, by Candrakirti: 172, 339, 343, 344, 347
pratisaṁkhyanirodha – cessation with knowledge: 120
pratītya-samutpāda – dependent origination: 21, 41
Pratiṣṭhāna – Paithan: 145
pratyakṣa – perception: 206, 207, 218
pratyakṣa kalpanāpoḍha – perception free of imagination: 207
pratyātma-vedanīya – to be experienced in oneself: 193
principle of sufficient reason 21

projection 49, 53, 59, 89, 138, 185, 186, 222, 224, 271, 324
pudgala – person, soul: 51, 71, 165, 254, 262
pudgalanairātmya – the being without substance of the Self: 165
pudgalavāda – idea that man has a soul: 77
Puggalapaññatti – *Description of Personalities*, work of Thera Abhidhamma: 77

Pulumāyi II , Gautamiputra Śatakarni: 171
Pure Land Buddhism 308
Puruṣapura – ancient capital of the Kushans: 79
Pūrvaśaila – sect of Mahasaṁgha: 142
Puṣpabhūti – royal house to which Harṣa belonged: 148, 149

Q

qí – vital force: 247
Qīngyuǎn – Zen Master: 290
quantum 20, 212

R

rāga – desire: 112, 244
Ratnagotravibhāga – *Exposition of the Jewel Box,* by Maitreyanatha: 199, 347
Ratnakūṭa-collection – *Pearl Peak Collection,* early Mahayana text: 141
Ratnavalī – *The Pearl Necklace,* by Nagarjuna: 172
realism 71, 102, 204, 211, 228, 285
rebirth 8, 27, 33, 34, 35, 37, 38, 40, 42, 43, 56, 57, 58, 60, 61, 62, 84, 86, 90, 155, 158, 163, 166, 167, 190, 214, 215, 218, 246, 255, 259, 283, 332
reductio ad absurdum 173, 174
relation 44, 66, 80, 81, 106, 110, 127, 176, 177, 178, 179, 181, 182, 209, 255, 262, 267, 272, 273, 274, 279, 280, 289, 308, 318
relativity 137, 138, 174, 179, 181, 199, 233, 265, 269, 272, 274, 286, 303, 308
religion 19, 27, 142, 143, 170, 297, 300, 303, 305, 307
rén – humanity: 243
renunciation 152, 274
representation 209, 210, 219, 220, 222, 223, 225, 226, 228, 254
rest 29, 34, 46, 50, 121, 166, 180, 238, 239, 253, 321, 330
retentions 256
retribution 56, 57, 59, 60, 68, 104, 105, 106, 107, 108, 124, 125, 205, 226, 227, 242, 244, 292, 322
Rinzai – founder of koan-school: 298, 316, 317, 318, 319, 320, 321, 330, 333
Rinzai-shu – Koan School: 317
root-causes 94, 97, 101, 185
roseapple –jambu: 54
Rújìng – teacher of Dogen: 320, 321, 322
Rúlái zāng – Tathagata garbha: 277
rūpa – form. matter: 42, 49, 78, 86, 91, 98, 103, 110, 154, 268, 269
rūpakāya – body of form: 157
Russell, Bertrand 20

Ś

śabda – sound, word: 206
śānti – peace: 156
Śaivism – Shivaisme: 142, 143, 144, 148, 149

S

Śakas – Scyths: 144, 146, 148
Śākyamuni – The historical Buddha: 31, 133, 134, 135, 157, 158, 341
Śāntarakṣita – hybrid idealist philosopher: 173, 175, 203, 340, 343, 347
Śāntideva – devotional thinker in Madhyamaka tradition: 172, 174, 175, 338, 339, 347, 348
Śāriputra – disciple of Buddha, said to be first abhidharmist: 75, 76, 78, 160
Śāriputrābhidharmaśāstra – independent Abhidharma work ascribed to Śariputra: 76, 77
Śaśāṅka – king of Bengal 147
Śikṣasamuccaya – *Compendium of the teaching*, by Śāntideva: 172, 348
śīla – virtuous conduct: 95, 152
śraddhā – trust: 95, 116
Śuṅga – royal house: 9, 143
śūnya – relative, empty: 154, 182, 191, 236, 254
śūnyatā – relativity, emptiness: 164, 171, 174, 186, 199, 218, 233, 235, 286
Śūnyatāsaptati – *70 Verses on Relativity*, by Nagarjuna: 172

Ṣ

ṣadāyatana – the six sensory fields: 42, 45
saddhā – trust: 95, 96
Saddharmapuṇḍarika – *Lotus of the True Law*, idealist Mahayana Sutra: 141
sādhumatī – Good Thought, 9th stage of the bodhisattva: 156, 157
Saichō – founder of the Hokke sect: 303, 304
sajātiya – from the same origin: 214
salvation 27, 72, 136, 139, 156, 174, 176, 304
saṁsāra – cycle of rebirth: 33, 40, 86, 163, 167, 238, 251, 252, 253, 257, 269, 275
saṁskāra – habitual tendencies: 41, 42, 44, 82, 91, 103, 107, 154
saṁskṛta – constituted: 82
saṁsthāna – shape, contour: 127
saṁtāna – stream of consciousness: 84, 100, 103, 181, 214, 261
Saṁtānāntarasiddhi – *Proof of Other Streams of Consciousness*, by Dharmakirti: 203
saṁtati – continuity: 99, 103, 214
samatā – sameness: 164, 193
samaya – moment: 84
samādhi – absorption: 95, 102, 111, 327, 332
Samādhirāja – *King of Samādhi*, early Mahayana Sutra: 141
samānāntara-pratyaya – immediately antecedent moment: 227

sāmānyalakṣaṇa – general characteristics: 209
saṁbhāra – preparations: 264
saṁbhoga-kāya: body of enjoyment: 158, 160
saṁgha – Buddhist community: 34, 300
saṁjñā – cognition: 49, 91, 103, 111
saṁkalpa – imagination, intentionality: 186, 191
Sāṁkhya – old, perhaps pre-Buddhist philosophy: 173, 174, 177
Samudragupta – a king from the Gupta family: 146
samūhaggaṇa – P. free synthetic act: 87
saṁvṛti – covered: 154, 160, 161, 166
saṁvṛtisat – conventionally true: 154, 160, 161, 166
saṁvṛtisatya – conventional truth 154, 160, 161, 166
Sāñci – town in Madhya Pradesh 30, 146
sañcita – accumulated: 214
Sandhinirmocanasūtra – *Sutra on the freeing of the Proper Meaning:,* Mahayana Sutra: 202
Saṅgītiparyāya – *Commentary on the Saṅgīti-sūtra,* work of Sarvastivada Abhidharma: 78
saṅkhāra – P. saṁskāra: 8, 82, 83
saṅkhata – constituted: 82
Sānlūn – Three Schools: 251
saññā – P. cognition: 91
Sanskrit 5, 30, 61, 71, 118, 140, 141, 173, 236, 305, 342, 343, 345, 348, 349
Sāramati – said author of Ratnagotravivhaga: 199, 202
sarūpya – conformity: 110
Sarvāstivāda – Old School holding that everything is in the three times: past, present and future: 8, 67, 70, 72, 73, 79, 80, 102, 106, 107, 111, 115, 116, 120, 121, 123, 124, 125, 128, 142, 143, 144, 165, 173, 226, 347
sati– memory, attention: 95, 96, 111
satkāyadṛṣṭi – the opinion that the body is substantial: 154
satori – Jap. enlightenment: 298
sattva – living being: 51
satya – truth: 166, 192, 240
Saurāṣṭra 171, 174
Sautrāntikas – School recognizing only the sermons: 9, 70, 71, 120, 123, 125, 126, 127, 128, 129, 201, 257
schema 222, 223, 225
schemata 222, 225, 226
Scyths 9, 144
selection 209, 221, 225, 290
self 9, 61, 90, 92, 94, 112, 136, 137, 138, 152, 160, 162, 165, 174, 178, 179, 180, 181, 182, 183, 185, 192, 213, 218, 224, 227, 239, 246, 248, 255, 258, 259, 263, 264, 268, 273, 279, 282, 283, 285, 288, 314, 315, 316, 317, 318, 327, 332

selfconsciousness 226
self-identification 258
selflessness 142, 155, 183
Sēngcàn – 3nf patriaech of Zen: 286
Sèng-yōu – writer of the *Hongming ji*: 243
Sëngzhào – Chinese Mādhyamika: 238, 241, 242
sensation 110, 111, 206, 207, 208, 209, 210, 215, 222
sensations 98, 209
sense data 48, 91, 103, 125, 127, 129, 199, 205, 210, 212, 236, 323
sense organs 87, 117, 127, 182, 216, 274
series 44, 45, 52, 84, 85, 86, 100, 102, 103, 105, 108, 109, 124, 125, 127, 129, 137, 181, 209, 212, 214, 217, 343, 344, 345, 348
shēng – generated: 270
Shénxiū – patriarch of northern Zen: 286
shí – mundzane: 241, 251, 255
Shíhán – School of stored impressions: 236
Shingon – Mantra School: 303, 305, 306, 307
shinjitsunintai – the real body of man: 325
Shinran – reformer of Jōdo shu: 300, 307, 308, 309
Shin sect – School of Shinran: 300
Shinto – Jap. natural religiom: 297, 305
shí xiāng – real state or quality: 241
Shōbōgenzō – *The Eye and Treasury of the Truie Law:* by Dogen: 298, 321, 322, 340, 346
sīla – P. good conduct: 95, 101
sīliang – manyanā, intellection: 254
Simuka – king, fiunder of Satavahana dynasty: 145
singularity 162, 164, 165, 166, 168, 224
skandha – the groups, lit.. branches: 118
Skandhagupta – Gupta king: 147
smṛti – memory, attention: 95, 96, 111
solipsism 228, 261
Sòng dynasty 234
Sōng period 237
Sōtō-shu – Soto School: 317
soul 23, 25, 39, 50, 51, 55, 71, 77, 103, 136, 137, 170, 175, 176, 246, 247, 248, 249, 250, 254, 308, 322, 326
space 9, 61, 84, 95, 99, 102, 104, 106, 107, 109, 110, 116, 117, 118, 120, 121, 127, 128, 134, 138, 156, 162, 180, 209, 212, 228, 261, 280, 313, 325, 327
sparśa – contact: 42, 45, 91, 111
speculation 33, 75, 170, 183, 222, 287
spontaneity 24, 25, 127, 180, 205, 226, 293, 322
Sthavira – early school of Buddhism: 71, 105, 158, 171, 348
stimulus 93, 108, 271

store-consciousness 198, 205, 256, 257, 258, 259, 260, 264, 278, 279, 284
stūpa – Buddhist memnorial: 146
styāna – sloth: 114
subconscious 42, 44, 45, 48, 59, 60, 83, 89, 90, 97, 100, 101, 108, 113, 198, 205, 227, 254, 256
subjectivity 52, 53, 55, 56, 180, 205, 315, 316
substance 55, 58, 84, 126, 155, 164, 165, 166, 170, 175, 179, 181, 187, 191, 193, 210, 249, 250, 268, 269, 270, 277, 278, 279, 282, 315, 322, 323, 324
subtle consciousness 9, 126, 129
Suchness 10, 163
sudden illumination 247
sudurjayā – 5th stage of the bodhisattva, hard to conquer: 154, 157
suffering 27, 33, 35, 36, 37, 38, 39, 40, 41, 42, 43, 45, 48, 51, 60, 71, 100, 101, 120, 129, 134, 135, 136, 137, 153, 155, 176, 184, 185, 192, 193, 218, 228, 275, 281, 327, 329
Suhṛllekha – *Letter to a Friend,* by Nagarjuna: 172, 344, 345, 348
Suí dynasty,– Ch. dynasty, from 590-717: 251
sukha – pleasure: 54, 92
Sukhavati-vyūha-sūtra – Sutra of the arrangement of paradise, Mahayana sutra: 307
sūkṣma-manovijñāna – 227
Sūn Chuò – Chinese scholar: 235
sūtra – sermon: 78, 140, 141, 159, 201, 233, 238, 267, 270, 276, 303, 304, 307, 328, 330, 338, 340, 341, 344, 346, 349, 350
Suvarṇaprabhāṣa-sutra – *Golden Radiance Sutra* – Mahayana sutra: 141, 348
Suzuki, D. T : 319, 344, 348
svabhāva – nature: 119, 180, 189, 198, 254, 261, 262, 338, 349, 350
svabhāvahetu – inference establishing essence: 216
svabhāvika-kāya – body of essence: 162
svalakṣaṇa – appearance, proper aspect: 207
svasaṁbhoga-kāya – body of self-enjoyment: 159, 160
sva-saṁvitti-bhāga –self experience part of consciousness: 255
svasaṁvitti-saṁvitti – reflective awareness: 255
svātantrika-school – School of Bhavaviveka, holds views of its own: 173
Syöng Myöng, – king of Paekche in Korea: 300

T

tad-anuvatthuka-mano-dvāra-vīthi – recollective and reproductive acts of consciousness: 89
tad-ārammaṇa – appropriation/identification: 89
Taishō-tripiṭaka: – Chinese/Japa-

nese tripiṭaka 234
tān'āi – rāga, greedy love: 244
Táng dynasty – Ch. dynasty, from 618-906.
taṇhā – P. thirst: 93
Tánluán – Chinese Mādhyamika: 308, 309
Tantric 305
Tarim Basin 144, 233
Tarkajvāla – *The Flame of Reason.* work of Bhavaviveka: 172
tathāgata – The thus become, name for the Buddha: 33, 157, 277, 284, 315
tathāgatagarbha – womb of the Buddha, the absolute: 164, 193
Tathāgataguhya – *Buddha's Secret,* Mahayaba Sutra: 141
tathatā – thusness, absolute: 138, 156, 158, 162, 163, 164, 166, 189
tatramajjhatatā – balance of mind: 95
tattva – truth: 187, 189, 192
Tattvasaṁgraha – *Compendium of Truth*, by Śāntarakṣita 203:, 340, 343, 347
tejo – fire: 98, 99
Tendai – Tiantai, Lotus School: 297, 303, 304, 305, 319
tertium non datur 177
tetralemma 10, 176, 177, 182
Thanesar – town between the Satlaj and the Jumna: 147
theory of knowledge 27, 126, 199, 204, 206
theosis 136, 152, 156
Theras 8, 71, 76, 77, 78, 81, 82, 84, 90, 99. 100, 102, 103, 108, 109, 110, 111, 112, 113, 115, 116, 120, 123, 124, 128, 337, 345. 346, 348.
Theravāda 45, 98, 211, 234
thīna – sloth: 94, 95
things in themselves 128, 178
thirst 5, 7, 36, 37, 38, 39, 40, 41, 42, 43, 44, 45, 46, 48, 93, 95, 101, 128, 154, 178, 214, 222, 223
thought-construction 182, 186, 189, 219
thusness 156, 263, 265, 277, 303
Tiāntái 267, 297, 303
Tiāntōng – a monastery in China 320, 321
time 9, 17, 20, 21, 22, 29, 31, 34, 46, 49, 51, 53, 54, 56, 57, 59, 65, 67, 68, 70, 78, 79, 84, 86, 93, 99, 100, 103, 104, 105, 106, 108, 109, 116, 117, 118, 119, 123, 124, 125, 126, 128, 129, 133, 134, 136, 138, 140, 144, 145, 147, 148, 149, 150, 151, 153, 154, 161, 162, 163, 166, 170, 173, 174, 177, 180, 183, 184, 188, 198, 201, 205, 207, 209, 212, 213, 215, 218, 219, 221, 226, 235, 237, 238, 239, 243, 247, 249, 251, 253, 260, 268, 272, 273, 274, 275, 277, 278, 279, 280, 281, 285, 288, 292, 300, 304, 307, 308, 314, 318, 319, 320, 321, 323, 324, 325, 326, 328, 329, 331,

332
Tokharoi – Greek name for Turuṣkas, not speakers of Indo-European tongue: 144
Tokugawa period – period of Japanes isolation, 1600-1854, also Edo period: 297
Tokugawa Shogunate – shogunate indicates military regime, see Tokugawa period: 329
Toramāṇa – king of the Huns: 147
to tí – essence in Greek: 303
tranquillity 34, 49, 95, 96, 121, 156, 299, 332
transcendental logic 199
transmigration 61, 126, 181, 246, 259, 326, 331
Triṁśikā – *Work of thirty stanzas*, by Vasubandhu: 200, 202, 254, 349, 350
tripiṭaka – three baskets: 29, 234
truth 9, 10, 11, 12, 27, 29, 35, 37, 38, 40, 41, 46, 54, 55, 56, 60, 66, 68, 78, 83, 100, 101, 102, 103, 109, 117, 120, 138, 154, 155, 156, 157, 162, 164, 165, 166, 167, 168, 171, 174, 175, 179, 183, 184, 185, 186, 187, 188, 189, 190, 191, 192, 199, 204, 207, 210, 211, 215, 216, 218, 219, 220, 223, 224, 226, 227, 228, 237, 238, 240, 241, 243, 245, 246, 248, 249, 251, 252, 253, 257, 262, 263, 264, 265, 268, 272, 273, 279, 287, 300, 304, 306, 314, 321, 328, 329, 331
Turki-sāhis – Turco-Mongolian tribe: 148
Turuṣkas – Turco-Mongolian tribe 144, 148
tṛṣṇā – thirst: 37, 42

U

udhacca – restlessness: 94
uniqueness 163, 164, 166, 175, 207, 209, 219, 221, 222, 224, 227
universal 13, 85, 103, 104, 126, 134, 142, 162, 179, 180, 181, 185, 190, 193, 198, 209, 213, 219, 272, 279, 280, 282, 283, 284, 285, 299, 300, 313, 315, 317, 318, 322, 326, 327, 331, 332, 333
universality 174, 183
universal Man 317
upaccaya – P. first of the three phases of development, rising: 99
upādāna – matter, substrate: 214
Upadeśa – Teaching: 145
Upaniṣad – Vedic esoteric doctrine: 139, 145
upāya – means: 155, 190
upekkha – P. equanimity: 92, 97
upekṣa – S. equanimity 116
upeya – goal, end: 190
Uttaratantra – Ratnagotravibhāga: 199

V

Vādavidhi – *Rules of Logic*, work of Vasubandhu: 202
Vaibhāṣikas – followers of the

Vibhāṣa, the Sarvastivada Commentary: 198, 209
Vaiśeṣika – Hindu School of natural knowledge: 173, 174, 177, 204, 205
Vaiṣṇava – Vishnuism: 135, 143, 146, 149
Vajracchedika – Diamond Cutter Sutra: 141, 330, 338, 340, 349
Vallée Poussin, Louis de la – translator of *Abhidharmakośa*: 79, 337, 347, 349, 350, 351
vāsanā – impregnation (of store-consciousness): 198, 205, 222, 256
vastumātra – thing in itself; 219
Vasubandhu – idealisy philosopher: 70, 79, 102, 112, 123, 135, 145, 147, 197, 199, 200, 201, 202, 204, 210, 212, 253, 254, 255, 286, 308, 309, 337, 341, 343, 344, 346, 347, 349, 350, 351
Vasumitra – Buddhist, probably Sarvastivada author: 70, 79
Vātsiputrīyas – early sect, believing in some kind of soul: 8, 71, 72, 76, 77, 204
vāyo – wind, air: 99
vedanā – feeling: 42, 45, 49, 91, 111
Vedānta – Brahmin philosophy about the absolute: 148, 149, 174
veil of afflictions 165
veil of knowables 183, 264
verification 215, 220, 306
Viṁśatikā – *Work of twenty verses*, by Vasubandhu: 200, 202, 338
Vibhaṅga – *Analysis*, Book of Thera Abhidharma: 77, 348, 349, 350
vibhajyavādins –Buddhists who accept only the present and that part of the past that hasn't as yet bore fruit: 119
Vibhāṣa – *Great Commentary* on the Sarvastivada Abhidharma: 67, 79, 102, 145
vicāra – reflection, pondering: 92, 112
vicarious atonement 136
vicikicchā – P. doubt: 94, 95
vicikitsā – S. doubt: 112
viśeṣa – distinction: 129, 216
vigilance 314
Vigrahavyāvartaṇi – *Exclusion of Opposition*, work of Nagarjuna: 172
vihiṁsā – harming: 115
vijñāna – perception, consciousness: 15, 41, 44, 49, 52, 82, 102, 119, 154, 198, 254, 256, 259, 279
Vijñānakāya – *Corpus on Consciousness*, work of Sarvastivbada ~Abhidharma: 78
Vijñānavāda – idealism: 200
vijñapti – mental consciousness: 99, 104, 124, 254
vijñaptimātra – theory which holds there is nothing but mental content: associated with Vasubandhu: 198

Vijñaptimātratā-siddhi – *Proof that all is mental content only,* work by Dharmottara, translated in Chinese and commented upon and elaborated by Xuanzang: 254, 255
vikalpa – imagination: 179, 182, 186, 189, 192, 206, 261, 314
vimalā – unstained :152
Vimalakīrti-nirdeśa-sūtra – *Instruction of Vimalakirti,* Mahayana Sutra: 233, 350
vinaya– order rules: 197
viññāna – P. perception, consciousness: 82
viññapti – P. object for consciousness: 99
vipāka – ripening of karmic fruit: 100, 254, 256
vipāka-vijñāna – maturing consciousness: 254, 256
vipaśyanā – introspection, form of meditation: 185
viprayukta saṁskāra – forces independent from consciousness: 103
viriya – P. energy: 92
vīrya – S. energy: 92, 154
visaya – P. object: 99
vitakka – P. thought: 92, 93
vital force 247, 248
vitarka – S. rational thought: 92, 112
viṣaya – S. object: 205
Viṣṇu – Hindu god: 139
volition 9, 44, 46, 48, 49, 55, 59, 91, 103, 104, 105, 106, 107, 108, 120, 124, 125, 137, 214, 227
vyāpti – ,logical implication: 15, 216

W

Watts, Alan: 298, 351
Wéishí sānshín lūn – Triṁśikā, Chin. translation of *Thirty Verses* of Vasubandhu by Xuanzang: 254
Whitehead 20, 21
wisdom 10, 12, 24, 25, 83, 95, 100, 101, 102, 111, 112, 120, 140, 154, 155, 156, 157, 158, 180, 183, 184, 185, 189, 193, 214, 238, 240, 241, 243, 248, 263, 264, 265, 269, 275, 284, 286, 287, 292, 313, 314, 316, 317, 323, 324, 325, 327, 328, 330, 332
Wisdom sūtras 163
Wittgenstein 16, 22
wú – non-being: 235, 238, 244, 245, 286, 314, 316
Wū – usurper emperess Zetian: 267, 285
wúwei – in Daoisn, non-activity: 261
wú xīn – no-mind: 314, 316

X

xiāngfēn – perceived part of consciousness: 255
Xiè Língyūn – author of *Discussion on Essentials:* 244, 245, 246
xīn – mind, spirit: 314, 316
xīn fā – mind reality: 316

xīng – nature, eseence: 261
Xīngkōng lūn – *Treatse on the Emptiness of Nature,* work by Dao'an: 236
Xīngsī – founder of Meditation Only School of Zen (Caodong): 317
Xīnwú – School of non-being of mind: 236
Xīyūn – Zen Master: 291
xuán – mystery: 241
Xuánzàng – Chinese idealist: 68, 70, 79, 253, 254, 255, 256, 264, 265, 267, 269, 270, 276, 278, 284, 286

Y

Yamaka – *Coupled Problems,* work of Thera Abhidharma: 77
Yamunā – Jumna, zijrivier van de Ganges: 147
yáng – male principle: 247, 301
Yaśasākara – Brahmin king of Cashmere: 149
Yaśomitra – late comentator of Abhiodharmakośa: 149
Yellow Emperor 248
yīn – female principle: 247, 301
yīng huī – necessities of the given moment: 241
yīshúshí – maturing consciousness: 254
yītāqĭxīng – paratantra svabhāva: 261
Yīxuán – Linji of Rinzai: 291
yoga 58, 197, 235, 329
Yogācāra – idealist school of Buddhism: 70, 128, 151, 160, 197, 198, 200, 202, 237, 345
Yogācārabhūmiśāstra – *Treatise of the stages oif the Yogacara,* ascribed to Asaṅga: 202
yōng – functions: 277
yŏu – being: 238, 251
yŏuwéi – the phenomenal, activity: 238
yuánchéngshíxīng – pariniṣpanna svabhāva: 262
Yuánhuī – School of causal combination: 236
Yú Dàosuī – representative of the school of causal combination: 237
Yuèzhí – Kushans: 144
Yú Făkāi – representative of the school of stored impressions: 237
Yuktiṣaṣtika – *Sixty Stanzas on Argument,* work of Nagarjuna: 172

Z

zāngshí – store-consciousness: 256
zazen – sitting meditation in Soto School: 313, 320, 321, 327, 328
Zazen-only school 317
Zen 13, 17, 55, 267, 285, 286, 297, 298, 313, 314, 315, 316, 317, 318, 319, 320, 321, 322, 328, 330, 333, 339, 342, 344, 351
Zétiān – emperess Wu: 267
Zhānrán – Zen Master 285

zhēndī – highest truth: 240
zhèngdāo – correct path: 253
zhèngzīzhèngfèn – reflective awareness: 255
zhēnrú – genuine thusness: 238, 263, 277
Zhēnyán, School of – Mantra School: 305
zhǐ – cessation: 281
Zhīdūn 236
Zhíkǎi – 3rd patriarch of Lotus School: 276
Zhīyán – monk of the Avataṁsaka School: 267
Zhōngguānlūn sū – *Commentary on the Madhyamaka Śāstra.* 235
Zhōnglūn sūjī – *Subcommentary on the Mdhyamaka Śāstra*: 235
Zhuāngzi – Daoist philosopher: 233, 238, 248, 249
Zhú Fǎwēn – teacher of the School of non-Being of Mind: 236
zīzhèng – aspect of self-consciousness : 255
Zoroastrianism 134, 135

www.ingramcontent.com/pod-product-compliance
Lightning Source LLC
Chambersburg PA
CBHW031307150426
43191CB00005B/112
9789077787403